Phonology in the
Twentieth Century

STEPHEN R. ANDERSON

Phonology in the Twentieth Century

Theories of Rules
and Theories
of Representations

The University of Chicago Press
Chicago and London

Stephen R. Anderson is professor of linguistics at the University of California, Los Angeles. He is the author of *The Organization of Phonology* (1974).

The University of Chicago Press, Chicago 60637
The University of Chicago Press, Ltd., London

Library of Congress Cataloging in Publication Data

Anderson, Stephen R.
   Phonology in the twentieth century.

   Bibliography: p.
   Includes index.
   1. Grammar, Comparative and general—Phonology—
History—20th century.   I. Title.
P217.3.A53   1985   414   85-2773
ISBN 0-226-01915-2

For Janine

CONTENTS

ACKNOWLEDGMENTS

This book originated in courses given at UCLA at various times, and at Stanford. It became a reality, however, when I was able to live in Geneva, Switzerland, for most of 1981–83. It is impossible for a linguist in Geneva *not* to spend at least a little time meditating on Ferdinand de Saussure, and everything else follows from that.

The present work owes much to discussions with many people over a number of years. Aside from students in courses where this material has been presented, I am obliged to the following for comments or suggestions relating to portions of the manuscript: Bill Darden, Eli Fischer-Jørgensen, John Goldsmith, Morris Halle, Paul Kiparsky, Peter Ladefoged, Roger Lass, Will Leben, Bill Poser, Eddy Roulet, Alan Timberlake, and Nigel Vincent. Fritz Newmeyer deserves special thanks for providing careful and eminently helpful comments on nearly the entire book. Finally, I would like to thank Outi Bat-El for her work in preparing the index. Naturally, none of these peoples should be blamed for my errors, omissions, and failures to follow their advice.

My time in Geneva, and much of the research and writing of this book, were supported during 1982–83 by a postdoctoral fellowship from the American Council of Learned Societies. The assistance of the ACLS both at this time and in the past has been invaluable to me, and I am very grateful to that body. Preliminary work during the spring quarter of 1982 was supported by a sabbatical leave from the University of California, for which I am also grateful. Research and library facilities were provided me during my stay in Switzerland by the linguistics department at the University of Zürich, whom I would like to thank here.

Finally, the support (personal, financial, and otherwise) of my wife Janine M. Anderson-Bays was also essential, both to our stay in Switzerland and to the writing of this book. I hope she will find in it some reasons to believe that the time was not only pleasant but worthwhile.

INTRODUCTORY REMARKS

This book is primarily concerned with the history of linguistics, but it is not simply *about* the history of linguistics. For one thing, positions are taken below on issues which, while they arise in a historical context, are discussed for their own sake, such as the motivation for assuming a significant level of phonetic representation in linguistics. Further, while the text traces the development of phonological theory in the twentieth century, the goal of this exercise is not only to contribute to the study of the history of linguistics per se. Our intent is to study this history in relation to a particular issue: the balance between *rules* and *representations* as components of a theory of language and, more particularly, as components of a theory of sound structure. It is our thesis here that current views on this issue can only be understood and appreciated in the context of the historical development of the field, and this leads to a presentation of the issue through the study of the forms it has taken in the work of various major figures over approximately the past hundred years.

In doing this, it will be necessary to present various conclusions and opinions concerning the history of linguistics. Some of these may be novel or controversial; often they will be incomplete (especially with respect to the position of figures discussed on other than phonological issues). The reader with a comprehensive interest in the history of the field should bear the more specific purpose of this study in mind when assessing the adequacy of its broader conclusions. We can hope, however, that the picture presented here of the development of twentieth-century linguistics does not seriously misrepresent it.

Why study the history of twentieth-century phonology?

It is reasonable to ask just how coherent an object of study the development of twentieth-century phonology is. Does it make sense, that is, to limit our attention to (a) the twentieth century, and (b) phonology? Of course, any study limited to part of a field runs the risk of losing touch with other parts of the same field which developed at the same time and in a relation of mutual influence. There is also a risk of artificially isolating the work of a given period from that which preceded it (and ultimately led to it). On both of these counts, though, the proposed limits of our scope can be defended.

The present choice of time span (roughly, the 1880s through the 1970s) is motivated by the fact that linguistics as practiced in the twentieth century evidently makes a fairly sharp break with its immediate past. Ferdinand de Saussure and Jan Baudouin de Courtenay in Europe, and Franz Boas in America, began to articulate views on the nature of language which obviously developed in many ways out of the issues discussed by previous generations of linguists, but which were also rather clearly at odds with the two dominant traditions of the time: on the one hand, rationalist traditional grammar as inherited from medieval philosophers and grammarians, and, on the other, the newer developments in comparative linguistics which were the particular achievement of nineteenth-century linguistics.

Around the turn of the century (liberally construed), several distinct figures contributed to the establishment of what was to become the new tradition in the study of language. Most of this innovative work was concerned with the development of a 'structuralist' view of language, though the early figures in its formation did not necessarily see their contributions in that light. In some cases, their influence was quite limited until somewhat later, and occasionally the interpretation of their work as 'structuralist' seems largely to have been imposed in retrospect. Nonetheless, 'structural linguistics' can be said to begin more or less simultaneously with the twentieth century, and to form a reasonably coherent and organic object of study.

Accepting the proposition that twentieth-century views on language are sufficiently distinct from their predecessors to warrant a separate study, we may then ask what justifies the exclusive concentration of the present work on phonology. This certainly does not represent a judgment that other aspects of the study of language are without interest; but it does recognize that, however general its goals in principle, structural linguistics in fact concentrated its theoretical attention on sound structure. Insofar as there can be said to have been a structuralist *theory* of morphology or of syntax, it was mostly a matter of importing into those domains the results that were felt to have been achieved by work in phonology. Though the poststructuralist development of the field can fairly be said to have given much more independent interest to syntax, it is probably also reasonable to suggest that, even here, many of our current notions of linguistic structure derive from structuralist views on the character of phonology. It is surely also fair to say for most of the linguists under consideration (at least up until the 1960s) that they would have wanted to be judged by the validity of their work in phonology, for it was here that the majority of them felt something had been achieved which constituted a fundamental advance in our understanding of the nature of language.

Granting, then, that a study of the development of phonology over the past century is potentially a coherent topic from the point of view of the history of linguistics, we can then go on to ask more generally about the methods and motives for such historical study. The history of linguistics is a field which has attracted considerable attention from a variety of perspectives, and we can identify a number of distinct motivations behind past research.

One possible reason that students of any field may look into its history is to find support for their current preoccupations and predispositions. We often find that our predecessors (preferably those with general reputations as savants, but in a pinch nearly anyone in the sufficiently distant past) were concerned with something we can interpret as the same thing we are working on, or that they made proposals that were similar in content, or at least in form, to our own. The parading of such precedents is sometimes seen as lending a kind of legitimacy to our concerns, or even an *imprimatur* to our views.

This 'roots' variety of history can be found from time to time in many fields, but it is arguably the case that it was particularly prominent in views expressed by generative linguists in the 1950s and early 1960s on the origins of their discipline. Specific examples would not be particularly illuminating at this point, though they will appear below; to the extent this attitude can be documented, however, it is somewhat ironic in light of the common criticism in antigenerativist writings that generative grammar was fundamentally iconoclastic and hostile to its past. It should be clear in principle that where we can identify historical discussions of this self-justifying type, we should be rather suspicious of their conclusions. Such inverted 'guilt by association' hardly serves as a valid substitute for argument. Its only possible validity is in countering the opposite assertion, that some current view is hopelessly outré.

An alternative (and intellectually somewhat more respectable) motivation for studying the history of one's field is the search for genuine insights and enlightenment. Few researchers feel that they have direct access to all of the truth that is worth seeking. Naturally, one looks to one's contemporaries for help, but unless we hold with particular rigidity to the view that historical development is a matter of monotonically nondecreasing progress, with the present always ipso facto more enlightened than the past, there is no reason not to treat our intellectual ancestors with similar respect. Many genuine insights arrived at in the past have gone unassimilated by the field at large, perhaps for want of an appropriate theoretical framework within which to place an observation or conclusion, or on account of the unfashionable character of some of its assumptions; or perhaps because of an unfortunate mode of expression or simply the obscurity of a particular investigator. In returning to the works of those who have studied our subject before us, we can always hope to find pearls that subsequent research has overlooked without warrant.

In adopting either of the motivations for historical research just considered, however, we run a serious risk of falsifying the thought of earlier scholars by attributing our concerns to them, or by putting their work into the terms of a present-day framework quite foreign to their point of view. Of course, that need not diminish the value of what we learn from such study about our own present projects, but it certainly makes for bad history qua history.

An example of this sort is furnished by Postal's (1964) remarks on Boas's phonological theory. Postal was responding to the remarks of Voegelin and Voegelin (1963), who had characterized Boas as a "monolevel" structuralist in the sense that he believed in only one structurally significant level of (phonological) representation. Basing his comments on a single paper of Boas's dealing with Iroquoian, which he admits is isolated and possibly not representative of all of Boas's work, Postal cites a number of instances in which Boas's locutions imply a conversion of one representation into another by phonological principles particular to the grammar of a language. From this he concludes that Boas must have maintained at least two levels of phonologically significant structure. Since one of these levels would clearly have to have properties that could not be discovered directly from the surface phonetic form by procedures of segmentation and classification, Postal suggests that Boas actually held a view on which abstract phonological structure is converted into surface phonetic form in a way quite similar to a generative phonology.

It is of course possible that Postal's view of Boas is correct (though we will suggest below in chapter 8 that it is not), but the methodology used to establish it is less than satisfying. In particular, it is only when we put Boas's words into a contemporary mouth that they have the implications Postal found in them. Avoiding anachronism, we see that Boas was simply using the rhetoric of traditional grammar for describing alternations. In those terms, to say "A *becomes* B (under some conditions)" is not to assert the antecedent existence of an A, which is later converted into a B if the conditions in question obtain. It means merely that where we might *expect* (perhaps on the basis of other, related forms) to find an A, but where the relevant conditions are satisfied, we find B instead. Such a mode of expression in describing alternations is quite general in nineteenth-century and earlier descriptions, and perfectly compatible with a view on which the sound structure of a form has only one significant level of representation. The development of generative grammar has led to a climate in which 'A becomes B under condition C' involves a relation between a more abstract representation (in which A appears) and a more concrete one (in which B appears instead); but this is not the only (or even the most direct) interpretation of such a way of talking about alternations. There is certainly no reason to attribute it to Boas, as Postal does.

Another, perhaps even more drastic, example of a similar sort is furnished by Lightner's (1971) criticism of Swadesh and Voegelin's (1939) classic paper on morphophonemic theory. Lightner discusses, in particular, Swadesh and Voegelin's analysis of the alternation found in English *leaf/ leaves* and other pairs in which a final voiceless fricative corresponds to a voiced segment in the plural. Swadesh and Voegelin represent the stem of English *leaf* as |liF| (as opposed to |bəlif| *belief*, with nonchanging [f]). Lightner raises the question of just what the symbol |F| in Swadesh and Voegelin's transcription signifies. He concludes (as they do) that it cannot be simple [f], since other forms ending in [f] (e.g., *belief*) do not show the alternation in question. Similarly, |F| cannot represent [v], since there are words ending in nonalternating [v] (such as *leave* 'furlough').

From these considerations, Lightner surmises that Swadesh and Voegelin must have intended their |F| to represent some other segment—say [f] with an additional feature, such as pharyngealization, glottalization, etc. Obviously, however, the phonetic value of whatever feature is chosen for this purpose will never be realized on the surface, since |F| is always produced either as [f] or as [v] without attendant pharyngealization, glottalization, etc. to distinguish it from other cases of [f], [v]. Therefore, Lightner concludes, Swadesh and Voegelin have used whatever feature they intend to distinguish |F| from |f| as a diacritic. The choice of a particular feature (e.g., [pharyngealized]) is totally arbitrary (so long as the feature chosen is not otherwise used in the language), and their analysis is ultimately incoherent in consequence.

The weakness of this attack on Swadesh and Voegelin should be evident. In fact, those authors give no reason to suspect that they intend the difference between |F| and |f| to be interpretable in phonetic terms at all. They are quite explicit about the fact that a symbol like |F| is simply an abbreviation for a morphophonemic formula (|F| = '/f/ in the singular, /v/ in the plural form'). In the spirit of the 1930s, such a formula is simply a statement of distribution (conditioned, in this instance, by morphological rather than phonemic factors). As such, it is phonetically (or phonemically) interpretable only by reference to its environment: in some environments, its value is /f/, while in others it is /v/. Nowhere, crucially, is it something in between, or somehow distinct from both.

At the time of Lightner's discussion, however, most generative phonologists believed that every symbol in an underlying (or 'systematic phonemic') form should be interpretable in terms of a uniform set of phonetic/phonological features. Thus, for Lightner, if |F| was not to be either /f/ or /v/, it had to be distinct from them in terms of some one of the (phonetically motivated) distinctive features provided by the theory. Whatever appeal this view may have today as a potentially restrictive theory of sound structure, there is no reason whatsoever to attribute such a position to Swadesh and Voegelin, who took some care to point out that their morphophonemic symbols were not to be interpreted directly as phonetic or phonemic. To do so and then present this as an argument against the coherence of their position is simply not a historically accurate way to approach their work.

Somewhat more defensible as a basis for doing history, it would seem, is a third possible motivation: one may simply wish to understand the past in order to know how the present came to be. So stated, this is a virtually empty formulation of the importance of history, but it conceals a more specific point. Many of the ideas, problems, research strategies, and emphases of a field, taken for granted by its practitioners and passed on to their students, have been derived in similar fashion from *their* predecessors. What is important is the fact that this process of transmission takes place without necessarily entailing that the notions passed on are rethought and justified anew at each step. As a result, we may find ourselves centrally concerned with problems which are really those of a previous generation, and which would have no particular claim on our attention if we were to redesign our field entirely on the basis of our current understanding of its object.

Often, that is, certain fundamental or guiding ideas of a field change, but without this having the result that all of the rest of its content is thought out again from basic principles so as to form a unified whole. It is of course true that many of the problems, etc., of a discipline remain the same through substantial change in theories, and the effort to rethink *everything* constantly to maintain complete consistency with innovations might well be thought prohibitive. The price of assuming a high degree of basic continuity, though, may well be the importation into the field of a certain amount of poorly digested conceptual residue: notions that were central for previous theories but have little or no relevance in light of current understanding. We may thus wish to study the history of our field, in part, just to identify such anomalous situations.

The recent development of generative grammar suggests that this latter motivation for studying history may be particularly apposite at the present time. This is because a major shift has occurred in the conception held by most researchers of the object of study in linguistics. Traditionally, linguists have assumed that their concern was with the study of *languages*, taken as (potentially unlimited) sets of possible sentences (or utterances, etc.) forming unitary and coherent systems. Gradually, however, the emphasis in research has shifted from the properties of languages to the properties of *grammars*, in the sense of systems of rules which specify the properties of the (well-formed) sentences in such a system.

The change involved is a somewhat subtle one, in that previous researchers who were concerned explicitly to characterize a language naturally presented their description in the form of a grammar; while present work, equally naturally, tends to identify the grammar under study by the sentences it specifies as well formed. Thus, both approaches involve simultaneous attention to objects of both sorts. However, where previous generations of linguists saw the presentation of a grammar as a way of satisfying the basic requirement of specifying a particular language, current interest is more on the evidence provided by individual grammars for the specification of the *general form of grammars*. A definite shift of the object of inquiry in linguistics is involved, though it is difficulty to formulate the issue with complete clarity.

Nonetheless, the change is highly significant for the conceptual structure of the field: the shift from studying sets of sentences to studying systems of rules results, at a minimum, in a change in the areas in which we might expect to find empirical contact between theoretical constructs and objects or structures in the physical (neurological, psychological, etc.) world. Chomsky (1981) has recently suggested that the empirical properties of 'languages' (in the sense of sets of sentences forming the system of communication within a given speech community) may be such as to render the notion an ill-defined one or, at least, an inappropriate one for systematic study. Since this notion has formed the basis of essentially all previous theories of language, the consequences of abandoning it are potentially rather far-reaching. There is no particular reason to believe a priori that theories of languages and theories of grammars are even commensurate with one another, and certainly not that the assumptions and results of a theory of one type carry over directly to theories of the other type.

Motivations for the present book

It is with regard to this issue that the present study should be situated. I suggest that the notion of linguistic *representations* is one that arises as the central object of study in a theory concerned with languages (construed as sets of sentences, words, utterances, etc.); while the notion of *rules* is one that arises particularly in connection with the study of grammars. Many of the central concerns of the field at present are fundamentally questions about the basic properties of representations; but if this is a notion that pertains particularly to theories of *languages*, and we accept the proposal that the appropriate object of study in linguistics is actually *grammars*, then it follows that concerns about properties of representations must at minimum be raised anew, and justified in terms of the logical structure we otherwise attribute to the field.

Let us make this issue more concrete within the domain of sound structure. As a result of the spoken character of language, the organizational foundation of the sound pattern of a natural language lies in the way it establishes systematic relations between (physically) distinct events. To characterize this sound pattern in a particular language is essentially to describe the range of variation that is permissible in such events if they are still to count as linguistically 'the same.' This problem evidently arises even for consecutive repetitions of the 'same' utterance, since it is in general possible for measuring instruments of sufficient sophistication to identify some differences, no matter how minute, between any two physical events. This is true even though physically distinct repetitions of a particular utterance may be completely indistinguishable from the point of view of a speaker of a given language.

From the point of view of the linguist, this sense in which differences always exist between distinct events may seem a mere technicality (however important it might be to a philosopher or a physicist). But a similar problem arises at rather grosser levels, in ways that only a linguist can address seriously. For example, in English the vowels of stressed syllables show considerable variation in duration as a function of the properties of a folowing consonant. *Ceteris paribus*, the 'same' vowel will be longest before a following /z/, shortest before a following /p/ or /k/, and intermediate in duration before voiced obstruents, nasals, etc. (cf. Lehiste 1970 for a review of the relevant facts). Nonetheless, we have considerable difficulty in saying that the *a*'s of, for example, *razz* and *rap* are (at least in English) anything other than 'the same'; and indeed, a nonlinguist may be quite reluctant to believe that they are not. The sound pattern of any language involves a large number of such regularities of pronunciation, which establish the more or less precise limits on the range and attendant conditions of variation in the 'same' sound.

It would be possible to present a set of examples illustrating a completely gradual transition between cases such as the length of English stressed vowels (as a function of following consonants) and others in which the differences involved are much more obvious. That is, related sounds may be physically very different indeed (and, hence, not the same at any level of phonetic analysis), while still counting as *linguistically* the same because they correspond to one another in different variants of the same larger linguistic unit (formative or morpheme). Thus, the [s] of *cats* and the [z] of *dogs* both represent the same component of the English plural marker (here, coextensive with the entire morpheme, but the [z] of *horses* is only a subpart of the same higher unit). Similarly, the [k] of *fanatic* is in some sense the 'same' as the [s] of *fanaticism*. At a yet higher level, we might say that there is a sense in which both *am* and *is* contain the same verb {*be*}; less radically, we may find that the same higher unit is represented by the same segmental content in different forms, as in Georgian *mo-k̦lav-s* 'kills' vs. *mo-k̦vl-a* 'killing'.

Whenever we study any of these sorts of systematic relations between sound forms, we seek to determine the range and conditions of variation in what counts as 'the same' lingusitic element. To determine this, we study the *rules* that make up the sound system of the language: systematic relations like (in English) 'vowels are longest before /z/, next longest before /n/, etc.'; 'word-final obstruents have the same voicing as a preceding obstruent'; '/k/ in many forms corresponds to /s/ if an ending beginning with a non-low front vowel follows'; (in Georgian) 'the sequence obstruent plus liquid (or nasal) plus /v/ does not occur; where we might expect it, we find the same consonants but with the liquid or nasal following the /v/'; etc. Statements of this sort, whatever formalism they may be couched in, are fundamentally expressions that establish correspondences between related forms: the form x under conditions A corresponds to the systematically related form y under conditions B. From the point of view of the identity of higher-level units, that is, the difference between x (under conditions A) and y (under conditions B) is insignificant: they count as 'the same thing'.

But whenever we say that (by virtue of rule R), x and y count as linguistically 'the same thing', the temptation is virtually irresistible to ask what that 'thing' is. When we propose an answer to this sort of question, we are no longer describing the rule relating *x* and *y*, but are rather proposing a *representation* of what they have in common.

In linguistics (or at least in the study of the linguistic role of sound structure), a basic insight was gained by distinguishing between *phonetics* and *phonology*. This was based on the realization that language-particular descriptions had to give some sort of account of each language's distinctive rules, in the sense above of systematic relations between phonetically distinguishable sounds that are identified under specified conditions by the language in question. It is arguably the case that the earliest clearly 'phonological' views within the Western tradition were primarily or exclusively theories of rules, and that the question of representations only arose somewhat later. Saussure deals with the problem of identity versus diversity at the level of individual segments, as do Baudouin de Courtenay and Kruszewski at the level of morphological units; but the issue of uniform representations for the sets of elements so related only came up years later.

Quite soon in the ensuing development of Saussure's, Baudouin's, and Kruszewski's ideas, though, attention came to be focused on the character of the presumed *invariant* representations which are apparently implied as underlying the *variants* whose relation is systematically governed by the rules of a language. As a result, most of the history of twentieth-century phonology is the history of theories of representations, devoted to questions such as 'What is the nature of the phoneme, morphophoneme, morpheme, etc.?'

From a strictly nominalist position, or even less extremely, we might argue that this issue rests on a logical error. The fact that *x* and *y* count as 'the same thing' doesn't need to imply the availability for study of such a 'thing' which they both are (a point made in a different but related context by Linell 1979). The fact that we can construct an expression 'the set of all sets which are not members of themselves' need not imply that such a paradoxical item has a claim to existence; and in general we must not be misled in our ontology by the possibilities provided by our metalanguage. But even a rather less radical critique, not denying the significance of underlying invariants in linguistic structure, might still argue that an exclusive focus on questions of representations leaves a great deal of the rule-governed regularity which characterizes linguistic variation unaccounted for. This is especially true if one accepts the shift of focus noted above from *languages* to *grammars* as the objects of linguistic inquiry.

In this work, the history of the balance between the study of rules and the study of representations (in the above sense) will be of primary importance. We hope to trace the sources of influence that have led to a concentration at different times on one or the other; and also to explore the ways in which facts that seem to fall clearly in one domain can be accommodated within a theory of the other. In this regard, it should be emphasized that it is not our intention to argue that one sort of consideration is *right* and the other *wrong* in a lingusitic theory. In fact, theories of rules and theories of representations deal with intimately interrelated and indissoluble aspects of the same linguistic structure. In order to understand that structure, however, both aspects must be appreciated, and this has certainly not always been the basis on which inquiry into sound structure has proceeded.

The historical origins of modern views: A concrete example

The motivation for a historical approach to the issues just raised is clear. When we seek to understand the conceptual bases of our own theories, we can only do so in light of the recognition that they are in part the residue of views held by others (our teachers and their predecessors). In order really to appreciate the logical content of our *own* views, then, it may be necessary, somewhat paradoxically, to approach this task through a prior appreciation of their historical antecedents—*taken on their own terms*. We must 'get inside' the position within which some problem originally arose in order to understand its motivations and logical underpinnings.

We can consider one example of such intellectual inheritance here. It is often taken as self-evident in phonological studies that underlying ('phonemic' or 'phonological') representations should contain only *distinctive* or nonredundant material. That is, in arriving at the phonological representation of a form, one of the steps involved is the elimination of all predictable properties, and the reduction of the form to the minimum of specification from which all of its other properties can be derived by general rule. For many, indeed, such a step establishes the fundamental difference between the 'phonological' and the 'phonetic' representation of a given form.

Sometimes, however, this elimination of redundancy turns out to have undesired consequences. Occasionally, two or more properties, each of which is predictable in terms of its environment, are interrelated in such a way that both cannot be simultaneously eliminated from phonological representations without reducing the generality of the resulting description. In such a case, we must conclude that a minimally redundant representation is not really to be desired.

In Russian, for example, it has often been noted that the difference between front [i] and back (or central) [ɨ] is not distinctive: [ɨ] appears after 'hard' (i.e., nonpalatalized) consonants, while [i] appears elsewhere. On this basis, writers such as Trubetzkoy (1939) concluded that the phonological unit /i/ (represented by [ɨ] after 'hard' consonants and by [i] elsewhere) is opposed to /u/ only in rounding, and to /e/ in height. A minimally redundant representation of this vowel then would not contain any value for the feature [±back], since this is uniformly predictable.

Many consonants in Russian belong to pairs of corresponding 'hard' and 'soft' consonants, but not all. Among those that are not contrastively paired in this way are the velar obstruents /k/, /g/, and /x/. Each of these appears in a phonetically 'hard' variant before back vowels ([u], [o], [a]) and in a phonetically 'soft' variant (phonetically, palatal) before front vowels ([i], [e]). Since the difference between the 'hard' (velar) and 'soft' (palatal) variants of /k/, /g/, and /x/ is thus perfectly predictable, these segments are presumably not to be specified for this property in a redundancy-free description.

But now it should be apparent that there is a problem. The backness of the vowel /i/ is predictable from the presence versus absence of a preceding hard consonant; but the 'hardness' of a prevocalic /k/, for example, is predictable from the frontness of the following vowel. In fact, the sequence /ki/ is always pronounced with a 'soft' [k,] and front [i] (as in [pušk,in] 'Pushkin'); but if neither /k/ nor /i/ is specified for backness, it is not clear how to describe these facts.

Of course, if /i/ is specified (redundantly) as 'basically' front, there is no problem: we need only say that (a) velars become palatals before front vowels, and (b) /i/ becomes [+back] after 'hard' consonants. Assuming that the difference between 'hard' and 'soft' consonants in Russian is a matter of the same feature ([+back]) as the difference between back vowels and front vowels, this set of rules expresses the assimilatory nature of the mutual accommodation between vowel and consonant in a quite appropriate way. If phonological elements are only specified for their nonredundant properties, however, the rule of velar palatalization cannot make reference to the frontness of a following /i/, and must be formulated as 'velars become palatals before a following nonlow, nonround vowel'. The fact that such vowels will in all cases be phonetically front (by virtue of the rule which makes /i/ front after 'soft' consonants) is thus treated as in principle quite independent, and the assimilatory nature of the change is completely obscured.

In such a case, an apparently redundant property must evidently be specified in phonological representations if the generality of the description is to be maintained. Of course, it might be claimed that this example is isolated and atypical of the structure of natural languages. In reality, however, the phenomenon of reciprocally dependent properties is quite frequent in language, although its consequences are not always recognized to be problematic.

The simplest case of this type, in fact, occurs so frequently that it is not generally even noticed. Suppose that two properties are completely predictable from one another (at least in some environment): for example, given a cluster of nasal plus stop in many languages, it is possible to predict the point of articulation of either from that of the other. Typically, we specify one of the properties (e.g., the articulation of the stop) phonologically, and include a rule to introduce the other (the articulation of the nasal, in this example). We must realize, however, that, from the point of view of eliminating redundancy, the decision to eliminate one of two such interdependent properties rather than the other is either completely arbitrary or at least based on ancillary principles of a somewhat ad hoc sort which are seldom made explicit or precise.

In the worst case, we may be forced to make choices that cannot be defended on principled grounds just in order to meet the requirement of eliminating redundancy. Among twentieth-century phonologists, only the British Prosodic school (see chapter 7 below) have been willing to take this point seriously enough to reconsider the basis of the role played by redundancy in linguistic descriptions.

We do not mean to defend here the opposite position, to wit, that predictable properties should be systematically included in phonological form rather than being eliminated and then reintroduced by rule. The point is, rather, to argue that there is at least an issue to be addressed, and that particular answers to the problem of how much information to include in phonological representations have other consequences, which require them to be justified on principled grounds. In particular, the position that such representations should be redundancy-free is not self-evidently correct. It is interesting to note that some speech scientists make exactly the opposite assumption: that the only linguistically significant representation of linguistic forms which speakers manipulate is one which is maximally specified down to very low levels of phonetic detail (Dennis Klatt, personal communication).

In fact (as we will have occasion to argue below), it is perfectly possible to develop a view of phonological forms which is consistent with the fundamental function of these representations in a grammar, but in which at least some predictable detail is present. Again, it is not our purpose here to argue for the correctness of such a view but only for the logical coherence of holding it. For many linguists, however, such a notion seems totally incompatible with the fundamental nature of the difference between phonological and phonetic form. It is worth asking why this should be the case: what *is* the relation between 'phonological' status and predictability, and how did the position arise according to which it is (all and) only *un*predictable properties that appear in phonological representations?

If indeed there are reasonable alternatives to that view, and positive arguments in favor of them, it is likely that the answers will come only from a study of the history of the relevant notions: phonological representations, and predictable (or redundant) properties. Consideration of these suggests two distinct sources for the strongly held conviction that predictable properties must necessarily be absent from phonological representations.

A possible motivation for this position is found in one interpretation of Saussure's notion of sound structure (though this is not, we will argue below, the only one, or even the one Saussure appears to have held), on which the units in phonological structures are *identified* with sets of properties setting them apart from other such units. The doctrine that "dans la langue, il n'y a que les différences" has often been interpreted as equating the phonological character of a sound with exactly those properties that distinguish it from others—no less but no more. Thus, there would be no room in such a representation for properties that were not distinctive.

Second, and for completely independent reasons, the development of the field of information theory during the 1940s and 1950s stressed the elimination of redundancy as a necessary step in identifying the information content of a message. Those who (like Jakobson, for example) identified the phonological form of an utterance with its potential information content were thus led to require the elimination of predictable information from phonological forms for this reason as well.

Either or both of these lines of reasoning may well be taken as quite persuasive, and may lead us to require that all redundant properties be eliminated from phonological forms. However, we should recognize that current views on this issue are often not the product of independent thought about the question itself but, rather, are inherited from previous researchers who reached them on the basis of considerations such as those just adduced, and provided them to us with the status of definitions. As a result, if we want to assess their value, we have to be able to reconstruct the arguments that led to them—and this implies reconstructing the logic of those who developed them.

To do this, we cannot simply look for our own concerns to be reflected in earlier work. We must instead try to understand how *our* work reflects *earlier* concerns. To see our assumptions and methodologies in the light of antecedent conceptual frameworks which gave rise to them, we must ask what earlier workers thought they were doing, and why, and how the results of their reflection were transmitted to subsequent generations, including ourselves.

In the present instance, for example, we can note that the interpretation given to Saussure's ideas by many of his immediate successors arose out of their own conception of 'structuralism' rather than out of any logical necessity inherent in Saussure's position, and that this weakens the force of their line of argument. Similarly, the constructs of information theory which seemed quite persuasive to Jakobson in the early 1950s would probably appear much less relevant to the study of natural language today, given our current understanding of the sheer bulk and internal redundancy of mental storage of information. Since the claim that 'Saussure said this', so it must be true, and the notion that information theory dictates such a view—two underpinnings of the redundancy-free notion of phonological form—can thus be argued to be less than persuasive in present-day terms, we might well want to reevaluate our assumptions in this area.

Until we justify in subsequent chapters some of the assertions just made about the history of phonological ideas, the argument just outlined cannot by itself carry much conviction. Nonetheless, it should serve to illustrate the general point. Despite what sometimes appear to be dramatic changes in scientific 'paradigms' (in roughly the sense of Kuhn 1962), it is often true that our agenda of issues was set for us (at least in part) by our predecessors. Similarly, the range of possible solutions to any given problem may well have been delimited by a previous generation in a way we would not find adequate today, but which we retain as a part of the cumulative conceptual structure of the field. In order to understand these issues, and to rethink them where necessary, we have to understand the considerations that originally led to them. That may often require a considerable effort, where the basic work in an area is remote from us in time and underlying assumptions.

The organization of the present book

As a result of these considerations, any historically based study of an important conceptual issue necessarily involves a great deal of more or less circumstantial biographical detail about influential figures. This book is no exception: it might be proposed, for example, to organize the subsequent chapters by issues to be addressed; but in fact our discussion centers in a thoroughly traditional way on individual figures and groups of figures, arranged in two parallel and more or less chronological sequences. Such a 'great man' approach to history may sometimes be inadequate to reveal the texture and motivation of events, but it can be argued that when we study the rather limited domain of the history of an individual intellectual discipline (such as linguistics) for essentially internal reasons, the nature of the problem as posed makes it essential.

Furthermore, we would argue that the character of the field until around the 1950s makes the limitations of an approach centering on individuals rather than issues comparatively innocuous. During most of the period studied here, linguists worked in much greater isolation from one another than is presently common, and the development of many issues can be identified with the work of particular scholars to a greater extent than would be possible in light of the present size and professional coherence of the community of linguists.

We start, then, by tracing in chapters 1 and 2 the development of phonology in the beginnings of 'structuralism' in Europe. This is based on a consideration of the work of Saussure, and especially of the views on sound structure which we can reconstruct from the *Cours de linguistique générale*. Although the views of Saussure only became influential somewhat after their initial expression, they nonetheless had a fundamental determinative influence (at least in the interpretation given to them by later linguists) on the development of the basic concepts of the field. Furthermore, the very nebulous character of Saussure's actual proposals in the area of 'phonology' (as this is presently construed) makes his work an ideal source in terms of which to introduce a variety of issues that play a role in the subsequent discussion. In this connection, chapter 2 introduces a range of ways in which Saussure's basic insights about sound structure could potentially be worked out—a typology of phonological theories which will prove useful in later chapters.

We then move on in chapter 3 to another of the initial developers of the field, Jan Baudouin de Courtenay, and his collaborator Mikołaj Kruszewski. Though rather less well known than Saussure (in substance, at least), Baudouin de Courtenay and Kruszewski also had a important formative influence on the field, especially on Russian and Eastern European linguists. We follow this influence in chapter 4 through the Moscow school and the early Prague school, and eventually to the work of Trubetzkoy and Jakobson. Jakobson's own later development of this work is discussed apart in chapter 5.

Though they do not fit into the linear development implied by these chapters, it is impossible to ignore the fact that there have been other forms of 'European structuralism' than that represented by the Moscow-Prague-Jakobson tradition. In chapter 6 we sketch the phonological side of glossematic theory (identified notably with the work of Louis Hjelmslev), which is of interest both because its details are comparatively less known than others in current discussion, and because it represents what is arguably the most abstract version of the doctrines of structuralism. A more radical break with a single developmental sequence is forced in order to consider work in the British tradition of prosodic analysis. The close conceptual relations between this point of view and current proposals about autosegmental and metrical structure in phonology require that we give in chapter 7 at least an abbreviated characterization of this theory, whose independence from all of the forms of structuralist (phonemic) phonology is well known—indeed, sometimes overstated.

We then return in chapter 8 to the beginning of the century, to trace the development of linguistics in North America. While the earliest linguists of importance on this continent (e.g., Whitney) may still be said to fall into the European tradition, this cannot be said of Franz Boas and his students, who originated a genuinely independent approach to linguistic problems. From Boas we continue in chapter 9 to Sapir and in chapter 10 to Bloomfield, and then treat in chapter 11 the way in which the views of these figures were (or were not) reflected in the influential theories of (post-Bloomfieldian) American structuralism. The particular problem of the status of morphophonemics in this theory leads us to an evaluation of the beginnings of generative phonology; in chapter 12 we attempt to sum up the relation (both real and imagined) of generative phonology to the two major strands (European and American) which constitute its past. Finally, in the unluckily numbered chapter 13 we venture into the dangerous (but irresistible) area of assessing some trends within generative phonology, broadly construed, since the publication of Chomsky and Halle's landmark work *The Sound Pattern of English* (1968).

This is hardly the first book to be written about the history of linguistics, or the first to deal with phonology in the twentieth century. Such works as Robins (1967), and especially Fischer-Jørgensen (1975) provide a wealth of invaluable information about the general history of the field, without which the present study would hardly be possible. Specialized studies, including a number of the articles in Jakobson (1971a) and Hymes (1974); Kilbury (1976); Stankiewicz (1972); Langendoen (1968); and Hymes and Fought

(1981) among many others have also been of great use. For the most recent period, Newmeyer (1980) has been invaluable, though his work concentrates its attention on the history of syntactic studies.

The primary concern of much of the existing literature dealing with the development of phonological theory, however, is to establish the external history of the figures and events involved in the development of the field, to clarify their influences on one another, and to present their views in responsible and coherent form. These are anything but negligible accomplishments; they do not, however, obviate studies of particular central issues and their origins such as the present one. If much of the substantive content of the chapters below can be found in the published literature, there is still a point in bringing it together in a different way, and in applying it to the problem which forms our focus.

While there is much that is well known and accepted about what we have to say below concerning various historical figures, there are also some places in which the interpretations to be presented diverge from commonly held views. This is particularly true with regard to Saussure, who made the task of subsequent historians immeasurably more difficult by not himself presenting any published account whatsoever of sound structure as a part of general linguistics. We are thus left to infer his position from rather sparse notes and from the codification his views received at the hands of his students and colleagues.

Substantiating a particular reading of Saussure raises another general issue. If the present work were intended exclusively as a contribution to the history of linguistics per se, it would be incumbent on me to establish this interpretation with extensive citations from the literature of Saussureana. Such an effort of scholarship would, however, take me rather far from my central concerns. I content myself here with suggesting what I feel to be a plausible view, and sketching its relation to the ways in which Saussure's work has generally been interpreted in the tradition. It is to be hoped that this view will be found sufficiently useful to warrant subsequent scholarhsip which may determine its justification as an interpretation of Sausure's own picture of sound structure. Similar (but perhaps less important) considerations could be raised in regard to my presentation of other historical figures as well.

Most of the work of establishing the facts concerning the history of phonology in the twentieth century has either been done by others, or would divert us from the purpose of examining the issue of how rules and representations relate to one another. It must also be stressed that no secondary source (such as the present book) can substitute for a close reading of the actual analyses presented by earlier authors, if one wishes to gain a real understanding of their views on language and its structure. Nonetheless, I hope that enough of a picture has been presented below to allow even those not familiar with the specialized literature to form a coherent and generally accurate view of the development of the field.

I

Ferdinand de Saussure

Conventional wisdom holds that the distinctive content of twentieth-century linguistics can in large part be traced back to the work of the Genevan linguist Ferdinand de Saussure. The literature displays, to be sure, a certain amount of jostling for position with regard to historical priority on particular points or the possible influences exerted on Saussure by others; furthermore, the details of just how Saussure acquired (or rather was given) such an influential status remain quite obscure (see Percival 1977). Nonetheless, it seems almost universally agreed that Saussure's views establish a genuine milestone, and the beginnings of what we think of as modern views on language.

Unfortunately, it is not always easy for those who approach the *Cours de linguistique générale* for the first time to see just what all the fuss is about. Many of the observations that seem to form the core of Saussure's system appear thoroughly obvious to the modern reader (when they are not quaintly obscure!), and it is not especially obvious why this should have been such an important book. The reason for this reaction is not simply that Saussure's views have now become the accepted starting point for the field, and are thus familiar; after all, we can appreciate the innovative nature of Copernican astronomy even though its basic results are by now common knowledge. Rather, the difficulty we have in understanding the importance of Saussure's views may be traced to their apparent obviousness in a completely prescientific sense. One has to be an astronomer, with specialized equipment and mathematical techniques at one's disposal, in order to make and interpret the observations that lead to the conclusion that the planets rotate around the sun, but it seems that anyone at all should be able to see the difference between a language as a system and speech as behavior, between the historical development of a language and its present state, and other cornerstones of Saussurean theory.

Indeed, many of his observations obviously had been made before by others, and Saussure's importance does not rest on the claim that everything he said was totally original. Rather, he brought a lot of observations together into a unified system quite at variance with the theories current in the first decades of this century in the scientific study of language. Despite their apparent self-evidence, we must realize that Saussure's basic premises were (in their historical context) thoroughly opposed to those underlying the way scientific linguistics was then being carried out. Furthermore, the very obviousness of many of Saussure's propositions, taken individually, lends the resulting totality a kind of immediacy that accounts for its persuasive, and ultimately revolutionary, character.

Saussure's own view of the importance of his enterprise was that he posed the basic question of *what a language is*, and held it to be the fundamental responsibility of linguistics to provide an answer. Although it may seem self-evident that this is what linguistics is about, we have to recognize that at the time it marked a basic shift in attitude. Others had taken it for granted that everyone knows what a language *is*, and that the questions suitable for scientific study are such as: How do natural languages evolve and change? Where did language come from in the first place? How is logical thought reflected in the structure of language? etc. The demonstrated successes of nineteenth-century comparative linguistics had focused nearly all of the scientific attention that was devoted to language on issues quite distinct from the essential character of linguistic systems, and it was Saussure's accomplishment largely to reverse this trend. As a result, post-Saussurean linguistics has been primarily devoted to synchronic, theoretical studies that are based (at least in principle) on descriptions of actual *états de langue*.

In Saussure's view, the serious study of language might be thought to have begun with the tradition of medieval speculative or philosophical grammar. This evolved, however, into what he saw as merely prescriptive studies, concerned not with what the system of a particular language is but, rather, with what it ought to be. Then, in the nineteenth century, the growing success of comparative linguistics shifted attention to the question of where particular language states come from. This view purported to provide an explanation of any given language in terms of its past; but since it resolutely denied the possibility of finding explanation in any specific present state of affairs, it resulted in an even greater diversion of linguists' energies away from the task of accounting for the basic problem of what a language *is*.

Saussure thus called for a refounding of the essentially synchronic study of language (note that it is difficult even to state this point without using the Saussurean vocabulary) on the basis of a search for explanation and for insight into the fundamental character of the object of study. On this basis alone, his place in the history of the field would surely be guaranteed. More than this, however, and in a more detailed way, Saussure initiated the focus which has dominated the field since on languages as *systems* (as his student Meillet put it, "où tout se tient"), rather than on the often atomistic study of particular elements. Much of the success of historical linguistic studies had come from concentrating attention on the histories of individual sounds (or limited groups of similar sounds); Saussure held out the hope that such a piecemeal (and ultimately fragmented) approach was not the only possible way to a genuinely scientific study of human language.

If a narrow focus on particulars loses sight of the systematic structure within which they find their linguistic place, the attempt to embrace all aspects of the phenomenon of 'language' in a single unified inquiry is also unsatisfactory, since it cannot fail to lead to incoherence. "Taken in its entirety, language is multiform and irregular; straddling several domains, simultaneously physical, physiological and psychological, it belongs both to the individual and to the social realm; it cannot be classified within any category of human reality, because there is no way to distinguish its unity" (Saussure 1916:25). The answer to this dilemma is quite simply to focus on the aspect of language that does furnish a unitary object of inquiry: the character of the underlying systems of particular languages. His work thus did nothing less than establish the fundamental character of the discipline since then.

For linguists, Ferdinand de Saussure stands as a dominating figure of great historical significance. It is therefore somewhat surprising to realize that in Geneva (where he was born and where he spent most of his academic life), he is far from the most famous bearer of the name de Saussure. His family was quite important in scientific and intellectual circles in Switzerland well before his birth in 1857, and other de Saussures have been more prominent than he was in Swiss history and culture. His great-uncle Horace-Bénédict de Saussure (1740–99), in particular, was a major figure in the development of the natural sciences in Geneva; he was especially celebrated for observations made on one of the first ascensions of Mont Blanc, which still form a basis for mapmaking in Switzerland. A number of other ancestors, dating at least to the beginning of the eighteenth century, played significant roles in a variety of scientific fields.

As a result of his family background, it was hardly surprising that the young Ferdinand de Saussure was sent to the University of Geneva in 1875 to study physics and chemistry. By this time he had studied (besides French and German) English, Latin, and Greek; and, indeed, at the age of fifteen he had written an essay on the reduction of all languages to a system of two or three basic consonants. He seems to have discovered early that he was more interested in pursuing linguistic studies than in physics and chemistry; and in 1876 he left Geneva for Leipzig to study Indo-European with such figures as Curtius, Braune, and Leskien (as well as Brugmann, with whom his relationship was rather limited and antagonistic). The next four years (with the exception of a year and a half studying Sanskrit in Berlin) were thus spent among the Leipzig 'Junggrammatiker'.

1876 was a significant year to arrive in Leipzig: this is generally considered the year in which, with regard to the developing theory of the neogrammarians, "everything seemed to happen at once" (Hoenigswald 1978). It was the year in which, among other things, Leskien formulated the doctrine of the regularity of sound change, Verner published his famous article on exceptions to Grimm's law, Brugmann presented his theory of the syllabic nasals of Indo-European (an event which had some impact on the young Saussure, since he had arrived at essentially the same conclusions some years before but refrained from publishing them apparently because of the extent to which they were at variance with then-accepted principles of Indo-European phonology); and Sievers published his *Grundzüge der Lautphysiologie*, which established the phonetic underpinnings of the theory of sound change. Saussure was thus immediately caught up in the sort of atmosphere that surrounds scientific revolutions.

His previous time spent studying languages and thinking about general problems in linguistics had evidently prepared him well to participate actively in this work. He had already in 1875 joined the Société linguistique de Paris, and some of his early work in Indo-European appeared in 1877. His major work, however, was the monumental *Mémoire sur le système primitif des voyelles dans les langues indo-européennes*, which appeared in Leipzig in December 1878 (though it bears the date 1879).

The influence of this work, which presented a comprehensive reconstruction of the vocalic system of Indo-European, is hard to exaggerate: it is by no means absurd to compare its influence on Indo-European linguistics with the influence of the *Cours de linguistique générale* on general linguistics. While the process was long and slow (and indeed, one could argue that it is still not complete), the gradual absorption into the field of historical linguistics of the point of view expressed in Saussure's *Mémoire* came to determine more or less completely the directions taken by the field. It presented a coherent picture of Proto-Indo-European as a system, and defined in an innovative way the problems which occupied subsequent research.

The most famous aspect of this system was the theory of "coefficients sonantiques"; these were the elements, like the liquids and nasals and the high vowels/semivowels (i/y, u/w), which could be realized either as vowels (when surrounded by consonants) or as consonants (when preceded by a vowel). Much of the originality and coherence of Saussure's proposal resulted from the fact that he included in the inventory of *coefficients* two elements which (at the time) were never attested phonetically in a straightforward fashion: they appeared only as some other vowel, or else through their influence on a preceding vowel.

These, of course, were the elements which would subsequently be called 'laryngeals', and the discovery nearly fifty years later by Kuryłowicz of direct (consonantal) reflexes of these segments in Hittite was generally considered as a striking confirmation of a brilliant conjecture on Saussure's part. The most important aspect of the 'laryngeals' in the *Mémoire*, however, was not the discovery of some additional Proto-Indo-European segments but, rather, the methodology which led Saussure to posit them. It was precisely by considering the Indo-European sonants *as a system* that he was led to conclude the existence of additional elements which, though not directly attested (as consonants), nonetheless behaved according to the rules of the system, and had effects apparent in the attested forms. This point of view, which seeks the coherence of the system constituted by a language (whether that language is observed directly or reconstructed) rather than simply investigating the history of the individual elements making up the system, was quite different from the dominant line in historical studies at the time. Partly on its own, and partly because of the dramatic success of the 'laryngeal theory', however, it has come to underlie most modern serious work in historical as well as general linguistics.

There is a reasonably direct connection between the *Mémoire* and Saussure's later views on language in the extent to which the notion of a linguistic system (as opposed to a simple inventory of elements) plays a central role in his work throughout. Another link between his Indo-European studies and his other work was his development in connection with the former of a rather elaborate theory of the structure of syllables and their importance for phonetics. The picture of phonetic structure that would later be developed (and presented slightly out of context by his editors) in the *Cours* is based on the notion that the actual phonetic value of a segment is a function of (a) its "phonetic species" (roughly, its basic articulatory/acoustic type, characterized e.g. as a static position of the articulatory organs) and (b) its position in the syllable (or perhaps in larger units in the spoken chain). We will return to the substance of Saussure's views on such issues of sound structure in the following chapter; for now we can simply note a connection between the phonetic presentation in the *Cours* and the issues dealt with in the *Mémoire* (especially the nature of the *coefficients sonantiques*, whose realization is essentially dependent on the role they play in syllable structure).

In contrast with the vast range of the *Mémoire*, the dissertation which Saussure presented in 1880 for his doctorate in Leipzig seems remarkably limited. This dealt with the uses of the genitive absolute construction in Sanskrit; and while there is no question that it was an extremely learned work, the efforts of later Saussure scholars to identify fundamental issues of linguistic structure addressed in it have not been notably successful. Its merit (and the mention *summa cum laude* which Saussure received at his defense) rested much more on a display of erudition than on lasting significance.

With respect to his published work, indeed, the *Mémoire* was nearly the only important thing Saussure ever wrote. During the ten years after his doctoral thesis, he produced several comparatively short articles devoted to particular historical problems in individual languages. Probably the most significant of these dealt with the accentual system of Lithuanian, but it seems that even here only a part of what he had to say ever appeared in print. And for the rest of his life he would produce virtually nothing more in written form.

Following his doctorate in 1880, Sausure left Leipzig (where it appears that a certain amount of tension had entered into his relations with the *Junggrammatiker*) for Paris. By the fall of 1881, he had been named *maître de conférences de gothique et de vieux-haut allemand* at the Ecole des Hautes Etudes; for the next ten years he taught a series of courses there, primarily in Germanic, but including also Greek and Latin in 1887–88, and more general considerations of Indo-European structure in his last years in Paris. His were among the first courses to be given in historical linguistics in Paris, and he attracted a comparatively large number of students—many of them, apparently, quite good (including Antoine Meillet, Maurice Grammont, Paul Passy, and others whose influence would later be fundamental in the field). He was also increasingly active in the Linguistic Society of Paris; he served in a variety of administrative capacities, and partly as a result of this he was in direct contact with most of the linguists of the time.

His career in Paris was thus a great success. His classes were important and well attended, and he was generally considered a natural candidate for a professorial chair and the Collège de France; in 1891 he was named to the Légion d'honneur. Nonetheless, he decided in that year to leave Paris and return to Geneva. A chair was created there for him as *professeur extraordinaire*, to teach Sanskrit and Indo-European. For the next twenty-two years, until his death in 1913, he taught in Geneva, where his students were many fewer and much less prepared. Indeed, with the exception of a few foreign students who came to Geneva specifically to study with him (such as S. Karcevskij), it is probably not unfair to suggest that hardly any of them achieved distinction in any area except the chronicling of Saussure's life during this time.

His written output, too (already rather sparse during his years in Paris), came to a virtual standstill. In part this seems to have reflected his general disenchantment with the conceptual bases of the field of linguistics. In a letter to Meillet (from 1894, quoted by Godel 1957:31), for instance, he says that he could not write anything sensible about the languages he was working on because it would be necessary first to undertake the immense task of showing linguists just what it is they do: i.e., to reconsider the very foundations of our conception of language. It is hard not to imagine that something other than this epistemological malaise was responsible for his nearly total retreat from the position he had made for himself in Paris, though there is no effective alternative to empty speculation about his reasons.

In any event, he was assigned (in 1906, on the death of another professor) responsibility for courses in general linguistics as well as his basic classes in Sanskrit and Indo-European, and the lectures that resulted have largely formed the basis of Saussure's reputation since. On three occasions (in 1907, 1908–9, and 1910–11), Saussure gave a course in general linguistics at the University of Geneva. When he died in 1913, he had not written any of this material in publishable form; indeed, he had destroyed the greater part of his lecture notes. As a result, we would be left with little but the reminiscences of his students if it were not for the activity undertaken by two of his colleagues.

Charles Bally and Albert Sechehaye had not in fact attended Saussure's lectures on general linguistics but were generally familiar with the position that had been presented in them (Sechehaye's wife, indeed, had been one of the students in Saussure's third and last series of lectures). They undertook, after his death, to reconstruct a book which Saussure *might* have written, on the basis of the little manuscript material that was available and, primarily, the notes taken by students in his lectures. The resulitng *Cours de linguistique générale* was published in 1916, and it is this work that is generally referred to when it is asserted that 'Saussure said' thus and so. The consequence of this method by which 'Saussure's' work was prepared for publication is that we have very little direct evidence for what Saussure actually said about most things, although the consistency of the student notes used by Bally and Sechehaye, together with the unpublished material which they and others (especially Godel, 1954, 1957; and Engler, 1968–74) have provided since give us a reasonable basis for judgment on many topics.

In a way, however, the indirectness of our access to Saussure's thought is thoroughly appropriate. After a rather critical reception accorded the first edition of the *Cours*, it gradually came to be well known during the 1920s and 1930s, partly through translations. It is worth noting that an English translation did not appear until 1959, which is surely responsible at least in part for the general lack of direct reference to Saussurean thought in British and American linguistics. Saussure's influence, such as it was, was exerted almost entirely through this book rather than through any actual linguistic work of his own or of his students. This effect was almost entirely posthumous, and as a result, his importance rests more on what people *thought* he said than on what he actually did say. The indirect way in which the *Cours* reflects his thought, then, helps to emphasize the exact nature of his influence on the subsequent development of specific areas such as phonology.

Despite the fact that Saussure's 'actual' views (whatever they were) were of less importance to the development of the field than the version that was presented by others, we will follow much other Saussure scholarship below in attempting to sort out what he himself had in mind in the areas most central to phonological theory. In part, this enterprise is interesting in itself (and not only for historical reasons); in part, it may serve to establish some perspective on the views others (especially those who considered themselves to be developing a Saussurean notion of 'structuralism') have attributed to him.

The Saussurean view of language, languages, and linguistics

Before approaching Saussure's work in phonology per se, we must discuss the general view of language usually associated with the *Cours de linguistique générale*, and therefore with Saussure. We are concerned here to identify the overall considerations that Saussure felt were relevant to the systematic study of language, and not with the study of sound structure in particular. The latter will form the subject matter of the following chapter. If the present discussion seems somewhat abstract and far from phonological concerns, the issues raised here form an essential preliminary to what follows.

A number of fundamental conceptual oppositions form a convenient framework for discussing Saussure's theory of language. The most basic (and best known) of these is the opposition between *langue* and *parole*: roughly translatable in English as 'language' vs. 'speech,' these terms are both opposed to *langage*, or Language in the most general sense. As we noted above, Saussure rejects this broadly construed notion as a coherent object of scientific inquiry, and focuses instead on the more limited notions of *langue* and *parole*.

The first of these, *langue*, is the aspect of language which represents our knowledge of the systematic correspondences between sound and meaning that make up our language (including the knowledge of what utterances are possible in our language, and what utterances are not). This 'knowledge' consists for Saussure of a system of *signs* (a notion to be further explored below), each of which can be identified with a particular association between sound and meaning. This system of signs constitutes the common knowledge of a speech community: it is therefore independent of the particular properties of any individual member of that community, or of any individual utterance that may be produced on a particular occasion by a speaker of the language.

Parole, on the other hand, is exactly the way in which this knowledge is put to use by individual speakers on particular occasions. For Saussure, this includes (in principle) not only the moment-to-moment details of speaker behavior but also the facts of articulatory and acoustic phonetics that characterize (even in a completely general, non-speaker-dependent way) particular words in the language. There is a certain amount of difficulty with this notion, as we will remark in the following chapter, but it follows in principle from the fact that what matters to the system of *langue* is not the form taken by particular signs but, rather, the fact that these signs are distinct from one another. Since what is not part of *langue* is part of *parole*, it follows that the phonetic form of words belongs to the latter, at least in the concrete details of their implementation.

It will be seen that (making allowances for other differences), the distinction between *langue* and *parole* is quite similar to one which other linguists since Saussure have made under other names. Basically, it is the difference between the system that underlies a language (which distinguishes it for example from other languages), and the use made of that system by the speakers of the language on individual occasions, subject to individual limitations of an idiosyncratic and/or situational nature. Though it is possible to argue (endlessly, it would seem sometimes!) about the precise extent of the parallel, the difference between *langue* and *parole* plays the same role in Saussure's theory of language as the distinction between *competence* and *performance* in the work of Chomsky and other generative grammarians.

Competence represents the knowledge attributed to an (obviously nonexistent) ideal speaker-hearer in a linguistically uniform speech community and is opposed to the details of how and to what extent individual speakers utilize that knowledge under realistic conditions and subject to extralinguistic limitations (*performance*). Competence is thus reasonably similar in character to

Sausure's notion of *langue*, making allowance for other differences between Saussure's and Chomsky's notions of the character of the system. In both cases, it is this distinction that allows the theory to "get off the ground" by giving a principled basis for delimiting the object of study in a way that idealizes away from the infinite variety of real-time events and focuses on their systematic aspect.

The exact character of *langue*, aside from its nature as a system of mutually opposed signs, is not easy to determine with precision from Saussure's writing. On the one hand, *langue* is said to be intrinsically social, in that it is present in a speech community rather than being complete in any individual. On the other hand, it is also described on various occasions as in some way psychological, and present in each member of the speech community. This psychological aspect of *langue* is often overlooked or downgraded in presentations of Saussure's views, but a careful reading of his own notes and those of his students suggests that it occupies a more central place than is sometimes assigned to it.

It is true that there are passages in which Saussure objects to a *purely* psychological interpretation of the nature of *langue*, but these objections are evidently based on two points. On the one hand, *langue* cannot be identified with something psychologically present in any particular individual, since it is the commonality of the system within a speech community that gives it a function as a basis of communication. This objection thus corresponds to the idealized character of *langue* mentioned above: just as the (idealized) competence posited by generative grammarians is not to be identified with the knowledge possessed by some individual speaker; *langue* is not to be identified with what could be found in the mind of individual members of the community of speakers. Nonetheless, both are notions with an essential reference to the structure of human knowledge and cognition, as is clear from the many references in Saussure's notes to the psychological nature of language.

On the other hand, Saussure objected to much that had been written on the psychological nature of language because it attempted to reduce the nature of language to general principles of human psychology, equally valid in domains other than language. Rather, Saussure insisted that a psychological study of language must take as its goal "to establish the scope of expression and to comprehend its laws, not in terms of what they have in common with our psychic organization in general, but on the contrary in terms of what there is that is specific and absolutely unique in the phenomenon of language" (quoted by Godel 1957:52).* *Langue* is thus not the object of study either of particular or of general psychology; but it is nonetheless to be studied in terms of the unique, specific properties of a psychological faculty, idealized away from its realization in specific individuals.

The importance of determining the properties of such a generalized linguis-

---

*Unless otherwise indicated, all quotations from Saussure's works are in my own translation.

tic faculty underlies another sort of confusion in the interpretation of Saussure's notion of *langue*. While this generally refers to the system underlying some particular language at some particular point in time, there are passages in the notes from Saussure's courses suggesting a more general sense: "Par l'observation de ces langues, il [le linguiste] tirera ce qui est universel (var: des traits généraux). Il aura alors devant lui un ensemble d'abstractions; ce sera *la langue*. *La langue* est un ensemble de faits généraux ⟨communs⟩ à toutes *les* langues. La langue est ce qu'on peut observer dans les différents langues" (quoted by Godel 1957:157). *Langue* is thus a construct that represents a distinctive but general cognitive faculty, which is realized in the systems of individual languages.

Over the years, it has become a common assumption that Saussure's view of language as essentially social rested on a notion of social fact derived from the work of Durkheim. It now appears that this picture results almost entirely from the claims of W. Doroszewski, who may well have intended thereby to reduce the apparent originality of Saussure's work (cf. Percival 1977:393–94, 397–98 for some discussion and further references on this issue, which is also discussed at length by Koerner 1973). The reference to Durkheim, in particular, is not substantiated by citations in the *Cours* or in the notes on which it was based; and the character of these notes (see, e.g., the several references to Whitney) would not lead us to expect that Saussure would omit mention of the source of such a fundamental notion as the ultimate ontological status of *langue*.

While there are no doubt similarities between Saussure's and Durkheim's conceptions of the social nature of such an institution as language, there is thus no reason to treat one as identified with (because derived from) the other. Saussure's references to the social character of *langue* seem to be based primarily on the fact that the system in any individual is something received (i.e., learned) from the community, and also that the systems of different individuals must necessarily be in conformity to the extent they allow the exercise of the communicative faculty of language. Such a notion is only obliquely related to Durkhaim's conception of a social fact.

The linguistic sign

As suggested above, the primary reason for distinguishing *langue* from *parole* is to allow the linguist to focus his attention on the former. *Langue* for Saussure is a system of *signs*, and the next basic issue to be clarified is the nature of these signs. Their basic character is that of a unity between a *signifiant* (a 'sound image,' the external or signifying aspect of the sign) and a *signifié* (a concept, the internal or signified aspect of the sign). The sign is not to be identified with either the *signifiant* or the *signifié* but, rather (and precisely), with the association that binds them together. It is the fact that [trij] means 'tree' (in English) that constitutes the sign, and neither the phonetic form [trij] nor the concept 'tree' by themselves are signs.

Importantly, both the *signifiant* and the *signifié* have the property of being in essence arbitrary. It is not hard to see that the range of possible sound shapes, since they differ in obvious ways from language to language, cannot be presumed as given antecedent to a particular language. It is also self-evident (once the question is posed) that, at least on the level of individual meaning-bearing units, the associations between sound and meaning are equally arbitrary: this follows directly from the fact that different languages have different words for the same things.

It is perhaps not quite so clear that the range of possible concepts (*signifiés*) is equally arbitrary, and Saussure spends a certain amount of effort arguing against the view that the inventory of signs in a language constitutes a *nomenclature*, or simply a set of associations between (phonetic) words and a set of antecedently given possible concepts. On the contrary, he argues, the range of concepts is just as much a function of an individual, language-particular sign system as is the set of phonetic forms. Different languages cut up reality in different ways: thus, French distinguishes a chair with arms, regardless of size (*un fauteuil*) from one without (*une chaise*) while English does not (or makes the different distinction between a (large) *armchair* and a (simple) *chair*). On the other hand English distinguishes between a *calf* and its meat used for food (*veal*), while French does not (using *veau* in both cases).

Beyond the fact that different languages have different (phonetic) words, different concepts, and different links between the two, however, the principle of the arbitrariness of the sign has a deeper sense. This is because, according to Saussure, the very notion of a sign as a constituent of a given *langue* is the result of our analysis, and the resulting sign has its reality only in the form of a relation between the terms of such an analysis. In other words, it is not the specific content of a given sign that gives it its existence but, rather, its relation to other signs in the same system—in particular, the fact that it is different from all of those other signs. This is the only kind of 'existence' a sign has (as a term of a linguistic analysis).

Thus, even if two languages contained superficially identical signs, with the same phonetic content and the same conceptual content, we still could not identify them as the "same" sign. Insofar as it is not the case that all of the rest of the signs in the two languages are the same (we assume there are at least some differences: otherwise we would not have two languages), the total network of relations differentiating each sign from others (within its language) differs from the corresponding network of relations in another language. Since it is these networks of differential relations which give a sign its existence as such, the two signs could not be identified.

This last point is worth underlining because Saussure attached a great deal of importance to the methodological issue on which it is based. Most commentators have devoted considerable attention to the claim that the sign's existence is purely formal and demarcative, but have sometimes given the impression that this was a somewhat metaphysical matter of faith. In fact, the purely differentiative and relational nature of the sign goes together completely with other aspects of Saussure's thought, as part of a general reluctance to attribute independent existence to the objects of an analysis conducted from the outside. In any given domain, there may be many different ways of analyzing a set of facts, each of which would yield different 'units' of analysis. The existence of any one of these 'units' is thus in no way antecedent to or independent of the analysis: their reality resides entirely in the extent to which they enter into some real relationship.

In discussing morphological analysis, for example, Saussure notes that in analyzing a form containing a prefix and a stem, the existence of the prefix (insofar as it does not constitute an independent word of the language) is limited to the relation betwen prefixed and unprefixed forms. Only the full words are accorded 'real' status, while their (inseparable) constituent parts derive their ontological status only as a way of representing the connections between members of parallel series. In general, Saussure seemed very reluctant to attribute 'reality' to purely theoretical objects; most of the terms of an analysis are thus names for relations between things, rather than 'things' themselves. When such an object as the sign is characterized as purely relational, we should interpret this not simply as meaning that the only way we can determine its properties is by examining the relations it enters into, but also as meaning that these relations are the only sort of existence it has.

The system of signs which constitutes (a particular) *langue*, then, is a purely formal pattern of relationships among linguistic forms. This system is deposited in each of the individuals in a speech community through their observations of acts of speaking (by other individuals). Once acquired in this way, the system forms the basis of the particular acts of speaking that a member of the speech community engages in. Thus, despite the essential conceptual separation of *langue* from *parole*, the two are quite intimately interconnected. The very development of *langue* depends on (observations of) *parole*—while any particular instance of *parole* only has the character it does by virtue of the underlying system of *langue*. This conception of the relation between language (considered as a system) and speech (considered as behavior) is not new with Saussure (as indeed the distinction is not), but he was perhaps the first to attempt to develop its consequences for the nature of language in general as fully as he did.

The relation of languages to their history

We come now to another of the cornerstones of the Saussurean view of language, his picture of the relation between language and language change. We can note first that, since linguistic signs are totally arbitrary (in the senses discussed above), there is no external constraint other than mere tradition within a community to keep them from changing. On the other hand, the arbitrariness of the sign also has the consequence that there is no possible basis for discussion that would convince members of the speech community to change the signs in use at a given time. This means that change in the system of *langue* itself would be completely irrational—and from this Saussure concludes (with what some might see as an exquisitely French turn of logic) that change in *langue* simply does not occur by itself.

Rather, change takes place in (particular acts of) *parole*; changes in *langue* result from the relationship between *langue* and *parole* which we discussed above, and are in no way motivated by the system itself. With regard to the motivations for (and thus the explanation of) change, recall that the *signifiant* of a sign is phonetic in character, and thus the details of its implementation belong to a branch of the study of *parole* which deals with phonetic phenomena. Phonetic change thus takes place entirely within *parole* (for reasons external to the nature of language), though it may have consequences for the system of *langue*—for instance, if it leads to a state of affairs in which the *signifiants* of two signs are no longer distinct.

This leads us to another of the famous dichotomies associated with Saussure's name: that between *synchronic* linguistics (or the study of a particular *état de langue* representing the language of a particular community at a particular time) and *diachronic* linguistics (the study of language from a historical point of view, including reconstruction as well as other aspects of the relation between historical stages in what we think of as the "same" language). From the point of view of what linguists actually do with their time, it was probably Saussure's insistence on the priority of the synchronic study of language that had more effect than anything else he said, for this resulted in an almost total reversal of the direction of the field.

It would seem reasonable that, if the primary goal of linguistics is, as Saussure had emphasized, to account for what a language *is*, an account of the nature of synchronic language systems must be its fundamental concern. If one is attempting to understand the nature of the knowledge we attribute to speakers of a particular language, it might appear that historical considerations could be excluded directly on the basis that (with the exception of the odd philologist) native speakers have no knowledge of, or even access to, the history of their language. Here, as in several other places, Saussure draws an analogy wth a game of chess. In understanding the nature of a given position in a game and the possibilities inherent in the present arrangement of the pieces at a particular point, an observer who has been following the entire game since its beginning has no advantage over one who arrives only at the point in question: for both, it is the *present* position (including the fact of whose move comes next) and nothing else that matters. The same might well seem valid in the study of language, and one would expect that the prority of strictly synchronic studies in linguistics would be established by merely pointing this out.

In arguing for the centrality of synchronic considerations, however, Saussure was challenging the central doctrine of the then-current neogrammarian view of explanation in linguistics: that historical study was not only important but, indeed, the *only* genuinely 'scientific' approach to the facts of language. Interestingly enough, the temptation of this view can be seen as being based on an essentially Saussurean insight: the arbitrariness of the linguistic sign. If the signs of a particular language are indeed completely arbitrary, then their present reality can have no possible present explanation. If we thus seek an explanation of the way things are, the best we can do is to show how they got to be that way: to establish such antecedent stages as we can, and a chain of sound "laws" relating them to one another and to the forms presently in use. This was the view of scholars such as Hermann Paul and Karl Brugmann, and the spectacular success of the neogrammarian methods in the study of Indo-European resulted in its overwhelming acceptance at the time.

For Saussure, however, such a theory was completely unsatisfactory as an explanatory account of the nature of language (or of particular languages). An obvious objection to the historical view is that it simply pushes the problem back: if we account for a present stage in terms of an orderly series of changes undergone by an earlier system, we are still left with no account at all of that earlier system itself. Where did *it* come from? The chicken-and-egg aspect of this problem is self-evident, but we might regard the difficulty as even more pernicious than that. This is because, in seeking antecedent stages from which to derive a present *état de langue*, we continually push the problem back into reconstructed systems which cannot even be observed (except inferentially, through the testimony of their modern reflexes).

A second, and even more fundamental difficulty with the historical notion of explanation was that, for Saussure, it completely falsifies the object of study. As we saw above, Saussure saw the locus of historical change (and thus the domain of operation of sound laws) as exclusively in *parole*. If we look to historical change for an explanation of a synchronic state, however, we are thereby attempting to reduce the facts of *langue* to facts of *parole*, which is totally illegitimate, given the basic conceptual distinctness of the two.

This is not to say, of course, that we cannot study linguistic change systematically. We can recognize that diachronically related stages of a given language represent distinct *états de langue* which are nonetheless systematically related, and thus that change does affect *langue* over time. As we saw above, however, the link between such related systems is, strictly speaking, outside of the domain of the study of *langue* itself. Through the operation of phonetic tendencies which affect acts of *parole*, a subsequent generation (having different primary linguistic experience to go on) may well induce a different system of *langue* on the basis of the observations of *parole* which they make—resulting in a linguistic change apparently affecting *langue*. The important point to make here, though, is that the motivation for the change is never in *langue* itself. The study of change is entirely dependent on the prior understanding of synchronic states in themselves, together with facts from a discipline external to the study of *langue* (i.e., phonetics, a branch of the study of *parole*). Historical studies thus can never yield an explanatory theory of the nature of *langue*.

One might well suggest that, while Saussure's view seems cogent with regard to phonetic change, the phenomenon of analogy surely represents a type of change motivated by the system of *langue* directly, and thus belongs to the study of *langue*. Saussure anticipated this objection, however, and provided an answer.

According to his conception of its nature, analogy constitutes an aspect of *langue* all right, but not change in *langue*, because analogy is claimed not to constitute a change at all. Rather, when we create an apparently novel analogical form, we are doing so (by the definition of analogy) by applying some rule of the system of *langue*: a rule which already existed prior to its application. We are thus simply realizing a latent possibility of the system, rather than effecting a change in it. Although it will be seen that this view of analogy saves Saussure's claim that the study of historical change is never a proper part of the study of *langue*, it is apparent that if it is carried to its logical conclusion, it results in such a broad a notion of the rules of the system that it is probably not satisfactory. Nonetheless, since Saussure gave very little attention to the problem of how to formulate the rules of a synchronic system, this consequence did not arise for him.

The central point of the Saussurean notion of linguistics, then, is that there is nothing that historical investigation can contribute to the study of synchronic linguistics, and it is this synchronic study alone that can yield explanatory answers to the central question of the field: the nature of a language (and, in general, the nature of *langue*). It might seem that in order to establish the priority of synchrony in the study of language, it would suffice to point out the considerations just discussed; it is therefore a bit hard to see why so much space is devoted in the *Cours* and in Saussure's notes to repeatedly exorcising the spirit of a historical approach from linguistics.

A consideration of the predominance of such historically oriented views at the time, however, quickly shows us why so much attention is devoted to this issue. When we recall the extent to which, at the end of the nineteenth century, historical linguistics was considered to provide a genuine explanation (and, indeed, the only scientifically valid one) for the facts of particular languages, we can see why Saussure felt compelled to return to this issue again and again, in every conceivable context. It is quite possible, in addition, that the purely personal factor of his own somewhat tense relationship with prominent figures of the neogrammarian movement during his student days in Leipzig had (at least subconsciously) something to do with the fervor with which he pursued this end.

Whatever the reasons, Saussure's work is most assiduous in eliminating from his formulations anything that bears the slightest resemblance to a historical approach to central linguistic problems. He probably realized that this attitude was in some ways slightly exaggerated, but felt that in the then-current climate of opinion there was "no danger in insisting above all on the nonhistorical side" (quoted in Godel 1957:45). This was no doubt true, and perhaps any less vigorous defense of the priority of synchronic considerations would have been less effective in reorienting the field toward its central problem. Nonetheless, Saussure's categorical rejection of anything with even an appearance of a historical basis had profound consequences for the delimitation of problems and possible solutions in the study of sound systems: consequences which Saussure might or might not have accepted, but which go well beyond the scope of his fundamental objections. We will see some of these in the next chapter.

2

Saussure's Views on Sound Structure

There is a decided lack of concrete evidence to be found in Saussure's own work for the way one ought to apply his general views to the specific problem of the sound structure of language. Although the nature of synchronic linguistic systems occupied his attention during most of his teaching career (at least after his return to Geneva), he only discussed such questions in his very last classes. Furthermore, he produced essentially no actual descriptions of individual languages, and we are thus deprived of most possible sources of evidence for his views.

The *Cours* itself is largely devoted to the general semiological problem of the nature of the linguistic sign, and says little that is very specific about the character of sound systems. There is, however, one important source of evidence in this work: the appendix to the introduction, which deals with (what we would now call) phonetics. This appendix represents a curious interpolation in the rest of the text, since unlike the remainder of the book, it is based not on Saussure's lectures on general linguistics but on a series of lectures given in 1897 on the theory of the syllable. Bally's own notes on these lectures, together with student notes on a similar presentation at the beginning of the first series of lectures on general linguistics in 1906, form the basis of the text.

It might appear that if this material is our primary source for Saussure's picture of sound structure, its comparatively early date compromises its relevance to his later views on general linguistics. The reappearance of essentially the same presentation in his later lectures, however, suggests that his ideas on these topics remained relatively stable. In addition to this appendix, it is also possible to cite some few notes of Saussure's own (Godel 1954), and some additional notes (evidently for a book on the subject) in a manuscript in the Harvard library that has been studied by Jakobson (1970). Finally, some conclusions can be drawn (especially concerning Saussure's view of alternations) from his courses in 1909–10 on Greek and Latin phonology (see Reichler-Béguelin 1980) and morphology (see Godel 1957). The overall picture that emerges is a coherent one, and does not suggest that the 1897 material in the *Cours* was unrepresentative of Saussure's later views.

The reason for dwelling on these purely textual issues is that, while Saussure's name conveys a sense of almost ultimate authority (at least for some), finding out what his actual opinions were on concrete issues is often all too much like the interpretation of the ancient oracles. A very sparse and limited text, full of suggestion but lacking in specifics, allows each interpreter to find what he wants, and thus to legitimize his own picture of the problem. No doubt the presentation in this chapter does not avoid such traps either, but there seem to be some fairly clear points in Saussure's presentation of phonetic problems, and we will attempt to stay close to these.

Sounds, sound images, and their study

We can recall that Saussure took linguistics to be the study of a certain class of *signs*, and that the signs in question have the character of uniting a (signified) concept with a (signifying) sound image. Most interpreters of Saussure have attempted to downplay the linguistic relevance of the sound images, but it seems to me that to ignore the question of what specific character they have is in a way to miss the point of Saussure's conception of language.

It is common, for instance, to cite the Saussurian doctrine that "dans la langue il n'y a que des différences . . . sans termes positifs" as evidence for the view that the particular elements composing the sound system are not legitimately the object of linguistic study. But to say that the linguist must be primarily concerned with *differences between* sounds is not by any means to reject entirely the study of the sounds themselves. While the linguist's main interest is in the system of oppositions between signs, these oppositions rest on the differences among sound images, and these differences themselves reside in the character of the sounds that are differentiated. Saussure thus stresses that the study of the formation and positive, physical character of sounds (the content of traditional phonetics) is not *in itself* a linguistic study: it is only when we consider the *relations* between sound images that we are studying the system of language. But his insistence on the sound image as one of the two inseparable faces of the sign makes it clear that insofar as their nature supports their differential function, these sound images are indeed an aspect of the object studied in linguistics.

We can perhaps make this issue more concrete by posing it in terms of our usual conception of a grammar today. Within such a grammar, we can identify two aspects of the description of the sound system of a language. First, the grammar provides a set of *representations* for linguistic forms, in the form of a system of transcription together with the principles for its interpretation. Such a system of transcription is generally taken to be fundamentally independent of any particular language, and its definition is given in universally applicable terms based on human linguistic capacities (rather than on the facts of an individual language).

Second, however, a grammar provides a system of *rules*, or principles particular to an individual language, which characterize some of these representations as (potentially) belonging to different signs, and others as (potentially) belonging to the same sign in Saussurean terms. 'Redundancy rules', for example, specify that if the representation corresponding to a given sign has some property P, it must also have (or, in some cases, may not have) some other property P'. Such rules specify the range of permissible variation in the realizations of a given sign, and thus (by implication) the characteristics that necessarily differentiate distinct signs. There are, of course, other sorts of regularity than those expressed in redundancy rules, and these are described by other sorts of rule. The general point should be clear: the rules of language (as opposed to the transcriptional system employed to represent forms in the language) are particular to that language, and, taken together, they characterize the system by which sound differences correspond to oppositions between signs.

Saussure's point, formulated in these terms, is clear: it is the business of the linguist to study not the nature of (phonetic) representations but the system of rules which underlies the differentiation of signs and thus constitutes a particular language. Seen in this light, however, the sound system itself is anything but irrelevant to the task of the linguist. Indeed, it is only on the basis of an understanding of the nature of sound images that the task of formulating the rules making up any particular system of signs can even be approached. We must arrive at a proper conception of these sound images in order to have an appropriate basis for the study of the system. For one thing, as we will note below, they are identified less with an *articulatory* characterization of utterances than with a somewhat more abstract and 'timeless' perceptual one. Yet they constitute the elementary units whose differentiation is the basis of the linguistic system.

It is sometimes suggested, nonetheless, that Saussure felt signs to be such abstract entities that the connection between the *signifiant* of a sign and a sound image per se is a completely accidental and contingent fact, unconnected with the nature of language. Indeed, it is insisted in the *Cours* that the material sound itself does not belong to *langue* but is simply the substance which supports linguistic expression ("*phonation . . .* is only the execution of the sound images"—cited by Godel 1957:82), and thus is a matter of *parole*. What is at issue here is the irrelevant or accidental character not of sound images as is sometimes suggested, but of *sounds*. These latter, for Saussure, are particular physical, articulatory implementations of linguistic possibilities, and thus belong to the study of *parole*. Sound images, on the other hand, have a timeless character as perceptual archetypes (1916:98); and while these serve as the basis of concrete acts of production or perception, they are not to be identified with them. These sound images, as essential (though not independent) components of the linguistic sign, are thus not excluded from *langue*.

To this interpretation it might be objected that Saussure explicitly says that phonetic implementation of sounds is not necessary, since the signs can be evoked by other means. It is, however, revealing to note the example Saussure uses to make this point: to wit, the possibility of transposing linguistic signs into writing. On the face of it, the expression of signs in writing has nothing whatsoever to do with sound images, since it involves a completely different, visual rather than auditory medium.

If we look at the context of this example in the notes on which the *Cours* is based, however (see Godel 1957: 193–94), the issue appears in a somewhat different light. In fact, for Saussure, writing bears a more or less direct relation (depending on the particular system) to the system of sound images, taken in its essential (rather than external, articulatory) character. The segmentation imposed by alphabetic writing systems, he feels, corresponds to a fundamental property of sound images. This is a point he makes explicitly in the *Cours* with regard to the Greek writing system: its segmentation reflects the parallel segmentation of sounds in perception, which is imposed as a part of the essential character of human speech perception. Alphabetic writing thus provides a sometimes imperfect, but largely accurate, representation of *sound images*, just as the articulatory formation of concrete sounds does. The relevance of the example of signs realized in writing, then, is not that *sound images* are inessential to *langue* but that (physical) *sounds* are. We must conclude, then, that an appreciation of Saussure's views on the system of language must be founded, in part, on his conception of the nature of sound images.

In the study of sound images, Saussure distinguishes essentially three approaches which can be seen as characterizing three distinct fields. To a considerable extent, these divisions correspond to those of later linguists, but although he often uses the same terms as those appearing in later work, he uses them in radically different ways. For the modern reader, the Saussurean terminology thus requires at least a note of clarification.

The nature of the linguistic sign (especially its linear character) and its realization in syntagmatic combinations leads directly to the study of *morphology*, in approximately the sense of subsequent linguistic theory. The spoken chain can be divided into discrete signs, and morphology is the study of the principles underlying such division. In various places, it is made clear that this segmentation of the chain is based on (synchronic) proportional analogies, which establish the relations between morphologically related words. As noted in chapter 1, Saussure is reluctant to attribute independent existence to the subparts of words isolated in this way, preferring to concentrate on the relations which underlie the divisions. For our purposes here, it is sufficient to note that divisions corresponding to different signs at least the size of the word are assumed to exist and to be real to the speakers of the language.

Individual signs in the spoken chain can be studied in terms of the mechanisms and principles by which their sound images are realized in speech, but this study is, by its nature, part of the linguistics of *parole* rather than of *langue*. Saussure calls this synchronic study of the articulation and acoustics of concrete sounds *phonologie*: it is essentially the same as what most linguists would today call *phonetics*. In the discussion below, we will use the modern terminology except where it is essential to call attention to Saussure's usage (in which case we will refer to this discipline as *phonologie*).

Saussure also distinguishes a discipline which he calls *phonétique*, but he uses that word in quite a different sense than we do today. Saussure's *phonétique* is not a synchronic study at all; rather, it is the study of the historical evolution and change of sounds. Like his *phonologie*, it is an aspect of the study of *parole*, since it is essentially based on the mechanisms by which speakers realize the signs of their language in concrete acts of speaking. Saussure had considerable faith (as had the neogrammarians) that the detailed study of the facts of speech would yield a comprehensive explanation of the mechanisms of sound change. To conform more closely to modern usage, we will refer to this study below as *historical phonetics* (except where Saussure's terminology itself is in question).

Saussure's usage of *phonologie* and *phonétique* is somewhat confusing to the modern reader, since essentially no one other than his student M. Grammont (from his years in Paris) followed his terminology. Nonetheless, both terms correspond to well-established aspects of the study of speech. Neither one provides us with a name for the study of sound images considered as a part of *langue*, however. The sound images that form one aspect of the linguistic sign differ from concrete sounds in essential ways (they are timeless rather than being realized in time, they are neutral between production and perception, etc.) and thus are not directly accessible to either phonetic or historical phonetic study. In fact, there is no reason to believe Saussure had any word for the study of the role of sounds in *langue*: this is simply an aspect of *linguistics*. Indeed, since he emphasizes many times in his lectures that the study of the linguistic sign must be based on the *simultaneous* study of the *signifiant* and the *signifié*, the pedagogical concerns which are so evident everywhere in his presentation of fundamental problems would probably have led him to avoid any term which would suggest an illicit separation of one face of the sign from the other.

'*Phonèmes*' and 'phonetic species'

To understand the nature of sound images, let us contrast them with the object of study in phonetics. Using the (not specifically linguistic) methods of physical investigation, we can study the units of sound in speech. These units have an articulatory side, and also an auditory aspect (called 'acoustic' by Saussure): they thus have "a foot in each chain," as he puts it—which does not mean that they are thereby *neutral* between the two ways in which we can study speech, but rather that both sides are relevant to their character. These concrete, actualized speech sounds, produced and perceived in real time in acts of speaking, are called by Saussure *phonèmes*.

Of all of the divergences between Saussure's terminology and that of later writers, this is undoubtedly the one which has given rise to the most misunderstanding. While the word 'phoneme' in its incarnations in various languages later came to designate a specifically *distinctive* sound element, it is quite clear that Saussure does not use it at all in that way. Rather, he intends by the word *phonème* simply a 'speech sound', with no connotations of language-particular distinctive character. When he speaks of the distinctive properties of these elements, he means by this simply that it is in terms of differences between speech sounds that the oppositions between signs are indicated in speech: this does not at all imply that the *phonème* itself is a unit whose content is limited to its distinctive function, as later phonologists would come to use the word.

In fact, for whatever historical interest this has, Saussure's use of the word corresponds to its original sense. According to Godel (1957; see also Jakobson, 1960), the word was coined by the French linguist A. Dufriche-Desgenettes, along with a number of other novel formations (which did not enjoy nearly as much success) in presentations to the Société linguistique de Paris in the early 1870s. For the originator of such a prominent term in linguistics, we know surprisingly little about Dufriche-Desgenettes: apparently his full first name is not even recorded. Aside from a few papers delivered to the Société linguistique of which either the text or a report appeared in its publications, we know him only as one of the charter members of the society. It is also recorded, however, that on one occasion he proposed the repeal of the society's constitutional provision against discussion of the origins of language (which he could not recall having approved at the time); in the absence of a seconder, the proposal was lost.

In any event, Dufriche-Desgenettes proposed the use of the word *phonème* as a substitute for the German *Sprachlaut*, and thus intended it simply as a designation of a (unitary) sound. The word was taken up by other linguists in Paris, and Saussure uses it in the Mémoire (though in yet another sense). In his work in general linguistics, it is clear that it designates what we would today call phonetic segments, considered as (ultimately unreducible) units in acts of speaking.

The integral and atomic character of Saussure's 'phonemes' is confirmed, for him, by the process of perception. On his view, when we perceive speech it is directly in terms of a sequence of internally homogeneous and atemporal acoustic impressions, corresponding to the sequence of phonemes. In the face of the measurable continuity of the speech signal, a process of segmentation is thus seen as built into the perceptual system (see the remarks above on the reflection of this segmentation in writing systems). Given the interest of nineteenth-century phoneticians in the transitions and continous character of speech, this is a rather remarkable suggestion. Saussure cites no source for it, and takes it as a self-evident observation. Nonetheless, it would be interesting to know where this view came from.

Since the unitary percepts corresponding to phonemes are internally homogeneous, we cannot analyze them directly. When we seek to describe phonemes, therefore, we do so in terms of their articulatory face, by describing the gestures of the vocal apparatus necessary to produce them. The actual classification of phonemes on this basis which Saussure gives is based directly on the phonetic views of Jespersen, with no particularly innovative features.

There is, however, a more abstract unit in phonetics than the phoneme. Phonemes are, by their nature, articulated in combination in the spoken chain. In particular, each phoneme occupies a particular place within a larger unit, the syllable. By virtue of its position in the syllable, a phoneme may have various characteristics which would differentiate it from other, similar phonemes. The most extensively described of these is the difference between *implosive* (dynamically closing) and *explosive* (or dynamically opening) articulations. In English [dɪd], for example, the initial [d] is explosive, while the final [d] is implosive: Saussure would thus transcribe the sequence as [d̓ɪd̕].

The articulations [d̕] and [d̓] are clearly distinct (quite independent of any issues of voicing, final release, etc.), and thus implosive and explosive segments constitute different phonemes. The difference between them, however, are based on the articulatory organization of a higher level unit (the syllable). When we abstract away from the differences due to this factor, we arrive at the *phonetic species*: a unit characterizable in terms of a non-time-varying position of the articulators, and thus the sort of description we usually give in phonetics. Both implosive [d̕] and explosive [d̓] belong to the same phonetic species, [D]. There are said to be a finite, though perhaps large, number of possible distinct phonetic species, whose characterization is not dependent on a particular language.

Saussure appears to hold that the auditory impressions corresponding to phonemes of the same phonetic species are the same, and thus that this unit is closer to the auditorily basic unit in speech than the phoneme itself. Specific phonemes are the positional realizations of phonetic species, where the variations among them are due primarily to general phonetic, rather than language-particular, principles. Fundamentally, it is syllabic organization that is being idealized away from here, and one can easily detect the relation of this view to the theory of *coefficients sonantiques* presented in the *Mémoire*. For example, one of the recurring examples of different phonemes belonging to the same species is Saussure's description of (prevocalic, onglide) [y], (vowel) [i], and (postvocalic offglide, or second element of a diphthong) [i̯] as members of the same species [I]. Aside from simple position in the syllable, however, there are other differences between phonemes that depend on their implementation in combination with other specific neighboring phonemes, and that may also be significant.

A comprehensive specification of the principles by which the same phonetic species corresponds to different phonemes depending on its specific position in the spoken chain would yield a sort of 'combinatorial phonetics'. Ultimately, the possibility of explaining historical changes within historical phonetics depends on the development of such principles, since the occurrence of change in *parole* is based on the detailed positional variation between phonemes. For example, Saussure considers the sequences [..Vgn..] and [..Vng..] (as well as other sequences of stop and sonorant) in the history of Germanic. The first (stop plus sonorant) developed an epenthetic vowel, while the second (sonorant plus stop) did not (and in this case, underwent assimilation). If we ask why this difference arose, we cannot provide an answer at the level of the phonetic species, where the difference is completely arbitrary. In principle, however, a consideration of the low-level variation between the phonemes involved would provide us with the basis of an explanation, since the resonant preceding the stop would be formed differently (and would thus be a different phoneme) from that following it. A corresponding difference would be present in the stops as well, of course.

Though Saussure was not in a position to provide such explanations in detail, he was clearly confident that a suitably worked-out theory of combinatorial phonetics would yield them. This faith that a sufficiently minute study of (synchronic) phonetic detail would furnish comprehensive explanations for phonetic change was a prevalent attitude at the time, arising from a fusion of neogrammarian studies on the regularity of sound change with the increasing observational sophistication of late nineteenth century phonetics. This notion of an explanatory historical phonetics (as based on combinatory *phonologie*) was carried considerably further in the studies of Saussure's student Grammont (e.g., Grammont 1933). It recurs (though perhaps for completely independent reasons) in some current work, such as the view of phoneticians like Ohala (see, e.g., Ohala 1979) that the substantive content of phonological rules can be exhaustively related to detailed facts of phonetics. Apparently, however, this remains a research program rather than a demonstrated proposition, just as it was in Saussure's time (cf. Anderson 1981).

The lingusitic representation of *signifiants*

Now that we have established the nature of the objects studied by phonetics (Saussure's *phonologie*), we can return to the question of the nature of the *signifiants* of linguistic signs. These are almost always referred to by Saussure as *images acoustiques*, or 'sound images', and characterized as a psychic reality that determines both the speaker's intentions and his perceptions. The sound image is thus neutral between production and perception: it is the pattern which the speaker attempts to conform to in production, and against which he matches external stimuli in perception, but its nature is not to be identified with either the one or the other. We can contrast this neutral character with the bivalent nature of the phoneme: the phoneme is a concrete sound, and thus has both a manner of production and a specific result in perception. The sound image, however, is *neither* produced *nor* perceived in individual, concrete acts of speaking; rather, it determines the category to which particular productions or perceptions are to be assigned.

When we speak, we attempt to produce a sequence of sounds that will conform to the sound images of the signs we are employing. The mechanism by which we do so is, strictly speaking, irrelevant to the character of those sound images, and thus of the signs themselves. Our listener in turn perceives our speech as having a certain meaning, by virtue of the fact that the value-assigning properties of a sign in his own system are activated when our acts of speaking conform to its sound image. The relation between sound images and particular productions or perceptions is thus rather like that between *types* of elements and particular *tokens* of those types. Of course, having observed that the difference between sound images and concrete sounds follows from their respective ontological status, we have still not said anything very specific about what sort of properties sound images have except that whatever these are, they must be sufficient to support both production and perception when the system of signs is employed in concrete acts of speaking.

In discussing the *signifiants* of linguistic signs, Saussure emphasizes repeatedly that what is essential to them is the fact that they differ from one another. In the study of *langue*, our interest is in characterizing these differences, which organize the individual signs into a system of relations. This is really the fundamental contribution which Saussure made to the development of linguistics: to focus the attention of the linguist on the system of regularities and relations which support the differences among signs, rather than on the details of individual sound and meaning in and of themselves.

At the beginning of the twentieth century, this was a necessary and timely shift in interest. The development of instrumental phonetic techniques to replace earlier, largely introspective methods resulted in studies so sophisticated that significance began to be lost in phonetic detail. Once we recognize the range of aspects of a speech event which it is possible to quantify, there is no apparent criterion by which we can decide that a given amount of detail is enough. We soon reach a point at which it is clear that while our measurements may well represent true observations of the speech event, they no longer represent things that are essential to its linguistic function. Nothing in the physical event (Saussure's phoneme) tells us what is worth measuring and what is not.

Saussure's distinction between concrete sounds and the *signifiants* of signs, however, throws such phonetic studies into immediate focus: the linguistic function of a phonetic property is determined by its role in separating (or not separating) productions or perceptions corresponding to one sign from those corresponding to another. For Saussure, the detailed information accumulated by phoneticians is of only limited utility for the linguist, since he is primarily interested in the ways in which sound images differ, and thus does not need to know everything the phonetician can tell him.

By this move, then, linguists could be emancipated from their growing obsession with phonetic detail. This still does not tell them much, however, about what the sound images they *are* interested in are like. The indication of (at least Saussure's conception of) their nature, though, is to be found in their name: *images acoustiques*, by its content (and also by comparison with the *impressions acoustiques* associated with the perception of concrete phonetic segments), suggests that these were simply idealized phonetic representations, fully specified for phonetic detail down to the level of the phonetic species (though not to that of the phoneme). The difference between the *signifiant* of a sign, and a phonetic representation (at the level of phonetic species) of an utterance making use of that sign is thus a difference not in the amount of information included but in the ontological status of the characterization. As we suggested above, this difference is rather like that between types and tokens.

The suggestion that the *signifiants* of signs are to be taken as specified for a considerable range of phonetic properties is quite contrary to the general interpretation in the literature of Saussure's views. Because of his insistence on the central nature of the *differentiating* properties of *signifiants*, it has been assumed that these should be taken as specified only for their distinctive properties. On this view, any property of a given phonetic species which does not serve to distinguish one sign from another within a given language should be left entirely unmentioned in the representation of corresponding *signifiants* in that language (though it might be specified, if distinctive, in the representation of *signifiants* in some other language).

In fact, however, this notion of partially specified *signifiants* is difficult to support on the basis of anything Saussure actually says. Nowhere does he say directly that a representation of signs (or rather, of their *signifiants*) would be fundamentally different in character (except for the difference in ontological status stressed above) from a phonetic representation. There is no suggestion, that is (even where he appears to be raising the issue), that there is a need for a distinct "phonemic" representation in what would come to be the post-Saussurean acceptance of this term.

Both what Saussure says and what he does not say imply that representations of *signifiants* are fully specified (to the same degree as phonetic species). For example, in discussing transcriptions, he suggests that a fully detailed phonetic transcription (noting all of the properties of individual phonemes) is really only useful for the physical scientist, and not for the linguist. The reason presented for this, however, is *not* that such a transcription would include redundant detail, but rather that it is clumsy and unaesthetic. A simpler representation, sufficient to indicate phonetic species, is quite satisfactory for linguistic purposes. We must remember that the representation whose linguistic significance Saussure is opposing is one whose degree of physical precision is limited only by the ingenuity of the phonetician and the accuracy of his measuring instruments—not one which simply includes some indication of properties which, while they may characterize a particular phonetic species, do not happen to serve distinctively in the individual language under investigaton.

The interpretation of Saussure's ideas here may seem somewhat paradoxical: after all, what characterizes a *signifiant* and gives it its value within a given system of *langue* is what distinguishes it from the other *signifiants* within that system. Thus, the study of *langue* must elucidate the distinctions or oppositions among signs, and it would appear that this goal is not consistent with a representation of *signifiants* which does not distinguish between distinctive and non-distinctive properties in the sound image.

This apparent difficulty results from confining our attention to the role of representations in a phonological description. To resolve it, we must recall Saussure's general reluctance to attribute 'reality' to units that result from a linguistic analysis. Rather, he preferred to assign 'reality' to the *relations* which such an analysis reveals between linguistic units. Returning to the conception of a linguistic description as consisting not only of a set of representations for linguistic elements, but also a set of rules determining the form and interconnections of these elements, we can see that the task of elucidating the system of differences among signs might well be construed as a problem to be solved by presenting the system of rules, without necessarily involving the choice of a set of representations.

Some approaches to the study of phonological differences

To make this suggestion somewhat more concrete, let us consider several different ways in which one might undertake to describe the differences among the (*signifiants* of) signs in a language. We can characterize these theories in terms of the properties they assign to a systematic notation for (language-particular) *signifiants*, which we will call a *phonological* representation, and the relation between this notation and the rest of the description (the rules). As we will see in later chapters, all of the approaches to be sketched below have in fact been taken at various times in the history of enquiry into sound structure, and they are thus not simply straw men.

At one extreme, we might decide to focus all of our attention on the set of phonological representations which the theory provides for forms in the language. We would then, in essence, ignore the status of rules in our description; but we could nonetheless come quite close to a description identifying the properties which distinguish signs from one another provided we could define phonological representations so that they will have exactly that character. On such a view, phonological representations would have to be specified *only* for the distinctive properties of the forms they correspond to. While a universally applicable theory of possible phonetic representations would presumably make provision for the indication of additional properties, not distinctive in the language in question, those would be 'left blank' in the representations of forms in this language.

Of course, we can imagine many implementations of such a theory, differing in particular in the inventory of properties they recognize as differentiating phonological elements (and particularly in the relation between these properties and phonetically observable ones). These differences are immaterial for the moment, since the characteristic of such a theory to which we wish to draw attention is its exclusive focus on defining 'distinctiveness', 'contrast', etc. in terms of the set of properties which are marked in phonological representations within a given language.

In fact, it is this sort of approach that has characterized most versions of 'phonemic' theory in phonology. Such a theory describes the differences between signs by defining a set of phonemes (no longer in Saussure's sense), each of which is a segment characterized for *all* and *only* those properties that set it apart from the other segments of the system. A phonological representation then consists of a sequence of such phonemes. Again, variations can be imagined: in some versions of this theory, for example, additional properties may be extracted and left unmarked when they are unpredictable within specific *sequences* of phonemes (thus, otherwise-distinctive point of articulation features in a nasal consonant may be omitted when it precedes an obstruent). For our purposes, what matters is that some criterion for 'distinctiveness' of a property, once given, is implemented as the definition of a notation which is free of all nondistinctive properties.

Of course, we must then define the relation between the phonological notation and the phonetic reality it stands for. This relation is a matter of a set of (in practice, often unstated) rules, which have the function of 'filling in the blanks' in the phonological representation: i.e., adding nondistinctive properties to the set which can be directly projected from the phonemic form. These rules are in some ways similar to those evidently posited by Saussure to relate phonetic species to *phonèmes* by adding phonetic detail which arises as a result of the combinatory environment in which a given segment is realized. Saussure's rules, however, are clearly not to be construed as part of the system of any particular language. They are rather a consequence of the (purely phonetic) universal mechanism of human speech production. As an aspect of *parole*, they do not belong to the system of *langue* in either the general or the language-particular sense. The phonemic rules required by the theory outlined above, however, are clearly not the same for all languages.

Phonemic representations *are* a part of the system of *langue*, however, and if these must be completed by a language-particular set of rules which specify them for additional (nondistinctive) properties, the question still arises of which aspect of language such rules should be regarded as belonging to. One extreme interpretation would have it that *only* the phonemic representations belong to *langue*, and that the rules as well as the phonetic realizations of forms belong to *parole*. In the long run, however, this is a difficult view to maintain. Many scholars have pointed out that the range of possible pronunciations of a given form is very much a part of the language in which it occurs. Even if all of the distinctive properties are produced correctly, a pronunciation which makes arbitrary changes in the nondistinctive properties must be excluded *by virtue of the system of the language in question*. This means that the principles which determine such nondistinctive properties must themselves be considered a part of the system, and thus of *langue*. It is very easy, however, to fall prey to the temptation to disregard the existence (or at least the systematic status) of these rules altogether, and to focus attention exclusively on the definition of a language-particular nonredundant phonemic representation for forms—as witness most of the phonemic theories of the twentieth century, which have paid little or no attention to anything except the appropriate definition of phonemes as elements of representations.

It is certainly such an interpretation which has most generally been given to Saussure's views, on the basis of his emphasis on distinctiveness coupled with his general lack of specific discussion of how to go about describing it. For many interpreters, the only conceivable way to realize Saussure's requirement that the system of sign-differentiating distinctions be the object of linguistic description was to define a representation with precisely that character. We have suggested above, however, that this is not a necessary interpretation of Saussure: on the one hand because he seems to speak of the *signifiant* of a sign in a way that implies a less abstract, more 'phonetic' description, not limited to distinctive properties, and on the other hand because of his general reluctance to set up a unit of analysis (here, the 'phoneme' in the post-Saussurean sense) and attribute reality to it. Yet he certainly felt that linguistic signs, and thereby their *signifiants* and *signifiés*, are 'real' if anything in language is.

A view of the sort just discussed can be called an *incompletely specified* phonemic theory, intending thereby that the phonemes are specified only for a limited range of properties (not that the theory is itself incompletely specified!). Its basic characteristic is that the elements of a phonological representation (the 'phonemes') are rather abstract elements, in the literal sense that they abstract away from some of the essential phonetic properties of actualized speech. Such an approach is not, however, the only way to realize Saussure's basic insight about the importance of the difference between distinguishing and nondistinguishing properties. We might also imagine a theory centering on a somewhat more concrete notion of what 'phonemes' are. Such a position could be developed in quasi-mathematical terms along the following lines:

Suppose that we have identified all of the phonetic segments which appear in utterances in a given language. Call this the class $p = (p_1, p_2, \ldots)$. Now suppose further that we have identified whether, for each pair (p_i, p_j) in p, the difference between $[p_i]$ and $[p_j]$ is capable of distinguishing one sign from another in this language (i.e., in presystematic terms, whether $[p_i]$ and $[p_j]$ contrast or not). Now let us divide the set p into subsets, such that each subset P_i

consists of at least one element [p$_i$] from p, together with all (and only) the other elements in p that do not contrast with [p$_i$]. As a result (making some—possibly strong—assumptions about the extent to which the relation of contrast is a well-behaved one), two segments [p$_i$] and [p$_j$] can be said to differentiate signs (potentially) if and only if they belong to distinct subsets P$_i$ and P$_j$.

Now from each one of the subsets P$_i$, let us choose exactly one representative phonetic segment, designated as [p$_i^*$]. We can call the set of ([p$_i^*$]) the set of *phonemes* of the language. For any utterance, its phonological representation is derived by replacing each phonetic segment by its corresponding phoneme: i.e., by the 'designated element' [p$_i^*$] in the subset P$_i$ of which the segment in question is a member. We can then give a set of rules which would allow us to derive phonetic representations from phonological ones, by identifying the conditions under which each of the members of a given noncontrasting subset P$_i$ occurs, and replacing the designated member p$_i^*$ by other members of the same P$_i$ under appropriate conditions.

This view, which we will refer to as a *fully specified basic variant* phonemic theory, differs from an incompletely specified phonemic theory in at least two important ways. First of all, instead of being identified for a small proper subset of the potentially relevant properties of segments (namely, exactly the distinctive ones), the 'phonemes' on this view are fully specified phonetic segments (though only a subset of those which appear in the language). And, second, the rules of the phonology do not 'fill in blanks' in such an incompletely specified segment to arrive at a phonetic form but, rather, *replace* one phonetic segment (the designated one, or 'phoneme') with another.

It should be clear that this second view, while quite distinct from the first, nonetheless allows us to satisfy Saussure's basic requirement that the system of distinctions among *signifiants* be described in the grammar. This is because, given any pair of utterances, we can determine immediately whether or not they correspond to distinct signs simply by comparing their phonological representations: if these are the same, the two could not be the realizations of distinct *signifiants*, while if the phonological representations are different, they must be. This is essentially the same as the way the notion of distinctness between *signifiants* is reconstructed in an incompletely specified phonemic theory: the major difference between them is the fact that, if phonemes are taken to be fully specified basic variants rather than incompletely specified clusters of properties alone, it is much more obvious that the rules (and not simply the phonemic representations) of the grammar play a significant role in the description of the linguistic system.

Nonetheless, it is difficult to argue that such a conception of the nature of phonological structure corresponds to that of Saussure. We have argued above that for him the representation of *signifiants* ought to be in terms of sound images that correspond to (specified) phonetic species, and in this respect the fully specified basic variant view corresponds better to Saussure's apparent picture than does the incompletely specified variety of phonemic theory; but the notion of rules that replace one specified segment type with another seems quite foreign to the presentation of sound structure in the *Cours* and other sources.

We might therefore propose a third variant of phonological theory, which makes no distinction between a 'phonological' representation and the representation of forms as a sequence of (sound images of) fully specified phonetic species. Such a theory would thus involve no systematically abstract representation that pays special regard to the notion of contrast. Self-evidently, this is not enough: the single representation assumed by this view does not suffice to solve the fundamental problem of describing the system of differences among *signifiants*. Given two such representations, we have no direct way of determining by inspection whether a difference between them corresponds to a potential difference between signs, or whether it falls within the range of permissible variation in a single sign.

This function would thus have to be performed not by the 'phonological representations' themselves but by a set of rules which specify both the range of possible representations in a given language and the relations that obtain among such representations. Such rules would be similar (in part) to a set of redundancy conditions applying to fully specified forms, as described in a generative framework by Stanley (1967). These include *positive* conditions ('every form in this language has property P'), *negative* conditions ('no form in this language has property P'), and *implicational* conditions ('if a form in this language has property P, then it also has property Q'). Among the latter, some conditions must admit disjunctions, in order to allow for free variation (e.g., in English 'if a form ends in a stop consonant, this segment may be either released or unreleased').

With this apparatus, we could claim to have fully captured the difference between (potentially) distinct *signifiants* and nondistinct variants. Given any two phonetic representations, that is, we are able in principle to determine their status in this regard by an appeal to such a grammar. First, we ask whether either (or both) violates any of the conditions stated as rules of the language. If so, of course, such a form is not a potential *signifiant* at all, let alone a contrastively distinct one. If not, we can then make an inventory of the differences between the two forms. Of course, if the forms do not differ at all (at the level of 'phonetic species'), we can claim that they could not correspond to distinct *signifiants*. If they do differ, however, we can then ask the following: is each individual difference between them related to a permissible disjunction found within some rule of the grammar? For instance, two forms in English which differ only in that one has a final unreleased stop where the other has a final released stop would satisfy this criterion by virtue of the disjunction found in the rule tentatively formulated above. If and only if there is some difference between the forms which does not meet this condition, the forms correspond to potentially distinct *signifiants*.

Though such a procedure may seem excessively complex when stated in such detail, it should be clear that it is in principle just as capable as the two preceding views of providing an explicit reconstruction of the difference between distinguishing and nondistinguishing properties of *signifiants*. Its crucial characteristic is the fact that it puts the whole burden of elucidating this difference on the system of rules rather than on the definition of a special sort of representation. On this view, the business of the linguist is the formulation of such sets of rules for particular languages—rules which represent the *signifiants* of language-particular signs, and the relations between them, in a direct fashion.

We do not mean to suggest that this third view of sound structure (which we can call a *fully specified surface variant* theory) gives a completely faithful picture of Saussure's own ideas. Nonetheless, there are a number of respects in which it would seem to be at least somewhat closer to those ideas than its competitors presented above.

By contrast with the 'incompletely specified' phonemic view, it does not require us to hypostatize the results of a linguistic analysis by attributing reality to a 'phonemic' representation distinct in principle from the sound images that govern our linguistic use of signs in production and perception. Everything that Saussure says on this issue implies that he did not conceive of the difference between the form of the *signifiant* and that of phonetic reality as a difference in degree of specification. Furthermore, as noted several times above, he preferred as a matter of principle to treat *relations* rather than abstracted *units* as having linguistic reality.

By contrast with the 'fully specified basic variant' view, however, this last picture does not require us to posit rules that change one segment type into another. As we will see below in the discussion of his treatment of alternations, such a formulation of linguistic regularities would also be completely opposed to his basic notion of synchronic linguistic structure.

A further potential advantage of the fully specified surface variant view of sound structure is that it settles the question, posed above, of what status nondistinctive properties have with respect to the distinction between *langue* and *parole*. If we formulate the description of these nondistinctive properties as a matter of language-particular rules, we are thereby attributing the range of permissible variation in phonetic species to the grammar of the language, and thus to *langue*. By contrast, the realization of a sequence of phonetic species as a sequence of concrete phonemes (in Saussure's sense) is a consequence of the human articulatory (and perhaps perceptual) system, and thus a matter of *parole* to be studied by phoneticians (although these details are also of interest to the linguist insofar as they furnish the grounds for an explanatory account of historical change).

It would thus appear that there is a logically coherent alternative to (post-Saussurean) phonemic theories as a way of realizing Saussure's basic goals in the description of sound systems. More to the point, there is also some reason to associate his views with such an alternative, rather than with a theory based on the notion of the phoneme as a direct embodiment of linguistic contrast. At minimum, there is no reason to claim that Saussure had a notion of the 'phoneme' in the sense that term later came to bear, or that he would have been better off if he had. Although on this view the *signifiants* of signs, as phonetically specified entities, would seem to have a positive character, this does not really separate such a picture from any other (e.g., a strictly phonemic one) as long as the elements of phonologically significant representation have any properties at all (e.g., distinctive ones). In any event, it is not the business of the linguist per se to study the properties of these representations: that is a matter for phoneticians. The linguist's interest is in the system of rules.

Indeed, one can maintain that the characterization of the system of *langue* on this account, since it consists simply in the negative and oppositive specification of what limits there are on variation and what *differences* among forms are possible, comes as close as possible to satisfying the Saussurean dictum that language is form, not substance. By localizing the description of the system of *langue* in the system of rules, rather than in the characterization of the entities which make up the *signifiants* themselves, such a system based on fully specified surface variants puts as much of the weight of linguistic description as possible on the description of linguistic forms and relations.

It is interesting in its own right to ask just how Saussure conceived of the sound-structural aspect of the system of linguistic signs. It is also useful, because the very nonspecific nature of this side of his theoretical presentation makes it possible to see his basic insight in quite general terms which admit of a wide range of possible realizations. Nonetheless, from the point of view of the history of linguistics, such an inquiry is almost beside the point: what matters about Saussure, in a way, is not his own work (of which we have next to none), but rather the infuence his *perceived* position had on later linguists.

In fact, his interpreters paid almost exclusive attention to one aspect of Saussure's thought: his insistence that a linguistic description must be primarily a description of the system that distinguishes one sign from another. Virtually all commentators interpreted this project in the form of a notion of linguistic representation (or 'phonemic transcription') which would reconstruct distinctiveness directly. The result was the proliferation of competing phonemic theories which we will see in discussion below, nearly all claiming in one way or another to be directly inspired by Saussure's basic insight. Arguably, all of these theories are fundamentally misguided, at least as far as Saussure is concerned. There is no reason to believe that he construed the system of *langue* in terms of a system of representation: indeed, it does not seem completely anachronistic to suggest that the fundamentally *relational* character of *langue* is closer in spirit to the contemporary conception of a grammar as a system of *rules*.

Saussure's description of alternations

Another topic which is worth examining both for its own interest and for its bearing on Saussure's general conception of linguistic structure is his treatment of alternations. We have thus far focused exclusively on the ways in which signs may be individually differentiated, but of course Saussure recognized that certain recurrent differences between signs within a given language may have a special status. When such differences are genuinely systematic, they may serve not only to keep signs apart but also (somewhat paradoxically) to link them to one another. The description of these relations is intimately related both to his view of the structure of *langue* and to the nature of the connection between synchrony and diachrony in language.

For example, in the history of Greek, intervocalic [s] was lost as a result of a phonetic change. Roots originally ending in [s] thus came to have two forms (with or without the [s]), depending on whether they were followed by a vocalic ending or not. The systematic character of the relation between forms such as *tre-ō* and *a-tres-tos* led to the conception (for speakers of the language) that there was "a correspondence [..] between radical groups such as *ne-/nes-*, *geu-/geus-*, as representing equivalent groups" (cited by Reichler-Béguelin 1980:47). Forms with and without [s] could thus be related despite this difference in their *signifiants*, and such a relation is called an alternation. Elsewhere, an alternation is defined as a "correspondence by which two specifiable sounds permute more or less regularly between two series of coexistent forms" (cited by Godel 1957:253). The reference to "coexistent *forms*" here is quite essential, since Saussure emphasizes at several places that an alternation is a *grammatical* phenomenon: "an opposition of form to form, not of phoneme to phoneme" (ibid.).

Every view of phonology must come to terms in some way with the phenomenon of alternation, even if only by rejecting it entirely as a principled aspect of sound structure. The fashion in which alternation is viewed and formulated may be taken as one of the primary 'diagnostics' of a phonological theory. Much of the program of generative phonology, for example, can be seen as founded on the attempt to reduce alternating surface forms to unitary underlying representations. By contrast a number of different versions of structuralist phonemic theory can be distinguished from one another largely in terms of the extent to which information about systematic alternations is allowed to influence the choice of a phonemic analysis.

The most obvious features of Saussure's attitude toward alternations can be derived in large part from his (sometimes overstated) views on the need to exorcise essentially diachronic facts from a synchronic description. As an example of the consequences of this, consider a common way of describing a pattern of alternation such as that found in Latin *capiō/percipiō*. It seems quite traditional to say that *percipiō* 'comes from' *capiō* by a rule that reduces [a] to [i] in medial syllables. For Saussure, however, this is completely wrong, since it imports a number of confusions into the synchronic system. Not the least of these is the impression that a historical change (the sound change by which [a] was replaced by [i] in medial syllables) is somehow a part of the synchronic grammar.

In Saussure's view, the synchronic fact is simply a systematic resemblance between two distinct signs (*capiō* and *percipiō*). Both signs are part of the system of *langue* (as is the resemblance between them), but this does not mean that either 'comes from' the other. If *percipiō* 'comes from' anything, it is earlier *percapiō*, and this is strictly a historical fact. The relation between earlier *percapiō* and later *percipiō*, though, is not a fact of *langue* but rather a fact of phonetic change, and thus a matter of *parole*. As far as the system of *langue* is concerned, what has happened is simply that the earlier opposition between the forms *capiō* vs. *percapiō* has been replaced by a different one: *capiō* vs. *percipiō*. At both stages, we have two distinct signs; and though the character of the distinction changes from one stage to the other, this change is not itself a property of the synchronic grammar (of either period).

Sometimes the alternation which results from a series of historical changes may itself become an essential part of the *signifiant* of a grammatical category. Thus, in early Germanic, the opposition between singular and plural in pairs such as *fōt* vs. *fōti* was carried by a distinct, separable ending *-i*. As a consequence of the sound changes of umlaut, unrounding, and final vowel loss, this was replaced in Old English by the opposition between *fōt* and *fēt*. At this point, however, it would not be correct to say that Old English *fēt* 'comes from' *fōt* by a synchronic rule of umlaut: rather, the language recognized the systematic character of the alternation as a possible relation between signs. Some signs whose *signifiants* contain back vowels are systematically related to other signs differing exactly in that their *signifiants* contain corresponding front vowels. In pairs like *fōt/fēt*, this relationship is itself seized on as a basis for the signified difference between singular and plural—just as any other difference in *signifiants*, such as a difference in their initial segments, or the difference between forms with and without a final [-əz], etc. might have been the basis for this opposition. The relation between forms, then, is a part of the synchronic system just as the range of possible elements of sound images is.

Despite the fact that such a systematic resemblance is a part of the synchronic grammar of the language, we must avoid saying that in pairs like *fōt/fēt* or *capiō/percipiō* we have a single unit (*fōt*, *capiō*) and a synchronic rule which changes this into something else under specifiable circumstances. In fact, neither at the later stage, where a systematic alternation is present, nor even at the earlier stage (where we had *fōt* versus *fōti*, or *capiō* vs. *percapiō*) did we have to do with a single unit. In synchronic terms, we have at each stage two distinct signs rather than a single unit. The 'change' is a fact of historical phonetics, "but its action belongs to the past, and for the speakers, there is only a synchronic opposition" (1916:219). To state a rule that changed one form into another would falsely give the impression of "movement where there is only a state." (ibid.)

Furthermore, it would be incorrect (according to Saussure) to say even that in the past there was a single unit in such cases, and that it underwent two divergent phonetic developments. It requires some reflection to understand this assertion, since it appears to be just such divergent development of an original unity that he previously invoked as the diachronic fact leading to the synchronic alternation. But in fact, he suggests, there was in every such case some difference in the forms involved even at the earlier period, and it is this difference which is *accentuated* (and not *created*) by the historical change.

This becomes clearer when we recall the importance Saussure attributed to the detailed study of combinatory phonetics, which would ideally reveal the minute differences between similar phonemes appearing in different positions in the syllable or other suprasegmental unit. Even if we had the same sequence of phonetic species in *fōt* and *fōt(-i)*, that is, the nonidentify of the two signs would lead to differences among the detailed phonetic properties of the corresponding phonemes. A [T] in final position is realized differently from a [T] preceding [i]—and thus, the [Ō] in *fōt* is in a different environment from that in *fōti*, which could lead in turn to a difference between these two [Ō]'s. If we had rules in our synchronic description which change one segment or form into another, not only would we risk importing diachronic facts illicitly into synchrony, but we might also be led to overlook a potential phonetic explanation of the change. For Saussure that explanation proceeds from the original difference between forms and not their unity.

Saussure's categorical rejection of the description of alternations by a unitary 'underlying' form and rules changing one segment into another had very important consequences for the development of the field. Subsequent generations of linguists, feeling that this rejection followed directly from the cogency of the distinction between synchronic and diachronic linguistics, adopted it as well. As a result, it was quite some time before *any* sort of 'morphophonemic' account was considered a respectable part of a linguistic description again. Saussure limited the characterization of alternations to a description of differences among surface forms, and in this he was generally followed (with some few exceptions which we will note in chapters below). As a result, the general topic of alternations was taken to be the matter of higher level studies (i.e., morphology) rather than a question of sound structure. The limitation on a particular technique of description which Saussure argued for was thus interpreted as a limitation on the range of data relevant to a phonological analysis: a much stronger restriction.

We must emphasize that, while Saussure had no sympathy for a description of alternations which posited unitary underlying forms and rules altering the character of segments, he certainly considered alternations to be a rule-governed aspect of sound structure. Rather, he took the rules involved to be ones which directly related one surface form (in a given language) to another, without assigning priority to either (or setting up an indirectly attested third form from which both are derived). As such, all of his rules have the character of 'lexical redundancy rules' (in the sense of Jackendoff 1975) or 'correspondences' (in the sense of Lopez 1979). A rule of this character may state an inferential relation between forms ('if the language contains a form with the properties {F}, then there may also exist a systematically related form with the properties {F'}'), but the relation is stated directly between the forms involved rather than in terms of derivations of either or both from some other (possibly more abstract) representations.

Such a nonderivational characterization may or may not be an appropriate way to describe alternations in the general case, but that is not the issue here. What is important to note is that Saussure attributed considerable importance to the description of alternations, and he was certainly ready to attribute 'reality' to the rules which described them. This reality was confirmed, in his view, by the phenomenon of analogy.

It will be recalled (from the previous chapter) that for Saussure the category of 'analogical change' did not constitute change in the system of *langue* at all, since he viewed analogical formations as consisting simply in the realization of latent possibilities inherent in the system of *langue* as it already exists. When a child uses the form *goed* instead of *went*, this does not constitute a change in the system, since the system already contains a rule to the effect that, corresponding to a given present tense verb base, there may be a past tense form which is the same with the addition of the suffix -*ed*. The form is thus inherent in the system, and the child's use of it does not constitute change. Of course, if the form *goed* eventually comes to replace the form *went* entirely, the loss of this latter sign does constitute a change, but the creation of the analogical innovation does not.

In order for this account of analogy to go through, it is necessary to recognize a wide range of alternations as encoded in the principles of the system of *langue*. Furthermore, at least in principle, it imposes a significant constraint on the operation of analogy, since an analogical formation is only possible insofar as the language contains (independently) a rule of alternation which supports the creation of the innovated form. Not simply any four-term proportional such as $A : A' = B : X$ is potentially a valid analogy; the proportion can only lead to the creation of an analogical form if a) some rule of the grammar relates A and A', and b) the same rule (potentially) relates B to some other form B' ($=X$). This limitation would prohibit, for instance, the creation of a new verb *heye* 'see' in English on the basis of the proportion *ear : hear = eye : X*. Such a spurious proportion could not be the basis of a possible analogical creation for Saussure, since the relation between *ear* and *hear* is quite isolated in English, and not based on any rule of the grammar. Saussure's position on the fundamental relation between possible analogies and existing rules of grammar is quite close to one that would be developed more explicitly by Kuryłowicz (see, e.g., Kuryłowicz 1949, 1964).

The interplay of the system of rules in determining the operation of analogy is carried quite far in some of Saussure's concrete discussions. A standard example of analogical creation is the replacement of Latin *honos* by *honor*, on the basis of the proportion "*ōrātōrem* : *ōrātor* = *honōrem* : *x*" (1916:226). The discussion of this example in his Greek and Latin phonology course, however (see Reichler-Béguelin 1980), shows that more is involved here than simply the existence of the three terms of which the proportion is composed.

In particular, the historical change of "rhotacism" in Latin had changed intervocalic instances of [s] into [r] (the detailed history of this change need not concern us here). As a result, many forms (such as *honōs/honōrem*) showed an alternation between [s] and [r] under determinate conditions, and this was, for Saussure, reflected as a rule of the grammar of Latin. However, many other forms (those with original [r], not [s]) showed an [r] that did not alternate with [s]. In these forms, intervocalic [r] was regularly related to final and preconsonantal [r].

Now given a form with intervocalic [r] (such as *ōrātōrem* or *honōrem*), one could not determine directly from it whether the [r] in question was one that alternated with [s] or not. Saussure suggests that it is precisely this indeterminacy (which we would today label 'opacity', after the proposals of Kiparsky 1973b) which provides the motivation for the analogical formation. This consists in substituting the regular pattern [r]:[r] for the alternation [r]:[s]. Both patterns are justified by rules of the grammar (one trivially, and the other by the synchronic, relational residue of rhotacism). The choice of the pattern [r]:[r], and thus the 'creation' of *honor*, is explicitly said to be due to the fact that "un paradigme tend à unifier le cadre dans lequel il court" (Reichler-Béguelin 1980:56). An appeal to the tendency of paradigms to be simplified is thoroughly traditional, of course, but Saussure's use of it here to predict the way in which an opaque interaction of rules will be resolved is rather similar to that found in more recent discussion.

Though Saussure does not explicitly point out the limitation of analogies to those based on existing synchronic rules, it follows from his conception of analogical 'change', and it is reasonably clear that he adhered to it in those places in which the problem arose (such as his lectures on Greek and Latin phonology and morphology). His formulation of particular analogical developments frequently involves an appeal to the rule-governed character of the alternation which supports them; and his rejection of other proposed accounts in terms of analogy sometimes rests on their lack of such a foundation. It is, obviously, difficult to delineate a priori just when a resemblance between forms justifies positing a rule of the grammar. It is therefore difficult to be sure that all of Saussure's specific historical discussions are in accord with his principle. This difficulty is by no means unique to Saussure's view, however. What is essential to recognize about his picture is that in principle, analogy is directly linked to the structure of the grammar, and in particular to the pattern of systematic alternations that form part of a given system of *langue*.

Saussure and the phonological tradition

This concludes our review of the principles of Saussure's phonological views. While there is very little in his work which is specific enough to serve directly as the foundation for concrete descriptions of phonological structure, most of the issues that have occupied the field since are at least raised, and a number of them have their origins there. We hope to have shown above that Saussure's conception of the system of *signifiants*, which makes up *la langue*, was not primarily in terms of a special sort of notation or representation for forms, but rather in terms of a system of rules which define the interrelations among forms. These include rules delimiting the range of forms in a particular language together with the range of variation permitted within the realizations of the same *signifiant*, and also describing the patterns of systematic alternation that relate one form to another within the system. All of these are aspects of the system which Saussure felt was real for individual speakers, and which formed the basis of the social, interpersonal character of language.

We do not intend to give the (anachronistic) impression that Saussure's views were 'wholly modern', of course. Among other clear limitations which set his system apart from much of today's work in phonology, his 'rules' were limited to the statement of unmediated regularities obtaining within and among surface forms, rather than deriving these (in at least some cases) from more abstract forms.

Other differences as well separate Saussure from phonologists of today. However, there is also a great deal he has in common with later phonologists, as well as a great deal that separates him from those who would come immediately after him (frequently invoking his name as the basis of their work). Aside from the introduction of principles (which often became mere slogans) such as the distinction between *langue* and *parole*, the separation of synchrony from diachrony, and the arbitrariness of the linguistic sign, Saussure's influence was primarily felt in a major redirection of efforts in linguistics. Where these had previously been aimed at somewhat atomistic historical studies based on phonetic detail, subsequent work has concentrated on the study of systems, of synchronic regularities, and especially of what is characteristic (perhaps universally) of overall language-particular grammars.

In all of these respects, later studies came to be founded on Saussure's own principles (though the same can not be said, it would seem, for the attempt to realize these goals largely through the means of defining a theoretically significant level of representation). As we noted in an earlier section, however, Saussure himself probably served more as the incarnation of a program which was in some sense 'in the air', reinforcing and legitimizing these views in others rather than constituting their substantive source. While the extent of his direct influence remains to be established with certainty, it appears to have been exerted in large part ex post facto.

3

The Kazan School: Baudouin de Courtenay and Kruszewski

A number of years before Saussure began to occupy himself seriously with questions of general linguistics, many of those very problems constituted the central concern of the Polish linguist Jan Baudouin de Courtenay and his students and colleagues (most notably, Mikołaj Kruszewski). Isolated in Kazan in central Russia, Baudouin's work was largely inaccessible to scholars in Europe, though it was known to at least a few of them. In the writings of the so-called Kazan school we find many of the same positions that would later be attributed to Saussure, and in many cases Baudouin's formulation of these issues, and his discussion and resolution of them, is considerably more explicit and lucid than Saussure's.

We do not study Baudouin and Kruszewski's views simply because they distinguished language from speech and synchrony from diachrony, however, or because they recognized the difference between phonetic properties that distinguish words and those that do not; or even because they were probably the first to use the word 'phoneme' in roughly its modern sense (as well as the coiners of the word 'morpheme'). Despite the fact that they addressed these issues well before Saussure did, their importance does not lie in their simple historical priority. This is because the views of European and American linguists on such matters derive, by and large, from the form in which they were presented by Saussure (or, at least, this was widely claimed to be their source). Given the overwhelming status of Saussure as the eponymous 'culture bringer' of modern linguistics, the fact that others had said much the same thing earlier would entitle the Kazan school to little more than a footnote of acknowledgement in works concerned with the subsequent development of those ideas. This is indeed the case for others who could also be cited as precursors of 'modern' ideas, such as the Swiss linguist J. Winteler (whose description of the Schwyzertütsch dialect of Kerenz in 1876 included an explicit discussion of what would later be known as the 'phonemic principle').

Aside from its status as a historical curiosity, there are at least two much more important reasons for contemporary linguists to study the theories of the Kazan school, one intrinsic and one historical. On the one hand, Baudouin and Kruszewski were much more concerned with notions corresponding to what we would now call 'rules' in sound structure than with the nature of representations. They arrived at the basic problem of how to understand the sound structure of natural languages through the study of ways in which phonetic distinctions take on meaning-differentiating function by being 'morphologized', and their central focus was on the nature of the relations between such morphologically linked (or 'alternating') forms. Unlike most of those who would come after them, they dealt primarily with questions of the typology and evolution of rules rather than with the nature of the elements which (from a phonological point of view) compose individual forms. The substance of their treatment presents insights (notably into the sources and nature of 'phonetic explanation' in phonology) which are arguably more profound than the opinions underlying much discussion of the same issues today.

On the other hand, the theoretical proposals and research emphases of Baudouin's work contributed to the subsequent evolution of phonological research, though not in a very direct way. While his teaching in general linguistics remained little known in Europe and America until quite recently, he did contribute significantly through his students to the formation of one of the two major schools of linguistic thought in Russia: the St. Petersburg (later Leningrad) school. As such, he exerted a subtle and indirect influence on those linguists studying in Russia who would later form the nucleus of the Linguistic Circle of Prague, one of the central sources for present-day linguistic ideas. Though somewhat tortuous, there is a path from the proposals of Baudouin de Courtenay to the basic assumptions of Trubetzkoy and Jakobson about the nature of language; and it is worth studying the former if we wish to understand the latter.

Biographical remarks

Although Baudouin's family came originally from the French aristocracy, they had lived in Poland for several generations when Baudouin was born in 1845 (in Radzymin, near Warsaw); and he himself felt a great loyalty to Polish cultural and political ideals throughout his career even though much of his life was spent outside Poland. After finishing the gymnasium, he began university studies in Warsaw, where he received a master of arts degree from the historical-philological faculty in 1866. Like Saussure, he spent a number of years studying Indo-European in various places (Prague, Berlin, Jena, Leipzig, and St. Petersburg) with prominent scholars of the day including Schleicher, Leskien, Brugmann, and Delbrück. In 1870, he received a doctorate from Leipzig for work on the nature of analogy, as well as a second master's degree (this time from St. Petersburg, where his Polish degree was not recognized) for a study of fourteenth-century Old Polish.

His supervisor in St. Petersburg, I. I. Sreznevskij, arranged a position for him there as docent (roughly, assistant professor) of comparative grammar beginning in 1870. The most notable result of his years in St. Petersburg seems to have been the opportunity provided by the Russian Academy in 1872 to do field work on Slovenian dialects in Austria and northern Italy. When it was published in 1875, his study of the phonetic systems of some of these dialects earned him a Russian doctorate. His political views and his somewhat contemptuous attitude toward Sreznevskij, however, resulted in his not being able to stay in St. Petersburg after his initial appointment, and in 1875 he was sent to Kazan (first as assistant professor, and after a year as full professor).

It is difficult to exaggerate the isolation of this provincial Tartar city in central Russian, and Baudouin was anything but pleased at having to work there. Nonetheless, it has sometimes been suggested that this isolation had a liberating and ultimately beneficial effect on his scholarship: if work appearing in Kazan was unlikely to be heard of in the intellectual circles of western Europe, it was correspondingly free of the pressures exerted by the dominant influences in those circles. Had Baudouin been entirely dependent on publication in journals controlled by the Neogrammarian figures of his day, it is unlikely that he would have produced much of what he did in general linguistics. Indeed, on those occasions when he or his students did submit work to such publications, it was received with considerable hostility (which Baudouin seems to have done his best to exacerbate with his rather sharp pen and abrasive personality). We may also note that Kazan had been (fifty years earlier) the place where N. Lobačevskij had published his work on non-Euclidean geometry. Whatever its frontierlike lack of amenities and distance from the main streams of academic life, Kazan does not seem to have been notably discouraging to creativity.

It was during his years in Kazan that Baudouin was most productive in general linguistics, whether because of his relative youth or because of his isolation—or because of the excited and stimulating group of students and followers he had there. Foremost among these was Mikołaj Kruszewski, with whom Baudouin quickly developed a very close working relationship. The historical literature in linguistics has contained a certain amount of discussion of the details of their collaboration, especially with regard to their relative priority in developing particular areas of the 'Kazan theory'. Baudouin's own discussions of these issues are of little help in resolving them, since he shifts between extravagant praise of Kruszewski's rigorous and scientific development of phonological problems, without which further progress would have been impossible, and the attitude that "Kruszewski merely gave another, finer form to what he had learned from some one else" (Baudouin de Courtenay 1895 [1972]: 150).

Like Baudouin, Kruszewski was born in Poland (in the town of Luck), in 1851. Again like Baudouin, he studied in the historical-philological faculty in Warsaw, but spent most of his time reading philosophy and psychology. He was particularly well trained in English philosophical logic, and the later development of his thought on linguistic matters would reflect this. After submitting an MA thesis in 1875 on a folkloristic topic, he wanted to continue his studies in linguistics, but was financially unable to do so. He had to spend several years teaching Russian language and literature to the daughters of the provincial nobility before he could take the suggestion of one of his advisers to go to Kazan in order to study with Baudouin.

After corresponding with Baudouin for some time and announcing his interest in developing a genuinely scientific foundation for linguistics, he arrived in Kazan in 1878 and immediately became an active participant in Baudouin's program of research and teaching. He was awarded a master's degree in 1881 for his thesis on *guṇa* alternations in Old Church Slavonic, a work which contained a substantial systematic chapter on the theory of alternations and which Baudouin praised extravagently in a published review. His 1883 *Sketch of the Science of Language*, a rather more comprehensive if occasionally somewhat tentative work, earned him a doctorate.

In 1884, Kruszewski fell victim to a progressive degenerative neurological disorder, and it is evident that Baudouin never managed to come completely to terms with the premature loss in this way of his young colleague. This is particularly and painfully clear in the obituary article that Baudouin wrote about him, which can only be called unbalanced (in more than one sense) and which shows us more about Baudouin's state of mind than it does about Kruszewski's work. Much of his denigration (here and in later works) of Kruszewski's contribution to their joint efforts thus must be seen as having little necessary connection with the facts.

In any event, there is little point in speculating on the relative contributions of the two, since it was essentially their joint work that developed the theoretical position that would subsequently be presented to others (largely, it is true, through Baudouin's teaching and writing). Most of the major themes can already be found in the programs of Baudouin's lectures before he had begun to work with Kruszewski, albeit in very programmatic form. Among these are the essential difference between the study of speech from a physical phonetic point of view and the study of the ways in which phonetic differences serve to distinguish meanings, the importance of the study of alternations for an understanding of sound structure, the relation between sound change and synchronic alternations, etc. It was through their joint efforts, though, that the substance and interest of the theory was developed.

In 1883, a chair of comparative Slavic grammar was established in Dorpat (Tartu, in Estonia), a location which Baudouin found much more appealing than Kazan and to which he immediately moved. Kruszewski was eventually (in 1886) appointed to Baudouin's chair in Kazan, but by that time his illness had already progressed so far that he was unable to accept, and he died in the following year.

Baudouin, in turn, became professor of comparative linguistics and Sanskrit in Cracow in 1893, a position which seemed to satisfy his most intense desires since he was at last in Poland. His pro-Polish feelings, however, appear to have been somewehat excessive for the Austro-Hungarian authorities, who were hardly supportive of Slavic nationalism within the empire. Since

Baudouin did not enjoy the equivalent of modern academic tenure, his contract was simply not renewed after five years, and he was forced to return to St. Petersburg. Here too he got into political difficulties, this time through his attacks on the tsarist suppression of national minorities, and he eventually spent some months in jail. Freed at the outbreak of World War I, he taught again briefly in St. Petersburg until he was invited to the chair of Indo-European linguistics at the University of Warsaw in the rèestablished postwar independent Poland. He remained there until his death in 1929.

The influence of Baudouin and Kruszewski, as one might expect, was primarily on Baudouin's students, especially in St. Petersburg, where his teaching was to some extent continued in the Leningrad school of Soviet linguistics. Their own work, though, was by no means unknown to linguists outside of their immediate circle. For one thing, unlike Saussure, Baudouin was intensely interested in detailed problems of 'hands on' linguistic description and in the consequences of theoretical ideas for the solutions to practical problems. He did a good deal of fieldwork, especially on Slavic dialects, and made a number of important contributions to comparative Slavic linguistics. Again unlike Saussure, he published a great deal during his lifetime; and if, like many others, he never accomplished the major synthesis of his ideas on general linguistics that he intended, we are still not at all lacking for direct evidence about his views. Nonetheless, since much of this body of writing appeared in rather obscure places and in languages not accessible to many Western scholars (Russian and Polish, in particular), his ideas were not widely known to his contemporaries.

One exception to this was Saussure, who had met Baudouin in 1881 at a meeting of the Société linguistique de Páris. Baudouin donated copies of some of his and Kruszewski's works to the Société and Saussure read them with interest. In his own notes and manuscripts, Saussure refers on more than one occasion to Baudouin and Kruszewski as having been "closer than anyone to a theoretical view of *la langue*, without departing from purely linguistic considerations" (Godel 1957:51; my translation). Saussure's ideas too, at least in his earlier work on Indo-European, were well known in Kazan. In 1880 Kruszewski had written an enthusiastic review of the *Mémoire*, and it is apparently from this source that he took the word 'phoneme' (then subject to a certain amount of evolution in its sense, which we will trace below, before it reemerged into the western European tradition in šomething like its current acceptation). Baudouin, too, wrote very favorably about the important innovations of method and emphasis to be found in the *Mémoire*.

There was thus a certain amount of interaction, including an exchange of several letters, as well as mutual appreciation between these two major sources of modern phonological thought. As far as direct influence is concerned, however, only Saussure's work was widely known until the recent (1963) publication of collections of Baudouin's papers in Russian and (less fully, in 1972) in English. A collection of Kruszewski's work in English translation has been promised for a number of years but, at this writing, has not yet appeared. Given the intrinsic interest of much of the Kazan school work, it is unfortunate that it has been known only through such secondary sources as Jakobson's review articles (Jakobson 1929, 1960, 1965); while invaluable, these inevitably reflect Jakobson's own strongly held views on what is and is not valuable in Baudouin's and Kruszewski's work.

The study of sound systems in the Kazan school

Just as many of Saussure's views grew out of his training in (neogrammarian) historical linguistics, much of what Baudouin and Kruszewski say about issues in general linguistics reflects their education and the opinions of the late-nineteenth-century linguistic community of which they were an isolated part. Nonetheless, even from his inaugural lecture at St. Petersburg, Baudouin establishes major differences of emphasis between his approach to the study of language and that of others. He suggests, in somewhat caricatural form, a number of different possible goals and methods for such studies, all of which must be rejected as inadequate or insufficient (1871; quotations below are from the 1972 English translation).

The linguist must not be content simply to amass data of a descriptive sort about particular languages "without attempting to explain their causes," since this attitude "avoid[s] the question of the usefulness and goal of gathering data" and "reduces science to a purely empirical endeavor, to some sort of meaningless game." On the other hand, the tradition of aprioristic, philosophical grammar, "which uses speculation and a limited knowledge of grammatical facts to construct grammatical systems that force linguistic phenomena into a logical strait jacket," is also unsatisfactory, since such a view would "violate and distort the facts for the sake of a narrow theory." While explanation is the only possible serious goal of genuine science, it must obviously not proceed in disregard of the *explicanda*. Finally, the reconstruction of the prior histories of languages through the use of the comparative method and other philological techniques is also insufficient since, if pursued for its own sake, it is simply a historical variant of the method of mere empirical description.

The science of language must, in fact, seek to understand the laws and forces that govern the nature and development of its object. For Baudouin, if the study of linguistic history—the major preoccupation of his contemporaries—is to go beyond the mere establishment and recording of historical facts and become genuinely explanatory, it must be based on an understanding of the *synchronic* nature of linguistic systems. There are two major reasons for this necessity, one somewhat practical and the other a matter of basic principle.

On the one hand, it is living languages that are directly available for study:

prior stages of linguistic history can be known only inferentially or, at best, through written records, which constitute only an indirect representation of a language, and not an actual language itself. Living languages must thus have basic priority as evidence for "the forces operating in language, and for the laws that govern its development, its life." We should note here that while Baudouin criticizes the descriptive, empirical study of languages for its own sake, he also stresses that a thorough knowledge of living languages is an essential preliminary to any attempt at theorizing and explanation.

On the other hand (and more importantly), it is in the forces that govern synchronic systems that we find the underlying principles leading to historical change. We must, therefore, give priority to the search for the general laws that govern the systems of living languages. This emphasis was particularly appealing to Kruszewski, whose arrival in Kazan contributed greatly to the stress put on such matters in Baudouin's work from that point on. Kruszewski hoped to be able to formulate a small number of fundamental laws of the nature of language, principles which would have the sort of richly deductive, explanatory scope attributed to the 'principle of association' in psychology.

Kruszewski's (and Baudouin's) goal, in the context of the prevailing interest in historical linguistics, was to make linguistics a natural science with an explanatory, not simply inductive, character. If linguists could be freed from their concern with history as the recording of more or less accidental events, they would be able to focus on what is truly essential to the nature of language. Accounts of linguistic structure could then be founded deductively on general laws of synchronic structure. It is interesting to note that half a century later, Trubetzkoy (1933) would claim as a major merit of the developing theory of (Prague school) phonology that it concerned itself with the search for such general laws—a methodological 'advance' which was in fact at the heart of Baudouin's and Kruszewski's thinking as well.

Kruszewski's approach to the synchronic structure of language was based on his earlier readings in philosophy, and particularly on his acquaintance with the English tradition of philosophical logic and psychology—Bacon, Hume, Locke, Mill, etc. On the basis of such typical positions as the attempt to reduce 'causality' to 'constant conjunction', these writers held out the hope that many philosophically important problems could ultimately be analyzed in terms of psychological notions, particularly the sorts of 'associations' that played such a prominent part in contemporary conceptions of the structure of the mind.

In his theoretical work, then, Kruszewski presents the nature of language as ultimately a network of two sorts of associations between linguistic forms: associations based on *simultaneity*, or parallelism of structure, and associations based on *sequence*, or frequent juxtaposition in larger structures. These are, of course, essentially the same as Saussure's notions of *associative* (called by later writers *paradigmatic*) and *syntagmatic* relations between forms. On the basis of such relations of simultaneity or sequence, words form families; these are also called 'nests', since the relation of one word to another results in further layers of relationship between the first word and others to which the second is, in its turn, related. Such a system of relational networks among forms is the structural basis of a language, and knowledge of such a system of similarities of morphological structure and contiguous combinability constitutes 'knowledge of the language'.

In order to formulate an explanatory theory of linguistic change, understanding the nature of such a system of associations is essential. This is particularly the case with regard to changes due to 'analogy' and 'folk etymology', which Kruszewski treated as instances of the same kind. According to his view, such changes illustrate the central role played by the factor of *reintegration* in language. For Kruszewski and Baudouin, language is not simply a matter of mechanical repetition but, rather, involves constant (re)recreation of the particular structures used in speech; thus, linguistic forms are constantly subject to the necessity of finding their place in the associative system.

It is this need to be continually reintegrated into the system that provides the pressure leading to analogical change and folk-etymological re-formation. When the past participle of German *essen* 'to eat', which we would expect to be **gessen* (< **ge-essen*) added an extra instance of the prefix *ge-* to become *gegessen*, we can attribute this to the fact that the form **gessen* did not seem to speakers to conform to the principle that German past participles are related to their stems by having the prefix *ge-* before the stem. The residue of subtracting *ge-* from **gessen* is simply *-ssen*, which does not seem to be the root; the entire form is thus integrated into the pattern of the language by taking it as the basis of a newly 'regularized' participle *gegessen*. Or, to take a case of 'folk etymology', when Old English speakers borrowed Latin *margarīta* 'pearl', this form was completely isolated in the system of their language, unrelated to any other form. By reanalyzing it as *mere-grota*, they were able to integrate it into a wider pattern of associations: in this form, it is a perfectly regular compound founded on the words *mere* 'sea' and *grota* 'grain'. In order to understand these and similar changes, we must begin with a substantial theory of the synchronic system of associations on which they are founded.

Interestingly, the interdependence between synchronic and historical understanding of the nature of language operates in both directions. Just as it is necessary to found diachronic explanations on an understanding of synchronic reality, so it is impossible to achieve a fully adequate account of this reality without an understanding of its development through historical change. It is for this reason, for example, that Baudouin de Courtenay criticizes the Sanskrit grammarians who "lacked a feeling for history and were unable to grasp the significance of gradual development, historical sequence, or chronology in general." It is this absence of an appreciation of language development which resulted in "the purely mechanical character of their grammatical rules; they give excellent prescriptions for the formation of all kinds of grammatical forms, but we would look in vain for a scientific explanation of the ways and means by which these forms originated" (Baudouin 1895[1972]: 147f.).

In light of Baudouin's general feeling that historical accounts of language are not per se any more satisfactory than other purely descriptive studies, it is not obvious how to take these criticisms of the Sanskrit grammatical tradition. It might be, of course, that he is simply reflecting the prevailing neogrammarian view that the only sort of explanation that can be given for the substance of a particular *état de langue* is historical, since any given state of affairs is ultimately the result of the accumulation of (individually accidental) historical facts that lead to it. Given the goal of the study in which Baudouin's critical remarks appear, however, there is a more interesting point to be seen in them.

Not only the substantive content of an *état de langue* but its very nature and character can be seen as a product of the nature of historical change. The facts of individual relationships between forms (as represented frequently in an alternation) are the result of historical change. For instance, the formal relation between German *Wort* 'word' and *Wörter* 'words' is in part a consequence of the historical change by which back vowels were replaced by front before endings (originally) containing a high front vowel, resulting in a synchronic alternation between [o] and [ö] in related words. The class of possible alternations, and thus of possible systematic linguistic relationships of this sort, is to an important extent a product of the class of possible evolutionary developments of linguistic systems, and thus an understanding of such relationships can be enlightened by the study of the character of linguistic change. The theory of alternations and their evolution which is presented in Baudouin (1895) is intended to have just this character: the range of possible alternations in synchronic grammars is presented as a consequence of the range of observed, possible developments of sound relations over time.

Baudouin's notion of the interaction between synchrony and diachrony is thus rather richer than the unbridgeable dichotomy seen by Saussure. Most of the theoretical work of the Kazan school, indeed, is devoted to exploring this relation in a positive spirit. In later sections we will sketch the proposals of Kruszewski and of Baudouin concerning the central role of alternations in the nature of language. In their views, the incipient cause of an alternation is to be found ultimately in phonetic factors, which are to be studied synchronically, as a matter of physics and physiology. The subsequent integration of the alternation into the system of the language is based on the synchronic associative principles underlying morphological relations in general, as is its capacity for modification and change in status. The sum of these evolutionary factors, which are, in turn, founded on synchronic ones, constrain and predict the range of alternations one might find in any given linguistic system. The essential nature of language and its development are thus indissolubly intertwined.

The nature of phonological structure

Baudouin distinguishes two aspects of the study of synchronic language systems: the *physical* and the *psychological*. In the particular domain of sound structure, the study of "the purely physical aspect of language" (the discipline for which present-day usage reserves the name 'phonetics') is called *anthropophonics*; this is the analysis of sounds from the physiological or acoustic point of view. Anthropophonics involves questions which could, in principle, be posed directly by physiologists or physicists, who have no special interest in language and speech per se, though the specific questions whose answers are of interest to the linguist are generally left unasked in these disciplines, appearing from a more general perspective to be matters of irrelevant detail.

It is the province of *psychophonetics* to deal with the other (nonphysical) side of the sound system of language. This has as its object "the *feeling for the language* of a given speech community" (Baudouin 1871[1972]:58; emphasis in the original), and treats a language as a particular system of sound/meaning associations that are related to one another in particular ways. In principle, psychophonetics is related to general psychology in much the same way anthropophonics is related to phsyics and physiology, but again the specific questions that are of interest to the linguist are likely to present insufficient interest to the general psychologist to motivate detailed study.

The psychophonetic aspect of sound structure is crucially based on "the analysis of sounds from the viewpoint of morphology and word formation" (ibid. p. 61). In part, this reflects the recognition that sound differences have a 'psychophonetic' value by virtue of the fact that they serve to distinguish words from one another. This basic notion of the distinctive value of (certain) sound differences, later called the 'phonemic principle', was a major concern of Baudouin's in his later years in St. Petersburg and Warsaw, perhaps under the influence of the prominence this idea attained in the wider linguistic community of the early twentieth century. It does not at all represent the primary emphasis of Baudouin's and Kruszewski's work during the period of their association in Kazan, however.

In fact, the main attention in their studies of 'psychophonetics' during this period was given to a phenomenon rooted in historical considerations. They observed that through the differential operation of phonetic changes in various forms, what was etymologically a single sound type might (in later historical stages of the language) come to be represented differently in different environments. When these different environments occur in related words, or in related forms of the same word, the result may be that the sound differences in question can come to serve as one of the factors—perhaps even the sole factor—separating morphologically distinct yet related forms from one another.

For example, in the history of English, the (originally purely mechanical) factors leading to the voicing of fricatives obtained in some denominal verbs but not in the corresponding nouns from which they were derived. Although subsequent changes eliminated other differences between the nouns and the verbs, the voicing distinction in final fricative consonants remained to differentiate such pairs as *cloth/clothe*, *house*([s])/*house*([z]), *calf/calve*, and others. In this way, an original purely anthropophonic difference has taken on psychophonetic value. There are also intermediate stages between differences that are strictly anthropophonic and those that are completely morphologized as in this case; an example would be the difference between umlauted and unumlauted vowels in German, generally a subsidiary marker of morphological differences found in association with some other marker (such as the diminutive ending -*chen*) rather than constituting the sole formal indicator of the morphological difference. The study of the character of such alternations and their role in the synchronic systems of languages occupies the central place in the Kazan school study of psychophonetics.

The centrality of alternations in the Kazan theory can be seen in the gradual mutation undergone by the notion of the 'phoneme' within this work. Kruszewski was the first to introduce this term in Kazan, having borrowed it as mentioned above from Saussure (and thus, ultimately, from Dufriche-Desgenettes). It will be recalled from the previous chapter that Saussure used the term *phonème* as an equivalent for the (phonetic) notion of 'speech sound', and we might expect that the contribution of Baudouin and Kruszewski was simply to shift the reference of this unit from anthropophonic to psychophonetic terms. In fact, the situation was somewhat more complicated than that.

Kruszewski took the notion of 'phoneme' not from Saussure's work on general linguistics (which of course did not exist in 1880), but rather from his earlier work on Indo-European, and specifically from the *Mémoire*. Saussure's use of *phonème* in that work was to refer to a historical unit: a (hypothesized) sound in the protolanguage ancestral to a given family, together with its reflexes in the each of the daughter languages. A 'phoneme' understood in this way is essentially an individual 'correspondence set' as one would identify these in the course of a historical investigation. Of course, if a single sound undergoes various sound changes in various environments, the resulting sounds remain members of the same 'phoneme' in this sense, regardless of how much they may diverge phonetically.

It was this notion, recast in synchronic terms, that Kruszewski took over. His first reference to 'phonemes' is, as with Saussure's usage, to a unit established by systematic comparison, but this time within a single language rather than across a family. When we compare instances of the same morphological unit in different words or families of words, we may find an alternation among distinct but anthropophonically related sounds, sounds that are ultimately related historically but no longer identical, being linked by the morphological relation which exists between associated categories. This is the basis of a 'phoneme' in a new sense: a set of alternating sounds occupying parallel positions within the same morphological unit in different families of words.

Although he asserted that this notion was essential to any scientific study of phonetics and morphology, Kruszewski did not immediately develop it further. He seems to have had in mind that each alternation constitutes a distinct 'phoneme' in a synchronic system; that is, that the 'phonemes' each consist of a set of alternating anthropophonic elements together with the conditions for the alternation. On this view, there is no reason why the same sound cannot belong to several different phonemes if it happens to participate in several different alternations. This is actually quite similar to the notion of 'morphophoneme' which Trubetzkoy was later to develop (see chapter 4 below), whose primary utility is to allow us to express the sense in which morphological elements are unitary despite superficial phonetic differences among their alternants. Suppose, for example, that we are dealing with a language like German in which final consonants are systematically devoiced. If we want to express the fact that the forms *Bund* [bʊnt] 'association' and *Bunde* [bʊndə] 'associations' contain the same morphological element, we can say that this element consists of the sequence [b], [ʊ], [n], and the unitary 'phoneme' ([t] finally, [d] before a vowel).

It seems to have been Baudouin who reinterpreted this notion slightly (but significantly), taking the 'phonemes' arrived at through the analysis of alternations to be the ultimate invariants of psychophonetic sound structure. In a language with a complex pattern of alternations, one might find that more than one alternation affects a single position within a given morphological unit. In Russian, for instance, we have both final devoicing and palatalization, with the result that [g] alternates both with [k] (in final position) and with [g,] (palatalized [g], occurring before front vowels). If we are to keep these alternations straight, we have a problem in representing a form like *kniga* 'book': the [g] which appears in the nominative singular of this form appears as [g,] before [i] in the genitive singular *knigi*, and as [k] in final position as in the genitive plural *knig*. We thus appear to have a single, three-way alternation ({[g]~[g,]~[k]}), whose relation to the two independent alternations of final devoicing and palatalization is unclear.

One way to resolve this difficulty is to take the 'phonemes' not as names for alternations, but rather as abstract, psychophonetic elements that alternate: for instance, we might say that there is a phoneme /g/ which participates both in the alternations {[g]~[g,]} and {[g]~[k]}. While in Kruszewski's usage a phoneme is close to being a name for a rule of alternation, Baudouin's change makes it into an element in the psychophonetic representation of morphemes which are subject to alternation. For both, however, alternations are crucial to defining the status of a phoneme.

From here, however, it is but a short step to a conception of phonemes in which alternations are no longer quite as central. If the invariant constituents of morphemes whose sounds alternate include phonemes, we can easily extend this notion to apply not only to obviously alternating elements, but also to sounds that show only 'low-level', anthropophonically determined variation (such as the different degrees of length of English vowels preceding voiced and voiceless consonants), and ultimately to those that happen to show no anthropophonic variation at all. The result is a homogeneous notion of phonemes as the ultimate invariant constitutents of morphemes. Morphemes then need not be thought of as made up of some simple sounds together with some phonemes (in positions where alternation occurs), but simply of a sequence of phonemes. In some positions, the phonemes may be subject to rules of alternation, but the alternations themselves are no longer pivotal for defining the very essence of a phoneme, and we arrive at Baudouin's conception of the phoneme as "the psychological equivalent of a speech sound" (Baudouin 1895[1972]:152). In his later work, Baudouin sought a conceptual foundation for this notion of phoneme in the distinction between external, anthropophonic reality and our psychological apprehension of that reality.

It is instructive to trace this development because it shows the gradual (and apparently quite natural) shift from a focus on regular relationships between morphologically associated forms, what we would now call rules, to a focus on invariant elements of the representation of the forms themselves that participate in such relationships. It appears to be a rather direct move to replace the claim that what is invariant in a given form is its systematic relation to other forms with the claim that each morphological element is made up of a sequence of invariant building blocks, parallel to, but different in status from, the speech sounds that make up its physical realization.

Most of the subsequent history of twentieth-century phonology would be devoted to the attempt to provide a satisfactory definition of these presumed invariant units. It is worthwhile to notice, however, that the issue of such an invariant element arises most directly as a consequence of the need to deal with the systematic *variance* represented by alternations. It is this systematic variation, with its fundamentally relational character, that language presents to us most directly. One way to organize this variation is to hypothesize underlying invariant units—indeed, judging from the history of the discipline, this is the most natural way for linguists to conceptualize such relations—but it should be borne in mind that this is not the only way to do so, or even the most transparent. As was suggested in chapter 2, for example, Saussure seems to have held a view of the phenomenon of variance and alternation that was much closer to an immediate account of the relations in question than to an account in terms of another kind of representation for linguistic forms, one given in terms of hypostatized invariants.

Kruszewski's theory of alternations

While it was Baudouin (in his lectures both in St. Petersburg and in Kazan) that had first brought up the importance of alternations for an understanding of phonological structure, it was Kruszewski who provided the first systematic treatment of the topic. His Kazan master's thesis contains a long initial chapter devoted to the status and classification of alternations, which was subsequently (1881) published separately in German. Baudouin was very impressed with this display of the "strictly logical analysis of general concepts" and with the "scientific character of Mr. Kruszewski's presentation."

After citing the general phenomenon of alternations among anthropophonically distinct sounds and introducing the word 'phoneme' as a way of referring to the unity of sounds involved in an alternation (as discussed in the preceding section), the bulk of Kruszewski's discussion centers on the classification of alternations into three types. In any alternation we can distinguish two factors: the sounds that alternate, and the conditions under which each one occurs. On these bases, we can establish a variety of dimensions along which alternations can differ from one another, and in terms of which they can be classified. Kruszewski's typology includes three categories.

Alternations of the first category meet four conditions, as follows. First, the cause of the alternation is directly determinate and immediately present, in the sense that the conditioning factors for the appearance of each of the alternating sounds can be identified in the environment. In terms of more recent discussion in phonology, we can restate this as the requirement that alternations of this category be fully transparent. Second, such an alternation must be general, in the sense of being insensitive to the morphological category of the words in which it occurs. This is, of course, the requirement that first category alternations be phonologically and not morphologically conditioned. Third, alternations of this category must be 'necessary' in that they have no exceptions and there are no cases in which one of the alternating sounds occurs under conditions which should require another. Finally, alternations of the first category involve sounds that are close to one another anthropophonically (i.e., sounds that differ from one another in only a limited number of phonetic properties).

Alternations of this category include a number of distinguishable types, although Kruszewski does not further differentiate them. For one, they include all of what is usually classified as 'subphonemic' or 'nondistinctive' variation, such as the distribution of vowel length in English as a function of the following consonant, or the alternation between [i] and [ɨ] in Russian as a function of the palatalization of a preceding consonant. They also include cases (called 'automatic alternation' in structuralist morphophonemic theory) in which otherwise distinctive segments alternate with one another, so long as the conditions for the alternation are transparent, phonological, and exceptionless: an example would be the alternation produced by (syllable-)final devoicing of obstruents in German, or the reduction of [o] to [a] in unstressed syllables in Russian. Though Kruszewski's own (limited set of) examples include only cases of the latter sort, it is clear (cf. Klausenburger 1978) that his definition and his intention apply to subphonemic variation as well. He appears to attach no importance at all to the question of whether the alternating sounds are independently distinctive (separate 'phonemes' in later, structuralist terms) or not (merely separate 'allophones' of the same structuralist phoneme). Sounds related by such an alternation are called *divergents*, and the alternation itself a *divergence*, using terminology introduced at about the same time by Baudouin.

It is important to be clear about the fact that Kruszewski's criteria for classifying an alternation as belonging to the first category are not simply taxonomic, in the sense of establishing a standard nomenclature; rather, they are intended to make a substantive claim about the range of possible alternations. This is evident from his claim that since all of the properties are inseparable, it is only necessary to establish *one* of the first three criteria in order to determine that an alternation belongs to this category. He does observe that the fourth criterion (phonetic similarity) is only a necessary one, and not sufficient, since alternations belonging to other categories may meet it as well. This contrasts with the first three conditions, which are both necessary and sufficient, such that any one of these is decisive for determining that an alternation belongs to the first category.

The empirical claim involved is thus a very strong one, and it suffices to find a single alternation in a single language that meets at least one of the first three conditions but fails one of the others in order to show that the classification needs to be modified or abandoned. In Latin, for instance, stress is assigned by a rule which ignores the final syllable; if the word is three syllables or longer, and has a penultimate syllable that is open and contains a short vowel, the stress is antepenultimate, while it is otherwise assigned to the penultimate syllable. This results in the well-known alternation in the place of the accent between *refēcit* and *reféctus* with penultimate stress vs. *réficit* with antepenultimate stress. This alternation appears to be completely transparent, and phonologically (rather than morphologically) conditioned; it must thus belong to Kruszewski's first category, but this presents a problem.

In particular, there are a few words in Latin with exceptional stress: *illíc*, for example, has final stress, reflecting its original form *illíce* where stress on the syllable that later becomes final is perfectly regular. In such a case, Kruszewski is confronted with a sort of Hobson's choice: either one preserves the exceptionless character of the accent rule by saying it applies to what is essentially the historical representation, in which case the alternation can no longer be said to be transparent, or one treats such words as exceptions to an otherwise transparent rule. In either case, the unity of the conditions defining alternations of the first category cannot be maintained.

Kruszewski himself did not have an enormous empirical base of established analyses with which to operate; it should also be stressed that he arrived at his claims deductively rather than making essentially inductive generalizations over the available data. It is thus not surprising that claims of this sort which one finds in his work are not hard to disprove, once one takes them seriously as empirical hypotheses. Nonetheless, what is worth stressing is the fact that his framework is intended to make such empirical claims about the notion 'possible alternation in a natural language'—a goal for linguistic theory which was quite revolutionary for its time, and which is not by any means met by all approaches to the nature of 'typology' in linguistics today. Much such work seems based on the assumption that a typology is sufficiently motivated once one shows that it establishes a useful taxonomy, and that it is unnecessary to require it to be explanatory in the sense of revealing necessary connections among phenomena. Naturally, taxonomies have their place in scientific discourse, in promoting concise and accurate formulation, but they should not be confused with theories. Kruszewski aimed to construct a genuine *theory* of alternations, and not simply a nomenclature for referring to them.

Sounds related by an alternation of the first category, or divergents, are considered by Kruszewski to be variants of the same sound, as opposed to those related by alternations of the second or third category. The different sounds that participate in alternations of the latter two types are called *correlatives*, and the two are quite similar (especially when both are opposed to divergences). Three general conditions are said to be applicable to an alternation of either the second or the third category.

First, it is impossible to determine directly the causes of such an alternation, and these causes may in fact be absent in particular forms. The 'causes' in question here are evidently the anthropophonic factors which provoke assimilation, dissimilation, etc. While the causes of a divergence are always present in the form itself (since such an alternation must be transparently phonetically conditioned), those of a correlation may be discoverable only through historical analysis, or indeed may be completely absent in particular cases (for instance, when a form is subject to an alternation as a result of analogical restructuring).

Secondly, an alternation of correlatives is not necessary, since either correlative may occur (in some forms) under the conditions appropriate to the other. The import of this is evidently not that there are no obligatory alternations whose conditioning is other than transparent and phonological, but rather that whatever phonological conditions one might associate with an alternation between correlatives, these are in principle violable in particular cases under nontransparent or morphological conditions. Finally, alternations among correlatives may involve more remote anthropophonic relationships (i.e., differences in a larger number of phonetic properties) than those among divergents.

Again, these conditions include an empirical claim, since the first two are said to be inseparable. Establishing either the nonphonological or the nontransparent character of the factors conditioning an alternation should thus suffice to establish the other as well and to identify an alternation as one between correlatives (and not divergents). Presumably, since divergents must be anthropophonically close, establishing the fact that the sounds involved in a given alternation do not meet this condition would also establish their status as correlatives, but Kruszewski is apparently somewhat uneasy about the value of this criterion by itself.

The difference between alternations of the second and third categories is essentially a matter of how completely an alternation is morphologized. An alternation of the second category may show partial dependence on morphological and nontransparent phonological factors. For instance, Icelandic *u*-umlaut is an alternation between *a* and *ö*. The vowel *ö* occurs when the vowel of the following syllable is *u*, but this alternation cannot be a divergence because (a) it is not transparent, since some instances of surface *u* are epenthetic and do not cause umlaut (e.g. *hattur* 'hat, nom. sg.'); and (b) it is not completely phonological, since *ö* occurs in certain morphological categories without a following *u* (e.g., *barn* 'child', but *börn* 'children'). The alternation would only be said to belong to the third category if it were completely linked to morphological categories: thus, German umlaut cannot be regarded as phonologically conditioned in any of its occurrences in the modern language, but only takes place in conjunction with a specified range of morphological categories. Under these conditions, however, an alternation of the third category is said to be obligatory (while one of the second category may not be obligatory even under those morphological conditions that can trigger it).

Kruszewski's classification is intended to be an exhaustive one, and constitutes not only a strong empirical claim about language but an elegant and conceptually parsimonious framework. It is also a well-motivated one, in the sense that its basic notions can be related to what Kruszewski considered the fundamental principles underlying the nature of language. Recall that, for him, a language is a system of associations arrayed on the two dimensions of simultaneity (or structural parallelism) and sequence (or contiguity within particular linguistic forms). It is clearly possible to treat alternations of the first category (divergences) as founded directly on sequential associations, since the conditioning factors are, *ex hypothesi*, always present in the phonological form itself to support such a syntagmatic relationship.

In alternations between correlatives, on the other hand, the conditioning factors reside not in other elements which are sequentially related to the alternating sounds, but rather in associative links the form bears to other, similarly structured forms: associations of simultaneity, or paradigmatic relationships. Such an association of simultaneity may be linked rigidly to some particular morphological category (in alternations of the third type), or it may be so linked only contingently or not at all (in the second category), in which case the association subsists only in the paradigmatic connection between particular related forms rather than in a systematic structural pattern which defines a morphological category. The range of alternation types which Kruszewski hypothesizes is thus intimately linked to the range of fundamental associative relations which constitute the essence of linguistic structure.

Baudouin's development of the theory of alternations

The logical structure of Kruszewski's account of alternations is a concise and elegant one, but the very strength of its empirical claims, in the presence of the limited range of data on which it is based and the small number of categories it provides, makes it difficult to use as the basis of a full and adequate account of many particular cases. Baudouin continued to think about these issues after his departure from Kazan and Kruszewski's death, and in 1895 he produced his own somewhat more comprehensive *Attempt at a Theory of Alternations*. For the *a priori* approach of Kruszewski the philosopher, he substitutes in large part the *a posteriori* approach of the empirical linguist. Making use of a rather wider (though still limited) range of factual material, he arrives at a classification of alternations which is logically somewhat less lucid but offers other advantages of its own.

After first introducing the general phenomenon of alternation as the synchronic analog of the comparison of etymologically related elements, Baudouin raises the general question of whether there is such a thing as 'phonetic change' in synchronic linguistic systems. He concludes that in one sense there is: often, he suggests, there is a discrepancy between our intended pronunciation and what we actually produce, owing to the intervention of various (anthropophonic) factors of accommodation. Such "substitution of an intended pronunciation by a possible one" is "the only type of phonetic change that may occur in the synchronic state of a language" (Baudouin 1895[1972]: 159f.).

An *alternation* in the strict sense, in contrast, is "simply the phonetic difference between etymologically related morphemes" (ibid.). The two are quite different in their basic nature, but there is nonetheless an intimate connection between them. This is due to the fact that "active, dynamic substitutions give rise to embryonic, incipient phonetic alternations; while the alternations which from a contemporary point of view seem to have no cause, can be traced back to substitutions which took place in the past" (ibid.). The investigation which follows these remarks is an attempt to found a theory of synchronic alternations on the fundamental interplay of synchronic and diachronic factors in the structure of language, alluded to in an earlier section of the present chapter.

Baudouin begins his account by introducing a number of parameters that can be used to classify alternations. First among these is the extent to which it is possible to determine anthropophonic causes for the alternation within the synchronic state of language (i.e., the extent to which the alternation is transparently phonologically conditioned). Alternations in which such causes can be identified are called *neophonetic*, while those in which they are absent or obscured are called *paleophonetic*. A second, parallel factor is the extent to which it is possible to identify "psychological causes" for an alternation, that is, the extent to which the alternation is associated with independently motivated morphological or semantic differences. Those alternations which are morphologized (or 'semasiologized') in this sense are called *psychophonetic*.

Third, alternations can be classified with respect to the role of "traditional or social" causes which maintain them, as opposed to active and independent synchronic factors. The presence of an alternation in a language may be due only to repetition and imitation (including the transmission of language from one generation of speakers to the next); that is, it may be learned as a more or less arbitrary fact about the language, rather than being motivated by some independent anthropophonic or psychological factor. With respect to the role of active anthropophonic factors, the alternations Baudouin calls *traditional*, which involve the learning of an arbitrary relationship between forms, are distinguished from others for conceptual reasons similar to those motivating the positing of 'rules' as opposed to '(natural) processes' in the theory of Natural Phonology (cf. Donegan and Stampe 1979). All paleophonetic alternations are *a fortiori* traditional, but neophonetic ones can become traditional as well, as we will note below.

Alternations can also be classified historically as to whether they arise entirely within the history of a single language or are the result of borrowing. Such a classification is only relevant to historical linguistics per se, however, since "from a synchronic point of view, all alternations are internal and peculiar to the given language" (Baudouin 1995[1972]:162). Similarly, alternations may be classified as to the difference between "individual and social causes," but this division is essentially a consequence of the nature of neophonetic vs. paleophonetic and traditional vs. nontraditional factors in their motivation.

Finally, alternations may be classified as to whether their causes are simple or complex. The cause of an alternation is simple if it is either purely neophonetic and not supported by tradition, or purely traditional and not supported by either neophonetic or psychophonetic factors. Alternations which involve both traditional and other factors have complex causes. Again, this dichotomy is strictly speaking reducible to others already introduced, but the possible complexity of the causes of an alternation plays a role in its subsequent development, and is thus worth pointing out despite its lack of logical autonomy.

With these parameters, Baudouin distinguishes three broad classes of alternations similar in content (and in name) to those distinguished by Kruszewski. First is the class of *divergences*, which can be defined simply as the class of neophonetic alternations. Within this class, however, we can distinguish two types: purely anthropophonic divergences, in which the phonetic motivation is still an active determining factor; and divergences which are genuinely alternations, in the sense that traditional (and not merely mechanical) factors play a role in them. Strictly speaking, only the alternating divergences are directly relevant to a theory of alternations, but these have their origin in purely anthropophonic divergences, share a number of significant properties with them, and are difficult to distinguish simply by observation.

The class of divergences as a whole displays a number of properties: (a) the alternating phonetic elements are not simply independent variants but are conditioned combinatorily by properties of the environment; (b) the conditioning factors are directly definable, or transparent; (c) the alternation is exceptionless; (d) the alternation is not correlated with 'psychological' (i.e. morphological or semantic) factors; and (e) the variation itself may go unnoticed by speakers, since its conditioning factors are phonetic rather than psychological. In contrast with Kruszewski's discussion (with which the overlap is self-evident), these factors are presented less as theorems that follow from the logical nature of the category of divergences than as empirical observations about the cases that fall within the class. Their role is to serve as the basis of more extended discussion of the evolution of divergences, and not to define the category itself.

A second class is that of *correlations*, which can be defined as paleophonetic, traditional, and (most importantly) psychophonetic alternations. These fully morphologized alternations, which we can again illustrate by the association of umlaut in German with particular categories (such as plural vs. singular, diminutive vs. nondiminutive) also display a number of correlated and characteristic properties: (a) the alternating sounds (the 'correlatives') are independent of one another and of their environments; (b) the cause of the presence of the alternation in the language is solely traditional transmission; (c) any anthropophonic causes are purely historical in nature; (d) each term of the correlation is associated with a morphological or semantic value; (e) correlations are exceptionless, by virtue of their association with psychological factors; (f) the correlatives may be arbitrarily dissimilar in phonetic terms; (g) when a correlation changes historically, the change may not be anthropophonically coherent at all; (h) a correlation may be extended to new forms in a given category without changing its nature, while other knds of alternation cannot be transferred in this way; (i) there are no substantive constraints on what kinds of correlations are possible, unlike the class of divergences where universal causal factors establish such contraints; and, finally (j) correlations are acquired gradually, while divergences are acquired directly by virtue of their anthropophonic motivation.

Finally, we have the class of *traditional alternations* in the narrow sense: the class of alternations that are paleophonetic, nonpsychophonetic, and of course traditional in the broader sense. There are two main subgroups of these: alternations that have developed from divergences by becoming in some way arbitrary, and those that represent the obsolete residue of formerly psychophonetic alternations. An example of the latter sort is the relation of [s] to [r] in English pairs like *was/were*, *rise/rear*, *snooze/snore*, etc. These alternations all share the first three characteristics of correlations (phonetic independence of the alternants, traditional transmission, and merely historical anthropophonic explicability). In addition, they are characterized by a conflict between their traditional support and the tendency to eliminate phonetic differences that are supported by neither anthropophonic nor psychological (semantic or morphological) factors. As a result, they tend either to be eliminated or to be associated with some morphological or semantic distinction so as to become correlations.

Having established a typology. Baudouin returns to his central concern: the origin of alternations and their evolution. Their origins he finds to lie uniformly in the class of 'purely anthropophonic divergences': mechanically predictable low-level phonetic variation which is typically outside of the consciousness of speakers, governed by universal constraints on production (and perhaps perception), and definitional for the class of 'incipient' or 'embryonic' alternations. The variation he has in mind here would include, for example, the tendency for vowel pitch to be slightly raised following voiceless consonants and slightly lowered following voiced ones; the tendency to lengthen vowels somewhat when a voiced obstruent follows; the typical perceptual effects of the formant shifts associated with nasalization of vowels; and a host of other effects studied more intensively by phoneticians than by phonologists. As long as they remain in this domain of "microscopic phenomena which can be detected only as a result of a concentrated effort," these divergences (while objectively real enough) do not suffice to establish a difference between the phonemes involved.

It is only when the differences become greater, so as to establish a perceptual difference between the sounds, that we can speak of a true alternation. The process by which such low-level variation can be 'appropriated' from the status of purely phonetic effects into the domain of linguistic structure has been called *phonologization*; this term appears recently in the generative literature (Hyman 1976), with earlier structuralist precedents such as the work of Jakobson, but Baudouin uses it as well in his later writing, and he was undoubtedly the first linguist to propose explicitly that all systematic phonological variation originates in the phonologization of phonetic detail. We can also note the parallel with Saussure's view, discussed in the preceding chapter, that the explanation of sound change is to be sought in a close study of the details of combinatory phonetic effects (his *phonologie*). For both linguists, advances in phonetic research in the nineteenth century had revealed a world intensely rich in minute variation, with the possibility that indeed no sound type is quite the same in any two distinct environments. For both, it is this infinitesimal detail that constitutes the raw material of linguistic variation and change.

The mechanism of phonologization is quite explicit: "The very fact that the words containing the respective phonemes differ on the one hand anthropophonically . . . and on the other hand psychologically, i.e. semasiologically or morphologically, introduces a difference between the seemingly identical phonemes that may eventually become perceptible" (Baudouin 1895[1972]:195). In other words, the fact that phonetic variation, however minute, is associated with differences between words makes it a natural candidate for becoming a factor *differentiating* those words. When this happens, the previously mechanical effect is elevated to the status of a linguistic alternation (a divergence, so long as the phonological conditioning factors remain transparent).

The process of phonologization only accounts for the existence of divergences: how are we to explain the appearance of other sorts of alternation? Baudouin hardly overlooks this issue, and his discussion of it is again clear and explicit. On the one hand, once an embryonic alternation has become a genuine divergence, the difference between the variants tends to increase, so as to emphasize the contrast between the two differentiated forms. As a result, the further maintenance of the alternation in its present form becomes dependent not simply on anthropophonic factors, but also on traditional ones. Thus, English-speaking children have to learn to lengthen vowels before voiced obstruents to a greater extent than is apparently anthropophonically motivated, and this effect has become a phonological rule of the language rather than a mere articulatory side effect (cf. Anderson 1981 and literature cited there). Such an alternation has become a traditional (though still neophonetic) divergence.

Subsequently, however, the original factors of the environment which produced the anthropophonic effect underlying the alternation may themselves undergo a change, obscuring its neophonetic character. This is of course a classic description of the development of opacity in an alternation: an example would be the fact that, for speakers of American English who replace both /t/ and /d/ by a flap /D/ in words like *latter* and *ladder*, the factor conditioning a difference in vowel length in the two words is no longer manifest in the surface forms. When this happens, we have a traditional alternation in the strict sense and no longer a divergence. The rise of such opacity in the conditioning factors of divergences thus furnishes a source of traditional alternations. Such a development is made possible by the fact that the variants of even a fully neophonetic divergence are rendered partially independent by the extent to which such an alternation becomes traditional as a side effect of phonologization.

As noted above, however, traditional alternations are unstable, insofar as they are dependent only on tradition for support and in conflict with the tendency to eliminate nonfunctional variation. They can be retained, however, if the variation in question is associated not simply with the difference between two arbitrary related forms, but rather with some morphological or semantic aspect of their relationship. When this happens, the alternation has become 'morphologized' (in present-day terminology), and has become a correlation.

The reduction of unstressed vowels in earlier German resulted in the conversion of the effects of umlaut to a purely traditional alternation; this alternation was maintained by associating the difference between umlauted and non-umlauted vowels with specific morphological categories rather than with anthropophonic factors. As a result, umlaut vowels appeared in forms where they had never been anthropophonically motivated, since the alternation was now a (morphologically conditioned) correlation. There is thus a clear source for alternations of this type as well, without departing from the idea that the origin of all alternations is ultimately to be sought in low-level anthropophonic variation.

Finally, over time the morphological support for a correlation may be eroded, through changes of either morphological or phonological sorts, or simply through a loss of the feeling of relatedness among certain lexical items. For instance, the alternation between [z] and [r] in the small number of pairs like *was/were* that can be cited in English is the residue of a once-productive alternation (the consequence of Verner's Law); this alternation was once associated with certain categories in the verbal system, but the general decay of verbal inflection has left these few isolated pairs with no systematic support. Such an alternation has reverted (from the status of a correlation) to being a merely traditional alternation and, if confined to few enough forms, may be lost entirely.

We can thus identify a 'life cycle' for alternations, which has considerable explanatory power. It fulfills Baudouin's original project of unifying the diachronic and the synchronic aspects of language, since each individual diachronic development is rooted in the character of the synchronic system within which it occurs, while the substantive character of a particular synchronic system can be seen to be the product of a chain of historical reorganizations of its basic material.

The result is probably the most nearly adequate framework proposed to date for discussing the issue of what constitutes a 'possible phonological rule in a natural language'. Any view of this issue must confront an apparent paradox: on the one hand, most rules are tantalizingly close to being explicable (or 'natural') in terms of phonetic factors, while, on the other hand, rules show no tendency at all to stick close to this phonetic explicability, and instead often become 'crazy rules' (Bach & Harms 1972).

Most views of phonology that have recognized this issue have 'solved' it by ignoring one side or the other. Either it is denied that there are any phonetically unnatural rules, with the apparent counterexamples being treated as not really rules of the grammar at all but simply quasi-systematic resemblances with no significance; or else it is argued that phonetic naturalness is not really a relevant constraint on phonological rules, and that the class of possible rules can be delimited and studied solely in terms of their formal properties within some appropriate notational system. Neither of these approaches has had notable success in dealing fully with the nature of phonological structure (see also Anderson 1981 for further discussion), and it may be argued that neither is as satisfactory as Baudouin's treatment of the problem in 1895.

The later history of 'Kazan phonology'

It would obviously be anachronistic to assert that the Kazan theory of alternations as represented in Baudouin's development of it sketched above is literally a theory of phonological *rules* in the sense of generative phonology, although the issues it addresses bear a striking similarity to those of modern work. There are numerous important differences: for example, Baudouin's alternations are not formulated in terms of deriving one alternant from another but, rather, as static relations between sounds occupying equivalent positions in related forms. As a corollary to this nonderivational character, the alternations are not sequentially ordered, and there is no notion of an intermediate structure between the most abstract and the most concrete. Additionally, there is no concern in Baudouin's (or Kruszewski's) work for the issues of formal expression which have played such a prominent role in recent phonology. Nonetheless, in the sense of the present work, the Kazan theory is primarily a theory of rules rather than a theory of representations, since its focus is the *relationships* between forms that establish the range of variation between linguistic elements, and only secondarily on the nature of some presumed underlying invariant elements themselves.

The theory of alternations that is embodied in this work must be said to have had only rather limited direct influence on the later development of the field. Meillet (a student of Saussure who became familiar with the Kazan linguists' work through him) makes use of the notion of alternation in various works on Indo-European (especially in his work on Slavic), and to some extent of the Kazan classificatory scheme; but his interest in these ideas was in a tool to be used in description rather than a theory to be developed. Others too have made occasional reference to Baudouin and Kruszewski, but (perhaps because of the inaccessibility of their publications, perhaps because other theoretical interests dominated) the content of the theory of alternations has remained largely unappreciated, at least until the recent publication in translation of Baudouin's work.

The most important possible direct impact of Baudouin and Kruszewski's work was probably on Jakobson's views (see chapter 5 below). Jakobson was certainly familiar with their work, and his own takes up some of the same themes. The division of alternations into automatic and morphophonemic in Jakobson's descriptions, with automatic alternations treated as a part of the phonology while the morphophonemic ones are more closely tied to the morphology, could be argued to have at least a part of its inspiration in Kruszewski and Baudouin's work. Similarly, the interest of Jakobsonian linguists in finding and describing the grammatical function of morphophonemic rules could be traced to the Kazan' discussion of correlations. Such notions are actually rather general ones, though, and however much they may have been suggested by a reading of the theories outlined in this chapter, they hardly constitute a development of the same program. In fact, we find little or no attention in the work of Jakobson and his students to the elaboration of a principled and comprehensive classification of alternation types, or (*a fortiori*) to the use of such a classification in the explanation of mechanisms of linguistic change.

As opposed to the theory of alternations, Baudouin's views on the nature of representations can be said to have had some more or less direct lineal successors. Recall that in the early work of Kruszewski, the notion of 'phoneme' was introduced essentially as a name for that constituent of a morpheme which underwent alternation. As we sketched above, this notion was gradually generalized so as to become a way of talking about sound types, rather than simply about alternations. In this way morphemes could be regarded as made up uniformly of phonemes rather than primarily of nonalternating sounds, with the admixture of a few phonemes to cover the alternating elements. In this form, the phoneme emerges fully as the central unit in a theory of the representation of linguistic invariants rather than as a tool for the study of variation. The nature of these 'phonemes' soon came to dominate linguistic discussion, including also much of Baudouin's work afer the Kazan period.

One thing which is consistent in all of Baudouin's writings, and which has been taken by later commentators as *the* defining character of his definition of the phoneme, is the psychological nature of this element. Already in his work on alternations, it is defined as "the psychological equivalent of a speech sound," and in general it is conceived as a sort of ideal sound image which exists in the speaker's mind and represents his (perhaps imperfectly realized) intention in production. In later discussion, the phoneme came to be associated particularly with the class of alternations defined as divergences. These have as their origins, as discussed above, precisely the speaker's inability—or, perhaps better, simply his failure—to produce an intended sound under certain conditions and the consequent substitution of some other sound. We thus arrive at the significant notion of a linguistically autonomous sound by "purging it of the accident of divergence" (quoted by Stankiewicz 1972:25).

The phoneme defined in this way constitutes a unit which is limited exactly by the range of transparent, phonologically conditioned variation. There is, for example, nothing against representing the final segment of German *Bund* as the phoneme /d/, since the alternation of final devoicing is a divergence. This conception of the phoneme would be further limited, however, in the later work of Baudouin and his students.

Baudouin himself had begun to devote more attention to the meaning-differentiating function of sounds (and thus of phonemes) in his post-Kazan work. It is perhaps worth noting that on several occasions he speaks of this function as associated not with whole phonemes but, rather, with constituent parts of them (*kinemes* and *acousemes*, elementary component gestures and aspects of the auditory nature of a sound). These are rather similar to the later conception of 'distinctive features' developed in the work of Jakobson and Trubetzkoy, as Jakobson (1960) pointed out. Baudouin did not pursue such an analysis in any detail, however.

The distinctive character of the phoneme was further emphasized in its treatment by his student L. V. Ščerba (1880–1944). Ščerba had studied phonetics in Paris with Rousselot and Passy before coming to St. Petersburg in 1909 to head the laboratory of experimental phonetics. He subsequently followed Baudouin's lectures there, though he was already familiar with his work in general. Since Ščerba's interest was most directly in phonetic structure, he was not primarily concerned with the theory of alternations (though he did write some on this topic in later years); he did, however, take over from Baudouin some of the latter's psychological approach to the definition of phonemes.

Partly on the basis of ideas he may have gotten from Passy's work, Ščerba was concerned to emphasize the distinctive or meaning-differentiating function of phonemes. As a result, he could not accept Baudouin's interpretation of these as defined by the full class of divergences: since [d] and [t] in German serve to differentiate words from one another, it would not do to represent one and the same sound sequence (e.g. [bʊnt]) by two different phonemic forms (/bʊnd/ and /bʊnt/) depending on morphological relationships. As a result, Ščerba's notion of the phoneme (which formed the basis of that associated with the Leningrad school of Soviet linguistics) could only treat two sounds as belonging to the same phoneme if they are members of a divergence which does not neutralize otherwise distinctive differences.

This is a reasonably natural (though hardly inevitable) development of Baudouin's notion, and it was in this form that the linguistic theories of subsequent years would approach the nature of the phoneme. But, by retaining Baudouin's psychological perspective on the phoneme as "a sound of the same intention" but of "different anthropophonic realization" (Baudouin 1895[1972]:171), Ščerba's conception acquires another aspect which was not so generally accepted. It seems quite plausible (indeed, necessary) on this view to regard the sound which represents the underlying intention of the speaker as a 'basic variant' which is transformed into various secondary variants under some (but not all) conditions. As remarked above, the Kazan notion of an alternation was not derivational in this sense (though sometimes Baudouin and Kruszewski do speak, unsystematically, of one member of an alternation as its 'basic variant'). Once we articulate the notion of phonemes as the psychological invariants underlying (a restricted class of) divergences, though, it is much more natural to adopt such a derivational picture, along the lines of the 'fully specified basic variant' view sketched above in chapter 2.

It was in the form of this 'Leningrad school' phoneme that Baudouin de Courtenay's views contributed to forming the climate of Russian linguistics in the period around World War I. It is perhaps ironic that a linguist whose most important and best-developed work in general linguistics concerned the notion of rules (in the sense of the present book) should be best remembered for helping to form a particular notion of phonological representations. In any event, the discussion that centered on the validity of the Leningrad conception of the phoneme was influential in determining the views of a later generation of linguists, who were in Russia at this time and who would subsequently form the nucleus of the Prague Linguistic Circle.

4

Prague School Phonology from the Moscow Circle through Trubetzkoy's *Grundzüge*

Work in phonology continued among Baudouin's students such as Ščerba and Polivanov in St. Petersburg, but in the years immediately preceding the Russian revolution an approach to the study of language developed in Moscow which was largely (though not entirely) independent of Baudouin's views. An interest in problems of poetics, literary analysis, and general artistic structure was combined with the influence of Slavic and historical linguistics in the discussions of a group of younger scholars, who were encouraged to develop this wide range of problems on the basis of the novel ideas they found in the works of Saussure and Baudouin. The result was an independent perspective on the basic issues in language and linguistics, much different from the rather phonetically oriented views of the St. Petersburg/Leningrad school.

The turbulence of the revolution and the period immediately following broke up this group, forcing many of them to emigrate. During the 1920s, however, several of the most important figures found themselves in or near Prague, where their collaboration was reconstituted and expanded around the activities of the Linguistic Circle of Prague. Besides their actual research, this group was particularly vigorous in presenting its point of view to the larger world of linguistics and in aggressively recruiting other scholars to the novelties of structuralist phonology. This crusading spirit may have contributed as much as did the actual results of their work to the Prague school linguists' success in essentially changing the character of European linguistics. Novelty and excitement, especially when combined with the activity of such powerful intellectual figures as Jakobson and Trubetzkoy, are often irresistible, as linguistics has seen in other contexts since.

It is interesting to note that the work usually identified as the virtual codification of Prague school phonology, Trubetzkoy's *Grundzüge der Phonologie*, was written by one who was not closely identified with the program of the earlier Moscow Circle, and who worked in Vienna rather than in Prague. Certainly other prominent members of the Prague Circle had other interests, and a full treatment of their views would have to go well beyond the discussion here centering on Trubetzkoy. Nonetheless, it is difficult to dispute the claim that in terms both of his centrality in discussions on specifically phonological issues and of his influence on later scholarship, Trubetzkoy represents the essence of

'Praguian' phonology. His intimate collaboration with Jakobson in the context of the Prague Circle, together with his role as perhaps its most prominent representative to the international community (both at the time and in the subsequent literature), makes his work the fundamental and most important statement of its views.

The background of the Prague Circle and the life of Trubetzkoy

The Moscow Linguistic Circle was founded in 1915 by a group of seven young Russian linguists, "having as its aim the study of linguistics, poetics, metrics and folklore" as stated in its authorization (quoted by Jakobson 1965:530). Central among these was Roman Jakobson, who was the president of the circle from 1915 to 1920; he and other members such as N. F. Jakovlev (a specialist in Caucasian languages) were noted for their contributions to more or less 'pure' linguistics, but from the beginning this group gave a very prominent place to what we would now consider interdisciplinary perspectives drawn from the study of art and literature, and especially of poetry.

Jakobson himself (born in 1896 in Moscow) was primarily interested in the study of poetry, and initially intended to specialize in literary history. In addition to the Linguistic Circle, he was also a member of several other innovative literary and poetic circles both in Moscow and in St. Petersburg. He was rather caught up in the general early twentieth-century interest in the analytical study of formal structure in art, architecture, music, and verse, but came early to the conclusion that the study of form in poetry could only proceed on the basis of an insignt into the structure of language. His early work was dominated by poetic considerations, and while this interest continued to be central throughout his life, his linguistic studies gradually led him to an involvement not only in questions of folklore, Slavic and Indo-European metrics, etc., but also in Slavic historical linguistics (the dominant concern of the linguistics faculty in Moscow) and eventually in general linguistics.

He notes (1962:631) that when he submitted a list of proposed readings to his adviser, the only item that was not approved as a part of his program was Ščerba's monograph on Russian vowels; and that, naturally, it was just this work with its background in Baudouin de Courtenay's (late) views on the nature of phonological structure and the phoneme that he read first. The notion of a unit of sound structure which represented exactly the aspects of the phonetic material that could serve to differentiate words from one another seemed the natural basis for an analysis which would extend to literature (and especially to verse) the study of formal relationships as in other arts.

Baudouin's work thus came to have an indirect influence on the early discussions of the Moscow Linguistic Circle, and another of its members soon introduced the views of Saussure. Sergej Karcevskij (born in 1884) had emigrated to Geneva in 1907, where he studied linguistics with Saussure, Bally, and Sechehaye. In 1917 he returned to Moscow, where he became a member of the

Linguistic Circle and presented the views of Saussure's *Cours* (just published) to his Russian colleagues. After leaving Moscow again in 1919, he spent additional time with Meillet (in 1920–22) and was awarded a doctorate in 1927 from Geneva, where he later taught. In his contributions both to the Moscow Circle and, later, in Prague, Karcevskij facilitated a familiarity on the part of both groups with the 'Geneva school' view of language.

By the beginning of the twentieth century, the notion of a *kružok* or 'circle' had a rather long history among Russian intellectuals. These small, semiformal societies were generally composed of young adherents of some more or less *avant-garde* view, who met in one another's homes for discussion. Since such groups (nominally devoted to literary concerns or the like) were also a source of much clandestine political activity, they unfortunately tended to arouse the interest of the tsarist police. In order to establish its own *bona fides* and thus avoid this consequence, the *Moskovskij lingvestičeskij kružok* operated under the auspices of the Moscow Dialectological Commission, associated with the Russian Academy of Sciences. The Dialectological Commission, itself founded in 1904 to provide a forum for young scholars interested in the study of Russian, was at the time the most active group engaged in linguistic and folkloristic research. Among its more active members was the Prince Nikolaj Sergeevič Trubetzkoy, with whom Jakobson and the Moscow Circle linguists thus came into contact.

Trubetzkoy was born in Moscow in 1890. His father, Prince Sergej Trubetzkoy, was a professor of philosophy at the University of Moscow and, at the time of his death in 1905, rector of the university. Evidently rather precocious, the young Trubetzkoy had begun to study the ethnology and ethnography of the Finno-Ugric peoples of Russia at the age of thirteen; and at the age of fifteen, he published two articles on the folklore of the Finns and that of the Voguls, Ostyaks, and Votyaks. Still in his teens, he also worked on the languages of the Paleo-Siberian group, sketching a grammar of Kamchadal and doing comparative work on this language and Chukchee. It is reported that V. Bogoraz, the most eminent specialist in Chukchee and Koryak at the time, was quite upset when he discovered that the promising scholar with whom he had been in correspondence for some time was in fact still of high-school age.

When he entered the university in 1908, Trubetzkoy wanted to specialize in ethnology and ethnography, but the faculty within which these subjects were taught in Moscow treated them as disciplines of the natural rather than the social and human sciences, as Trubetzkoy would have preferred. He thus began to study in the department of philosophy and psychology, but soon discovered that it was impossible to pursue his main interests within this program either. As a result, he transferred in his second year to the department of linguistics. Here too his studies were not concentrated on his primary area of interest, since the required program was mostly devoted to Indo-European historical and comparative grammar, but he decided to continue for primarily methodological reasons. Linguistics seemed to him to be based on more rigorous grounds than any other branch of the human sciences, and Indo-European studies were obviously much better developed than any other branch of the field and thus the best place to learn its methods.

In 1911 Trubetzkoy spent his summer vacation in the Caucasus with Professor V. Miller, president of the Moscow Ethnographic Society and a specialist in Ossetic. On this trip he began work on the languages of the Northwest Caucasian family; and, indeed, for the rest of his life he would devote a considerable share of his scholarly attention to these languages as well as those of the Northeast Caucasian group. In 1913 he presented his thesis in lingustics, dealing with the range of expression of the future in Indo-European, and was accepted into the faculty of the department. After spending 1913–14 studying in Leipzig (where he came into contact with Leonard Bloomfield, who was there at the same time) with Brugmann, Leskien, and others, he prepared for his doctoral examinations and gave the required two public lectures to qualify for the doctorate, after which he was made the equivalent of an assistant professor. He began by teaching Sanskrit, and intended to add Avestan and Old Persian the following year, but by 1916 his attention was drawn irresistibly to questions of methodology and to historical Slavic phonology.

The linguistics faculty in Moscow at this time was completely dominated by the views of F. Fortunatov, who had developed an essentially neogrammarian position on historical reconstruction in a particularly formal and rigorous way. In 1915, A. Šaxmatov published a comprehensive reconstruction within this tradition of the history of Russian and of common Slavic, a work which Trubetzkoy felt exemplified perfectly all of the faults in Fortunatov's methodology. He presented a highly criticial analysis of Šaxmatov's work at the Moscow Dialectological Commission, which created a furor. As a result of this confrontation, he decided to devote his efforts to substantiating his position in detail, and intended to write his own *Prehistory of Slavic*. This project became something of an obsession with him over a number of years, and most of his attention was for a time concentrated on studies related to it.

In the turmoil of 1917, Prince Trubetzkoy was forced to flee Moscow. Escaping through the Caucasus (where an independent republic existed briefly in the period immediately after the October revolution), he found a temporary refuge in Rostov, but soon had to be evacuated again. In the process, nearly all of his notes and manuscripts were lost, including drafts of parts of the *Prehistory*. During 1920–22, he occupied a position in Slavic philology and comparative linguistics at the University of Sofia in Bulgaria, but as political conditions once more became difficult for him there, he was forced to move again. Hoping to find a position in newly independent Czechoslovakia, he settled "temporarily" in Vienna, where he was offered a chair in Slavic philology. In fact, he occupied this position for the rest of his life.

In the meantime, Jakobson too left Russia and took up his studies in Prague in 1920. He contacted Trubetzkoy at this time in Sofia, and an extensive series of letters between the two began at this time. Their contents (published by Jakobson 1975), continuing up to Trubetzkoy's death, provide valuable insights into the development of the notion of 'phonology' during this period as well as their authors' attitudes toward their own work and that of others.

In this period, Trubetzkoy was primarily interested in Slavic historical questions related to his *Prehistory*, and the early correspondence with Jakobson is dominated by such issues. Jakobson himself was largely occupied with questions of poetics and metrics, as illustrated in his first major work, *On Czech Verse* (published in 1922); but as a natural development of this along lines suggested already in discussions of the Moscow Circle, he was increasingly interested in the more general notion of sound structure in language. His attempts to interest Trubetzkoy in the development of the theoretical study of phonemic patterns received little more than polite response at first; but in 1926, Jakobson found the key to Trubetzkoy's attention.

In a long letter outlining the significance of phonological studies for historical change, he suggested that a genuinely explanatory and predictive theory in this area could be supplied by a consideration of changes as taking place not blindly and fortuitously in sounds but, rather, functionally in phonological systems. The interpretation of sound change as motivated by the structure of such systems could thus replace what Jakobson saw as unsatisfactory in the neogrammarian and Saussurian views; but obviously it was necessary first to have a clear idea of what such systems were like and of the laws governing their structure.

Trubetzkoy was immediately persuaded that in such a direction lay answers to the questions of methodology in historical linguistics that had preoccupied him for so long, and from then on the direction of his work changed radically. Though he continued to teach and to do research on historical Slavic matters, his primary interest became the study of regularities in synchronic phonological systems. He soon saw that his earlier plan for his *Prehistory* would have to be totally rethought from the new point of view; and, indeed, in the face of his new goals, the *Prehistory* rapidly disappeared from view. Instead, he concentrated his attention on studying the phonological systems of as many languages as he could find adequate descriptions of, in order to uncover in this inductive fashion the basic regularities governing phonological patterns.

The cooperation between Trubetzkoy and Jakobson was further enhanced, and given an organizational vehicle, by the founding of the Linguistic Circle of Prague. The Czech professor V. Mathesius had admired the atmosphere and work of the Moscow Linguistic Circle, and in 1925 explored the idea of starting a similar group in Prague with his student B. Trnka, Jakobson, and Karcevskij (who was also in Prague at this time). In October of the following year, the *Prazsky linguistický kroužek* held its first meeting, and the group rapidly attracted a number of Czech (and other) linguists to its discussions as well as Trubetzkoy from nearby Vienna. As with its predecessor in Moscow, the

Prague Circle involved literary and philosophical figures as well as linguists: Husserl and Carnap, for example, as well as several novelists and poets addressed its sessions. Nonetheless, its primary activity (at least as far as it affected the outside world) was the development of a 'structuralist' perspective on language, and particularly on phonology.

In the manner of artistic and literary movements of the time, this development found early expression in manifestos presented to international gatherings. It must be recognized that despite the earlier work of Saussure, Baudouin, and their followers, the character of linguistic research still had not fundamentally changed. The field was dominated by historical studies of the atomistic, neogrammarian sort on the one hand, and by detailed observational phonetic studies on the other. The notion of a language as a system of *related* elements (rather than a more or less disjointed collection of independent ones) had as yet had little impact on the methodological premises of linguistic investigations. Similarly, the notion that a linguistically significant description of the sound system of a given language should explicate the ways in which distinct forms are differentiated from one another, rather than providing a uniformly fine-grained account of the acoustic and/or articulatory events associated with the production of particular words, had still not effectively emancipated phonetic studies from the obsession with masses of detail in which they were effectively mired as intrumental techniques of observation were refined.

The phonologists of the Prague school thus felt they were leading a sort of crusade against entrenched fundamental misconceptions, and they adopted an aggressive, sometimes confrontational approach in the effort to put across their ideas. As often happens in such circumstances, the very feeling of novelty and lively activity generated by the 'phonological movement' proved irresistible to many, especially younger scholars. Trubetzkoy himself, as indicated in his letters to Jakobson, saw in an almost Manichaean fashion a field divided between those who were "with us" and those who were not. The ranks of the former swelled significantly with each passing international gathering.

The work of the Prague Circle focused immediately on preparations for the upcoming First International Congress of Linguists, to be held in The Hague in 1928. For this meeting, a set of general questions about the nature of the field and its methods had been formulated by the organizers, and participants were invited to prepare propositions addressing these issues. In response to the question "Quelles sont les méthodes les mieux appropriées à un exposé complet et pratique de la grammaire d'une langue quelquonque?" Jakobson (1928) prepared a set of propositions outlining and arguing for the basic goals of phonology. Intended to address the perceived failures both of neogrammarian historical linguistics and of phonetics, these propositions (which were signed also by Trubetzkoy and Karcevskij) advocated a fundamental change of direction in linguistic research. While obviously controversial, they were in fact enthusiastically approved by many participants at the Congress, encouraging their formulators to further efforts (assuming this was needed).

According to Jakobson's proposals, the tasks of phonology are (a) to identify the characteristics of particular phonological systems, in terms of the language-particular range of significant differences among "acoustico-motor images"; (b) to specify the types of such differences that can be found in general, and in particular to identify 'correlations', or recurrent differences that serve to characterize multiple pairs of elements (as e.g. voicing separates p from b, t from d, etc.); (c) to formulate general laws governing the relations of these correlations to one another within particular phonological systems; (d) to account for historical change in terms of the phonological system (rather than the individual sound) which undergoes it, and especially to construe such changes as teleologically governed by considerations of the system; and, finally, (e) to found phonetic studies on an acoustic rather than an articulatory basis, since it is the production of sound that is the goal of linguistic phonetic events and that gives them their social character. In this program, there was undoubtedly something to offend just about anyone who accepted the then-current assumptions of the field.

While Jakobson's propositions diverged from the practice of other linguists in all of their major respects, this was especially true in his urging a concentration on the system of distinctive sound differences to the exclusion of other phonetic facts, and in proposing a teleological, system-determined conception of linguistic change. It is by no means clear that the latter notion ever really prevailed: while historical studies came soon to be cast in terms of changes undergone by the phonological system, the role played by the system in *motivating* change generally in a teleological fashion was stressed more by theoreticians (e.g. Martinet) than by the mainstream of practicing historical linguists (which is not to deny that Martinet himself did substantive work of a historical nature).

In descriptive studies, on the other hand, the eventual victory of the 'phonological' perspective was virtually complete. Its essential insight was basically no different from Saussure's: in order to study the sound system of a particular language, it is necessary to focus on the ways in which sound differences do or do not differentiate distinct forms within that language. The fact that Jakobson posed this basic principle in an explicit and persuasive way, at a time when the field was prepared to recognize the deficiencies of the alternatives to it, led to its acceptance. Though this did not take place overnight, the dominance of purely phonetic and historical studies gave way before long to analyses concentrating on the distinctive function of sound elements.

It is necessary to recognize that the specific way in which the Prague linguists intended to carry out this study (to wit, by establishing systems of elements composed of exactly the distinctive properties of phonetic entities) is not the only way it could be pursued. Recall the discussion above in chapter 2 concerning different conceptions of phonemic representation, and different ways of carrying out the essential aspects of Saussure's program. Nonetheless, many linguists accepted the notion that studying exclusively the distinctive elements (or 'phonemes' in one specific sense) was a necessary concomitant of abandoning a naive phonetic approach to language—in part, probably, for the simple reason that it was in this concrete form that the basic insight of phonology was presented to them.

After the Hague congress, the Prague Circle immediately began preparations for an International Congress of Slavists to be held in Prague in 1929. Again at this meeting, a set of 'theses' was formulated in the name of the Prague Circle, circulated at the congress, and discussed. These theses extended and refined the lines suggested by Jakobson at The Hague, and again resulted in both controversy and conversions. Indeed, it appears (according to Jakobson 1965) that the controversy engendered by the circle's theses was sufficiently ardent that the proceedings of the plenary sessions (at which their point of view was the most prominent) were mysteriously 'lost', and this volume of the congress's *Transactions* was never published.

During the 1930s the growth and international prominence of phonology and the Praguian approach to it was prodigious, though this was more a matter of individual scholars than of whole institutions. Academic employment was anything but abundant, and the onset of the depression hardly improved this. Jakobson was only offered a regular faculty position (as professor in Brno) in 1931, and then a combination of economic difficulties and academic political opposition had the result that he was not officially nominated until 1933. Even then, he was not confirmed (and thus received no salary) until the following year. Trubetzkoy had a secure position in Vienna, but most of his teaching was committed to Slavic rather than to general linguistics or phonology per se.

Nonetheless, Jakobson and Trubetzkoy were in contact with most of the important figures in the field, as well as a significant number of the less prominent ones. Some of the former, such as Sapir, Meillet, and Vendryes, proved receptive in varying degrees to their ideas, and these consequently became more widely known. In Prague itself, the Linguistic Circle initiated a series of *Travaux du cercle linguistique de Prague* with a set of studies prepared for the Slavistic Congress in 1929, and these became the primary forum for discussion of Praguian phonology. Following on their successes at the congresses of the preceding years, the Prague linguists organized an International Phonology Meeting in 1930, which was attended by scholars from a number of countries. In 1932, an International Phonological Association was established in connection with the International Permanent Committee of Linguists (CIPL), the body responsible for organizing the international congresses of linguistics. This association distributed copies of Trubetzkoy's *Anleitung zu phonologischen Beschreibungen* to its members in many countries.

Dedicated attention to matters of organization and 'public relations', as well as intellectual ones, together with a nucleus of ardent supporters, thus secured a central place for Praguian views in the development of linguistics in the 1930s. This development was greatly complicated, however, by the economic difficulties and political crises which upset both communication and the careers of many individual linguists.

Trubetzkoy began work on a comprehensive synopsis of the central notions of phonology, incorporating analyses of numerous languages as well as the theoretical principles underlying phonological theory. Increasingly affected by a heart ailment, he was particularly eager to see this project completed. In 1938 (perhaps partly as a result of an especially unpleasant Gestapo raid on his apartment, when many of his papers were destroyed or confiscated), he suffered a final attack and died on 25 June. He managed to complete a draft of the first (and principal) volume of his introduction just before his death, and this was published as *Grundzüge der Phonologie* in the Prague *Travaux* series in 1939. This work has generally been regarded as the most comprehensive single presentation of Prague school views on phonology, and it is to the system presented there that we now turn.

Units in phonological analysis

Although it had become clear to most linguists by the 1920s that something besides careful phonetic observation was necessary in analyzing the sound systems of particular languages, there was no general agreement on exactly what this might be. In particular, the relation between phonetics and the emerging discipline of 'phonology' continued to create controversies. Among these were the role played by the phonetic identity (and identifiability) of the properties that function in a (language-particular) distinctive way, the relative roles of the properly distinctive and the merely identifying functions of the sound image, and the extent to which phonetic and phonological analyses must refer to each other.

Trubetzkoy's discussion in his *Grundzüge* starts—with explicit reference to the prior work of Saussure and Baudouin de Courtenay—from the distinction between the *Sprechakt*, or concrete act of speaking, and the *Sprachgebilde*. The latter is the system which underlies, as a complex of socially determined values, actual concrete acts of speaking: it is this system which enables these acts to represent meanings for both the speaker and the hearer. Evidently, the distinction between *Sprechakt* and *Sprachgebilde* is the same in its essence as that between Saussure's *parole* and *langue*.

On the basis of the fundamental difference between these two aspects of the structure of a language (its material realization on the one hand, and the system of distinctive values underlying this on the other), Trubetzkoy concludes that with respect to the study of sound systems, two distinct disciplines must be kept separate. *Phonetics*, as the science of sounds in their concrete physiological, acoustic, and auditory aspects has quite a different object, and employs quite distinct methods, from *phonology* or the science of the functional distinguishing role of sounds within a linguistic system. Of course, these two disciplines are not totally separate, in that they refer to one another's results. The phonetician pays more attention to the material basis of those distinctions that have a linguistic function, while the phonologist starts from the phonetic data showing that the functional opposition between particular sounds is realized in such and such a way. Aside from this sort of friendly 'handshaking', however, phonology as the science of the functional utilization of sounds remains quite distinct in its goals and procedures from phonetics.

The phonetician, in order to realize the ideal of this discipline, must rigorously exclude from the investigation all reference to the distinguishing, functional nature of speech sounds. Indeed, not even the conventional segmentation of speech is available to phonetics *a priori*, since it rests on the distinguishing function of segments of sound; and this is of course notoriously difficult to reconstruct *a posteriori* on purely phonetic grounds. These imperatives result in a necessarily atomistic study of particular sound types, taken in isolation from one another except insofar as they reveal similarities of formation or acoustic structure. The phonologist, on the other hand, must make an equally rigorous effort to limit attention to the strictly distinguishing properties of opposed elements, observing the attendant nondistinctive properties only long enough to reject their relevance as soon as they are shown to have that character.

As a practical result of this separation, the systematic aspect of the relations between the invariant elements of the phonological system and the actual variation found in phonetic form tends to fall between two stools, and has no place in description. Phonology in these terms only has room for a study of the invariant representations, and the rules governing the systematic variation in realization shown by phonological elements have at best an uneasy place in the phonological description (and none at all in phonetics). In consequence, the only way to describe such systematic variation is to incorporate it into the definitions of elements of the phonological representation. We will see this below in the notions of the archiphoneme and of neutralization, and in the concept of the morphophoneme.

In defining the basic elements of phonological structure, Trubetzkoy starts from the functional notion of opposition or contrast. A phonological opposition exists between two sound sequences when the substitution of one for the other (perhaps within some large sequence) results in a different meaning. This may mean either a different word or, to cover the case of accidental gaps, a sequence which represents no word at all in the language under study. 'Contrast' here clearly means 'contrast on the surface': there is no provision for differences between words other than those that are provided with a direct phonetic implementation. In light of subsequent more abstract views of phonology, we might be tempted to take this as a sort of empirical claim about the range of differences that can possibly have linguistic relevance, but to do so would be at the very least anachronistic. The linguists of the Prague Circle and most of their contemporaries (with a few isolated exceptions such as

Sapir) took it as self-evident that if one wanted to study the ways in which words are differentiated from one another, the only conceivable starting point is the overt phonetic manifestation of their differences.

Given two words that contrast, we can presumably identify the phonetic material in terms of which they differ. Such a stretch of sound is called a 'phonological unit'. For example, the contrast between *phonological* and *phrenological* allows us to isolate the material represented by *-o-* and *-re-* in these words as phonological units. When other pairs share subparts of these units, this fact allows us to decompose them into smaller subunits. Thus, the contrast between *Fred* and *fraud* provides us with the basis for decomposing *-re-* into a sequence *-r+e-*. When this analysis has been carried to the point that the units arrived at cannot be further decomposed, the resulting elements represent the *phonemes* of the language.

As we will discuss in the following chapter, Jakobson later argued that a crucial misstep in this process is its limitation to the decomposition of the sound material into a sequence of linearly concatenated units. For him, the Saussurian conception of the sign as essentially linear involves an erroneous limitation, and this must be overcome by admitting also a decomposition of phonemes into their simultaneously occurring components if the ultimate units of phonological structure are to be uncovered. Such a further analysis is not involved in Trubetzkoy's notion of the phoneme, and his conception of the role played by the simultaneous distinctive properties carried by this element is somewhat different from Jakobson's.

Trubetzkoy at first presents the process of analysis of sound material into successively smaller constituents, based on functional contrasts, as a definition of the concept of 'phoneme'. It soon becomes clear, however, that such an analysis serves a rather more limited role: it merely reconstructs the phonetic segmentation of the utterance (which it will be recalled is not presumed by Trubetzkoy to be available from phonetic considerations alone), and still results in phonetically 'complete' elements, or 'linguistic sounds'. These elements consist of a vast range of properties, nondistinctive as well as distinctive, and the phonological analysis must go further to separate the functional wheat from the phonetic chaff if the ultimate contrastive units of language are to be reached. What must be done, that is, is to identify for each pair of 'linguistic sounds' arrived at by segmentation whether or not they contrast with one another, and, if they do, what phonetic property provides the basis of this contrast. The phoneme can then finally be defined as "the sum of the phonologically relevant particularities borne by a sound image."

It will be seen that the definitions thus given of the basic units of phonological structure are couched in terms of analytic procedures that could (in principle) be applied to objective phonetic data from a given language in order to arrive at its inventory of phonemes—and not in terms of some presumed antecedently given entity such as Baudouin's "psychological equivalent of a speech sound," which must merely be *identified* rather than reached as the end product of analysis. Partly a product of the general climate of operationalism in science that characterized the intellectual atmosphere of the 1930s when the *Grundzüge* was written, this is also a consequence of the stress put by Trubetzkoy on the social rather than individual nature of the *Sprachgebilde*. If the linguistic system is not a part of any particular individual but, rather, exists as a set of social norms or conventions among the members of a speech community, it follows that its essence cannot be either physical phonetic or psychological.

In his earliest writings on phonological topics, Trubetzkoy had in fact made use of definitions of the phoneme that rested on a psychological foundation, partially under the influence of Baudouin de Courtenay's ideas on the subject. Indeed, Twaddell (1935) lumps Trubetzkoy together with other proponents of the notion that the phoneme is a "mental or psychological reality" on the basis of the position taken in his early important work on vowel systems (Trubetzkoy 1929). By the time of the *Grundzüge*, however, he had come to reject such a notion. This was partly because of his acceptance of a social rather than an individual foundation for the linguistic system, but also in part (perhaps, indeed, primarily) because the psychological definition appeared to give no basis for the analytic isolation of the strictly *distinctive* properties of the sound image.

As he notes, if we think of the 'psychological image' of an intended pronunciation, we have no reason to believe that this consists only of its distinctive properties. Indeed, "acoustic-motor representations correspond to each of the phonetic variants, to the extent that the articulation is controlled and regulated by the speaker. Neither is there any reason to consider some of these representations as 'conscious' and others as 'unconscious'. The degree of consciousness of the articulatory process depends only on practice. By special training, one can become aware of the nonphonological properties of sounds. . . . The phoneme thus cannot be defined either as 'phonic representation' or as 'conscious phonic representation' and thus be opposed to the linguistic sound or the phonetic variant" (Trubetzkoy 1939[1949]:42).

The operative term in this argument can be seen to be 'representation'. Evidently, so long as we confine our description of the phonology of a language to the choice of a set of representations for utterances, the full set of acoustic-motor instructions apparently entailed by the notion of a psychological image of intended pronunciation will fail to distinguish distinctive from nondistinctive properties. The anecdotal character of our actual awareness of phonetic detail also contributes to make such consciousness far from satisfactory. From this it appears to follow that an adequate representation would have to be of a rather different nature, and that the psychological conception of phonological structure must be rejected. Trubetzkoy relies here on the strongest form of the proposition that a phonological theory is limited to being a theory of representations, and it is clear that his argument leads to a conception of the phoneme as a unit of such representations consisting of all *and only* the distinctive properties of a given sound segment.

In previous chapters, we have explored the possibility of attributing significance within a phonological theory not only to the set of representations it provides for utterances, but also to a set of rules that describe relations between them. On such a view, it would be possible to maintain that the phonological representations of utterances include phonetic detail, either in the 'fully specified surface variant' form suggested in chapter 2 as an interpretation of Saussure's position, or in the 'specified basic variant' form attributed in chapter 3 to Baudouin (and even clearer for Sapir; cf. chapter 9 below). Within such a theory, it would be possible to rehabilitate the psychological conception of the phoneme—at least as far as Trubetzkoy's argument is concerned. Within the limitations implicitly placed by Trubetzkoy on the content of a phonological theory, however, his conclusion follows that an adequate definition of the phoneme must restrict the content of these units to their phonologically distinctive properties.

While the phoneme thus came to be identified with the sum of the phonologically relevant properties of a sound, this does not at all exhaust the content of the Praguian theory of phonological structure. The most characteristic feature of this view, indeed, was not the exclusion of nondistinctive properties (which the Prague school linguists shared with most other positions at the time) but the extent to which the phoneme was regarded as embedded within a system of structured oppositions. The system of phonemes was not considered as simply an inventory of building blocks of sound structure from which words could be constructed by concatenation, but rather as a whole in which each element entertains specific and distinguishable relations of fundamental importance with each of the other elements to which it is opposed.

The study of such phonemic systems rests essentially on the elucidation of the properties which underlie the oppositions between phonemes. For Trubetzkoy, at least, these properties are phonetic ones, and furthermore, by virtue of his rejection of a psychological character for the system, they must also be properties which are observably present in the speech signal. This position was rigorously pursued to its conclusions: for instance, if the phoneme is something which is actually present in the speech signal, it must be the case that a set of sounds can only be regarded as variants (or realizations) of the same phoneme if they share some unique subset of phonetic properties which are not present together in any other sound not belonging to that phoneme. As something identifiable in principle in the physical acoustic realizations of particular utterances, such an externally construed, nonpsychological phoneme was directly in line with the formal and socially based conception of language and linguistics promoted by the Prague school.

It might well appear that if the phoneme is something that can actually be found by analysis in the speech signal, the substantive side of such a phonological theory must reduce to an inventory of the phonetic dimensions that are available to serve as the bases of linguistic contrasts. Indeed, much of the *Grundzüge* is devoted to a survey of such properties, giving examples of particular languages in which they serve contrastively in order to demonstrate their right to inclusion in a universal phonological theory. It is important not to be misled by this, however, for an exhaustive catalogue of potentially phonological parameters was pursued less as a goal in itself than to make it possible to compare the systems of different languages, to organize and classify the sets of oppositions obtaining within particular languages, and ultimately to state general laws governing the structure of such systems and their role in motivating and directing historical change.

The ultimate goal of the Prague school theory of phonological structure, then, was not simply descriptive in the sense of providing an enumeration of all of the contrasts that could be observed empirically in natural languages, though it included this project as a subsidiary aim. Rather, it was explanatory, and intended to elucidate general laws from which these empirical observations could be shown to follow. For example, by relating both oppositions of pitch (tone) and those between palatalized and nonpalatalized consonants to a single dimension of 'tonality', Jakobson and Trubetzkoy (cf. Jakobson 1929) came to the conclusion that no language could display these two contrasts simultaneously and independently. When this observation is raised to the status of a 'law' governing phonological systems, we predict, for example, that when a language develops the opposition of palatalization, it must subsequently lose any independent tonal (pitch) contrasts. The particular claim here is not actually valid, since there exist languages (such as the Szechuan Chinese dialect studied by Scott 1956) in which palatalization and tonal contrasts are independent; but this does not alter its value as illustrative of the *aims* (if not necessarily the accomplishments) of Praguian phonology in the domain of phonological explanation.

The structure of phonological systems

While phonemic systems are founded in Trubetzkoy's view on physical properties of the sounds that realize their elements, the analysis of a particular system does not reduce to a simple task of phonetic description. In general, it is not possible to tell from the phonetic properties of a segment in isolation (even given a universal inventory of potentially distinctive parameters such as that proposed in the *Grundzüge*) just how it should be characterized phonemically. This is because it is not merely its phonetic identity that matters phonologically but, more importantly, what other segments it is opposed to in the language in question.

In English, for example, we find stops at labial, dental, and velar positions that are quite parallel phonetically. Nonetheless, their phonemic content is not similarly parallel. If we consider /t/, for example, we can see that this segment is phonologically *voiceless* (because it is opposed to /d/), *non-nasal* (because opposed to /n/), *dental* (because opposed to /p/ and /k/), and a *stop* (because opposed to /s/ and to /θ/). In contrast, /k/ is voiceless (because opposed to /g/), non-nasal (because opposed to /ŋ/), and velar (because opposed to /p/ and to /t/); but given the absence of a velar continuant /x/ in English, /k/ is not *phonologically* a stop. Of course it is not a fricative either: it is simply not specified in any way for this property (though the phonetically similar /p/ and /t/ are both specified as stops).

Indeed, even knowing the range of segments to which a given phoneme is opposed does not make its phonological analysis self-evident. This is because any given opposition may provide a number of potential dimensions simultaneously, along any one of which the contrast might be established. The requirement that all nondistinctive properties must be eliminated, however, means that not all of these features can be simultaneously present in a given phoneme (assuming they co-vary). For example, in considering vowel systems, we often find (among the nonlow vowels of a language) a contrast between /u/ and /o/ on the one hand, and /i/ and /e/ on the other. These differ in terms both of rounding and of backness, and we must establish in each particular case which of these properties is the phonologically relevant one.

The answers to such questions are found in the interaction of language-particular factors with general laws governing the structure of phonological systems. In Russian, for example, when we consider the phoneme /i/, we find that it may be phonetically either front [i] or mid-back [ɨ], depending on its consonantal environment. Similarly, /u/ is phonetically less back after certain consonants than after others. Since frontness is not invariably present in the realizations of /i/ and absent in realizations of /u/, it follows that the two must be opposed to each other in rounding instead.

Trubetzkoy contrasts this state of affairs with that obtaining in Japanese, a language which also has the vowels /i/, /e/, /u/, /o/ and /a/. In Japanese there is a contrast between palatalized and nonpalatalized (dental) consonants which appears before the vowels /a/, /o/ and /u/; before /i/ and /e/, however, only the palatalized segments appear. On the basis of this regularity, Trubetzkoy argues that /i/ and /e/ must be opposed to /u/ and /o/ in terms of backness rather than rounding. This follows from the further fact that /a/ (which patterns like /u/ and /o/ in this respect) is back, but not round. A parallel argument bearing in the opposite direction is based on the facts of Northern Ostyak: in this language, the vowels /u/, /o/, /ɔ/ only occur in initial syllables, while the vowels /a/, /ɛ/, /e/ and /i/ appear in noninitial syllables as well. Since /a/ (which is phonetically back as well as unround) patterns like the other nonround vowels rather than like the other back vowels, Trubetzkoy concludes that the /i/-/u/ opposition in this language is based on rounding rather than on backness.

In other languages, other facts resolve similar questions. In many languages with /i/, /e/ and /u/, /o/, for example, we find more than one low vowel. When we find a back unrounded /ɑ/ and a front unrounded /æ/, as in certain Montenegrin dialects of Serbo-Croatian, we can identify the contrast as one of backness (in the nonlow as in the low vowels). On the other hand, when we find a back unrounded /ɑ/ and a back rounded /ɔ/, we must treat the contrast of /i/ vs. /u/ as one of rounding on the analogy of the only possible account of the contrast in the low vowels.

Such arguments make an implicit appeal to a principle which has since been taken as absolutely fundamental to the choice of a set of phonological dimensions in a universal theory: the notion that the features defined by such a set ought to facilitate the definition of 'natural classes' whose relevance is displayed by some common behavior shown by their members as opposed to nonmembers of the class in question. Trubetzkoy never articulates this principle as an explicit basis for the choice of one possible proposed feature over another in analyses, but he makes constant implicit appeal to it in the decisions he makes and in the way he uses particular examples to support his choices such as those just reviewed.

We have noted that much of the *Grundzüge* is devoted to a presentation of a putatively exhaustive set of phonetic dimensions along which phonological contrasts can be established in any natural language. This presentation is intended to serve as a descriptive framework for the higher purpose of developing a substantive phonological theory: in particular, the development of universally valid laws governing the structure of phonemic systems.

The first step in describing such systems is to establish the set of phonemes which contrast in the language, and Trubetzkoy presents a set of explicit procedures for accomplishing this. Some of these procedures, such as the tests for whether a given stretch of phonetic material should count as a unitary phoneme or as a sequence of two—for example, the choice between affricates and sequences of stops plus fricatives—are somewhat ad hoc and ultimately unsatisfactory, as has been argued in the subsequent literature; but it must be admitted that the problems they address are among the classic chestnuts of the field, and that no one else has ever solved them to general satisfaction.

In any event, there is a difficulty of principle here. In Trubetzkoy's account of phonological structure, this is strictly an external construct, based on a social reality and arrived at by a set of fixed procedures. There is in fact no sort of 'external' evidence which could count as confirming or disconfirming particular analyses, and it is difficult to argue convincingly that a given procedure or use of language-internal evidence, as in the establishment of oppositions in the fashion described in the preceding paragraphs, yields incorrect results— except on the basis of aesthetics or a sort of presystematic intuition of what the solution 'must be'. The extent to which any external evidence exists to confirm a given solution is another of the standard problems of phonology, and of course it is by no means uniquely a problem for Trubetzkoy's views. It exists there nonetheless, and perhaps in an exacerbated form as a result of the extent to which he separates the phonological system from any other, independently verifiable, aspect of language.

Having established the set of contrasting phonemes, the analyst next asks about the nature of the oppositions among them. It is the totality of these oppositions that yields the phonological system of the language. Since any two phonemes (and not simply those that differ in only one or two properties) must be regarded as opposed to each other, many of these oppositions are based on quite a few phonologically relevant properties at once. Of course, if all pairs of phonemes differed in an essentially global way, the resulting system would be no different in substance from a simple inventory. Interestingly, however, some oppositions are based on only one property or some small number of related properties, and sometimes some one property serves as the (only) distinction within more than one pair of opposed phonemes. It is this kind of opposition that gives phonological systems an interesting internal structure, and it is the analysis of this kind of structure that led Jakobson to emphasize in his propositions for the First International Congress the search for 'correlations' or recurrent oppositions that allow the decomposition of other alternations into component parts.

For the interpretation of such structure, Trubetzkoy proposes that oppositions can be classified along several simultaneous dimensions. For instance, oppositions can be distinguished between those that are *isolated* in that exactly the same combination of features does not serve to distinguish any other pair of phonemes in the language and those that are *proportional* (or recurrent). Most phonemes in a given language, taken pairwise, will as already remarked form isolated oppositions. In English, for example, the opposition between /d/ and /m/ is isolated, since the combination of features in which they differ (a labial nasal vs. a voiced dental stop) does not recur as the basis of any other opposition in the language. It is the proportional oppositions that are of special interest, such as that between English /p/ and /b/ (whose difference, voicing, reappears as the minimal difference between /t/ and /d/, /s/ and /z/, etc.).

We can also distinguish between *bilateral* and *multilateral* oppositions. When the same phonetic property distinguishes more than two phonemes along the same dimension, the resulting opposition is a multilateral one. Trubetzkoy treats place of articulation as a single dimension, and thus /p/ vs. /t/ vs. /k/ constitutes a multilateral opposition if we assume these phonemes do not differ in any other feature. When exactly two phonemes are distinguished minimally on a given dimension, though, we have a bilateral opposition such as voicing in English (since there is no third value other than 'voiced' and 'unvoiced', holding other properties constant). As we will see in the next chapter, Jakobson differed from Trubetskoy on the question of whether any oppositions were in fact multilateral, but Trubetzkoy's framework includes at least some properties that could serve as the basis of multilateral oppositions.

Additionally, it is possible to distinguish oppositions in terms of their 'logical' character. When two phonemes differ in that one contains a particular property which is lacking in the other, Trubetzkoy calls such an opposition a *privative* one. The opposition between phonemes with and without an added nasal resonance, for example, is privative. In contrast, when two phonemes differ in that they contain different properties (rather than one simply having a property that the other lacks), the opposition is *equipollent*. The difference between vowels with and without rounding, for example, is generally to be regarded as privative, while that between front and back vowels is equipollent. A final possibility of this sort is a *gradual* opposition, in which both phonemes possess a given property but to varying degrees. The opposition between mid and high vowels for instance is generally a gradual one based on their relative degree of openness.

There is further subdivision of the types of opposition in the *Grundzüge* and other work of Trubetzkoy and the Prague school, but these basic categories should give the flavor of the types of classification proposed. It is interesting to note that despite the amount of effort expended on such definitions and distinctions among types of opposition, the resulting typology plays hardly any role in the theory. The proposed laws of phonological structure generally make no reference to oppositions by type but are, rather, based on the specific substantive content of particular oppositions.

Among these laws, for example, is the proposal that if a language distinguishes between a set of 'bright' (front and/or unrounded) vowels and a set of 'dark' (back and/or rounded) vowels, either the two sets have the same number of elements, or there is exactly one vowel which is neutral between them, and this is the most open vowel in the system. If the language further distinguishes a third class intermediate between the 'bright' and the 'dark' vowels (e.g. a set of central unrounded or front rounded vowels), there cannot be more members in this set than in the set of 'bright' vowels. Such principles make no essential use of the logical classification of oppositions, but only of their substantive content.

There is one partial exception to this: a class of *correlations* is defined from the earliest writings of the Prague phonologists, which in Trubetzkoy's work is characterized as the set of proportional, bilateral, privative oppositions. The correlations have a unique role to play in the description of what we would now interpret as morphophonemic phenomena, especially those connected with the notion of neutralization. We will return to these questions in a later section.

Suprasegmental properties

Trubetzkoy's survey of phonological contrasts in natural languages and his proposed set of parameters for a general theory constitute the foundation of subsequent efforts to delimit such a universal set of features. For the most part, the actual dimensions he discusses are rather traditional ones, though the addition of acoustic terminology in some definitions had consequences that were unfamiliar at the time. It would take us too far afield to discuss his proposals in any detail here, but in one respect we must at least sketch his views, since they constituted innovations in an area which has only rather recently been rediscovered within generative phonology.

The bulk of the proposed phonological features in the *Grundzüge* relate to properties of the traditional phonetic segment, and the fundamental status of this unit in Trubetzkoy's view of phonological structure is beyond question. Nonetheless, he also devotes considerable attention to properties whose association with segmental structure is at best loose. This is a real departure in Prague school theory from previous accounts of phonology, and these were the first linguists in a modern sense to devote really serious attention to the domain of 'prosodic' features. This is of course a rather natural outgrowth of the attention paid by the originators of Praguian theory (especially Jakobson) to problems of poetic structure as the original inspiration for their interest in language.

Trubetzkoy's theory of prosodic features is based on the insight that some properties naturally appertain not to particular segments but to entire syllables. He sketches a view of the structure of syllables, which are constructed around an obligatory nucleus made up typically of a vowel or vowels (but in some languages also including certain consonantal elements). He then argues that while properties such as distinctive tone are typically realized as part of the articulation of the segment(s) making up the nucleus, it is an error to treat them as properties of these segments themselves. Rather, he says, they are properties of the syllable, with the peculiarity that they are realized in a particular portion of the syllable's structure.

Beyond recognizing the syllable as the locus of assignment of tone and accentual properties, Trubetzkoy also recognizes that the role played by a segment within a syllable may itself constitute a distinctive phonological dimension. Here what is in question is the difference between 'syllabic' and 'nonsyllabic' forms of what is otherwise the same segment type. The former make up part of the nucleus while the latter do not, but there may be no other independent property distinguishing them beyond that of their integration into syllabic structure (a point that had been made before by others, including Saussure; cf. chapter 2). This is the case, for example, with the difference between high vowels such as /i/ and /u/ and the corresponding semivowels /j/ and /w/, and also with the syllabic (vs. nonsyllabic) resonants like /r̩/ and /l̩/ that are found in some languages (Czech and Serbo-Croatian, for example). Sometimes even obstruents may be syllabic, as Trubetzkoy argues for Mandarin Chinese.

In many cases the difference between syllabic and nonsyllabic forms of a segment may be completely predictable and thus non-phonological, when it is entirely determined by the consonantal environment for example, but in other languages the same phonetic difference may be independently contrastive. As with the earlier discussion of the identification of phonemic contrasts, he gives a number of procedural principles for deciding when apparently syllabic consonants should be analyzed as displaying the 'correlation of syllabicity' and when they should be treated as sequences of a reduced vowel and a nonsyllabic consonant. The exact content of these rules is not particularly interesting in itself; they are not free of the ad hoc nature of other such procedurally oriented definitions, and probably raise as many problems as they answer. What is significant is the recognition that among the properties that may have phonological relevance are some that cannot be assigned to the segment itself in any natural way, but rather reflect the distinct ways in which one and the same segmental content may be integrated into a larger structure (the syllable).

This notion plays a particularly important role in Trubetzkoy's account of the nature of linguistic quantity, to which he devotes a good deal of attention. He notes first of all that while many languages have a contrast among long and short vowels, this contrast may have very different status in different systems. He then argues that while such length is often to be treated as a (segmental) feature, there are also cases in which a long vowel ought rather to be regarded as composed of two (or, at least theoretically, even more) subunits called *moras*.

A number of circumstances are cited in which such decomposition of long vowels is warranted. Most obviously, this may be the case when (at least some of) the long vowels in a language arise from the juxtaposition of two morphological elements, the first of which ends in a vowel and the second of which begins with one; or from the loss of intervocalic consonants, leading to sequences of identical vowels, etc. Besides such cases, where the compound nature of the resulting long vowel is patent, however, it is also possible to argue for a similar decomposition on other grounds. For instance, if a language contains some diphthongs which are analyzed as vowel sequences, and the long vowels of the language display some important similarity of behavior with these diphthongs such as attracting the stress, then it is justifiable to treat them as 'diphthongs' made up of two identical elements.

Again, it may be the case that certain prosodic oppositions are limited to syllables containing long vowels or diphthongs, in which case the treatment of long vowels as made up of two (or more) moras is also indicated. In Lithuanian, for example, long syllables can bear either falling or rising accent (or be unaccented), while short syllables only contrast as accented vs. unaccented. Treating the difference between rising and falling accent as a matter of which mora in a long syllable bears the accent allows a simple and natural account of this complex accentual system, justifying the decomposition of the long vowels.

Not all languages in which long and short vowels contrast provide evidence of the sort Trubetzkoy regards as warranting the analysis of the long vowels into moras, however, and in other cases we must regard such a contrast as a simple one of 'intensity' applying to a single segment. The same phonetic material (a long vowel) may thus be analyzed differently in different languages, depending on whether it represents simply a segment with a particular property (increased intensity) or the integration into a single syllabic nucleus of two distinct but segmentally identical moras.

A third phonological interpretation of phonetic quantity distinctions is also proposed, which is even more interesting from the point of view of syllable structure. In some languages, he suggests, the difference between long and short vowels depends not on a property of the vowels themselves but on whether the vowel is 'free' in its syllable or 'checked' by a following consonant. It might appear that what is involved in the 'correlation of close contact' (or *Silbenschnittkorrelation*) is simply a matter of the difference between vowels in open and in closed syllables, but it is evident from the examples he gives that this is not what Trubetzkoy has in mind.

Central among these is the case of Hopi, which appears (on the basis of observations by Whorf) to show not two but three degrees of vowel length. A minimal set of three forms displays this contrast: [păs] 'very' with extrashort vowel; [pas] 'field' with middle quantity; and [pās] 'calm' with a fully long vowel. From the fact that all three of these forms are monosyllables ending in a consonant, and thus closed syllables by any natural criterion, it is clear that the difference between simply open and closed syllables is not what is at issue here.

Trubetzkoy argues that two separate oppositions are at work in Hopi. One of these is a contrast between long and short vowels on the basis of the difference between two moras and one: the longest vowel quantity (that of [pās] 'calm') differs from the other two in that it represents a bimoric long vowel while the others contain only a single mora. But in that case, how are we to distinguish [păs] 'very' from [pas] 'field'? This, he claims, is based on whether the following consonant interrupts (checks) the articulation of the vowel or not—a matter of whether the consonant itself is incorporated into the nucleus. We could represent the difference structurally in terms of the notation used in the recent generative literature for describing the internal constituency of syllables (though Trubetzkoy himself does not propose a graphic representation of the contrast):

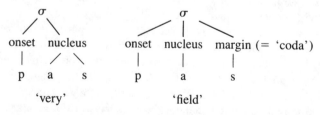

Other representations of this analysis could be imagined (see Anderson 1984 for further discussion of this and other claims of Trubetzkoy and Jakobson about the treatment of quantity as they might be interpreted in the framework of present-day metrical phonology), but the essential aspect is the treatment of a postvocalic consonant as distinctively falling either within or outside the nucleus of its syllable. In Hopi, this is argued to provide an immediate account of the absence of the extrashort quantity in open syllables, where there is no consonant available to check the vowel. The absence of a free vs. checked contrast in the genuine (bimoric) long vowels suggests the rather natural constraint that no more than two units can appear in a single nucleus: either two vowel moras (yielding the greatest length) or one vowel and one consonant (yielding the shortest).

Trubetzkoy argues that the *Silbenschnittkorrelation* is the basis of length contrasts in a number of languages, including English and German. For our purposes, the greatest interest of this proposal lies not in the analysis of individual languages, however, but in the theoretical innovation it involves. One and the same sequence of phonemic units is here allowed to compose both members of a pair of contrasting forms which differ exclusively in the way in which this material is organized into higher-level units.

Had subsequent research pursued the substantially enriched conception of phonological structure on which this proposal is based, there might have been important consequences; but in general later phonologists maintained until quite recently a notion of representations as composed simply of a linear sequence of discrete, homogeneous segments. Discussion of the syllable was not of course completely lacking, and the British school of prosodic analysis in particular discussed the notion of phonological properties that inhere in the syllable and its internal organization (see chapter 7 below). It does not seem unfair to say, however, that no thoroughgoing integration of segmental and syllabic structure was developed as the basis of a theory of phonological structure until the recent advent of metrical phonology.

Within the scope of more orthodox prosodic features, Trubetzkoy presents a rather restrictive theory of tonal distinctions. He first makes it clear that the phonological significance of the pitch of a given segment lies in its relative and not its absolute value. This point, by now so familiar to phonologists as to seem self-evident, has significant consequences for an understanding of the nature of phonological distinctions in general, and it provided an eloquent demonstration of the superiority of the phonological perspective over the purely phonetic in analyzing particular languages.

At the time Trubetzkoy wrote, even rather sophisticated observers of tonal phenomena (such as C. M. Doke in his work on Zulu) tended to get mired in largely irrelevant detail, since they concentrated on the measurable phonetic facts of pitch rather than on the phonologically more significant question of what tonal possibilities existed contrastively in a given environment. By concentrating his attention on the relative pitch distinctions that operate in particular positions, Trubetzkoy brought much more clarity to the analysis of tone. In the process, he demonstrated the fundamental difference between a phonological property (e.g., 'high tone') and its phonetic realization (which might be anywhere within a very wide range of actual pitch values).

Trubetzkoy distinguishes in his account between 'tone register' contrasts (differences in simple relative pitch) and 'tone movement' contrasts (such as that between a rising and a falling tone). The latter are recognized only for languages in which long vowels exist, and are analyzed into sequences of moras. In this way he ultimately reduces the inventory of available tone features to a set of relative levels, since he can then analyze a falling tone as a sequence of a relatively high tone on the first mora of a long vowel followed by a relatively lower tone on the second mora, with a rising tone being represented as the reverse sequence. By admitting only (logically) level tones, he succeeds in tremendously simplifying the range of possible tone systems.

Further simplification results from his claim that only three tonal registers need be recognized phonologically in any given language: a 'normal' register, and tones either above this or below it in relative value. Where more tone registers appear to exist, he argues that they are illusory. The additional values are either the result of nondistinctive phonetic modification, as when a low tone on a final syllable is lower than low tones elsewhere, or else some additional distinction such as a difference in voice quality is operative. Similarly, some apparently nonstationary tones are argued to be either nondistinctive variants of basically level tones, or the consequence of some other dimension interacting with voice pitch.

Both of these major factual claims of his system, that phonologically nonlevel tones can only occur on bimoric vowels and that three tone levels are sufficient to describe all languages, have been shown in recent years to be false (see Anderson 1978 for a summary and references). It has been demonstrated, in particular, that contrastive tone contours in some languages can occur on phonologically short vowels. Nonetheless, the development of a notion of tonal representation as 'autosegmental'—i.e., as partially independent of segmental structure—allows us to maintain the essence of Trubetzkoy's claim, which is the proposal that contour tones can always be decomposed into sequences of levels and need never be recognized as primitives of a tonal feature system.

Trubetzkoy's system for the description of tones is quite close in spirit to those accepted today. This is especially true if one takes literally the claim at the beginning of his discussion of prosodic properties that features like tone are associated not with segments on a one-to-one basis but, rather, with larger units such as the syllable. If this view is consistently worked out, the supposed dependence of tone contours on the complexity of the syllable nucleus is seen to be not a necessary consequence of other aspects of structure (though it would of course be an interesting empirical claim if it were true) but an unmotivated stipulation.

In a number of regards, Trubetzkoy's position can be clearly distinguished from that of other early phonological accounts of tone, such as Sapir's work and especially that of Pike in the United States in the 1940s and 1950s. These works differ from his in recognizing both contrastive tonal contours (distinct from sequences of levels) in some languages, and a larger number of levels. In the latter claim they appear to be validated by the existence. of languages in which at least four, and possibly five, tonal levels cannot be further reduced (see Anderson 1978 for references); but with reference to the structurally more interesting claims concerning contour tones, Trubetzkoy's position seems at minimum to be a defensible one.

Within his study of prosodic properties, Trubetzkoy proposes a number of potentially general laws governing the structure of phonological systems, in line with the Prague school program of formulating such principles as the ultimate aim of a phonological theory. Some of these can be seen to be logical consequences of the framework in which they are formulated: for example, the claim that tone-movement contrasts only occur in languages in which the long vowels are analyzed into moras follows largely from the fact that the very existence of such contrasts provides sufficient evidence to require the decomposition of long vowels into moras. Others, however, such as the proposal that languages cannot display simultaneously a contrast of freely distributed (stress) accent and freely distributed quantity (aside from the contrast between 'free' and 'checked' vowels, which does not count as 'quantity' in the relevant sense), seem to be genuine empirical propositions.

This proposed incompatibility of free stress and free quantity (which dates back to Jakobson's proposals at the first International Congress of Linguists) elicited a considerable amount of discussion devoted to either disproving it or showing that it followed from other principles. It is possible to argue that when the notions of 'free stress' and 'free quantity' are properly formulated within the framework of metrical phonology, the generalization proposed by Jakobson anad Trubetzkoy follows as a theorem from independent properties of the two (see Anderson 1984). At minimum, we must regard this generalization as a fruitful hypothesis.

Neutralization, archiphonemes, and markedness

We return now to the formal (rather than substantive) nature of the phonological theory presented in the *Grundzüge*, and in particular to the dimensions along which this theory classifies phonemic oppositions. In addition to the parameters of this sort which we discussed above, there is one more which is of fundamental importance for Trubetzkoy's views: the difference between oppositions that are *constant* and those that are *suspensible*. If the opposition between particular pair of phonemes is constant, this means that either one can appear (in contrast with the other) in any environment. Suspensible oppositions, on the other hand, are those for which there is at least some environment in which the two phonemes involved cannot contrast with each other. In such a position, the opposition between the two is said to be *neutralized*. For example, in Russian or German, only the voiceless members of voiced/voiceless pairs appear in final position, where they thus do not contrast with the corresponding voiced segments. We say, then, that the opposition of voicing (a correlation, in terms of the classification discussed above) is neutralized in this position in these languages.

Where an opposition is neutralized, we can then ask what the phonemic entity is that appears in the position of neutralization. Taking the case of Russian or German final voiceless obstruents as a concrete instance, we can note that in both languages, phonemes such as /p/ vs. /b/, /t/ vs. /d/, etc., can be identified in positions where voicing is not neutralized, but what of the phonetic [p], [t], etc., that occur finally? If we assume that no other neutralizations are involved, these apparently have all of the phonological properties of other instances of /p/, /t/, etc—except that, since they are not opposed to voiced segments, they cannot contain *any* value for the property of voicing (by the definition of the phoneme, since no such value would be distinctive in this position). As a result, such an element must consist of exactly the features common to /p/ and /b/, /t/ and /d/, etc., but lacking the feature which elsewhere separates the members of these pairs.

Such an element, identical with the subset of features common to a pair of phonemes whose opposition is neutralized in some position, is called by Trubetzkoy an *archiphoneme*. The existence of archiphonemes is an immediate consequence of the possibility that oppositions may be suspended in certain positions, together with the definition of the phoneme as consisting of all and only the properties that distinguish it from other elements of the system. For Trubetzkoy, the archiphonemes in a system constitute additional elements of the system beyond the inventory of phonemes: thus, the system of German or Russian contains the archiphoneme /P/ (representing the features common to /p/ and to /b/) as well as the individual phonemes /p/ and /b/. Since archiphonemes are essentially related to (and indeed implied by) independently established oppositions, however, they are not generally presented as distinct units in phonological systems.

Since archiphonemes are implied by the neutralization of particular oppositions between segments which are nondistinct along all other dimensions, and since they are themselves phonemic entities, it follows that only certain pairs of phonemes can have a corresponding archiphoneme. In particular, the segments involved must share some set of common properties which distinguish them from all other elements of the system. Thus, for example, an archiphoneme /P/ representing the neutralization of /p/ and /b/ in final position in German is possible, since its content (the features common to /p/ and to /b/) is that of an 'oral labial stop', properties which set it apart from any other phoneme in the language. Even though /h/ and the velar nasal /ŋ/ do not contrast anywhere, however, an archiphoneme representing the two is impossible since the only feature they have in common is that of 'consonant', and there are of course many other consonants from which this element would not be distinct.

In his definition, Trubetzkoy argues that only bilateral oppositions can be neutralized and thus represented by an archiphoneme. His claim here is based on a logically incorrect argument, however. He reasons that if, in German, only /b/ and not /d/ appears before /l/, it is still not possible to say that the opposition between /b/ and /d/ is neutralized and represented by an archiphoneme in this position, since such an archiphoneme could only be identified as 'voiced oral stop', and there is another voiced oral stop in the system (/g/) from which it would thus not be distinct. From this it can be seen that a proper subset of the segments involved in a multilateral opposition cannot be represented by an archiphoneme without destroying the distinctness of this unit from the other elements of the same opposition.

While this argument does indeed show that not all instances of the apparent suspension of a multilateral opposition can be coherently represented by an archiphoneme, it certainly does not suffice to show that *no* multilateral oppositions are so neutralized: it is simply necessary to be sure that the entire opposition is effectively neutralized in a given case, and not simply a proper subpart of it. Consider the common case of a language which, in prevocalic position, contrasts several nasal consonants (along the multilateral dimension of place of articulation), but in which preobstruent nasals must always be homorganic with the following consonant. Surely in such a language we would want to say that an archiphoneme /N/ (defined simply as 'nasal consonant') represents the multilateral opposition in the position of neutralization. Such an element is completely well formed by all of the other defining criteria for archiphonemes.

Assuming that any phonological opposition can be neutralized and represented by an archiphoneme in particular environments, then, so long as the resulting archiphoneme remains distinct from all other contrastive phonemic elements occurring in the given position, the next question is that of the phonetic realization of such elements. Trubetzkoy notes that an archiphoneme may be represented by a segment identical with other realizations of one or the other of the phonemes involved (as with the case of the final voiceless stops which represent German or Russian obstruent archiphonemes), or its phonetic realization may be different from any segment that occurs in other positions. This is the case, for example, with the voiceless unaspirated stops which appear in English as the realization of neutralized obstruents /P/, /T/, and /K/ after /s/. The one thing which is determinate, of course, is that the realization of the archiphoneme must contain the properties which define it; that is, which are common to the neutralized phonemes it represents.

This notion that the phonological identity of a segment may be determined only *relative to a particular environment* is one which is not unique to Prague school phonology. As we will see in chapter 7 below, it constitutes the central tenet of Firthian 'polysystemic' analysis, and a central reason behind the rejection of phonemic analysis altogether by his school. In the context of American phonemic theory (which we will discuss in chapter 11), Twaddell (1935) had arrived at rather similar notions by a completely different route, as Trubetzkoy recognizes in a passage of the *Grundzüge*. Taking into account simply the distribution of individual phonetic segments, Twaddell had observed that the range of distinctions present in some positions is quite different from that in other positions, and thus that the distinctive value of the same segment under different environmental conditions may be quite different. Twaddell's terminology is quite different from Trubetzkoy's (or Firth's), but the issue being addressed is essentially the same one.

There are interesting differences among these views. Firth and Twaddell both arrived at their conclusions by considering distribution alone, and not the logical character of particular oppositions; in Firth's case, the result was a radically different, nonphonemic approach to phonology which is not easy to compare with Trubetzkoy's views. For Twaddell, on the other hand, there is no limit to the range of sets of phonemes whose opposition may be neutralized, while we have seen above that on Trubetzkoy's account only oppositions between segments which retain a common core distinguishing them from all other phonemes can be neutralized. In Trubetzkoy's summary of Twaddell's position, he does not appear to recognize this difference, and rejects Twaddell's view only because it is a more complex way of arriving at the desired end than his own definition. In particular cases, however, different analyses would result: for instance, Twaddell's principles would recognize the equivalent of neutralization even between a single pair of phonemes that for Trubetzkoy formed part of a multilateral opposition. Since neither Trubetzkoy's theory nor Twaddell's contains any independent criteria by which alternative claims of this sort can be assessed, however, it is difficult to pursue such issues much further.

Among the possibilities for determining the phonetic realization of an archiphoneme, we can distinguish 'external' from 'internal' causes. This is essentially the difference between realizations that are in some way motivated by phonetic properties found in the segment's environment (e.g., assimilation to the value of a neighboring segment) and those that are not related to anything beyond the definition of the segment itself.

When no contextual properties determine those of the variant appearing in a position of neutralization, we can make the important distinction between the *marked* and the *unmarked* terms of the opposition neutralized. This notion is fundamentally a logical one: it is assumed that for any bilateral opposition, one of the terms differs from the other in possessing a special 'mark' which the other lacks. As a result, many oppositions are characterized as 'logically privative' even though they may not be based on a property which is phonetically privative.

This notion of the markedness of a term of an opposition should not be confused with another notion introduced in the *Grundzüge*, that of the 'naturally marked' term of a phonetically privative opposition. This refers to the phoneme in such a pair that possesses the phonetic property defining the opposition (e.g., the voiced member of a voiced/voiceless pair). It is generally possible to determine from the phonetic basis of an opposition which of its members (if either) is the 'naturally marked' phoneme. In contrast, the '(logically) marked' term of an opposition has this status for reasons internal to the phonological system of the language, and cannot be determined by phonetic criteria.

The notion of (logical) markedness is not restricted to phonetically privative oppositions. Whenever *any* opposition is neutralized, if the variant that appears is not externally conditioned (i.e., if its phonetic properties are not determined by those of some element in the environment of neutralization), Trubetzkoy assumes that it is the logically unmarked member of the pair that must appear. In German or Russian, for instance, the devoicing of a final obstruent is conditioned by a boundary element rather than a segment with phonetic properties, and thus the appearance of voiceless sounds in this position cannot be regarded as externally motivated. They must therefore constitute the logically unmarked members of the opposition. The concept of markedness which thus appears for the first time in Prague school phonology is tied directly to the nature of neutralizaton. This notion would be pursued further in the work of Jakobson and (in somewhat different form) of Chomsky and Halle, but we will not further develop Trubetzkoy's use of it here.

External causes may determine predictable nonphonological properties of fully individuated phonemes as well as archiphonemes, of course, and the possibility of such determination has interesting consequences. In particular, it allows Trubetzkoy to escape, in princple, from the argument given by Halle (see below, chapter 12) against the acceptance of a phonemic level which is based specifically on the difference between contrastive and noncontrastive properties.

This by now rather familiar argument is based on the facts of voicing assimilation in Russian, a system in which the contrast of voicing is not symmetrically distributed. That is, some segments (e.g. /t/ and /d/) enter into voiceless/voiced pairs, while others (e.g., /č/) do not contrast with a corresponding segment of opposite voicing. As a result, Halle contended, a general rule for Russian voicing assimilation could not be formulated if a phonemic representation of the sort based precisely on contrast was required for every utterance. This is because the assimilation of voicing to that of a following obstruent will necessarily be a morphophonemic effect for segments entering into the voicing opposition, but a subphonemic, phonetic effect for those that do not show such a contrast. As a result, the grammar of Russian would not contain any single statement of what is evidently a single generalization, but rather two disconnected and only accidentally related substatements, located in different portions of the grammar.

Consider now how the facts treated by Halle would be described in Trubetzkoy's framework. Let us assume that each morpheme has a representation in the dictionary of the language in which its phonemes are specified maximally (within a system established on the basis of contrasts displayed in maximally differentiated positions). When a morpheme ending in an obstruent is immediately followed by another beginning with such a segment, the voicing of the first obstruent is assimilated to that of the second (though if an obstruent-final morpheme is followed by a sonorant, no adjustment takes place). In schematic terms, we can identify the various possibilities with the following sets of representations:

Lexical form:	{t+l}	{t+b}	{d+l}	{d+b}	{č+l}	{č+b}
Phonemic form:	/t+l/	/T+b/	/d+l/	/T+b/	/č+l/	/č+b/
Phonetic form:	[t+l]	[d+b]	[d+l]	[d+b]	[č+l]	[ǰ+b]

Note that this analysis involves an archiphoneme /T/, representing the neutralization of the contrast between /t/ and /d/ before a following obstruent. This archiphoneme contains no value for the feature of voicing by virtue of the fact that that feature is not contrastive in the position of neutralization. Phonemes such as /č/, which do not contrast with some other segment in voicing, do not contain any value for this feature.

Now consider the principles involved in describing this situation. First, of course, we need a statement of neutralization: the correlation of voicing in obstruents is suspended in preobstruent position. Note that this statement is a perfectly general one, and need not distinguish between two classes of obstruent. It is simply a statement that this property is not a contrastive one in certain positions, and results in the replacement of certain phonemes (specified for voicing) by archiphonemes in the relevant position in a representation which is genuinely phonological in Trubetzkoy's sense.

Second, we need a statement to the effect that the phonetic value of voicing in an obstruent is externally conditioned by that of an immediately following obstruent. This principle assigns the noncontrastive property of voicing to archiphonemes (like /T/) and phonemes like /č/ alike when they are followed by a voiced obstruent. Again, the statement in question is completely general, and is not divided into two parts (one to accommodate the segments that show basic voicing distinctions, and one to accommodate the others like /č/).

While it is true that the resulting description contains two distinct statements, it is not obvious that it involves the sort of pernicious decomposition of a generalization that Halle argued resulted from a phonemic level based on contrast. The two statements here have rather distinct logical roles (one describes a limitation on the appearance of a certain contrast, and the other describes certain nondistinctive details of pronunciation). Each is perfectly general, and thus no generalization goes unstated; at worst, the two can be faulted for referring to the same environment, but this is surely not as forceful an objection (if indeed it is one) as the one Halle leveled against the rather different phonemic theory associated with American structuralism, which we will discuss in chapter 12.

Further, we can see that the presence of both a statement of neutralization and a principle of external determination of the phonetic realization of certain phonemic entities is completely independent of the asymmetry in the distribution of voicing in Russian obstruents. The same two statements would be required even if Russian contained no unpaired segments like /č/. It is not because the phonemic level distinguishes the treatment of contrasting and noncontrasting segments that the voicing assimilation facts are specified by two logically distinct statements. Trubetzkoy's view, then, can be said to be relatively free of at least this one problem associated with a surface-contrast-based view of the phoneme.

While Trubetzkoy can, thus, escape Halle's argument (a point made also by Johns 1969), there is actually little reason to believe that he would have accepted its force in any event. In fact, it rests on the claim that a uniform rule of variation should be stated in a single, general way; but Trubetzkoy's phonology assigns no genuine role to the statement of such rules per se. As we have remarked above, his view of phonology is confined to a theory of the (phonological) representations of utterances. Rules enter into such a theory only incidentally, as part of the definitions of the individual elements which occur in such representations. The device of archiphonemes is simply a way in which certain facts of rule-governed variation can be systematically built into such definitions of phonological invariants. As we have seen above, there are certain principled limits on the range of cases in which archiphonemic descriptions involving neutralization are possible; and Trubetzkoy's theory could be interpreted as embodying a claim that the linguistic significance of such variation among segment types is limited to this class of cases.

Morpho(pho)nology

In fact, however, Trubetzkoy makes provision for a somewhat wider range of potentially significant variation between distinct phonemic entities. In two short articles (Trubetzkoy 1929, 1931) he describes the outlines of *morpho(pho)nology*, a discipline which is to treat in general "the study of the morphological use of a language's phonological means." This field is argued to have three major tasks: (a) the study of the phonological structure of morphemes; (b) the study of the combinatory changes in sound undergone by a morpheme when it enters into combination with other morphemes; and (c) the study of sound alternations which have a morphological function. There is essentially no reference to these topics in the *Grundzüge* (they were to be dealt with, among others, in a projected second volume which was never written), but they play a role in much of Trubetzkoy's descriptive work, and especially in his description of Russian morphophonemics (Trubetzkoy 1934).

The first subpart of this field, the description of the phonological structure of morphemes, is only to be distinguished from phonology insofar as genuinely morphological conditioning is involved. When some morphological class (such as roots, stems, or affixes; or nouns, verbs, etc.) is subject to particular structural limitations (e.g. monosyllabicity, the triconsonantal character of Semitic roots, special restrictions on the consonants that can begin or end a verb stem), and where these limitations are not similarly imposed on all surface forms of the language, they are to be stated as part of the morphophonology. For instance, a language might allow only monosyllabic roots but impose no limitations at all on the length of complete forms: in that case, the monosyllabicity of roots is a morphophonological matter. Restrictions on possible consonant clusters, syllable structure, final consonants, etc., which apply to the language as a whole, on the other hand, are simply an aspect of the phonology proper. This posited branch of morphophonology is clearly the direct ancestor of the systems of *morpheme-structure conditions* which would form an essential part of (at least early) generative descriptions of phonological systems.

The remaining two branches of the study of morphophonology both involve the treatment of alternations between distinct phonemes. They differ in that the last treats alternations that directly signal differences between morphological categories (the *correlations* of Kurszewski and Baudouin; cf. chapter 3), while the branch identified as *b* above deals with alternations that are conditioned in some way by the environment rather than serving a directly symbolic function.

This does not include those 'alternations' which can be described completely by the devices of neutralization and the specification of how the corresponding archiphonemes are to be phonemically realized. Thus, in Russian /riba/ 'fish' vs. /riPka/ 'minnow', we say that the opposition between /b/ and /p/ is neutralized before obstruents, yielding the archiphoneme /P/; and this in turn is represented by the externally conditioned value /p/ before voiceless /k/. Such statements form a part of the phonology itself, as we have already seen. Precisely because /b/ does not contrast with /p/ *before another obstruent*, this is not an alternation between independent phonemes, and thus not morphophonemic in character. Similarly, of course, the 'alternation' between phonetic variants of a single phoneme belongs to the phonology. It is only cases of alternation between phonemic elements which contrast with one another (e.g., the vowel alternation in French *fleur* 'flower' vs. *floral* 'floral', conditioned by the stress and by the nature of the following affix) which are assigned to the morphophonology, a discipline intermediate between phonology and morphology.

The method by which morphophonological description is to be carried out is through a new kind of structural entity, the *morphoneme* (a term derived from the works of Baudouin's student H. Ułaszyn). "Every alternation corresponds in the linguistic consciousness to a *morphoneme*, i.e., the totality considered as a morphological unit of the phonemes participating in the alternation in question" (Trubetzkoy 1934: 30). This unit is quite explicitly not a kind of unitary basic form underlying the sounds in question but, rather, a "complex idea," made up of the several individual phonemes which alternate in the corresponding position in related forms. Trubetzkoy takes quite seriously the fact that each of the alternating segments is equally copresent in a given morphoneme, and even goes so far as to claim that, as a result, the linguistic awareness of the form of morphemes which involve one or several alternations is vaguer and less distinct on the part of speakers than in the case of nonalternating morphemes.

The important thing to note about Trubetzkoy's morphonemes is that they are an attempt to describe morphophonemic variation entirely in terms of the definitions of a new class of units in the representations of forms, rather than directly in terms of rules governing the ways in which invariant representations can be realized. Each alternation is equated with a list of alternants together with the conditions in which each occurs: it is this list which is taken as a *Gestalt* and equated with the corresponding unitary morphoneme. These units should not be confused with the elementary constructs of a theory in which morphophonemic representations are given in terms of basic segment types which then undergo modification in order to arrive at a surface phonemic form. Equally, Trubetzkoy's morphonemes are not simply ordinary phonemes together with some special mark.

Thus, in Russian we find an alternation between /k/ and /č/ in e.g. /ruka/ 'hand' vs. /ručnoj/ 'manual'. We might describe this fact by saying that a morphoneme /k/ (a sort of 'ideal' [k]) is replaced by [č] in certain forms. Alternatively, we might say that the morpheme for 'hand' ends in some sort of special /k/-sound: perhaps with an additional feature not otherwise utilized in Russian, like 'glottalized', or perhaps with a purely arbitrary, nonphonological diacritic such as [+alternating] (so that /k*/ = /k,+alternating/ ≠ /k/). This alternating /k/ (=/k*/) then becomes /č/ in some environments and /k/ in others. Each of these views would involve describing the alternation between /k/ and /č/ in terms of rules of the grammar: rules to turn either /k/ or /k*/ into /č/ under specified circumstances (and into /k/ elsewhere). Neither of these positions is Trubetzkoy's, however. The morphoneme underlying the /k/-/č/ alternation here is not to be identified either with an ideal /k/, or with a /k/ that bears a special mark: rather, it is a complex segment consisting essentially of a list of alternants (/k/ and /č/) together with the conditions under which each occurs.

It is evident that this view of morphophonemic representation has its own distinctive consequences. For example, it is impossible in this framework to state conditions of relative precedence (rule orderings) among alternations, since each alternation is treated as a global unit independent of all other units. On the other hand, it would be possible to make use of the distinction between a segment that shows an alternation (in forms related to one at hand) and the same segment that never alternates, in conditioning the variants of some other alternation. For instance, one might distinguish the alternating velar stop at the end of *eclectic* (cf. *eclecticism* from the nonalternating one in *bolshevik* (cf. *bolshevikism*); the former represents a morphoneme $\{/k/\sim/s/\}$ while the latter is simply /k/. One could then in theory use this difference to condition some other alternation—say, a rule that fronted vowels before alternating but not nonalternating surface /k/. This latter possibility is not available (without the special introduction of 'global rules') to a phonological theory that treats morphophonemic elements as homogeneous with ordinary phonemic elements.

Trubetzkoy of course made no effort to explore these (or other) distinct consequences of his view of morphophonemic alternations: at the time he wrote, it was still a major innovation to accord systematic status to any such notion at all. Indeed, subsequent discussion of Trubetzkoy's ideas in the area of morphophonemics was largely critical of his suggestion that there was anything in particular to account for at all, and his concrete proposals concerning the nature of morphonemic form were not really taken up by anyone. Even Jakobson, in works such as his 1948 article "Russian Conjugation," makes use of a notion of morphophonemic representation which is much closer to that of Bloomfield (see below, chapter 10) than to Trubetzkoy's.

For our purposes, the most important aspect of Trubetzkoy's view of the morphoneme is the extent to which it is of a piece with the other constructs of his theory of phonological structure. This theory is almost exclusively a theory of the invariant elements of phonological representations, and accords minimal status to the rules which govern variant realizations of these representations. As a result, any systematic variation which is to be incorporated in a description must be accommodated in the definitions of particular elements. Trubetzkoy carries this program out in a way which recognizes a range of types of variation in natural language (subphonemic phonetic variation, variation resulting from the neutralization of particular oppositions in particular positions, and more general sorts of alternation, both automatic and morphological in nature); but consistent with his basic position, all of these alternations are treated by appropriate definition of elements in phonological representation.

Probably no linguist since has attempted to encompass so much of the sound pattern of natural language entirely within a theory of representations as he did; and a detailed study of the capacities and limitations of the descriptive framework that he provided would no doubt cast a good deal of light on the conceptual scope that such a program is adequate to deal with. Unfortunately, attention in subsequent years focused largely on the limited area of phonemic form as delimited by surface contrast. Only in the late 1950s and early 1960s did the full range of Trubetzkoy's concerns reemerge in a prominent place in phonological theory, bearing by then the clear impression of the form in which they were passed on to later linguists by Roman Jakobson.

5

Roman Jakobson and the Theory of Distinctive Features

During his years in Czechoslovakia, and especially in the thirties, Jakobson's views on phonology were developed very much within the context of his co-operation with Trubetzkoy and the other members of the Prague school. If Jakobson was clearly the leading spirit of this partnership in many ways, it is still somewhat difficult to disentangle his individual contributions from Trubetzkoy's; and as with the relation between Kruszewski and Baudouin de Courtenay during their 'Kazan period', it is probably unprofitable to attempt to do so. Of course, the two disagreed on many points (mostly of detail), as attested in their letters; but it was only after Trubetzkoy's death in 1938 that Jakobson's own position began to diverge in significant ways from that underlying their earlier collaborative work.

In March 1939, shortly after the German invasion of Czechoslovakia, Jakobson managed to escape to Denmark. After only a few months it became clear that this was no real refuge, and he went to Norway; when Norway was occupied in its turn, he went to Sweden, where he stayed until 1941. In that year he left for New York. During 1942–46 he was active in what had become the French University in exile, the École Libre des Hautes Études. He was in close contact there with the anthropologist Claude Lévi-Strauss, who was greatly taken with the possibilities of applying 'structuralist' methods derived from linguistics (as he learned it from Jakobson) to the social sciences more generally. After the war, Jakobson stayed in New York until 1950 as professor at Columbia.

Jakobson was by no means universally acclaimed in the United States. On the one hand, he found some of his old antistructuralist opponents from Europe who had similarly taken refuge there. Partly by the sheer force of his personality, however, he was quite able to dominate these influences; and he and a new generation of his students quickly became central to the discussions of the Linguistic Circle of New York (founded in 1934 on the model of the Prague Linguistic Circle) and to much of the work published in its new (1945) journal *Word*.

On the other hand, however, he also encountered opposition from American linguists. Some of this seems to have been based purely on regrettable and not always very subtle xenophobia, but much also represented a genuine conflict of scientific views. By comparison with the radical positivist and operationalist climate of thought among the members of the 'post-Bloomfieldian' generatïon (which we will treat below in chapter 11), then dominant in the Linguistic Society of America and in American universities, Jakobson's position seemed wildly idealistic. By insisting on the importance of unobservable 'meanings' (the *signifié* of the linguistic sign) as well as the supposedly 'hard data' of phonetic fact (the *signifiant*), Jakobson seemed to threaten a retreat into what many American linguists considered more of a recidivist metaphysics of language than proper 'science'.

Even the most patently 'scientific' (because highly technological) aspect of Jakobson's position—the appeal to data from acoustic research, which had progressed greatly by the end of the 1940s—was widely considered illicit. This was because of the use he made of it: in proposing a universal system of phonological description founded on properties that could be defined independent of particular languages, Jakobson threatened the position of presuppositionless, fundamentally agnostic analysis that many believed was essential to objective linguistic description.

Nonetheless, although they did not succeed in changing the basic directions of American linguistics overnight, Jakobson and his students continued to gain prominence and influence, representing in some ways the 'official opposition'. American linguists' hostility toward Europeans abated somewhat in the early 1950s: Hockett published a favorable review of Martinet's work in 1951, and Hjelmslev taught in the 1952 Linguistic Institute. Jakobson was elected president of the Linguistic Society of America for 1956, representing in some ways the seeds of a fundamental reorientation of research away from an increasingly sterile obsession with purely procedural issues. Especially among Slavists, though, Jakobson had already become a genuinely central figure by that time. In 1950 he was appointed professor of Slavic and general linguistics at Harvard, and soon thereafter (on the strength of his interest and work in the acoustic structure of speech) he also became professor (later Institute Professor) at MIT. He continued to be associated with both institutions (though forced to retire officially from Harvard at the mandatory retirement age of seventy) until his death in 1982.

Origins of the distinctive feature theory

Most of the central aspects of Jakobson's view of phonological structure can be identified in the prewar Prague school picture presented in Trubetzkoy's *Grundzüge*, but their elaboration nonetheless resulted in a distinctly individual position. This position was taken over in largely intact form by (at least early work in) generative phonology, and it is important to be clear on its basic elements and their motivation.

Trubetzkoy's theory was, as described in the preceding chapter, primarily a theory of systems of *phonemes*: ideal segmentlike constructs reduced to their distinctive minimum, and identified only by their opposition to the other elements of the same system. Although he says in places that phonemes should be regarded as composed of features (which would seem to imply logically that features, not phonemes, are the minimal building blocks of sound structure), this formulation is due to Jakobson and in some ways foreign to the actual thrust of Trubetzkoy's work. He seems to have regarded the individual features that are the basis of phonemic oppositions more as characterizations of the dimensions along which systems of phonemes are structured than as actual units having autonomous ontological status.

This is perhaps a rather subtle distinction: if the phonemic units of Trubetzkoy's analyses are identifiable only in terms of the distinctive dimensions along which they are opposed to other units, the difference between this and saying that the properties themselves are the basic units, combined into clusters of simultaneously co-occurring elements which are in turn concatenated sequentially, seems more a matter of philosophical than of linguistic significance. Nonetheless, Jakobson's insistence that it is features, not phonemes, that are the fundamental units of linguistic analysis has some consequences for the range of issues addressed by the theory.

In Jakobson's view, Saussure was fundamentally mistaken in a number of his basic propositions about the nature of language. We have already had occasion to note Jakobson's opinion that it was misleading for Saussure to stress the absolute separation of synchronic and diachronic aspects of language, since this would rule out a teleological interpretation of change in terms of the properties of the system undergoing it. He also took exception, however, to what Saussure regarded as two of the most basic properties of the linguistic sign.

One of these was the claim that linguistic signs have an essentially sequential character, which Jakobson took to imply an analysis that stops with units the size of the segment. According to his own position, it is necessary to continue the analysis until the autonomous simultaneous components are reached: a matter only of degree of precision, like the decomposition of morphemes into phonemes after words have been analyzed into morphemes, and not a fundamentally different procedure; but not one that can be allowed to be impeded by an insistence on linear arrangement of the constituents of the sign.

Second, Jakobson felt that the doctrine of the arbitrariness of the sign had to be subjected to important qualifications. While it is of course true that signs are arbitrary in that the link between a particular *signifié* and a particular *signifiant* is established by the conventions of the linguistic system, this does not imply that the sorts of things that can serve as potential *signifiants* are constrained only by the necessity to be different from one another. In particular, language has an essentially spoken character, as a result of which the *signifiants* are necessarily to be found in their logically primary form in the structuring of sound. Furthermore, not just any differences in sound are potentially relevant phonologically: a universal inventory can be given of the small set of *distinctive features* that function to differentiate *signifiants* in natural languages. Insofar as the *signifiant* of any sign in any language must be made up of these same elements, the arbitrariness of the sign is considerably restricted. Of course, if this view is to have cogency, it is necessary to establish a plausible set of candidates for the status of universal distinctive features. These features must be defined generally enough to be applicable to the wide range of phonetic phenomena observed to differentiate forms in the languages of the world; but precisely enough to make specific claims about what is and is not a possible phonological system, thus giving the theory empirical content. Much of Jakobson's writing on phonological topics was directed precisely toward refining the proposed inventory of these universal features.

The system of Trubetzkoy's *Grundzüge* can fairly be described as the first attempt to provide such a universal framework of the features that are exploited for phonological purposes in the languages of the world (as opposed to purely phonetic descriptive frameworks). The set of parameters proposed there involved a fairly large number of features. Each was provided with a general, language-independent definition, but some of these definitions were articulatory in character while others were based in acoustics. Within the overall framework of segmental features, different sets were proposed for vowels and for consonants. The proposed classification of oppositions allowed for a number of different types, including for instance both bilateral and multilateral oppositions.

In all of these respects, Jakobson's views gradually came to differ. Jakobson reports that he and Trubetzkoy had already differed by 1938 on the issue of whether truly multilateral oppositions should be recognized. Seeking a framework which would provide a maximally uniform notion of phonological opposition, he noted that most of the features in the *Grundzüge* system were in fact bilateral, and suggested that those few that apparently were not might actually be decomposable into two or more bilateral oppositions (a proposal of which Trubetzkoy appears to have remained unconvinced). In 1938 Jakobson developed his position in a talk to the Prague Linguistic Circle, and subsequently at the International Congress of Phonetic Sciences in Ghent.

In this paper, Jakobson (1939) considers the most obvious candidate for a multilateral opposition, the parameter of place of articulation in consonants. All previous descriptive frameworks had treated the differences among labial, dental, palatal, and velar consonants (as well as those at other positions) as completely parallel, aligned along a single dimension. Jakobson proposed, however, that this apparent uniformity in fact represented (at least) two distinct features.

One of these, differentiating labials and velars on the one hand from dentals and palatals on the other, can be defined both in articulatory and acoustic terms. *Grave* consonants (labials and velars) are formed with a relatively large, undivided oral resonant cavity, resulting in a relatively low frequency region of prominence in their acoustic spectrum; while *acute* consonants (dentals and palatals) are formed with an oral cavity divided into two smaller resonators, resulting in a relatively high-frequency region of spectral prominence. Cross-classifying with this difference is that between *posterior* (later called *compact*) consonants (velars and palatals), formed with a constriction relatively far back in the mouth, and *anterior* (later called *diffuse*) consonants, the labials and the dentals which are formed with a relatively front constriction. In acoustic terms, Jakobson (1939) identifies compact consonants only by their relatively greater perceptibility; in subsequent formulations, they were described as having a concentration of energy in the central region of the acoustic spectrum (as opposed to diffuse consonants, which lack such a concentration). Regardless of their specific definitions, however, if these features are accepted, the result is a theory in which multilateral oppositions can arguably be dispensed with entirely.

Developing the theory of distinctive features

At least three major points follow from this analysis: the logical character of the distinctive features, the substantive nature of their definitions, and the homogeneity of their application to sounds of all classes. Each of these represents an important theme in Jakobson's later work.

First, of course, is the exclusive role played by binary oppositions in the resulting theory. Jakobson consistently argued that the principle of binary oppositions is absolutely fundamental to language, and has its basis in the nature of our mental processes. He notes later that individual nerve cells appear to function on a strict 'on/off' basis, and suggests that this property is reflected in the structure of language (though he does not discuss the fact that the muscles which actually implement articulatory gestures are by no means binary in their control possibilities). With the reduction of consonantal place of articulation to a set of binary oppositions, this program is largely accomplished in the domain of phonological features. Additional place of articulation distinctions beyond the basic four (e.g., the difference between velars and uvulars) are argued to be treated in terms of other binary properties. He claims, for example, that uvular stops in most languages are actually affricates, and thus relatively *strident*—noisy, or affricated—by comparison with velars. There is thus no need to recognize a distinct uvular point of articulation for consonants, since an independent dimension is available to contrast uvulars with other sounds.

One further candidate for the status of a multilateral opposition must also be mentioned, in part because its status continues to be controversial today. The difference among high, mid, and low vowels (perhaps with still further height distinctions) is much less easily decomposed into binary features than is consonantal point of articulation. One proposed solution was to make use of additional properties (similar to the use of stridency mentioned above for consonants): many height distinctions, for example (such as [i] vs. [I]), can evidently be reduced to differences in *tenseness*. There still appear to be at least three irreducible degrees of vowel quality distinguished only by height, however. To describe these, Jakobson at one point proposed that a single feature was involved, but that it took three values: $+$, $-$, and $\pm$ (or perhaps o, for 'unspecified'). Yet this is transparently not a binary opposition in any interesting sense, and most presentations of Jakobson's framework rely on dividing the parameter *compact/diffuse* into two features: [$\pm$compact] and [$\pm$diffuse], with mid vowels specified as [$-$compact, $-$diffuse].

Another important aspect of the theory presented in Jakobson (1939) and subsequent work is its striving to provide every feature with definitions in both articulatory and auditory terms. Relying on the fact that language is in its essence a spoken system, Jakobson surmised that its primitive terms must have an objective, external basis in the acoustic signal as well as in the articulatory activity of the speaker (and the auditory perception of the hearer). In practice, the transformations from articulation to acoustics and from acoustics to articulation are not unique (since more than one articulatory configuration can give rise to the same sound, and the same configuration can produce more than one sound); therefore, what we really want, in addition to these, is an auditory or perceptual definition, since we speak in order to be understood.

This insistence that the distinctive features are identifiable directly in the signal at all three stages (articulatory, acoustic, and perceptual) limits the range of properties that can be encompassed to those with a direct surface realization. Whatever their importance in other terms (e.g., morphophonemics), abstract differences between forms cannot count as 'phonological' in the strict sense. We will explore in chapter 11 some of the motivations behind this limitation of phonology to surface properties (which is of course not at all limited to Jakobson's position); for Jakobson, it seems to follow directly from the basis of language in speech communication, and the need to provide simultaneous objective definitions of features at all levels of the speech communication process.

Another important aspect of Jakobson's position which is already present in his first major paper on phonology after Trubetzkoy's death is what we might call the 'one mouth' principle: the requirement that the same apparatus be used to describe both vowels and consonants simultaneously, rather than providing separate sets of features for these two classes of sounds. The division between grave and acute consonants is first presented as parallel to that between grave and acute vowels (the grave vowels being back, and the acute vowels front); and the three consonants *p*, *t*, and *k* are said to be arranged perceptually in a triangle which is quite parallel to the vowel triangle of *u*, *i*, and *a*. Such a parallel is obviously suggested by the insistence on an acoustic and auditory perspective, and not only an articulatory one. If this proposal is to be realized, however, it is necessary to frame the definitions of the distinctive features in rather general terms, so as to make them applicable simultaneously to the rather different structure of vowels and consonants (as well as the intermediate classes of glides and liquids).

This elimination of the difference between features for vowels and features for consonants, in its turn, paves the way for the most striking aspect of the Jakobsonian system. As a general program, this system assimilates as many traditional phonetic dimensions as possible to one another, bringing them together under a single general definition wherever this is possible and they cannot be shown to function independently of one another. The result is a radical reduction of the number of features recognized (from around forty in Trubetzkoy's system to roughly a dozen), and a much greater utilization of this minimal set of dimensions in the languages of the world—potentially leading to a richer universal theory of phonological systems and their structure.

Some of the reduction in the number of distinctive features in Jakobson's system is provided by framing definitions in terms of relative, rather than absolute properties. The import of this is that each feature is defined in terms of a general, language-independent set of properties—but the segments distinguished by a given feature may still be determinable only on a language-particular basis.

For example, Jakobson (1962b) cites the fact that Bulgarian has two vowels in each of the following classes: front unround (/i/, /e/), back round (/u/, /o/), and back unround (/ə/, /a/). The three classes can easily be distinguished by means of the features grave/acute (separating back from front vowels) and flat/nonflat (separating rounded from unrounded vowels). Within these classes, however, the question of the appropriate way to characterize the distinctions involved remains. /i/ and /u/ are high vowels, /e/, /ə/, and /o/ are mid, and /a/ is low; so we would appear to have to do with three vowel heights. But Jakobson argues that in each class we really have to do with a difference between a *relatively* higher (more diffuse) vowel and a relatively lower (more compact) vowel—and thus we can differentiate the members of each pair by the same feature, without regard to the fact that the [+diffuse] member of the [+grave, −flat] pair (namely, /ə/) is actually articulated at the same height as the [−diffuse] members of the other two sets.

The fact that features are to be interpreted as distinguishing segments in terms of their relative (rather than absolute) possession of some property has important consequences for the general program of making maximal use of a minimal set of potentially contrastive dimensions. It can also be regarded as a way of encoding certain information about rule-governed variation into the definition of elements of a phonological representation, similar to the role played in Trubetzkoy's theory by the archiphoneme and the morpho(pho)neme (see chapter 4). As should be evident, Jakobson's theory is just as much a theory of representations as Trubetzkoy's, with little explicit place for a notion of 'rule' except in the definition of elements of these representations.

The role of relative feature definitions in this program is clear from Jakobson's examples. For instance, he often cites the fact that in Danish, initial [t] and [d] contrast, while postvocalically we find [d] and [ð]. By interpreting the opposition in both positions as one between a relatively tense and a relatively lax obstruent, we obtain the desired result of identifying initial [t] with postvocalic [d], and initial [d] with postvocalic [ð]. But another way of looking at the same analysis is to observe that, by treating features as defined relatively, we are able to provide a uniform phonological representation for certain sets of phonetically distinct segments [t] and [d], [d] and [ð]) which alternate with one another under definable conditions. The definitions of the phonemic elements /t/ and /d/ and their opposition thus incorporate what is in effect a rule of postvocalic lenition. Such analyses are subject to the constraint that the alternating segments be sufficiently similar to one another phonetically for the device of relative feature definitions to be sufficient to describe their relation; but this still allows a considerable range of variation that might be described by rules that convert one segment type into another to be described directly in terms of constant representational elements.

The program of collapsing phonetically distinct contrasts into a single phonological dimension was already important in Jakobson (1939). In that paper, for instance, it was suggested that a distinct place of articulation did not have to be provided for affricates since these could be distinguished from plain stops in the same general articulatory/acoustic region by means of the property of *stridency* (noisy release). The same parameter also can be used to make other place-of-articulation distinctions such as that between bilabials and labiodentals, between alveolars like English [s] and interdentals like English [θ], etc.; and since uvulars in most languages are more affricated than the corresponding velars, this distinction too can be included under stridency.

In Jakobson's later development of the distinctive feature system, several other features subsume a number of phonetically distinct dimensions. The most dramatic of these, perhaps, is the feature [±flat] (see Jakobson, Fant, and Halle 1952), which includes distinctions of (a) rounding, (b) retroflexion, (c) velarization, and (d) pharyngealization. The feature [±checked], in its turn, encompasses ejection, implosion, and clicks. In each case, an important empirical claim is made by bringing the several contrasts under a single feature, to the effect that no language will ever display two or more of the contrasts covered by a single feature independently. Of course, this does not mean that a language cannot, for example, have both rounded and retroflex consonants (since both would contrast with plain consonants by being [+flat])—but only that the two cannot be independently contrastive under otherwise identical conditions. Thus, the contrast of retroflexion might appear in dental stops and fricatives, and rounding in velars, without violating the claim made by the definition of the feature [Flat].

The adequacy of Jakobson's distinctive features

The limited inventory of very general features which form the system presented in Jakobson's work (e.g., Jakobson, Fant, and Halle 1952; Jakobson and Halle 1956) can be seen to make very strong empirical claims about the range of possible phonological systems in natural languages. As can be expected, the investigation of a wide range of languages which has been stimulated by these claims has turned up a certain number of problems for the Jakobsonian system. For example, a number of languages in Australia have stops and nasals at six points of articulation: labial, interdental, alveolar, postalveolar (retroflex), palatal, and velar. The labial, palatal, and velar positions pose no problems, but apparently all of the interdental, alveolar, and postalveolar segments must be treated as [acute, diffuse]. The feature [flat] can be used to distinguish the postalveolar position from the others, but the interdental and alveolar positions remain unseparated. While the feature [strident] might be called into play for this purpose in the case of the stops, this is obviously unsuitable as a description of the difference between interdental and alveolar nasals, and the Jakobsonian system does not seem to provide any more adequate alternative.

A variety of languages post logically similar problems. Chipewyan, for example, is reported to contrast two affricates in the dental/alveolar region ([t͡s] vs. [t͡θ]); since stridency is already employed to separate affricates from the corresponding stops, it is not available to make this further distinction as well. Also, as with the problem posed by the Australian systems noted above, some languages (e.g., Greenlandic Eskimo) present a contrast between velar and uvular nasals which cannot plausibly be described as based on stridency. It appears, then, that more points of articulation must be recognized than the four basic ones provided by the Jakobsonian system; and this entails the addition of some further features (assuming the framework of binary oppositions is maintained).

There are also some problems for the generalization represented by the definition of the feature [flat]. This feature predicts that no language will have more than one independent contrast out of a set consisting of rounding, retroflexion, velarization, and pharyngealization. In the northwest Caucasian languages Ubykh and (the Bzyb dialect of) Abkhaz, however, independent contrasts of retroflexion and rounding are reported among affricates in the alveopalatal region. Ubykh also displays independently contrastive plain, rounded, pharyngealized, and rounded-pharyngealized uvular stops. Bzyb ·Abkhaz has uvular fricatives of five distinct types: plain, rounded, 'palatalized' (involving an increase in the length of the constriction), pharyngealized, and rounded-pharyngealized. A contrast of rounding is also reported for distinctively pharyngeal fricatives in some languages of the Salishan family, such as Colville. In the Athabaskan language Chilcotin, it appears that velar obstruents show independent contrasts of rounding and velarization (where the latter also appears in dental obstruents, and is manifested largely as a modification of adjacent vowels). In vowel systems, the Northeast Caucasian language Tsakhur has a vowel system including two high back vowels ([ɨ] and [u]) that contrast in rounding (as well as [i], [e], [a] and [o]); each of these vowels appears with contrastive pharyngealization as well.

From the above observations, we can conclude that several detailed claims made by the Jakobsonian feature system concerning the complementarity of certain contrasts are not borne out. For most of the cases in which two or more traditional phonetic dimensions are united under a single feature in this system, in fact, it is possible to find languages in which these dimensions are independently contrastive. On the other hand, we should not let this cause us to lose sight of the essentially marginal nature of such cases: the problematic contrasts are exhibited only in languages of rather unusual structure, such as those of the Northwest Caucasus and the Northwest coast of North America, which are noted for their exuberant consonantal inventories. As generalizations about the vast majority of the world's languages, the complementarities predicted by the Jakobsonian system are overwhelmingly valid.

A different sort of objection to the comprehensive adequacy of the Jakobsonian system for the description of natural languages is due originally to McCawley (1967a). He points out that a complete description of any language within such a system would require not only a set of phonological representations for forms, but also a set of principles (a) supplying the values of redundant features; and (b) interpreting the distinctive features in terms of their particular articulatory and acoustic realization. That is, given the fact that a given segment is characterized as e.g. [+flat], it is still necessary to specify whether this means that it is rounded, pharyngealized, retroflexed, or velarized. This set of principles specifying the non-distinctive aspects of speech may be impossible to formulate in a satisfactory way if it is based on representations given in a system like Jakobson's.

To illustrate this problem, McCawley cites facts from Arabic. Arabic has a set of pharyngealized consonants (the 'emphatics') which are contrastively [+flat]; it also has three vowels /a/, /i/, and /u/ which involve a rounding contrast and thus another use of the feature [flat]. The contrasts involved are not independent (rounding is only contrastive in vowels, and pharyngealization in certain consonants), so a problem of the sort discussed in the preceding paragraphs does not arise; but another difficulty appears as a result of certain non-distinctive facts about Arabic pronunciation.

In particular, vowels adjacent to a pharyngealized consonant are predictably pharyngealized themselves. To describe this, we might say that vowels become (predictably) [+flat] when preceded or followed by a [+flat] consonant. But when we now come to interpret the feature [+flat], we need to say the following: (a) in consonants, [+flat] means 'pharyngealized'; (b) in vowels that are high and back, [+flat] entails 'rounded'; and (c) in vowels adjacent to pharyngealized consonants, [+flat] entails 'pharyngealized'. The problem, of course, is that this last statement duplicates the principle by which [flat] is redundantly assigned to vowels adjacent to [flat] consonants. Other formulations of the specific rules involved could be proposed, but there does not appear to be any description which does not involve such a duplication.

This argument bears on the adequacy of the Jakobsonian feature system so long as we accept the assumption that the same set of features (including [flat]) is to be employed both to specify the contrastive values of the phonological representations of forms and the nondistinctive or redundant properties of their pronunciation. In numerous places Jakobson insists that a description of the redundant features as well as the distinctive ones must be included in an adequate theory of language; but he never proposed a real theory of these redundant features which was separate from the theory of distinctive features. The assumption might thus be warranted that it was intended to employ the same set of features to describe both distinctive and redundant properties. As McCawley points out, this is exactly the assumption adopted by Halle in such early generative work as Halle (1959), and indeed quite generally until the revisions in the basis of the feature system proposed in Chomsky and Halle (1968). Nonetheless, McCawley's argument from Arabic makes it clear that whatever the value of the Jakobsonian framework for the description of the distinctive properties of phonemic forms, an adequate treatment of the relation between these forms and actual pronunciation must be based on a rather different set of features which does not involve the collapsing of distinct but complementary phonetic properties under a single dimension of contrast.

Once we see that such a (nonminimal) set of general phonetic parameters plays an essential role in the description of natural language systems, we must then ask what the motivation is for assuming a separate, minimal set of specifically *distinctive* features. For Jakobson, such a special status for the system of distinctive features is motivated by the unique status of the representations which they characterize: representations in which only the distinctive properties of a form are registered, with all predictable or redundant information rigorously eliminated. Of course, if it were true that no language could employ, for example, both rounding and retroflexion independently, then characterizing any particular contrast as phonologically one or the other would leave this predictability unexpressed; and so the conflation of complementary features forms an integral part of the definition of phonemic forms as strictly distinctive, and nonredundant. In Jakobson's view, the existence of a level of representation defined by exactly this property of nonredundancy follows directly from the Saussurean insight that the linguistic significance of a form lies in the way it differs from other forms. Nonredundant phonemic representations characterize these differences directly and explicitly, thus apparently expressing the linguistic essence of particular forms.

The absence of predictable features from the essential nature of the linguistic *signifiant* appeared self-evident to Jakobson. Directly echoing Trubetzkoy's rejection of Baudouin's conception of the phoneme as the psychological equivalent of a speech sound, Jakobson and Halle (1956) argue that such a psychological picture is based on a fallacy: "we have no right to presume that the sound correlate in our *internal* speech or in our speech intention is confined to the distinctive features to the exclusion of the configurative or redundant features."

The extension of this observation to the claim that utterances should be provided with a distinct phonemic form devoid of all configurative or redundant features rests on the assumption that phonological theory is fundamentally a theory of *representations*, and that the only way to characterize limitations on the variation that does or does not count as corresponding to the 'same' linguistic unit is by defining a level of representation that will have exactly that property. If, as we have argued above (in chapter 2), it is also possible to characterize this variation and its limits by means of *rules* that relate representations not specifically defined by this property, then the motivation for a separate system of distinctive (as opposed to more generally phonetic) features disappears along with the necessity of such a level of representation.

We might still motivate the Jakobsonian system of a minimal set of phonetic features by the argument that, even though this specific proposal about their substantive content may be in need of refinement and revision (as the observations above about their empirical adequacy suggest), it is still overwhelmingly the case that many phonetic dimensions are in overall complementary distribution in natural languages. Thus, even though a tiny minority of languages do indeed exploit both rounding and pharyngealization separately, most treat only one or the other (or, obviously, neither) of these as potentially contrastive under any given set of circumstances. If a fully adequate set of features along Jakobsonian lines could be constructed, this might allow us to express such generalizations about natural language.

Before admitting a set of features constructed on this basis, however, we must ask exactly what the insight is that characterizes it. In fact, the possibility for generalization in the Jakobsonian system rests essentially on the auditory foundation of the features themselves. This suggests that what is really at issue here is a rather direct pragmatic fact, rooted (as Jakobson so often insisted) in the basis of language in speech communication. We could formulate the relevant generalization approximately as follows: the more nearly similar two phonetic parameters are in their auditory correlates, the less likely they are to function as independent cues to the identity of particular forms. Put in such a way, the generalization appears to be almost a truism: the harder it is to distinguish which of two properties is intended, the harder it is to use them independently as cues to the intended form of an utterance. By showing that, for example, all of the properties brought together under the proposed feature [flat] are highly similar in their acoustic consequences, Jakobson and his coworkers provided just this basis for the observation that these properties are by and large not treated as independent cues in perceptual identification, and thus in the structure of languages.

But, of course, this generalization is a relative one and not absolute: as long as two properties are not absolutely identical in their acoustic and auditory consequences, there is still the possibility that they will show up in some language as independent. This is exactly the case with the wide range of auditorily marginal distinctions exceptionally exploited by languages like those of the Northwest Caucasian family; and the fact that these cues are usually reinforced in such languages by other (redundant) ones simply stresses the unusual nature of the situation.

Indeed, the role played by this generalization is considerably broader than that of simply predicting what contrasts can co-occur within a given phonemic system. When we state it in terms not of (surface) distinctive properties, as in Jakobson's system, but in terms of the perceptual cues used to identify linguistic forms, it has other clear consequences for the evolution of phonological systems.

For example, there is no serious question that the properties of voicing in obstruents and tone in vowels constitute quite independent dimensions of contrast, which must be separated in any adequate framework for phonological description. Nonetheless, both of these have the property that one of the acoustic cues utilized in their perception is the frequency (in relative value or direction of change) of vocal cord vibration. As is well known, voiced obstruents induce a lower pitch on the immediately following portion of a vowel, and (certain kinds of) voiceless obstruents induce a relatively higher pitch in the same way. Though attempts have been made to attribute both of these effects to the same features, there are excellent reasons to assume that they are quite independent (see Anderson 1978): it happens, however, that the articulatory mechanisms involved in controlling obstruent voicing have as side effects a perturbation of the frequency of vocal cord vibration. Further, there is some evidence to the effect that such perturbations can be among the cues utilized perceptually for the identification of obstruents as voiced or voiceless. The role of fundamental frequency in the case of distinctions of tone is obvious.

Thus, we have to do with two independent dimensions of contrast, which happen to have some auditory similarity (in that they share in part a perceptual cue). We must, of course, recognize a basic distinction between the phonological properties in question and the auditory cues which allow a listener to identify them: otherwise, we would be unable to describe the independence typically shown by tone and voicing. Equally, however, we must recognize the consequences of the auditory relationship which such a shared cue establishes between properties. To the extent that they are both identifiable (at least in part) on the basis of evidence from the acoustic value F_o, the independence of tone and voicing is likely to be compromised in the same way as that of the various properties brought together by Jakobson into a single feature on the basis of a (nearly) uniform auditory definition.

In this case, we can see the action of the generalization above in the fact that, in the evolution of a number of languages (especially in the Sino-Tibetan family), voicing distinctions have been reinterpreted as distinctions of tone (and perhaps vice versa, though this is more controversial). The mechanism involved is evidently the following: given the auditory similarity between the two, they are likely to be interpreted as related rather than independent; and at that point, a property other than the originally intended one may be taken to be the independent variable. The pitch perturbations provoked by voicing distinctions were reinterpreted as representing autonomous tonal contrasts, and the change in phonological structure is thus a consequence of the auditory relation between the two parameters. We see here the effect of the same generalization that accounts for those instances of complementarity between phonetic dimensions which Jakobson's system attempts (in too absolute a fashion) to capture. Jakobson's insight concerning the importance of auditory considerations is a very real one, but it is relevant to other areas than the delimitation of a universally adequate feature system for phonological description.

Kindersprache, Aphasie und allgemeine Lautgesteze

Although the development of Jakobson's thought in regard to the system of distinctive features took place over a long period, its high point was perhaps his 1941 monograph on child language, aphasia, and phonological universals. The work was written in Norway, while he was more or less constantly on the move before settling in the United States. It attempts to bring together facts from a wide variety of areas whose relationship we now take for granted (largely as a result of Jakobson's ideas) but which were then treated by rather different disciplines. The purpose of this enterprise, of course, is to bring this putatively extralinguistic material to bear on the analysis of synchronic phonological systems, to enable us to understand on a more general basis what is 'natural' about natural languages, or why they are as they are. This was undoubtedly the first attempt within modern linguistics to create a genuinely explanatory theory of linguistic systems by establishing logical and empirical connections between the data of linguistic analysis per se and other, independent domains.

At the time Jakobson wrote, the available data concerning language acquisition, language dissolution in aphasia, the general bases of auditory perception, and other areas to which he refers were largely fragmentary from a linguistic point of view. As a result, some of his factual assertions about language cannot stand as empirically valid today; but if the linguistic relevance of this material is now much better understood, and the available data much greater both in quantity and quality, it is primarily because of the wealth of suggestive implications Jakobson found in what was available to him in 1941. It is a considerable tribute to his insight that, if the ensuing forty years of research have revised many points of detail, the broad outlines of his bold synthesis continue to be confirmed.

He begins with the study of the most obviously linguistic material available (which was, however, largely the result of studies by nonlinguists): the course of acquisition of a first language by children. It is necessary first of all to argue that this material is indeed *linguistic* in character: that is, that the deviations in children's early speech from the system of adult language really are based on linguistic principles and have a systematic character which is relevant to the understanding of linguistic systems, rather than being based merely on physical, perceptual, or conceptual limitations inherent in uncompleted development. While one cannot of course completely neglect the influence of such limitations (where they can be shown to exist), Jakobson argues that the vast majority of deviations in child speech that had been recorded could in fact be understood and organized by the terms and categories of linguistic systems; and that they thus represent authentically and systematically *different* systems rather than simply imperfect command of the adult system.

Jakobson also notes that the data of language change support the relevance of child language to adult language. When we examine the sorts of change found in the evolution of a variety of languages, we often find that they correspond closely to the reductions or changes shown by child language with regard to its adult model. This suggests, of course, that much of language change has its basis exactly in these alterations made by the child: that the child's innovations are in some instances taken up and continued in adult systems, and that this forms an important source of raw material for change. The systematic, linguistic nature of the modifications made by the child is shown by the fact that, in many instances, it cannot be claimed that sound types altered in early language are at all unpronounceable (and thus due to possibly extralinguistic limitations of development). They may well appear elsewhere in the system as modifications of other sounds, and in any case many modified sounds are well attested in earlier stages of the child's development.

The proposal that change has its roots in child language was not new with Jakobson: Grammont (among others) had earlier observed striking similarities between the two, and devoted considerable attention to them as a source of data for his theory of change. There are also some remarks by Baudouin de Courtenay that can be seen as recognizing the relevance of child language for the class of anthropophonic processes which, as discussed above in chapter 3, serve as the foundation of all alternations in adult language systems. Nonetheless, Jakobson's use of these connections is more ambitious than that of his predecessors. He wants not simply to refer to observations about child language as a factual source for a theory of linguistic change: he wants rather to establish the point that adult language systems are as they are because they necessarily develop in a particular systematic way that can be studied in the form of child language.

Jakobson notes that before the onset of genuine meaningful language, the child goes through a stage of 'babbling', in which typically a vast array of sound types are produced (including such comparative *exotica* as clicks, nasal vowels, obstruent liquids, etc.). More or less suddenly, however, this enormous diversity disappears, to be replaced by a radically reduced inventory of sounds in the child's first real words. This corresponds, according to Jakobson, to the transition from a stage in which the babbling is pure sound, pure expression, to a point at which sound production is employed in the service of expressing a distinctive function. Babbling can be regarded as serving the purpose of a sort of preliminary 'tuning up' of the articulatory and auditory apparatus, establishing the range of gestures of which this apparatus is capable and their acoustic consequences, but without utilizing the resulting sound for any (nonemotive) meaningful expression. As soon as sound comes to constitute the *signifiant* of a linguistic sign associated with a *signifié*, however, a fundamental change takes place in the range of productions thus utilized. Where once nearly any sound from nearly any language could be found in the child's babblings, the first words typically involve very few: [p], [m], and [a], for example.

This radical reduction in variety had largely confounded earlier attempts to ascribe a systematic course to language development: how can it be that, if children are observed to produce nasal vowels at six months, such sounds appear to be beyond the capacity of a two-year old? For Jakobson, the answer is clear: after the babbling period, when language becomes endowed with distinctive function, it is not the articulations of sound types that need to be developed, since these are already well established. Rather, it is the use of distinctive oppositions that is lacking, and which must be built up piece by piece.

Evidence for this proposition comes from several sources. First, of course, the fact that postbabbling language acquisition does not consist in acquiring the articulatory skill to produce a wide variety of sounds is shown by the very diversity of content of babbling itself. Second, however, even during the period of development of genuine language, the child often gives evidence of controlling a wider variety of articulations than are available for distinctive exploitation. Frequently, sounds that are missing from the child's meaningful language nonetheless appear in purely expressive uses (interjections, onomatopoeia, imitations, etc.). Further, a sound that is missing in one class of words may well appear in others as a substitute for some other sound, when a sort of 'chain shift' of segments occurs.

The essential point Jakobson draws from these data is that the process of developing the system of distinctive uses of sound is qualitatively quite independent of the development of mere articulatory control. Furthermore, once the issue is clarified in this way and attention focused on the emergence of a genuinely linguistic system of sound values, a striking conclusion emerges: the order of development of sound distinctions is roughly constant across languages, in a sequence independent of the nature of the language being acquired. Thus, all children begin with a minimal opposition of a single vowel (roughly [a]) and a single consonant (generally labial [p]). Consonantal distinctions arise with a difference between a nasal ([m]) and an oral ([p]) segment type; and subsequently with a split in point of articulation between grave (labial) and acute (dental) sounds. Within vowels, the first split is between compact (low) and diffuse (high) segments. With regard to manner of articulation, stops arise before fricatives, and both before affricates. The consonant/vowel distinction precedes the emergence of liquids or glides, and sonorant liquids precede obstruent liquids. Some distinctions, where they are to appear, arise only very late: e.g., nasal vs. oral vowels; oppositions between liquids; clicks, ejectives, implosives and other nonpulmonic airstream mechanisms, etc.

The uniformity of the sequence in which these segmental distinctions are acquired seems quite general. Of course, a child acquiring a language which simply does not have a given opposition obviously does not introduce it simply because it is the next thing in the chain of development. The predictive role of these generalizations is relative to the set of oppositions present in the language ultimately to be acquired: their sequence follows strict lines (though some of these lines, such as those governing e.g. vowel quality and consonantal manner distinctions, may be largely independent of one another) which (for any given set of oppositions) are related in the same way in the development of any language.

An important corollary of the determinacy of this developmental sequence is the prediction it makes about possible phonological systems. Since the child must acquire stops before fricatives, and both before affricates, the prediction is made that a system with only fricatives and not stops, or with stops and affricates but no fricatives, could not be acquired, since an essential step toward the development of such a system would in each case be missing. Now in fact there are languages with stops but no fricatives (many languages in Australia, for example), but not vice versa; and while there are many languages with stops and fricatives but no affricates, there are no languages attested in which affricates are contrasted as a class with one or the other of stops and fricatives but not both.

In fact, Jakobson argues, the other apparent laws of phonological development attested in acquisition data are similarly mirrored in implicational universals governing the structure of possible phonological systems. If phonological opposition B systematically arises after opposition A in development, then no language will be found (he suggests) which employs B but not A. The logic of this situation is apparent, but its importance is absolutely fundamental. It establishes, if valid, both a set of highly restrictive constraints on phonological systems and an explanatory grounding for the content of these constraints in the process of language acquisition.

Further confirmation of the outline of Jakobson's proposed implicational relations among oppositions is provided by the complex data of aphasia studies. In these cases, one finds, at least grossly (the interpretation of the details of aphasia studies is often highly problematic), a mirror image of the developmental sequence of language acquisition. Again, as in the case of babbling, it is necessary to distinguish the linguistic use of sound oppositions from the mere production control of the sounds involved. In the case of aphasics, it is necessary to separate disorders involving genuine motor difficulty (e.g., dysarthria) and those involving specifically linguistic defects. In these latter cases, as with the babbling and expressive uses of sounds by children, one sometimes finds that sounds which have apparently been lost to the linguistic system are nonetheless controlled by the patient, in expressive speech for example. The patient may be obviously quite able to make a given sound, but not to use it linguistically.

In general, when we focus on deficits that are authentically linguistic in nature, we find that the sequence in which phonological oppositions are lost is constant, and that these losses follow implicational hierarchies which are the direct reverse of those governing acquisition. Thus, distinctions like nasality in vowels or that between obstruent and sonorant liquids are among the last to be acquired, the least common in the languages of the world, and the first to be lost in aphasia. On the other hand, distinctions such as that between vowels and consonants, or between compact and diffuse vowels, grave and acute consonants are the first to be acquired, essentially universal in their distribution, and the most resistant to loss in aphasia. The solidarity thus demonstrated by these various realms is a thoroughly remarkable discovery.

The data Jakobson dealt with were not by any means completely unknown to other students of language, but his synthesis was the first importantly comprehensive one. The innovative basis which allowed him to bring order to these areas and their relationships was the notion of contrast as the basis of phonological systems. Previous researchers had tried to deal with some of the same problems, and had proposed hypotheses of uniform development in acquisition or dissolution in aphasia, but had always been confounded by a wealth of obvious counterexamples to any apparent hypothesis. This was clearly because they framed their proposals in terms of order of acquisition or loss of *sounds* rather than of linguistically functional oppositions. Of course, in that case both babbling in infants and the absence of apraxia as a general correlate of aphasia are inexplicable.

Even less successful were attempts to explain apparent uniformities of development by a sort of 'ontogeny recapitulates phylogeny' principle, according to which child language should show important similarities to 'primitive' languages. As Jakobson shows, this position fails miserably in the face of the fact that, where agreement can be achieved on what might be such 'primitive languages', their range of phonological segment types is often much greater than those of familiar European languages (the supposed developmental acme). A concentration on phonetic data makes either the acquisition or the aphasia data a chaotic jumble; but the notion of phonological contrast brings it into dramatic focus.

While Jakobson of course conceived of the phonological oppositions which play such a fundamental role here directly in terms of surface contrasts present in the speech signal and endowed with distinctive function, it is evident that the facts are not that specific. Actually, the key insight is that the *linguistic* use of sound properties (at whatever level of abstraction this might be found) follows certain implicational relations that are independent of matters of motor control and the other aspects of physical implementation. Subsequent investigation might well turn up evidence specific enough to indicate that it is precisely surface contrast that is subject to these constraints (and not, for instance, abstract morphophonemic contrast or the linguistically governed use of noncontrastive properties), but neither Jakobson's original empirical basis nor the much greater accumulation of similar, better-described data since then seem to support such a claim.

Overall, Jakobson brings together an enormous range of data from various domains, and makes it clear not only that all of these aspects of language fall together in a coherent unity, but also that there is presumably a uniform organic basis for many of the fundamental structural regularities of human language. Furthermore, this uniformity is specific to language qua language, and not reducible (or perhaps even related) to other, nonlinguistic aspects of human physiology, neurology, perception, etc. (For some additional general discussion of this issue in phonology, see Anderson 1981.)

It is only fair to observe that Jakobson himself saw the basic principles at work here rather differently: he attempts to show, in the later sections of his work, that there are connections between the structural regularities governing language and broader (especially perceptual) properties of human mental organization. It is striking, however, that exactly these sections are notably speculative in character, in contrast to the firm empirical thrust of the observations about relations among acquisition, change, aphasia, and phonological universals. However suggestive they may be, the proposed connections between linguistic and nonlinguistic perceptual development cannot be regarded as established by Jakobson's work.

On the other hand, the insight that language is distinct in important ways from the other faculties with which it interacts plays an absolutely fundamental role in achieving the important systematization of various perspectives on this capacity. While subsequent studies of the uniqueness of a language faculty as the factor integrating data from many points of view have not always explicitly recognized Jakobson's pioneering role in achieving this insight, his work clearly underlies most of what has been done in this area.

Information theory and Jakobson's legacy

In discussing the Jakobsonian program of reducing all phonological oppositions to a minimal set of uniformly binary oppositions, we identified above at least two motivations for taking such a direction. First, of course, is the fact that certain phonetic parameters are indeed similar to one another in their auditory consequences; and if "we speak in order to be understood," such similarities should be reflected in the range of possible systems of contrast in natural languages. The other side of the same coin is that, if certain parameters are indeed mutually exclusive as the basis of contrasts *ceteris paribus*, an explanation for that complementarity must be provided. Basing the features on their auditory definitions seemed to hold out the hope of providing such an explanation by making the relevant observations about which properties can be independently exploited within the same system follow from the fundamental definitions of phonological theory.

Another influence on the development of Jakobson's thinking about the nature of distinctive features, however, came from the area of information theory. Recall that from his earliest writings about phonological structure, a phonemic representation (and the system of phonemic elements that compose it) was seen as expressing exactly what distinguishes one linguistic form from another: a logically 'pure' distillation of the contrastive relation between forms, purged of all redundant and accidental properties. This picture came to be reinforced by considerations from outside the field of linguistics proper.

In the 1940s and 1950s, the mathematical theory of communication developed largely on the basis of electrical engineering considerations involved in optimizing the transmission of information over limited channels. A major goal of this theory was to provide a mathematical expression of the amount of information contained in a given message, and of the corresponding predictabilities and redundancies in the expressive system (or code) underlying the message. It is quite obvious that this goal is highly similar if not identical to that of providing an expression of just what and how much separates linguistic forms from one another. Analyzing the phonemic system on which such linguistic contrasts are based appears simply to be a particular instantiation of the general problem of information theory, as applied to the particular domain of human natural languages.

Jakobson seized on the connection between information theory and his view of phonology (as did, in the other direction, workers in the former domain such as E. Colin Cherry), and expressed the view in a number of papers (e.g., Jakobson, Cherry and Halle 1952; Jakobson 1961) that the generalized mathematical theory of communication would provide a rigorous scientific basis for the interpretation and analysis of phonological systems. It is hard not to see a certain amount of fascination with the impressive mathematical apparatus of this theory in Jakobson's espousal of it. When one reads papers such as that of Jakobson, Cherry, and Halle (1952), in which extended calculations are presented of the precise probabilities of occurrence of particular segments, features, and sequences of features (transition probabilities) in a given corpus of linguistic text, it is difficult to see these as reflective of fundamental insights into the nature of the language in question. It is of course possible to count a great many things in such material, and to apply statistical measures of arbitrary sophistication to the numbers obtained in this way, but the evidence for the linguistic significance of such activity is anything but obvious.

In any event, it is a fundamental notion of information theory that an optimal coding system for the transmission of messages in a given domain is one that makes maximal use of a minimal set of basic contrasts. Binary decisions are both logically and empirically easier to make than ternary or, in general, n-ary ones, and thus ideal for coding information. Furthermore, if all information is represented in consistently binary fashion, it is quite easy to derive a uniform measure of the information content of a given message: this is simply the number of binary decisions it is necessary to make in order to differentiate it from all other possible messages in the same system. A code based on a minimal number (in principle, $\log_2 N$, where N is the number of contrastive elements that must be distinguished) of strictly binary properties is thus the optimal way of representing information from this point of view.

Obviously this conclusion, together with the emphasis on isolating the distinctive from the redundant properties in a given message, dovetailed perfectly with the conception of phonemic structure Jakobson had arrived at independently; and it served to reinforce those aspects of his system. In the course of the 1950s and 1960s, his presentations of phonology relied increasingly on the results of the mathematical theory of communication as the underpinning of the uniformly binary, redundancy-free distinctive-feature representations proposed as a general theory of human language sound patterns.

It is important to note, though, that there is a major premise which is suppressed in the direct application of the results of information theory to natural language: this is the presumption that human language is in fact based on the optimization of the use of its information channel. That is, while it may well be a desirable engineering goal to exploit the communicative capacity of a given channel to its fullest, it is by no means obvious that the empirical facts of human language are founded on the same considerations. But if they are not, of course, a theorem about the properties of an optimal coding system or its implementation in message transmission, no matter how rigorously demonstrated, may be completely inapplicable as a description of the properties of natural language.

Indeed, what has been learned in recent years about the way language is stored mentally, produced, and understood gives us little reason to believe that a principle of optimization and avoidance of redundancy has the fundamental role in its essential character that Jakobson imagined. On the contrary, everything about actual language use seems to be characterized by massive amounts of redundancy—redundancy which is not apparently 'added on' in the mere process of implementation but, rather, is always and essentially copresent with the supposedly more fundamental 'distinctive' elements of structure. There is, thus, no reason to believe that the nature of language is somehow to optimize the representation of information first, and then (incidentally, as an almost accidental property of the physical means at its disposal) to embellish this with certain predictable concomitants. As a result, there is little basis for assigning a special status to a representation of exactly this distinctive core;

and correspondingly little basis for transferring the results of the mathematical theory of communication to the study of language unchanged.

This is in no way to deny the importance of attempts to determine which aspects of language structure are predictable from which others, and to find generalizations about the distribution of linguistic properties where they exist. We mean here only to point out that the existence of predictabilities in language does not license us to ignore a given variable once it has been shown to be dependent on another, as the focus of research in information theory would suggest. A full understanding of the nature of language—and of the real bases of the predictabilities we do find—requires that we pay attention to all of its systematicity, and not only to some minimal set of independently variable parameters.

Regardless of the original motivations for Jakobson's enthusiastic acceptance of the relevance of information theory to phonology, it had practical consequences for actual research in this area which to some extent have persisted long after their original basis has been forgotten. The notion that underlying (or phonological) representations ought only to be specified for the distinctive properties of forms, and that a set of quite different statements (redundancy rules) should then provide the values of redundant features, derives directly the position that phonological forms should provide a uniform measure of the information content of an item, and that the characterization of the difference between distinctive and redundant properties is the central issue to be addressed by a theory of phonological representations.

Early generative phonological descriptions devoted considerable attention to organizing the distinctive features exploited in a given language into maximally symmetric 'decision-tree' structures, organized to exploit redundancies in a way that minimized the number of features specified in any given instance (thus expressing the irreducible information content of forms). While such representations of the interrelationship of features soon disappeared from descriptions (at least by the mid-1960s), the philosophy behind them has remained to some extent in the form of unstated methodological principles of analysis. Whenever two or more ways of characterizing the properties of a given form are available (for instance, specifying the location vs. specifying the vowel quality of a stressed syllable), it is taken for granted by most phonologists that the only correct solution is one which allows other information about the form to be predicted as well (and thus treated as redundant), to the exclusion of an alternative that does not have this consequence.

It is perhaps not too far-fetched to see Jakobson's interest in the mathematical theory of communication as the source of much that has been written on the topic of 'evaluation measures' as well. Recall that uniform binary oppositions play an essential role in codes within that theory, since they admit of a consistent measure of information content which allows the comparison of forms and descriptions. Given two different coding systems for the same set of messages, the system designated as (more nearly) optimal is that which minimizes the number of choices measured in this way. Within generative grammar, the basic problem of an explanatory theory was posed quite early: such a theory must provide a basis (or an *evaluation procedure*) for determining which of a set of alternative descriptions is more likely to represent the descriptively adequate grammar of a language. The specific proposal that this requirement will be satisfied by a feature-counting metric, defined over an expression system for rules and representations that is based on a uniform set of binary features supplemented by appropriate abbreviatory conventions, amounts to the claim that the phonological systems of natural languages constitute optimal coding systems in an information-theoretic sense.

This is not to suggest that aspects of phonological analysis which generative phonology inherits from Jakobson's views have gone undiscussed; on the contrary, the role of redundancy and its proper expression in a grammar, as well as the basis of an evaluation procedure for grammars, constituted major topics of discussion in the early generative literature. Nonetheless, this debate has generally accepted as a basic postulate the idea that the purpose of phonological representations is to express exactly the unpredictable aspects of a form, and that the way to do that is by eliminating all predictable properties from such representations. While writers have stressed the empirical nature of the hypothesis that feature counting over a particular notation constitutes a valid evaluation procedure for grammars, discussion of this issue has concentrated exclusively on the choice of abbreviatory devices and other aspects of the notation.

We should consider the fact, however, that the conceptual motivation of the notion of *phonological representation* has undergone some significant changes between Jakobson's views and those of most contemporary phonologists. Jakobson, as we have argued repeatedly above, saw phonemic representations as the essential expression of the communicative content and distinctiveness of a linguistic form. This view leads directly to minimal, redundancy-free representations which are specified for as little as possible.

Over time, however, the rather different concerns of linguists such as Baudouin de Courtenay and Kruszewski have reasserted themselves: on this view, the role of a phonological representation is to provide the basis for the description of alternations. If we want to express what various alternants in different but related forms of the same higher-level linguistic unit (morpheme, word, etc.) have in common, and what properties of their environment condition the appearance of these variants, this purpose may turn out to be better served by a representation in which redundant detail is specified in phonological form (though constrained by rule, so as to express its predictability). The result may be a view of phonological form along the lines of the 'fully specified (basic or surface) variant' theories sketched in chapter 2. This is not a *necessary* consequence of accepting the importance of alternations for determining phonological form; but once segmental distinctiveness alone is no longer the definitional basis of this representation, the question is at least an open one.

Similarly, once the possibility of such nonminimal representations is taken seriously, we might want to question the appropriateness of the feature-counting sort of strategy for defining an appropriate evaluation metric for grammars. While the formulation of such a procedure is argued by many to constitute the central issue of explanation in an explicit linguistic theory, little if any substantive progress has been made in this direction since the early days of generative phonology. Many 'constraints' and 'general principles' have of course been proposed in the literature as forming important parts of such an evaluatory metric, but these have generally proven unformulable in terms of any natural notion of feature counting. If the basis of a prejudice for feature counting as the only rigorous or explicit kind of metric that would satisfy the demand of explicitness is indeed rooted in considerations of optimal coding taken from the field of information theory, and these concerns are now regarded as not directly relevant to natural language, we might well want to reexamine the entire issue of how evaluation procedures are to be expressed.

Clearly, much of the conceptual capital of generative phonology is inherited from Jakobson's work (as will be discussed further in chapter 12). The basic system of distinctive features, despite the modifications it has undergone in subsequent work, has its roots firmly in Jakobson's theory. Similarly, the basic research goals of phonological investigation, including the formulation of explanatory general laws, and the integration of accounts of historical change, language acquisition, and language pathology into a theory of synchronic systems, were most forcefully expressed in his work. Nonetheless, not all of the foundations of his views (when these are made explicit) would find general acceptance among generative phonologists; and it is important to examine particular points derived from those views to see how comfortably they can be integrated into our present framework of assumptions.

6

The 'Glossematic' Theory of Louis Hjelmslev

Many American linguists have a somewhat caricatural picture of the difference between their own work and that of their European colleagues. In North
America, according to a common view, linguistic research is heavily oriented
toward the description and analysis of concrete linguistic data from real languages. Theoretical proposals, if not actually arrived at inductively from such
practical study, are at least constantly confronted with as wide an array of
factual material as possible. In Europe, on the other hand, most research on
language falls more within the province of speculative philosophy than that of
empirical linguistics. Linguistic theories are spun out of essentially aprioristic
considerations, with only an occasional nod toward one of a small range of
embarrassingly obvious standard examples. If a paper on 'the morphosyntax
of medial suffixes in Kickapoo', bursting with unfamiliar forms and descriptive difficulties, is typical of American linguistics, its European counterpart is
likely to be a paper on 'l'arbitraire du signe' whose factual basis is limited to
the observation that *tree* means 'tree' in English, while *arbre* has essentially
the same meaning in French.

The gross distortions in this picture (which is obviously unfair to both
sides) nonetheless conceal a grain of truth. Much European work in the theory
of language *is* concerned with philosophical problems of the nature of language; and for reasons growing out of the historical development of the field
in America (see chapters 8–11 below), much American work focuses on problems of fieldwork and the description of a wide array of linguistic structures.

If there is one major figure in the history of linguistics who comes closest to
embodying the sort of thing Americans expect of Europeans, it is surely Louis
Hjelmslev. His writings (with only a few exceptions, and these essentially unknown outside Denmark until the publication of volume 2 of his *Essais linguistiques*, 1973) are almost exclusively concerned with questions of Theory
(with a capital T): philosophical discussions of the nature of the sign and
arcane discussions of the proper application of unfamiliar terms, proceeding
with little or no reference to actual linguistic material. It is not unfair to suggest that much of what Hjelmslev wrote is close to impenetrable for the modern (especially North American) reader. This results in part from his exuberant coining of new terminology, combined with frequent highly idiosyncratic

uses assigned to familiar words. All of this terminological apparatus is quite explicit and internally consistent, but the extremely dense and closely connected nature of his prose and the lack of reference to concrete factual material which might facilitate understanding makes the reader's task an arduous one—with few obvious rewards along the way.

Hjelmslev has, however, generally been regarded with considerable respect, and a citation (at least in passing) of his name and of the theory of glossematics has long been a near-obligatory part of any discussion of fundamental views on the nature of language and linguistic theory. Especially during the 1950s, his work was widely praised (both in Europe and North America) for its 'rigorous logic', his demand for 'explicit formulation', and the exent to which he developed certain Saussurean (or at least Saussure-like) ideas to their ultimate conclusions—some would say, indeed, a reductio ad absurdum.

Despite the wide range of work in which Hjelmslev is cited, however, and the generally positive terms of such references, as well as the number of languages into which his work has been translated, there is very little evidence that the actual practice of linguists (aside from some of his immediate students and colleagues, as well as Danish dialectologists more generally) has ever been significantly influenced by specifically Hjelmslevian ideas. Indeed, much of the praise to be found has the character of lip service. One hesitates to make such a suggestion without positive documentation, but the parallel that comes to mind is the behavior of the audience in the story by Hjelmslev's compatriot H. C. Andersen about the emperor's new clothes. Perhaps the favorable references to Hjelmslev's work are due to a sense of awe inspired by the undoubted elaborateness of the structure, combined with a lack of understanding of just what he was getting at (but a feeling that it must be very significant), rather than representing respect born of profound appreciation of his ideas.

Hjelmslev's view of the structure of language deserves to be better understood than it has been; not, perhaps, because his views and formulations would be assented to if discussed in detail but, rather, because he did raise some important fundamental issues in ways no one else did at the time. His discussion of these issues can be argued to suffer from important limitations. In part, these limitations stem from a vision of linguistic structure which he in his turn inherited from others. The study of this relationship may shed light on the way in which even rather independent work is shaped by the context of assumptions in which it develops. The other side of the same coin is the extent to which that context determined the reception of his work by others: again, the reaction to Hjelmslev's views by his contemporaries is worth considering.

In addition to these considerations of an admittedly historical nature, Hjelmslev's work independently merits examination by phonologists. Despite the generally abstract emphasis of his writings, he did do a certain amount of linguistic description. Although his treatments of Danish and French phonology and Baltic accentuation are rather summary and incomplete, it is still clear that he had interesting ideas concerning what a phonological description should consist of, and what relation should obtain between such a description and the data it is based on; and these were quite at variance with much other work of the time.

The discussion below will thus focus on relations between Hjelmslev's views and those of others, and on the novel features to be found in his descriptive practice. This chapter certainly does not form part of a strict linear sequence with the immediately surrounding ones. Instead, it aims to present an alternative view of the proper development of a 'structural linguistics', representing an approach distinct to a considerable extent both from that represented by Trubetzkoy and Jakobson and from those we will consider in later chapters.

Hjelmslev's life and career

Hjelmslev is clearly the most notable figure in the development of structural linguistics in Denmark, but he is far from isolated in the linguistic history of that country. Especially in relation to its size, Denmark has produced a remarkable number of distinguished linguists: among names from the past one can mention Rasmus Rask, Karl Verner, Holger Pedersen, and Otto Jespersen, to cite only those that would figure in any general history of the field. More recent scholars of international reputation include Viggo Brøndal, Paul Diderichsen, Søren Egerod, Jørgen Rischel, and especially Eli Fischer-Jørgensen. More important for an understanding of Hjelmslev's work than any of these individuals, perhaps, is the general fact that a 'critical mass' of scholars interested in general linguistics has long existed in the country. Hjelmslev thus had a constant supply of colleagues and students with whom to exchange ideas and encouragement in the development of his own rather individual views. The sketch of his life below is based primarily on Fischer-Jørgensen (1965, 1975).

Louis Hjelmslev was born in 1899 in Copenhagen. His father was a mathematician and a prominent figure in Danish academic administration at the time, who served as rector of Copenhagen University in 1928–29. It is superficially appealing to credit Hjelmslev's inclination toward highly abstract, 'algebraic' theory to his father's influence; yet not only did Hjelmslev himself deny such influence, but the sort of work he did seems rather at odds with the specifics of his father's research (which sought precisely to provide a *less* abstract foundation for geometry, grounded more directly in experience than in purely theoretical constructs). In addition, Hjelmslev's own use of mathematical terms in ways far removed from their technical acceptation in that field suggests that any influence from his father was in the form of a general intellectual atmosphere rather than any specific mathematical training.

In 1917, Hjelmslev entered Copenhagen University, where he studied Romance and (later) comparative philology with a number of distinguished figures, especially Holger Pedersen. Through Pedersen's influence he became interested in Lithuanian, and spent the year 1921 doing research in Lithuania which resulted in his 1923 master's degree for a thesis on Lithuanian phonetics. The year after he received his MA was spent (somewhat against his will, it appears) in Prague, where his knowledge of traditional Indo-European studies was developed. He was much happier to spend 1926 and 1927 in Paris, where he studied with Meillet, Vendryes, and others; the attachment to things French formed at this time was a lasting one, as shown in the fact that during his entire career the bulk of his writing in languages other than Danish was in French.

In 1928 he produced a book (*Principes de grammaire générale*) which aimed ambitiously at providing a general theoretical foundation for the study of language. The continuity between this book and his later work is evident from its goal of developing an abstract formal "system within which the concrete categories are found as possibilities, each having an exact location defined by the conditions for its realization and its combination with other categories" (Fischer-Jørgensen 1965:vi). This work was so uncompromisingly theoretical in nature that Pedersen was unwilling to accept it as a thesis for the doctorate, requiring instead that Hjelmslev produce some piece of research more directly grounded in factual material. As a result, he produced his *Etudes baltiques* in 1932, a rather traditional work of historical phonology dealing with Baltic phonology and especially with the principles governing suprasegmental factors in these languages: tone, accent, and quantity. Aside from earning him a doctorate, this study also served as a source of examples defining important research problems in his later work.

During the same period, he also undertook (by request) the editing of the manuscripts and other writings of Rasmus Rask. He published three volumes of Rask's manuscripts (in 1932, 1933, and 1935) with commentary. A final volume, consisting of Rask's letters and further commentary, was published much later by his student Marie Bjerrum. Hjelmslev was obviously fascinated by Rask both personally and intellectually: he considered that the general evaluation of this scholar was completely misguided, and argued in a paper given in Paris in 1950 (published in 1951) that the major goal of Rask's work, especially toward the end of his rather short life, was not the development of historical linguistics (the connection in which his name is generally cited), but the development of a general typology of linguistic structure in terms of which a basically ahistorical comparison of languages would be possible.

There is a certain amount of anachronism in the resulting picture of Rask as a pioneer of structuralism, but probably less than is claimed by Diderichsen (1960) in his attack on Hjelmslev's interpretation. The central issue in this controversy has been whether Rask had a clear notion of the difference between typological and genetic comparison as the basis for discussing linguistic relationships. Though he probably did not, and thus should not be credited with an explicit theory of synchronic linguistic structure, his interest seems clearly to have been in the question of how languages are to be compared with one another, and not simply in how they evolve. Unfortunately, Rask fits too conveniently into the conventional wisdom about the development of comparative historical linguistics in the nineteenth century, and (outside of a narrow circle of specialists) Hjelmslev's view, based on a serious and extended study of all of the available material, has not been seriously integrated into standard histories of the field.

Hjelmslev's work in phonology can be said to date from 1931, the year of the International Congress of Linguists in Geneva. At that meeting the phonologists of the Prague school were actively proselytizing for their novel approach to sound structure (see chapter 4 above). One result of this was the formation of 'phonological committees' in various research centers; and Hjelmslev participated in the creation of such a committee in Copenhagen under the auspices of the Linguistic Circle of Copenhagen (also founded in 1931, with Hjelmslev as an active initial member). The initial goal of this committee was to produce a phonological description of Danish, but Hjelmslev's work tended more toward the creation of a general theory of sound structure (and of language in general), especially after he began to work together with Hans Jørgen Uldall.

Uldall, born in 1907, had studied English in Copenhagen with Jespersen and, in 1927, in London with Daniel Jones. After teaching briefly in Capetown (where he substituted for D. M. Beach at the remarkably young age of twenty-two) and London, he went to the United States in 1930 to do fieldwork on American Indian languages under Boas. While there, he worked especially on Maidu; he received his MA from Columbia under Boas's supervision in 1933, and returned to Copenhagen (where he had no real job awaiting him, a problem that was to plague him for most of his professional life).

The collaboration between Hjelmslev and Uldall began shortly after his return, within the context of the 'phonological committee'. Its first concrete result was a paper 'On the Principles of Phonematics', presented to the International Congress of Phonetic Sciences in London in 1935. While the picture of 'phonematics' presented in this paper is quite close in spirit to Praguian 'phonology', it also diverges quite clearly in important details. For instance, Hjelmslev and Uldall reject both the sort of psychological definition of phonemes (as the 'psychological equivalent of a speech sound' or as the 'intention' underlying realized speech) characteristic of the very earliest Prague school work under the influence of Baudouin de Courtenay, and also any sort of purely phonetic definition which would identify phonemes with external physical properties of the speech event. Instead, they require that phonemes be defined exclusively by criteria of distribution, alternation, etc., within the linguistic pattern, as foreshadowed already in Hjelmslev's earlier *Principes de grammaire générale*.

The differences between Hjelmslev's views and those of the Prague phonologists were quite explicit; indeed, this is a point Hjelmslev insisted on many times. Virtually all of his papers dealing with sound structure contain at least as an aside, and sometimes as the main point, a reproof of 'phonology' as making an important conceptual mistake in basing its analysis on considerations of substance—especially on phonetic properties. Hjelmslev's interaction with both Trubetzkoy and Jakobson involved a considerable amount of mutual criticism, though it was never especially bitter or personal in tone on either side. Relations between glossematics and other forms of structural linguistics seem never to have been particularly warm either, however.

Since 1934, Hjelmslev had been a reader in comparative linguistics in Aarhus, where Uldall had joined him in order to continue their joint work. In 1937, Hjelmslev succeeded Pedersen in the chair of general linguistics in Copenhagen (though Uldall was still without a regular job). By this time, the two had decided that their views on phonematics could be combined with Hjelmslev's earlier work on grammatical categories (represented in his *Principes*, and also by the 1935 book *La catégorie des cas*) into a general theory of language. Both felt that this was the first approach to language that treated it in itself and for its own sake rather than as a combination of the objects of other, nonlinguistic disciplines—such as psychology, physiological and acoustic phonetics, etc. A distinct name seemed warranted to emphasize this difference from previous 'linguistics', and thus was born the field of *glossematics*.

In order to give substance to glossematics, Hjelmslev and Uldall wanted to provide a complete set of definitions and concepts that would constitute a rigorous, internally consistent framework of principles, founded on a bare minimum of terms from outside the system. Such a theoretical apparatus would specify the sorts of formal system that count as 'languages' in the most general terms, and also what constitutes an 'analysis' of a language.

The latter notion is described in glossematic writings as a set of 'procedures' of analysis—probably an unfortunate term, since it suggested the sort of field procedures a linguist not knowing a given language might actually apply to arrive at an analysis of it. In fact, the notion of 'procedure' in glossematics is a specification of the form a finished analysis takes, not the way one arrives at it. To say that texts are made up of paragraphs, which are made up of sentences, which are made up of clauses, etc., is to say nothing at all about how to go about dividing up an actual text in practice, and glossematics had no real practical hints to offer on this score. Rather, it was assumed that the linguist went about learning and analyzing a language using any methods or shortcuts that turned out to be convenient: only after arriving at an analysis was it to be organized so as to conform to the glossematic 'procedure'.

Hjelmslev and Uldall kept developing and elaborating their analytic framework and system of definitions, with the hopes of publishing soon a detailed *Outline of Glossematics*. In 1936 at the International Congress of Linguists in Copenhagen, they distributed a pamphlet of a few pages, identified as a sample from a work of this title "to be published in the autumn." No year was specified for this "autumn" however, and it became a standing joke among linguists in Copenhagen. Such a long-delayed but much-referred-to work, supplying the conceptual underpinning for a good deal of other work, cannot fail to remind linguists of a more recent vintage of the *Sound Pattern of English*.

In 1939, as the war was beginning, Uldall finally was offered a more secure position—in Greece, with the British Council. His departure effectively severed the glossematic collaboration during the war years, but the two continued to work independently on what they still considered their joint project. Hjelmslev completed a sort of outline of the theory, but felt he ought not to publish it in Uldall's absence (it was ultimately published in 1975, as a *Résumé of a Theory of Language*). Instead, he produced in 1943 a sort of introduction to the theory and its conceptual basis, under the title *Omkring sprogteoriens grundlæggelse* (translated into English in 1953 with some minor revisions as *Prolegomena to a Theory of Language*).

Though Hjelmslev at least claimed to regard this as a sort of 'popular' work, indeed a work of "vulgarization", it is surely one of the densest and least readable works ever produced in linguistics. It is largely through this book (and reviews of it), however, that linguists outside Hjelmslev's immediate circle came to know anything about the substance of glossematics. In 1952, he taught in the Linguistic Society of America's Summer Linguistic Institute, where he had an opportunity to present his views to a North American audience. This event certainly made glossematics better known outside Europe, but does not appear to have produced many converts to the theory.

Hjelmslev and Uldall continued to work independently on the theory over the following years, but were unable to spend much time together. Uldall was briefly in London, and held a succession of positions in Argentina, Edinburgh, and later in Nigeria; he was able to spend 1951–52 in Copenhagen, but by this time it appears that his and Hjelmslev's views had come to diverge significantly. They still hoped to bring out a unified *Outline of Glossematics*; in fact, Uldall published part 1 of such a work in 1957, but Hjelmslev found himself unable to write his proposed part 2 on the basis of Uldall's presentation. Uldall himself died of a heart attack in 1957; and Hjelmslev's own time during the 1950s and early 1960s was increasingly devoted to university administrative tasks rather than to the further development of glossematics. Though he produced a number of papers on particular topics, including at least one (*La stratification du langage*, 1954) with a general scope, he never published any more comprehensive description of his theory beyond that in the *Prolegomena*. He died in 1965.

Hjelmslev's notion of an 'immanent' linguistics

Following de Saussure, Hjelmslev regarded languages as a class of sign systems: the essence of a language is to define a system of correspondences between sound and sense. The analysis of a language, then, involves describing each of these two *planes* and their interconnections. The domain of the Saussurian *signifié*—the 'meanings' of signs—Hjelmslev calls the plane of *content*, while the domain of the *signifiant* is the plane of *expression*. Each of these planes in any given language has its own structure: words (or morpheme-sized units, to reduce attention to elements the size of a minimal sign) are realized by a sequence of segments in the expression plane; and their meanings can be regarded as combinations of smaller componential units in the plane of content. Importantly, these two analyses of the sign are not conformal, in the sense that units of expression are not related in a one-to-one fashion to units of content. The word /ram/ in English can be regarded as a sequence of /r/ plus /a/ plus /m/ in the plane of expression, and as the combination of (male) and (sheep) in the plane of content, but there is no detailed correspondence between the two analyses.

Hjelmslev considered that previous (and contemporary) linguistics had failed to provide an analysis of either content or expression in terms of its own, strictly linguistic or *immanent* structure. In particular, the linguistic analysis of content had been directed toward an account of linguistic categories of meaning based on general aspects of human mental or psychological organization; while the analysis of expression had attempted to reduce this aspect of linguistic structure to the study of general acoustics or physiological phonetics. In his opinion, other linguists were attempting to study the categories of language as special cases of more general domains, each of which (in particular, psychology and phonetics) constituted a more comprehensive field that was in principle independent of the special properties of language.

For Hjelmslev, all such moves are fundamentally mistaken, in that they obscure or deny the specifically *linguistic* character of language. The only way to study language in its own right, according to him, was to develop a notion of linguistic structure completely independent of the specifics of either phonetic realization or concrete intentional meanings. The radicalism of Hjelmslev's project lies in its seemingly paradoxical proposal to study systems of correspondence between sound and meaning with methods that are to be completely independent of either sounds or meanings. His critics, needless to say, did not fail to point out and even exaggerate the apparent contradictions of such an approach.

We will discuss the basis and justifiability of this program below. At this point it is worth pointing out, however, that in embracing it Hjelmslev became the first modern linguist to campaign specifically against the notion that 'naturalness' in linguistics is to be achieved by reducing facts of linguistic structure to facts from other, not specifically linguistic, domains. This issue was often ignored in later structuralist discussion, or misstated (as when Hjelmslev is cited simply as advocating the analysis of linguistic structure without appeal to meaning, ignoring the fact that phonetic facts are in his terms just as irrelevant as semantic ones).

Indeed, in the strongly positivistic atmosphere of scientific studies in the

1930s, 1940s and 1950s, it seemed hard to take seriously an approach to language that renounced at the start a foundation in operational, verifiable external facts. It would, in fact, be a mistake to equate the kind of program against which Hjelmslev was actually reacting, one that saw the goal of linguistics as the reduction of language to nonlinguistic principles, with empiricist approaches to the field in general. In advocating the complete independence of linguistics from both semantics and (more importantly) phonetics, however, Hjelmslev left few substantive points of contact between his view of glossematics and the empiricist linguistics of his time—except for an appeal to rigor and explicitness, a kind of 'motherhood' issue that no linguist could possibly fail to applaud. The fundamental presuppositions about the role of 'naturalness' in linguistic structure against which Hjelmslev aimed his appeal for an immanent linguistics were not really discussed by most of his critics. These concerns would reappear later, however, in the context of post-*Sound Pattern of English* generative phonology under conditions that make substantive discussion easier to engage (see chapter 13 below, and Anderson 1981).

Hjelmslev argues for the independence of linguistics from external considerations (at least from the phonetic facts that might be thought to play an essential role in the plane of expression) by claiming that in fact the same linguistic *system* can be realized in radically different media. In particular, the linguistic system of a given language can be realized either orally, in the sounds studied by phoneticians, or orthographically, by symbols of an alphabet. Even within the limits of phonetic realization, he suggests that arbitrary replacements of one phonetic segment by another (so long as the same number of contrasts remain, and the pattern of distribution, alternation, etc., of contrasting elements stays the same) would have no effect on the system. If [t] and [m] were systematically interchanged in all German words, he suggests, the result would still be identically the same system as that of standard German.

Additionally, the same system could be realized in systems of manual signs, flag signals, morse code, etc.: a potentially limitless range of ways to express what would remain in its essence the same linguistic system. If this is indeed the case, the system itself can obviously have no intrinsic connection with phonetic reality (to the exclusion of other possible realizations). Reviewers and others discussing glossematics replied that (a) orthographic and other systems are obviously secondary in character, parasitic on the nature of spoken language and developed only long after spoken language had arisen; and (b) in any event, such systems do not in general display the 'same' system as spoken language.

To the first of these objections Hjelmslev replied that the historically secondary character of writing, etc., is irrelevant, because what is important is the *possibility* of realizing the system in another medium, not the fact of whether this possibility was or was not realized at some specific time. As to the supposedly derivative character of writing, Hjelmslev quite simply denied that writing was invented as a way of representing (phonetically prior) speech: he maintained that writing represented an independent analysis of the expression system of language. If sound and writing both serve as realizations of the same system of elements composing the expression side of signs, it is only natural that they should show close correspondences; but the lack of detailed isomorphism between the concrete facts of phonetics and orthography in all known writing systems, together with our obvious lack of knowledge of the specific motivation and procedures of the inventors of writing, make the point at least moot.

The content of the second objection noted above is that when one studies the system of, for example, English writing in Latin characters, one arrives at a rather different system than when one studies English phonetics. Written English does not have contrastive stress (or any stress at all, for that matter); it makes some contrasts spoken English does not (e.g., *two* vs. *too* vs. *to*), and vice versa (e.g. *read* [rijd] vs. *read* [rɛd]); the distinctive features of the letters involved (insofar as this notion can be carried over into such a domain) establish rather different candidates for the status of natural class than do phonetic criteria; and so forth. Again, it is possible to argue that this is beside the point: Hjelmslev was quite ready to concede that in practice rather different systems of expression form (e.g., those corresponding to phonetic and to written norms) might be matched to the same system of content form as variants of the 'same' language; but what matters is the fact that in principle it would be *possible* to develop a writing system that would mirror the same system of expression as that operative in a given spoken language. Indeed, an adequate system of phonemic transcription (perhaps representing phonemes as graphic feature complexes, somewhat along the lines of the Korean Hangyul orthography) would serve to make Hjelmslev's point in principle.

Discussion of Hjelmslev's views in the literature, thus, cannot really be said to have effectively refuted his position on the independence of linguistic structure from external considerations. It would have been to the point, perhaps, to question whether it is really accurate to say that the character of the system would remain unchanged if arbitrary substitutions were made in the realizations of its elements. After all, the whole thrust of neogrammarian explanation had been that the character of a synchronic state of language results from the cumulative history of its accidental details. If such a state represents a system, indeed, that fact must in some way grow out of a combination of specific particulars; and those particulars must have an influence on the development and maintenance of the system's internal equilibrium. Though such an exclusively historical view of language largely disappeared (outside of some Indo-Europeanist circles, at least) with the rise of structuralism, most linguists would still agree that the working of sound change and analogy (both crucially, though not exclusively, based in the details of the external form of signs) contribute to the formation of the linguistic system. If that is so, arbitrary changes in the external form of its signs could not be said to leave the system of a language essentially unchanged. The principal objections made to Hjelmslev's radical position do not seem to have been based on grounds such as these, however.

Basic terms of glossematic analysis

To make explicit the separation he intended between the system and its manifestation, Hjelmslev proposed a system of terms that has not always been well understood since. Fischer-Jørgensen (1966, 1975) discusses and clarifies this terminology and its history. First of all, he proposed to distinguish between linguistic *form* and linguistic *substance*: 'form' is the array of purely abstract, relational categories that make up the systems of expression and of content in a given language, while 'substance' is constituted by some specific manifestation of these formal elements. Since the system itself is independent of any concrete manifestation, and any such manifestation only has a *linguistic* reality insofar as there is a system underlying it, Hjelmslev maintained that "substance presupposes form but not vice versa." Although by the logic of the terms in question this proposition is essentially tautologous, it was considered one of his most controversial assertions. This is, of course, because it is in this claim that the independence of linguistic structure from phonetic (and semantic) reality becomes concrete.

A particular linguistic substance is regarded as the manifestation of a given linguistic form in a particular *purport*. This latter is a kind of 'raw material' subject to being used for linguistic purposes, but which has no linguistic character in itself unless shaped by a linguistic form into a linguistic substance. Hjelmslev uses the image of a net (representing form) casting shadows on a surface (the purport) and thereby dividing it into individual cells or areas (the elements of substance). The complete range of human vocal possibilities (considered as a multidimensional continuum) constitute one sort of linguistic purport, which can substantiate the manifestation of a linguistic form (e.g., the sound pattern of English) in a substance (roughly, the 'phonemic' system of English in structuralist terms). In the nature of things, the same purport may be formed into different substance by different systems (e.g., the same space of vocal possibilities is organized differently by different languages), just as the same form may be 'projected' onto different purport to yield different substances (as when both phonetic and orthographic manifestations can serve to substantiate the system of expression of the same language).

The notion of purport is reasonably clear in the domain of expression (given the ideas of 'form' and 'substance' in their glossematic sense), but it is not so obvious that there is a range of potentially different 'purports' available to substantiate the content plane of language, although the putative independence of language from semantics implies that there ought to be.

The analysis of each plane, content as well as expression, involves a search for the set of constitutive elements of signs within that plane and for the principles governing the organization of these elements into larger units. The specific glossematic implementation of this search is the 'commutation test', according to which two elements of linguistic substance in a given plane manifest different elements of linguistic form if the substitution of one for the other leads to a change in the other plane. In one direction, this is quite standard structuralist procedure: phonemic contrast exists between two phonetic elements when substitution of one for the other leads to change of meaning.

An innovation in glossematics consists in the fact that the same procedure is supposed to be applicable in looking for minimal elements of content as well: thus, substitution of {male}+{sheep} for {female}+{sheep} leads to a change in expression (from *ewe* to *ram*), and so establishes {male} and {female} as different elements of content form in English. It must be added that this program of analyzing content form as well as expression form by essentially the same procedure remained a purely theoretical one, with no substantial, extended descriptions of the glossematic content form of particular languages having been produced. In general, the complete symmetry of the two planes (expression and content) was a major tenet of glossematic theory; but in the absence of serious studies of content form, it remained a point of principle with little empirical content.

We can note that the 'commutation test' sounds like an eminently practical procedure; indeed it resembles in its essentials the sort of thing students of field linguistics in North America were being told to do in studying unfamiliar languages. Seen in that light, however, it would seem to compromise the claim that substance presupposes form but not vice versa: if the only way form can be elucidated is by such a manipulation of the elements of substance, its independence seems rather limited. But here it is important to note that Hjelmslev did not at all mean the commutation test to serve in this way: as observed above, he felt linguists engaged in field description should make use of whatever expedients helped them arrive at an analysis (including an operational analog of the commutation test, if that proved useful), but that the validation of the analysis was completely ex post facto, and not to be found in the procedures by which it was arrived at. In other words, the analysis could perfectly well come to the analyst fully formed in a dream: the role of the commutation test was to demonstrate its correctness as a formal system underlying a particular association of content substance and expression substance.

The goal of linguistics, in glossematic terms, is the development of an 'algebra' (or notational system) within which all possible linguistic systems can be expressed. Such a theory specifies the range of abstract possibilities for the systems of expression form and content form in all languages, independent of particular manifestations of such systems in specific substance. Each of the 'grammars' specified by such a theory is simply a network of relationally defined formal elements: a set of categories available for forming suitable purport into substance.

The elements of such a network are themselves defined entirely by their distinctness within the system (their commutability), and by their possibilities of combination, distribution, alternation, etc. The element of English expression form which we identify with the phoneme /t/, thus, is not definitionally a voiceless dental stop but, rather, something that is distinct from /p/, /d/, /n/, etc.; that occurs initially, finally, after /s/, etc.; that alternates with /d/ (in the dental preterite ending), etc. The labels attached to such minimal elements of expression form (and to corresponding elements of content form) are completely arbitrary, as far as the system is concerned: their identity resides entirely in their relations to other elements, not in their own positive properties. Such a view is clearly (and explicitly) an attempt to realize Saussure's notion of *langue* as form and not substance.

As we have emphasized repeatedly above, it is this complete independence between linguistic form and its manifestation in substance that is both the hallmark and the most controversial aspect of Hjelmslev's view of language. Taken in a maximally literal sense, for instance, this separation seems to preclude any sort of even halfway coherent analysis of actual languages: if we ignore 'substance', how are we to identify the initial and final variants of a single phonetic type (e.g., [k])? Indeed, how can we even identify initial [k] when followed by [i] with the [k] which is followed by [u]? If we carry out a consistent analysis based on identifying elements only by their possibility of commuting with others under given distributional conditions, we arrive at an analysis in which, for example, there are ten contrasting units initially before [i], eight initially before [u], and six finally; but what basis do we have for identifying the units found in one position with those found in another, except their substantive (phonetic) resemblance?

For Hjelmslev, the answer to this problem did not lie in conditions on the possible form of grammars. In the general case, a variety of different forms will be available for the same set of concrete linguistic facts. The theoretical validity of any proposed formal interpretation of a linguistic system is assured by the fact that (a) it satisfies the commutation test (in that exactly those changes in one plane that result in changes in the other are registered as changes between distinct elements of the system), and (b) it satisfies the oddly named 'empirical principle' in that the system itself is internally consistent, exhaustive (i.e., accounts for all of the facts), and as simple as possible (in that it posits a minimal number of constitutent elements in each plane). We will return to the 'empirical principle' (and especially to the notion of simplicity it contains) below; for the moment, it is sufficient to note that this principle considerably underdetermines the formal interpretation of a given linguistic usage.

The solution to the problem of providing a phonetically plausible formal interpretation of a given usage lies rather in the way in which a linguist matches a potential formal system (selected from the range of possibilities given by the theory) to match that usage. The linguist chooses that one of the formal possibilities which is most *appropriate* to the substance, in that it provides the best and most straightforward match between formal and substantive categories. Thus, there is nothing in the nature of linguistic form that *requires* the linguist to choose the 'right' system (as long as the system he chooses is one that satisfies the empirical principle, and accounts for commutation)—but there is nothing in the theory that *prevents* him from doing so, either. The principles that govern the appropriateness of particular formal interpretations of linguistic usage fall outside of the study of form per se, as they must if substance is to presuppose form but not vice versa.

This answer, while logically adequate, is unlikely to satisfy those who feel Hjelmslev's separation of form from substance is too radical. On the one hand, he is undoubtedly correct in insisting that the system of language is centrally governed by properly *linguistic* principles, principles which cannot be reduced to special cases of the laws of physiology, physics, general psychology, logic, etc. But on the other hand, the categories of linguistic form show too close a correspondence to those of substance to allow linguists to treat this relationship as some sort of extrasystemic consideration, or even as a colossal accident. By and large, the regularities of distribution, alternation, and similar properties of linguistic elements operate with reference to *phonetically* natural classes, have *phonetic* explanations (at least in part), etc.

Further, we see that linguistic systems when expressed in other media than the phonetic show a similar dependence on, and determination by, the properties of that medium. Striking demonstration of this has come in the research on manual (or 'sign') languages conducted in recent years. When Hjelmslev wrote, the only such systems that were generally considered by linguists were systems of finger spelling, in which manual signs serve in a more or less direct way to represent letters of an established orthography—itself, in turn, representing a spoken language. With increasing attention to signed languages in their more general form, however, it has been realized that these often represent unique, autonomous systems that are radically different in structure from (and not essentially parasitic on) spoken languages. An introduction to the basic properties of manual languages and their distinctness from spoken languages is provided by Bellugi and Klima (1979). The organizing principles of these systems, the natural classes of elements that function in linguistic regularities and the principles of historical change operating on the elements, etc., can only be understood in terms of the specific characteristics of their manual implementation—suggesting that a similar understanding of phonetic implementation is essential to an account of spoken languages.

Language seems paradoxically to be subject in its essence to its own proper set of organizing principles, while its concrete details can be largely related to extralinguistic factors. This contradiction is nowhere resolved (or even admitted) by Hjelmslev, but his work has the merit of stressing one side of the question so strongly as at least to raise the issue. Many other investigators have asserted the autonomy of linguistic structure, but few have been willing to follow this proposition in its most absolute form nearly so far. Probably the only view of phonology to pose the problem and a concrete solution to it is that associated with Baudouin de Courtenay and Kruszewski (cf. above, chapter 3): here the extralinguistic factors serve as constraints on the raw material that enters the linguistic system, while the system itself is subject to its own distinct set of principles. As we have already noted, this is more a program for research than a concretely articulated theory, but it does propose an account of what must be considered the most central issue raised by Hjelmslev: the relation between form and substance in linguistic structure.

There are numerous other issues in general linguistics that are addressed by Hjelmslev's work, but considerations of space preclude further discussion here. On the basis of the overall account given above of the conceptual foundation and goals of glossematics, we shall now discuss the proposals made within that theory concerning sound structure, and their instantiation in particular descriptions.

Hjelmslev's approach to the description of sound structure

The abstract character of the issues treated thus far in the present chapter and their distance from actual empirical descriptions of particular language data are completely typical of the writings for which Hjelmslev is known. His study of such theoretical topics was not, however, carried out in as near total isolation from concrete factual material as is sometimes believed. His early training in Indo-European studies, for example, involved the study of a range of languages necessary to pursue that kind of research. His work on Baltic (especially Lithuanian) for his doctorate involved direct fieldwork, and forced him to pay attention to a set of descriptive problems in the domain of accent to which he would return numerous times in his later, theoretical writings.

In addition, he developed descriptive analyses of at least two other languages in some detail: French and Danish. The description of French is known primarily from a summary by Fischer-Jørgensen of lectures Hjelmslev gave in 1948–49 (Hjelmslev 1970). The analysis of Danish is presented in an outline by Hjelmslev himself (Hjelmslev 1951), again representing lecture material rather than a finished paper per se. Despite its incompleteness and inconsistencies, the analysis presented of Danish is quite interesting and substantial; it has remained little known because it appeared only in Danish in a comparatively obscure publication. Recently, however, an English translation has been published in the second volume of Hjelmslev's *Essais linguistiques*.

Of special help to present-day readers is the fact that Hjelmslev's analysis of Danish has been presented and extended by Basbøll in a series of two articles (Basbøll 1971, 1972; cf. also Fischer-Jørgensen 1972). Basbøll's aim is to demonstrate the potential descriptive scope of a strictly glossematic analysis of sound structure, and he stays explicitly within that framework in explicating, improving, and further developing Hjelmslev's analysis. According to Fischer-Jørgensen (1972), a number of Basbøll's proposed modifications represent points that Hjelmslev and others had discussed informally and with which Hjelmslev was more or less in agreement.

The sketchy analyses of Danish, French, and, to some extent, Lithuanian that we find in Hjelmslev's work perhaps raise more questions about the descriptive methodology that should be attributed to the theory of glossematics than they answer. Nonetheless, it is possible to gain a reasonable idea of what such descriptions would look like in practice from a study of the material referred to above, especially that dealing with Danish. The few other descriptions that have been produced under the label of glossematics are not, unfortunately, reliable as indicators of Hjelmslev's own views (cf. Fischer-Jørgensen 1975). Within the scope of this chapter, we cannot address all of the points of interest raised in Hjelmslev's work. We attempt here only to give a notion of the dimensions along which his views differed from those of his contemporaries, and especially to present his views as they bear on the central issues of this book.

For Hjelmslev, the analysis of the expression system of a given language starts from the set of elements that commute (or contrast) with each other. These are all at least candidates for the status of elementary constituents of the expression system; as we will see below, however, the inventory may later be reduced if there are reasons to represent some items as combinations or variants of others.

Within each of the two planes of language, the elementary constituents of linguistic form are called *taxemes*. These are the minimal units that can be arrived at in any particular analysis: in the plane of expression they are roughly the 'size' of a segment (or phoneme). The point of introducing this terminology was (at least in principle) to emphasize the independence of glossematic notions of linguistic form, and especially its relation to substance, from their 'phonological' counterparts (primarily the views of the Prague school and those of Daniel Jones). The essential difference is supposed to lie in the fact that taxemes are elements of pure linguistic form, having no necessary connection with substance. The taxemes could, of course, be manifested phonetically: in that case, the units of phonetic substance that manifest them are called *phonematemes* by Hjelmslev. These are roughly units similar to structuralist phonemes, if we construe these as segments given a 'broad phonetic' characterization from which most or all nondistinctive phonetic detail is omitted.

The taxemes can be further dissolved into combinations of prime factors called *glossemes*. In scope, these units are comparable (in the plane of expression) to distinctive features; but their analysis is purely formal and universal, and depends in no way on the actual phonetic content of the segments manifesting the taxemes. The glossemes in the plane of expression are called *cenemes* and those in the plane of content *pleremes*. Hjelmslev sometimes refers more generally to elements as 'cenematic' or 'plerematic' (i.e., as units of expression and content, respectively); and to 'cenematics' and 'pleremat-ics' as the study of expression and the study of content. Since the analysis of taxemes into glossemes has much less systematic significance for the questions of interest to us here, we will ignore these terms below and treat taxemes as the minimal units of linguistic form in each of the two planes.

The taxemes of expression form are themselves defined by the network of relations into which they enter. In his 1935 (preglossematic) treatment, Hjelm-slev divides the rules characterizing these into three classes: (a) rules of grouping, which specify the distributional, clustering, etc., properties of elements; (b) rules of alternation, which specify the replacement of one element by another under specified grammatical conditions; and (c) rules of implication, which specify replacements that take place under phonematic conditions. This last definition cannot be taken literally, since phonematic realization is only one possible manifestation of linguistic form (others being orthographic, etc., as discussed in previous sections). The distinction being made is nonetheless clear: alternations involve two or more distinct expression-forms that correspond to the same content, where the choice between them is determined by conditions only represented on the plane of content; while implications involve conditions for the occurrence of one or another form that are present in the expression plane itself.

These three classes of rules, incidentally, are asserted by Hjelmslev to be mutually exclusive in governing the relation between particular phonema-temes. This would entail, if correct, the claim that two segments which alternate (under either grammatical or phonological conditions) cannot be system-atically related in cluster formation. He illustrates this by arguing that in German the voiced and voiceless obstruents which alternate in syllable-final position do not co-occur in clusters. No one has ever actually examined this claim in any detail; if true, it would be a remarkable fact indeed about the sound patterns of natural languages.

The notion that the units of a linguistic analysis are to be defined in terms of their role in a network of rules is maintained in Hjelmslev's later, more strictly glossematic work, though much heavier emphasis there is put on rules governing distribution than on the principles of alternation. The basic idea is clearly related to (and in part derived from) the same proposal by Sapir, discussed below in chapter 9.

Another influence on Hjelmslev in this regard can be traced in his papers on linguistic reconstruction, an enterprise in which he believed that the purely relational character of taxemes is strikingly shown. The reconstruction of earlier, unattested stages of a language (or family) proceeds in a way that is completely independent of any actual claims about the pronunciation of that ancestral language, at least in principle. The result is the establishment of a system of pure relations, whose terms are correspondences among phonological elements in related systems, but are not themselves phonetic realities. In this connection, he invokes the notion of 'phoneme' as used by Saussure in his *Mémoire*: an element in the system of a reconstructed language, as attested by a unique set of correspondences in the daughter languages. As we have seen above (chapter 2), Saussure's later use of the term *phoneme* in the sense of 'speech sound' was from Hjelmslev's point of view diametrically opposed to this, but in fact Hjelmslev had read the *Mémoire* and been impressed with it long before he devoted serious attention to Saussure's work in general linguistics.

While the distinctions among expression taxemes are purely formal and relational, they usually correspond to surface phonetic differences as well. This is not always the case, however, since substance (here, phonetics) does not alone indicate what is most important about an element of the linguistic system: its function, or role in the system of relations. For instance, in his description of French, Hjelmslev notes that schwa must be kept phonologically apart from [œ], not because they differ in any phonetic way (they do not, at least in 'standard', conservative French), but rather because schwa can be latent (deleted) or facultative (optionally inserted) under specified conditions, while the presence of [œ] is constant in a given form. It is precisely its behavior with respect to certain rules that establishes schwa as a distinct element of the system of French expression form.

Differences of this sort between formal and substantive categories in language show up most clearly when we consider the role in Hjelmslev's system of (a) neutralization or syncretism; and (b) reductions in the inventory of taxemes due to representing certain elements as combinations or variants of others. We discuss these two aspects of glossematic description below.

Neutralization is defined as the "suspension of a commutation" under some specifiable conditions. The result of the fact that certain (otherwise contrastive) elements fail to contrast under the conditions in question is an *overlapping*; the element that occurs in this position is called a *syncretism*. For example, syllable-final voiced and voiceless obstruents fail to contrast in German, and so the final element of words like *Bund* and *bunt* (both phonetically [bunt]) is the syncretism 't/d'.

Clearly, a syncretism in this sense is similar to an archiphoneme in the Prague school sense (cf. chapter 4 above), but there are also several differences between the two concepts. For one thing, syncretisms are not limited (as archiphonemes are) to cases in which the elements which fail to contrast share certain properties to the exclusion of all other phonological elements in the language. Such a condition would make no sense in Hjelmslev's system, since syncretisms involve elements of linguistic form and not substance, and phonetic features are aspects of substance. Also, syncretisms are not limited to the neutralization of binary oppositions, a condition on archiphonemes imposed somewhat arbitrarily by Trubetzkoy, as noted above in chapter 4.

Finally, and perhaps most importantly, syncretisms are only posited when there is an actual alternation involved (as in the case of German final devoic-ing), and not in cases where a particular contrast simply fails to appear in a given environment (as in the case of English stops after [s], where only pho-netically voiceless, unaspirated elements occur). The latter are treated simply as instances of defective distribution of certain phonological elements: it is a fact about English stops that, while the voiceless ones appear after [s], the voiced ones do not. Although Hjelmslev maintained that evidence from alter-nations was necessary to the positing of a syncretism, he did not in fact always adhere to this in his practice. Thus, he posits an abstract consonant 'h' in French (to account for the well-known class of *h-aspiré* words, which begin phonetically with a vowel but behave in liaison as if they began with a conso-nant). This segment is uniformly syncretic with $\emptyset$ (i.e., it is never realized phonetically), despite the fact that there are no alternations to support the syncretism.

On the other hand, once a syncretism is established between certain ele-ments in a certain position, the same analysis is extended to other forms which do not happen to show any alternation. Thus, German *ab* is said to end in the syncretism *p/b* (not simply in *p*) even though it does not alternate, since other alternating forms establish the syncretisms of voiced and voiceless obstruents in this position.

This treatment leads to a difference between two conditions under which a syncretism may occur. In the case of alternating forms, related words provide evidence of which element is basic to the syncretism (thus, *Bunde* establishes that *d* underlies the syncretism *d/t* of *Bund* 'bund/t'); while no such evidence is available for nonalternating forms (e.g., *ab*). The syncretism in the lat-ter case is said to be *irresoluble*, as opposed to the *resoluble* syncretism in 'bund/t'. Naturally, the question of whether a given syncretism is resoluble or not is a property of individual forms, not of syncretisms themselves, since a syncretism that was irresoluble everywhere would lack the sort of basis in ac-tual alternations necessary to establish it in the first place.

Syncretisms are divided into several sorts, though the difference is pri-marily terminological. When the opposition between two elements is sus-pended in favor of one of them (as when both voiced and voiceless obstruents are represented syllable-finally in German by voiceless ones), the syncretism is called an *implication*. When the representative of a syncretism is distinct from either element (e.g., the neutralization of various unstressed vowels in English as schwa), it is called a *fusion*; the same term is applied to a syn-cretism represented by either of the neutralized elements, in free variation. An example of this latter situation is furnished by Danish, where syllable-final *p* and *b* do not normally contrast, but where the syncretism can be pro-nounced as either voiced or voiceless. A special case of a syncretism is a *la-tency*: this is a syncretism between an overt taxeme and $\emptyset$. A French form such as the adjective *petit*, for example, ends in a 'latent' *t*. In fact, in Hjelm-slev's analysis, all final consonants in French are latent (unless followed by a vowel, such as a schwa—itself latent in final position under most circumstances). That is, there is an implication of a consonant to Ø in this position.

Syncretisms form a part of the phonological system of a language, and a representation on the plane of expression in which all syncretisms are indicated has a systematic status. When all possible syncretisms are resolved (including the supplying of latent elements, a process called *encatalysis*), we obtain another expression representation which also has systematic status. Such a notation, in which all possible resoluble syncretisms are resolved, is called *ideal*, while the notation with syncretisms indicated is called *actualized*. It is the actualized notation that is directly manifested in substance as a series of phonematemes, but the ideal notation that serves as the basic expression form of a sign. Diagrammatically, the relation among these elements of a description is as follows:

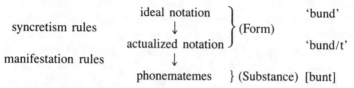

Hjelmslev's ideal notation for expression form is certainly rather abstract. It clearly cannot be recovered uniquely from surface forms, for example, which is a condition of great importance in most other schools of structuralist phonology. His descriptions make clear that, in practice, it is quite similar to representations that in other schools were called morphophonemic, or to the underlying representations of generative phonology. A number of important differences separate Hjelmslev's picture of sound structure from that of generative phonology, however. One of these concerns the actualized notation, which corresponds to nothing in a generative description, but which is assigned systematic significance in glossematics. On the other hand, the multiple (unsystematic) intermediate representations in a generative or classical morphophonemic description have no correspondents in Hjelmslev's picture, since his rules all apply simultaneously rather than in an ordered sequence.

Another difference lies in the fact that no syntactic or other grammatical information is in principle allowed in ideal notations—leading, as Basbøll (1971–72) shows, to rather labored analyses in cases where different word classes show systematically different phonological behavior. This constraint follows, of course, from the fact that such information concerns content, while ideal representations are an aspect of linguistic expression, and the two planes are quite distinct in Hjelmslev's view. As a result, grammatically conditioned alternations are represented as the relation of two systematically different expressions that correspond to the same content, while phonologically conditioned variation is represented as a relation between a single ideal expression form and its various actualized correspondents.

The role of simplicity in a glossematic description

The distance between Hjelmslev's 'cenematic' representations and phonetic ones is further increased by the fact that he makes every possible effort to reduce the taxeme inventory by treating some elements as variants or combinations of others. To this end, he makes extensive use of aspects of representations that others might consider arbitrary.

An important role in this respect is played by the notion of 'syllable' (cf. the following section). Since Hjelmslev explicitly denied that any phonetic definition of syllables was relevant to their identification and delimitation, he was largely free to posit them wherever they seemed useful. For example, he noted that, in German, only [z] and not [s] occurs in undoubted syllable-initial position (e.g., when word-initial); while [s] occurs to the exclusion of [z] in undoubted word-final position. Medially, the two contrast in, e.g., *reisen* ([z]) vs. *reissen* ([s]); but here Hjelmslev proposes to treat the contrast as a matter of the location of syllable boundaries—'rai.sən' vs. 'rais.ən'. In this way the two segments are reduced to positional variants of a single one. Similarly, the small number of superficially contrastive instances of the 'ich-Laut' [ç] in German (in e.g. *Kuhchen*, as opposed to *kuchen*) are treated as differing in syllabic position ('ku.xən' vs. 'kux.ən'), removing the need to posit a rather counterintuitive phonological difference between velar and palatal fricatives (see chapter 11 below for the attempt to represent this difference within American structuralist theory as depending on another sort of inaudible boundary element).

Similarly, a single segment may be represented as the manifestation of a cluster. In Danish (and other languages), [ŋ] can be represented as manifesting 'n' before 'k' or 'g', where 'g' is itself often latent in this situation. Thus, apparently distinctive [ŋ] can be treated as the only overt manifestation of the cluster 'ng'. In this instance, the single segment does not actually manifest a cluster per se; but the difference between [n] and [ŋ] is the difference between simple 'n' and 'n' forming a cluster with a latent 'g'.

Somewhat different formally is Hjelmslev's proposed reduction of aspirated stops [p], [t], and [k] in Danish to clusters of 'b', 'd', and 'g' with 'h'. In fact in initial position, the stops *p*, *t* and *k* in Danish are aspirated, and thus an analysis of 'p' as 'bh', etc., would be phonetically realistic; but there are two objections to this. First, the phonetic fact is entirely a matter of substance, and as such strictly irrelevant to the analysis of form. More importantly, though, Hjelmslev in fact writes 'hb', 'hd', and 'hg' in most cases rather than 'bh', etc., and there is no phonetic justification whatever for this.

Actually, this raises a classic problem which is as real for any other theory as for Hjelmslev's: how far should an analysis go in reducing surface diversity to a small number of basic elements? In its most extreme form, such reduction would allow every language to be reduced to a system of one or two underlying elements, such as the 'dot' and 'dash' of the Morse code. Hjelmslev explicitly renounces any such reduction, saying reductions should only be made when they are not 'arbitrary'; but it is precisely the problem to provide a suitable notion of 'arbitrary' to constrain analyses. Intuitively, the reduction of [ŋ] to 'ng' is less arbitrary than that of [p] to 'hb', but (especially in the absence of considerations of substance) it is hard to make this intuition precise. It cannot be said that Hjelmslev provided any explicit criterion for when a proposed reduction is allowed, and when it is disallowed as 'arbitrary'.

One might argue that, in fact, the principle Hjelmslev appeals to in distinguishing syncretisms from defective distribution is of relevance here: that rules have to be founded in alternations (in the most general sense of the term) in order to be justified. This condition would allow the representation of nasal vowels in French as ideal sequences of vowel plus nasal consonant, for example, as argued by Hjelmslev, and perhaps the representation of Danish [ŋ] as 'ng'. It would, however, prohibit the representation of Danish *p*, *t* and *k* as combinations of 'b', 'd' and 'g' preceded by 'h' (though Hjelmslev does attempt to adduce evidence from alternations in loanwords such as *lak* [laǧ] vs. *lakere* [laǧhe':rə]). More drastically, it would prevent any sort of analysis in which two segments that are in complementary distribution (but do not alternate) are represented as the same underlying element: for instance, Hjelmslev's treatment of Danish syllable initial [t] and final [d] as representing the expression taxeme 't', while initial [d] and final [ð] represent 'd'; or his elimination of the vowel [œ] from the Danish vowel system, as a variant of [ø].

In fact, while the requirement of an alternation to support a rule makes obvious sense in the case of syncretisms, it is not clear how such a condition could be coherently formulated with reference to rules of manifestation—and most of the problematic cases of possibly spurious reductions fall in this area. Hjelmslev does indeed argue for the plausibility of certain reductions to manifestation rules by invoking productive rules. For example, in discussing quantity in Lithuanian, he notes that there are certain semiproductive alternations between long and short vowels; and then observes that the same alternation, in terms of its grammatical conditioning, relates the vowels [a] and [o], and [e] and [ė] (with the first of each of these pairs occurring in the categories that show short vowels, and the second in categories that show long vowels). On the basis of this rule, he concludes that [o] and [ė] should be treated as the long correspondents of [a] and [e], respectively. Since his analysis treats long vowels as clusters of short vowels, this allows him to eliminate [o] and [ė] completely from the inventory of Lithuanian expression taxemes (treating them as 'aȃ' and 'eȇ', respectively). It is by no means clear, however, that similar arguments can be provided for all cases in which some segment is eliminated from the inventory by treating it as a manifestation of another.

For Hjelmslev, the overriding condition motivating the reduction of taxeme inventories is that portion of the 'empirical principle' referred to above that requires a description to be as *simple* as possible. In fact, the meaning of 'simplicity' here is quite clear and explicit: the simplest description is the one that posits the minimum number of elements. On this basis, subject to the essential but unclarified prohibition of 'arbitrary' analyses, the linguist must obviously make every reduction possible.

Interestingly enough, the notion of minimizing the number of elements posited in an analysis has two quite distinct senses for Hjelmslev, with rather different implications. On the one hand, of course, it refers to minimizing the taxeme inventory: it is in this way that the reduction of Danish [p] to 'hb' is motivated by the principle of simplicity. In addition, however, the principle is used to motivate the positing of syncretisms.

This is because an analysis which assigns two different expression forms to the same content form (i.e., which treats an alternation as grammatically conditioned or suppletive) is taken to posit more 'elements' (here, in the sense of sign expressions) than an analysis which assigns a single, constant expression form to a single content form. Thus, the principle that morphological elements should be given unitary underlying forms wherever possible (often taken to be a hallmark of generative phonology, and of morphophonemic analysis) is a governing one in glossematic analyses. Of course, not all differences in the expression of a single element of content can be so treated, as Hjelmslev recognizes: English *be*, *am*, *are*, etc., cannot be described by rules of syncretism in the plane of expression. A considerable range of (often, rather idiosyncratic) alternations *are* so treated, however: in his analysis of French, Hjelmslev proposes a specific rule that makes the sequences 'sə', 'fə' latent before 'z' to account for the small number of unusual words like *os* ([os] 'bone', pl [o] with the ideal notation 'osəz') and *bœuf* [bœf] 'ox', pl [bø] with the ideal notation 'bœfəz').

It is essential to recognize that the notion of simplicity invoked by Hjelmslev is only applicable to inventories, whether of taxemes or sign expressions, and not at all to the rules or other statements of systematic relations that enter into the analysis. This is at first sight somewhat at variance with his overall theoretical premises: after all, the units (taxemes, etc.) of the analysis only have their existence insofar as they are defined by the network of rules and relations into which they enter; so it would seem reasonable to claim that the primary way in which an analysis is 'simple' is in having simple rules. Nonetheless, it is clear that simplicity of rules plays little systematic role in Hjelmslev's thinking. For example, the elimination of [œ] from the expression taxeme inventory of Danish is a comparatively limited gain in comparison with the complexity of the rules which are necessary to predict it as a variant of 'ø', but this consideration is never raised in relation to the analysis, and it would appear that it was quite irrelevant to the decision to make the reduction in question.

Given that the elements of the analysis are supposed to derive their reality only from the rules that relate them, a condition such as that part of the empirical principle which requires their number to be minimized seems quite unfounded; but we must recognize that Hjelmslev probably approached the issue from a rather different vantage point. After all, previous linguistics (including the earlier forms of structuralism with which he was familiar) had discussed sound structure in terms of a theory of *phonemes*, elements which represented in one way or another the minimal contrastive constituents of sound patterns. Hjelmslev argued that these minimal elements of form should be derived in a purely immanent way from the relations among them, and to that extent emphasized the role of the rules in grounding an analysis; but he does not seem to have escaped in his own thought from the tendency to hypostatize the terms of these relations. Though his is clearly a theory that differs from others in the ontological status assigned to 'phonemes', it is still primarily a theory of units rather than a theory of relations in its actual content and application. As such, the notion that simplicity of relations (and not simply of inventories) should play a role in the theory does not seem to have occurred to him.

To the claim that simplicity of rules played no part in Hjelmslev's notion of phonological theory, two partial exceptions come to mind—one more significant than the other. On the one hand, he maintained consistently that the following constraint applied to consonant clusters in all (or at least nearly all) languages: if $C_1C_2C_3$ is a possible cluster, then both C_1C_2 and C_2C_3 must be possible as well. In other words, all clusters of more than two elements must be made up of sequences that are well formed in a local, pairwise fashion as well. It is this constraint, in fact, that causes him to represent Danish [p] as 'hb' rather than 'bh' in many cases: if a cluster such as [pl] were represented as 'bhl', this would violate the condition because 'hl' is not otherwise possible in Danish.

The relevance of this constraint to the simplicity issue comes from the fact that it might be seen as a requirement that the rules of consonant clustering be 'simple' in the particular sense that the rules for long clusters be reducible to the rules for shorter ones. The notion that this is a question of simplicity of rules, however, does not seem very plausible. Hjelmslev fairly clearly regarded this generalization about clusters as having the status of an independent principle of linguistic structure, and not at all as a theorem to be derived from the requirement of simplicity applied to the rules of an analysis.

Another fact is perhaps more significant. Recall that, as stated above, a large number of formal analyses are typically provided by the theory of glossematics for any particular language, where the choice among them is to be made on the basis of which analysis is most appropriate to the substance in which the language is realized. This cannot be interpreted otherwise than as the requirement that the rules of manifestation be maximally simple. Of course, since the rules of manifestation are not an aspect of linguistic form per se at all, it is clear that the requirement of simplicity in the empirical principle (a principle that governs the range of possible linguistic forms) cannot be responsible for this; but it is nonetheless a consideration which would have a role to play in a more fully elaborated glossematic theory of sound structure.

Simplicity of rules, then, may play a role in the relation between linguistic form and its manifestation, but apparently not in the rules underlying linguistic form itself. From this, and the expulsion of all phonetic (or 'substance') considerations from the analysis of form, it might seem that the theory is hopelessly unable to deal adequately with the nature of linguistic structure. One could maintain, for example, that no analysis of German can be said to describe the sound *pattern* of the language unless it treats the changes of /b/ to /p/, /d/ and /t/, etc. in syllable final position as aspects of a unitary fact; and it is only the requirement of simplicity of rules, combined with the definition of the segments involved as a substantive natural class, that has this consequence.

To this objection, Hjelmslev would probably have replied that it states the issue backwards. In his terms, that is, it is the fact that /b/, /d/, /g/, etc. undergo syllable-final devoicing that establishes the link among them, not their phonetic similarity. Different languages containing the same segments may assign them quite different phonological properties (a point made most explicitly by Sapir; cf. chapter 9 below), and so phonetic properties cannot be taken as diagnostic in themelves of whether or not a class of segments is phonologically 'natural'. The very fact that the implications affecting all of the voiced obstruents in German have the same form is what constitutes the similarity among the segments involved—not the substance property of voiced implementation.

Of course, to make this notion more explicit it is still necessary to develop a notion of when a set of implications (or other rules) are relevantly 'similar' to one another; but it is clear that such a notion of rule similarity, implicit in glossematic notions, could be formulated in a purely immanent way—that is, based on the form of rules rather than on the substantial content of either rules or segments. In fact, it was just such a principle of formally based rule collapsing that underlay the notion of simplicity characteristic of early work in generative phonology. In this theory it was in effect proposed that the only intrusion of substance into this question was through a universal phonetically based notation system (the set of distinctive features) for linguistic forms. A perceived failure of this theory due directly to its attempt to disregard the substance of rules (as opposed to representations) was responsible for the addition of the notion of 'markedness' in the final chapter of Chomsky and Halle (1968).

* These issues take us increasingly away from the theory of glossematics, at least as far as it exists in Hjelmslev's writings and analyses. It is worth noting, however, that that theory raises rather directly a number of questions that are less evident in relation to other forms of structuralism, and that would only be treated systematically in much later work.

Nonsegmental structure in glossematic phonology

Finally, we wish to mention briefly another aspect of Hjelmslev's theory which distinguishes it from most of its contemporaries, and which has considerable relevance to present-day work. This is the attention he paid to phonological structure and properties that cannot be localized within the scope of a single segment. Of course, other theories of phonology recognized the existence of a certain range of 'suprasegmental' properties, and in fact the major contribution of the British school of prosodic analysis (cf. chapter 7 below) was precisely in this area. Nonetheless, Hjelmslev is unique among structuralists in the importance he accorded to questions of syllable structure and prosodic phenomena within a primarily segmental framework.

Hjelmslev regarded a text as organized in a hierarchical fashion: into paragraphs each of which can be divided into sentences, which can in turn be divided into clauses that are divisible into phrases, etc. Of particular interest for phonological analysis, a phrase (which can represent a complete utterance by itself) is divided into syllables, and each syllable is divided into segments. Syllables thus play an important role in organizing the utterance: they are the building blocks of phrases, and the domains within which the distribution of segments is to be specified.

It might be possible to give a phonetic definition of the syllable, but (as noted above), this would be irrelevant to the analysis of linguistic form even if such a substance-based characterization were available. What matters to the analysis of linguistic form is a functional definition of the syllable, and Hjelmslev proposes several at various stages in his writings. The one he finally settles on, which appears prominently in his descriptive work, is the following: a syllable is the hierarchical unit of organization that bears one and only one accent.

To understand this, we must of course ask how an 'accent' is to be defined. The answer rests on Hjelmslev's view of the nature of phonologically relevant properties. In the course of an analysis (i.e., a division of a text into successively smaller hierarchical units), one eventually arrives at units that cannot be further subdivided (essentially, at the division of the utterance into segments). These units can be said to *constitute* the chain that is a text. But in addition to these, other relevant properties appear in the text which are not localized uniquely in a single such unit. Examples of such properties are intonations (which occur over an entire utterance), stress (which occurs over an entire phonetic syllable), pitch accents in languages like Lithuanian, which occur over a sequence of vowel(s) and following sonorants, etc. Another example is the stød in Danish: though this is realized as a quasi-segmental element (a glottal stop, with associated perturbation of laryngeal activity), Hjelmslev analyzes it as a signal for certain types of syllable structure. The stød is a property of certain segmental patterns within a larger hierarchical unit, rather than a segment per se.

Such an element that "characterizes the chain without constituting it" is called a *prosodeme*; these are in turn divided into two types: *modulations*, which characterize an entire utterance as their minimal domain (e.g., intonation patterns that characterize questions), and *accents*, which do not (e.g., stress, pitch accent, the stød, etc.). It is in terms of this notion that Hjelmslev defines the syllable as a hierarchical unit bearing one and only one accent.

This theory bears some resemblances to recent proposals concerning 'metrical phonology', at least in outline. Both depend essentially on the notion that utterances are organized into hierarchical units, and both claim that certain properties are associated with units at one level while others are associated with units at another level. The view of stress as a property of syllables, for example, can be opposed to the view of stress in, for example, Chomsky and Halle (1968), which treats it as a property of individual vowels (just as, e.g., height, backness, or rounding is a property of a vowel). As opposed to metrical phonology, Hjelmslev appears to treat stress not as a relation between syllables but as a property (typically 'strong stress' vs. 'weak stress') which is assigned to a particular syllable. Since 'weak stress' presupposes 'strong stress', though, and this relation might appear at several levels, it may well be that apparent differences between Hjelmslev's view of the nature of stress and that characteristic of metrical phonology are merely a matter of notation.

An interesting aspect of Hjelmslev's theory of syllable structure is that he uses it to define the notions of vowel and consonant. A vowel is defined as a segment that can constitute a syllable by itself, or as one that has the same distribution as such a segment. Consonants are segments that do not fall into this category and that can appear in various positions dependent on vowels. The definitions offered are not always as precise and adequate as one might wish, but the view of syllabicity that is involved is fairly clear. Syllables, that is, contain an obligatory nucleus and various optional peripheral positions (which depend on the particular language). A segment occupying the position of the nucleus is ipso facto a vowel (regardless, as Hjelmslev points out, of its articulatory properties: liquids, nasals, and even some obstruents can be 'vowels' if they occupy the appropriate position in the syllable), while a segment whose dependence on such a nucleus has to be specified within the syllable (i.e., part of an onset or syllable-final margin) is ipso facto a consonant.

The syllable as a hierarchical unit thus has properties (e.g., accents) associated directly with it, rather than with its constituent segments; it also has an internal structure which is essential to defining the traditional notions of vowel and consonant. As a hierarchical unit of linguistic form, it must of course first be identified in terms of some relational properties it exhibits, and the basis of the unit in these terms is its role in the statement of segmental distributions. For Hjelmslev, this was an extremely important fact: the syllable is the domain within which the grouping properties of segments are defined, and (aside from special restrictions that refer to boundaries of the larger unit, the utterance) this is the only such unit.

He explicitly denies, for example, that there are any grouping restrictions that apply precisely to units of the size of a morpheme, insofar as this is not coextensive with a syllable. This impossibility is claimed to follow from the separation of the planes of expression and content: morphemes, as content units, have no autonomous existence on the expression plane. Any limitations on the distribution of expression units must thus be stated in terms of properties of the expression plane, and it is exactly there that syllables have their reality. Actually, since Hjelmslev appears to count sign expressions as units whose inventory should be minimized, it is not clear that this consequence follows; but it is clear that Hjelmslev intended the syllable to have this central role of being the locus of distributional restrictions.

Hjelmslev's theory of the syllable and the specific definitions he gave led to some rather bizarre consequences. For example, a 'syllable' properly speaking is a hierarchical unit with one and only one accent; and accents are defined in a way that recognizes their existence only when they are constrastive. A language like French, then, with predictable stress (and no other apparent candidate for the status of accent) has no accents, and thus no syllables. This consequence is typical of Hjelmslev's intellectual style: he liked very much to use the consequences of a rigorous set of definitions to derive striking, indeed shocking conclusions. In this case, the hierarchical unit (relevant to the statement of distribution) in French that corresponds to a syllable is called a pseudo-syllable.

Another such strange conclusion results from the definition of a 'consonant'. A segment only qualifies for this status insofar as its distribution within the syllable has to be specified; thus, a hypothetical language with exclusively (C)V syllables, in which the distribution of any consonant is completely determined by the fact of its belonging to a specific syllable, would have no 'consonants'. The consonantal segments, that is, could be treated as a sort of prosodic property of their syllables. In fact, he describes the earliest reconstructable stage of Indo-European as having this property: all syllables were open, and instead of having 'consonants' in the strict sense, the language had a large inventory of 'converted prosodemes'. This is claimed to be an unstable situation, which led to radical restructuring of the Indo-European phonological system.

Though there is considerably more to be said about Hjelmslev's view of nonsegmental structure in phonology, we close the discussion here. The point of citing this aspect of glossematic theory is not to argue that Hjelmslev had important insights here that have otherwise been lost, but simply to point out the central role he assigned to such structure. Most other forms of structural phonology concentrated their attention on segmental structure alone, and attempted insofar as possible to treat other phenomena (such as stress and accent) as segmental properties. Here as elsewhere, the theory of glossematics occupies a unique position within the structuralist tradition, one which is closer in some ways to that of present-day phonology than to those of his contemporaries.

7

J. R. Firth and the
London School of Prosodic Analysis

The six chapters which precede have been concerned with the development of phonological theory in continental Europe; the six which follow will trace its evolution in North America. The present chapter is devoted to a summary sketch of the approaches to sound structure taken by linguists in Great Britain; but its location in our exposition should not in the least be taken as a claim that British linguistics somehow forms a bridge or connection between these other two major traditions. If anything, the very independence of the theories to be discussed here from either the continental European or the North American models will serve to emphasize the separateness of these two main components of the present book.

The study of sound structure in Britain (generally referred to there as *phonetics*, whether or not it also includes the material called phonology by others) warrants a book-length study of its own, by virtue both of its long history and of the theoretical novelties it presents. For the modern linguist, the aspect of this history that is most intriguing is the theory of *prosodic analysis* associated with J. R. Firth and his students at the School of Oriental and African Studies in London University; but the origins of this view and its relation to the phonetic tradition represented by such great names as Henry Sweet and Daniel Jones would surely be worth exploring as well. To date, however, there have been few general discussions of prosodic analysis and its background beyond the brief sketches of Robins (1957a, 1963) and the critical summary (from the point of view of early generative phonology) by Langendoen (1968).

If there are two features which characterize the study of language in Britain, at least up until the early 1960s, these are its insularity and an emphasis on pragmatism rather than principles. Indeed, while linguists elsewhere would probably resent having either of these attributes associated with their work, British writers have often shown what seems to others a strange pride in the completely homegrown character of their tradition, and its emphasis on the practical and the ad hoc at the expense of broad conceptual and theoretical results.

The British certainly were not the first to concern themselves with the nature and relations of the sounds of language, but (as pointed out in detail by Firth 1946 and Abercrombie 1948) this study has a particularly long and important past in the work of English grammarians, orthoepists, and other scholars going back to the fifteenth century and beyond. This tradition concerned itself largely with the study of *English*, and was to a great extent self-contained rather than developing in relation to comparable scholarship elsewhere.

This concentration on the apparently local problem of the description of English, in the general context of British independence in scientific and philosophical inquiry, was coupled in some cases with personal attitudes: Sweet, for example, had a highly unfavorable opinion of the methods and results of German philological scholarship, and set out specifically to provide a viable (and suitably British) alternative to it. Over time, a model for the scientific investigation of language arose which took its problems, its methods, and the criteria for its critical evaluation almost exclusively from British sources—resulting in a growing lack of connection with work being done anywhere else.

As late as 1969, Robins could suggest (in a review of Langendoen's book cited above) that the fact that neither Firth nor any of his students attempted an "adequate statement of his linguistic theories . . . must in part be attributed to the lack of an adequate challenge to Firthian linguistics during the Firthian period." True, "American linguists were little interested in British development," and perhaps the general level of international scholarly interchange was lower than what we are accustomed to today—but it is at least equally clear that British linguists showed little or no interest in seeking such interchange. If there was no effective alternative to Firth in British linguistics, and thus no stimulus to him to clarify his position, this was because the possibility of looking for such alternatives outside Britain itself was not the kind to be seriously pursued.

The pragmatic character of British approaches to scientific linguistics was aptly summed up by Householder (1952a) in his review of Daniel Jones's book *The Phoneme*: "The European asks: 'Is it true?', the American: 'Is it consistent?', the Englishman: 'Will it help?'" Jones's book, for example, has a subtitle promising to describe, for the phoneme, *Its Nature and Use*, and it quickly becomes clear that a primary consideration for him in choosing among theoretical views of the phoneme is the question of which approach yields the most immediate benefits in areas such as language teaching. Indeed, a fundamental motivation for phonetic research in Britain, from the early orthoepists through Bell, Sweet, and Jones was the issue of how to teach the pronunciation of foreign languages. Benefits for our theoretical understanding of the nature of language in general were definitely of subsidiary (even though not inconsiderable) interest in this enterprise.

A similar eschewal of abstract theoretical concerns for practical ones can be identified in the commitment on the part of Firth and his students to 'polysystemic' analyses. As we will discuss below, the content of this is the claim that whatever sort of analysis works best in a given limited area should be adopted for that area—even if this analysis is unrelated to or, worse, inconsistent with the analysis provided for some other area of the same language. There is no reason at all, on this view, to present a unified or coherent picture of an entire language insofar as particular disconnected approaches to it yield better results in limited areas.

As a consequence of this concern with results rather than general principles, most of the concerns of both continental European and North American scholarship about language have seemed foreign to British linguists—even those who felt motivated to explore other approaches—and vice versa. It is thus somewhat forced to present the development of linguistics in Great Britain in the present context, given the extent to which our attention has been dominated by questions of little essential interest to the major figures in British linguistics.

Nonetheless, there are several areas in which British research provides essential perspective on the work of other schools. First, Daniel Jones's theory of the phoneme provides us with a new conceptual foundation for this element, one not covered by the classification suggested in chapter 2 but which is quite close to the view that would later become the consensus position for many American structuralists. Second, British linguistics has consistently been much more thoroughly based on detailed, accurate phonetic observation than work elsewhere, and is important to an understanding of the relation between phonetics and phonology. Third, Firth's work was essentially the only major approach to linguistics in the period 1935–57, which questioned the central role of the phoneme in phonological analysis. And finally, the introduction by Firth and his students of the notion of 'prosodies' anticipates in many ways such recent developments in generative phonology as 'autosegmental' theory. The similarities and differences between these pictures certainly merit more than the minimal discussion which considerations of space allow us below.

Henry Sweet, Daniel Jones, and the British phonetic tradition

Though we could trace the roots of British phonetic research considerably farther back, a convenient starting point for the present discussion is the work of Henry Sweet, one of the first in England to stress the scientific status of an inquiry into the facts and mechanisms of speech. Sweet was born in 1845; after studying various languages, as well as some German philology at the University of Heidelberg, and spending some time working in an office, he entered Oxford at the age of twenty-four. While there, he began the series of studies on the history of English (especially Old English) which would establish his reputation as the premier Anglicist of his day. Unfortunately, his student career at Oxford had a disastrous conclusion: he was given a fourth-class degree, a result so bad as hardly ever to be given, and generally reserved for those about whom the examiners cannot decide whether they are fools or geniuses. This effectively foreclosed the possibility of a professorial chair at Oxford, a source of bitterness which became progressively greater to Sweet throughout his career.

The series of specialized studies, grammars, collections of texts, and student handbooks devoted to Old and Middle English which Sweet produced between 1869 and 1885 certainly established his stature as a philologist (though they did not earn him the desired chair in 1876, 1885 or—at his final attempt— in 1901), but it was his work on phonetics which is of greater interest to us here. This interest was probably stimulated originally by Melville Bell's (1867) book *Visible Speech*, an attempt to provide a scientific system for recording the facts of speech in terms of a representation of the articulatory gestures involved in its production. Sweet's own *Handbook of Phonetics*, first published in 1877, served as the standard reference work on phonetics in English for generations.

Aside from presenting the facts of articulatory phonetics (based primarily on impressionistic observations), Sweet's *Handbook* is of interest to the modern phonologist in presenting an early version of Saussure's 'phonemic insight'. Sweet distinguishes clearly between two related forms of phonetic transcription: 'Narrow Romic' and 'Broad Romic'. The former, narrow transcription, is intended to present as accurate as possible a representation of all of the facts relevant to the production of a transcribed utterance which the phonetician can describe. The notational system for Narrow Romic transcriptions is explicitly intended to be valid cross-linguistically, and equally apt for the presentation of utterances in any human language. Broad Romic, in contrast, is a language-particular representation: such a transcription should "indicate only those broader distinctions of sounds which actually correspond to distinctions of meaning in language." Though he does not use the word *phoneme*, Sweet makes it clear that a system of Broad Romic transcription for a given language should provide distinct symbols only for those elements whose interchange could (potentially) serve to distinguish words from one another: the phonemic principle.

Sweet's Broad and Narrow Romic transcriptions serve different ends: the former is practical in intent (since if it is adequately defined, such a representation provides all of the information necessary to describe the pronunciation of any transcribed form within a given language with a minimum of apparatus), while the 'scientific' Narrow Romic was intended to provide "an accurate analysis of sounds generally," and was thus "too minute for many practical purposes." There is clearly a relation between the two other than their disparate goals, however: a Broad Romic representation differs from a Narrow one precisely in omitting mention of those phonetic properties that do not serve to distinguish meanings. In other words, Broad Romic representations can be regarded as identifying incompletely specified basic variants, in terms of the discussion in chapter 2. These can (in principle) be converted into fully specified Narrow Romic forms by the addition of (nondistinctive) phonetic detail.

Sweet thus ranks (along with J. Winteler, Baudouin de Courtenay, and others) among those who explicitly discussed the fundamental principle of phonemic analysis well before the publication of Saussure's *Cours*. In fact, it is quite clear when we look into the history of virtually every tradition in the study of language that transcriptions which record only those distinctions that serve to distinguish one word from another within a given language were not only the basis of the original reduction of languages to writing but were perfectly familiar in the theoretical study of language as well, rather than the innovation many writers on phonemic theory in the 1930s and 1940s claimed.

Nonetheless, it would be equally unreasonable to interpret Sweet as a phonemic theorist in a modern sense, since his concern was exclusively to devise a practical system of transcription. The real innovation in structuralist phonemic theory, beginning with Saussure and (especially) the Prague school, was the notion that the set of phonemes (or elements of a Broad Romic representation) in a given language form a system with an important internal organization. It is not the notion of a phonemic representation per se that sets off twentieth-century phonology from its phonetically oriented predecessors but, rather, the conception of this representation as composed of elements requiring study and analysis in their own right. 'Structuralism' in phonology should not be identified with the discovery of phonemic representations.

Sweet himself published descriptions of the phonetics of a number of other languages, and beginning in 1885 turned his attention more toward general linguistics than to his earlier work in English. He supported himself largely through private teaching of English, and served as the model for Professor Henry Higgins in Shaw's *Pygmalion*. In 1902, after his final failure to secure a professorship at Oxford, he was named a Reader in Phonetics there. To get the university authorities to establish such a position required him to convince them of the proposition that "phonology is not only the indispensable foundation of all philology, but also that no department, from the highest to the lowest, can be investigated fully without it, whether it be accidence, syntax, or prosody, or even that fundamental problem—the origin of language." The chair in comparative philology did not, he argued, provide adequate coverage of this crucial area, and eventually his rather limited position was approved. By this time, though, he was so embittered against the academic establishment that his final years at Oxford were characterized almost as much by a series of embarrassing incidents stemming from his feelings of persecution as they were by his actual accomplishments. He died in 1912.

Though Sweet's conventional academic career was professionally disappointing to him, his impact on the study of language in Britain was enormous. In the period between 1869 and 1885, his influence was the dominant factor in the principal organization in Britain devoted to the study of language, the

Philological Society; he was president of the society in 1877 and 1878. As Wrenn (1946) says, he "founded the modern science of phonetics, made it the basis of all linguistic studies, while at the same time becoming the best practising phonetician of his age. He provided the first handbooks on phonetics, the first accurate and scientific recording of the sounds of living languages in his presentations of Welsh, Swedish, etc., in the Philological Society's *Transactions*, and the best treatments of English pronunciation and orthography till then obtainable." He also introduced a notion of phonological (as distinct from purely phonetic) representation, and in general established the basis for subsequent phonological studies in Britain.

Sweet's influence thus led to the establishment of phonetics as a distinct discipline in British universities, especially in connection with the teaching of languages (both foreign languages and English for foreigners). This development was not limited to Oxford; in 1903 a series of evening lectures began at University College, London, on phonetics as applied to French, and other lectures were given there on general phonetics with special reference to English and German. In 1907, a new lecturer was appointed at University College in the area of phonetics, Daniel Jones. It was largely through his efforts that the 'London School of Phonetics' grew and prospered in the coming years.

Jones was born in 1881 in London. During his school years, he studied a number of languages, though his Cambridge B.A. was in mathematics. His father had pressed him to study law, and he did earn an M.A. in this, but never practiced as a lawyer. In 1900 he studied German phonetics at Marburg with William Tilly and, in 1905–6, French phonetics with Paul Passy in Paris. Passy was almost literally a father figure to him: he married Passy's daughter, and it was through Passy's influence that he was asked to lecture at University College at the beginning of 1907. He was offered a regular appointment later that year (shortly after completing his law degree and being admitted to the Bar). Over the ensuing years, he built his lectureship into a substantial department of phonetics. He was also a major force, together with Passy, in the International Phonetic Association, and served as coeditor (later sole editor) of *Le maître phonétique* for much of his career. His London appointment was upgraded to the status of a reader in 1914, and he was made professor in 1921. He continued to teach and direct the department at University College until 1949; after his retirement, he pursued his research as professor emeritus until his death at the age of eighty-six in 1967.

Passy and Sweet were undoubtedly the major influences on Jones's early career, but in 1911 he came into contact with Ščerba, who discussed with him Baudouin de Courtenay's notion of the phoneme (at least as it had been taught in his later St. Petersburg years; see chapter 3 above). Another of Baudouin's students, Tytus Benni from Warsaw, provided Jones with a more extensive opportunity to discuss these ideas two years later. "The immense importance of the theory then became very clear to [Jones], especially in its relation to the construction of phonetic transcriptions, to the devising of alphabets for languages hitherto unwritten, and in general to the practical teaching of foreign spoken languages. Consequently by about 1915 the theory began to find a regular place in the teaching given in the Department of Phonetics at University College" (Jones 1957).

The stress on practical applications of the notion of phonemic representation in this remark is entirely characteristic of Jones's attitude, as it had been for Sweet (and Passy, who also urged students of language to "ne noter dans les textes que les différences significatives"—in order not to "rendre les textes phonétiques illisibles"). Jones goes well beyond Sweet in developing an articulated notion of the phoneme as a basic constituent in a theory of language (see especially his 1950 book *The Phoneme*), but the motivation for his theoretical choices is always practical rather than one deriving from general scientific considerations.

This is particularly clear in his discussion of the definitional basis of the phoneme. Jones observes that at least two different conceptions of the phoneme can be distinguished. On the one hand, phonemes can be thought of as psychological constructs, "a speech-sound pictured in one's mind and 'aimed at' in the process of talking" (Jones [1957] 1973:190). This picture, a version of the 'fully specified basic variant view' identified in chapter 2 above, Jones correctly attributes to Baudouin. On the other hand, "viewed from the 'physical' angle a phoneme is a family of uttered sounds (segmental elements of speech) in a particular language which count for practical purposes as if they were one and the same" (ibid., p. 191). We will return below to the precise content of this view, but it is fairly clear that it is distinct from the psychological conception introduced above.

The remarkable thing about Jones's discussion of the choice between these two ways of founding the concept of the phoneme is that in a number of places he expresses a preference for the 'psychological' view, finding it conceptually superior, yet he consistently opts for the 'physical' definition on practical grounds. "When it became necessary for me to come to a decision between the two, I found it in the end impossible to escape the conclusion that the physical view of the phoneme is on the whole better suited to the needs of ordinary teaching of spoken languages and (in spite of Sapir's experiences) for those who are called upon to reduce to writing languages hitherto unwritten or to improve on existing unsatisfactory orthographies. I find the physical view more easily comprehensible to the ordinary student of languages than any other" (ibid., p. 192). This concern for considerations relevant to the design of orthographies recalls the work of Kenneth Pike in America, whose 1947 book *Phonemics* bears the subtitle *A Technique for Reducing Languages to Writing*.

Jones's physicalist view of the phoneme is not, in fact, one that can be equated with any of the pictures presented in chapter 2 above. Over a number of years (starting in the 1920s) he successively refined the definition referred to above, arriving in his 1950 book at the conception of a phoneme as "a family of sounds in a given language which are related in character and are used in such a way that no member ever occurs in a word in the same phonetic context as any other member" as a definition which is "as precise as words can make it" (ibid., p. 195). A phoneme on this view, then, is not itself a sound (either completely or partially specified, physical or psychological) but, rather, the name of a *set* or *family* of sounds. This view is a physical one in the sense that the individual members (or, as they were called in American practice, *allophones*) of a phoneme are concrete, fully specified sounds—but the phoneme itself, as the name of a set, is an abstraction of a higher level.

We can note that the stated basis for including different sounds in the same phoneme is not their failure to distinguish meanings of words. It is the fact that they never occur in the same phonetic environment: in other words, that they are in *complementary distribution* (American terminology which Jones explicitly accepts, though he does not use it). This was not by any means an accident, but a reflection of Jones's belief that "any reference to meaning is out of place in a physical definition of the phoneme. It is incumbent on us to distinguish between what phonemes *are* and what they *do*. *Phonemes* are *what is stated in the definition. What they* do *is to distinguish words from one another*" (ibid., p. 195; italics in original). The elimination of meaning from the definition thus does not follow (as it would for American structuralist phonemicists—see chapter 11 below) from a general rejection of meaning as a valid linguistic category; it results from considerations of conceptual clarity.

Jones's work involved the study of a wide variety of languages: he wrote book-length descriptive studies of languages as diverse as Cantonese, Sechuana, Sinhalese, and Russian, as well as descriptions of English pronunciation that can still claim to be in their way definitive. His theory of phonological structure, however, is clearly limited to a particular (practically oriented) view of the nature of phonological representations. Regularities of relationship among forms do not enter significantly into this picture, which is founded entirely on the notion of segment-sized phonemes as the fundamental units of linguistic sound structure.

Much of the theoretical apparatus of Jones's book *The Phoneme* is devoted to clarifying the basic properties of the object of study in linguistics. He believed that a coherent analysis can only result from the study of phonological properties of (isolated) words, in the speech of individual speakers within a uniform speech style, and developed a set of terms (*variphone*, *diaphone*, and others) to support this conception. He was also concerned to reserve the word *phoneme* for standard segmental units, and proposed (in contrast with much American usage) the terms *toneme*, *chroneme*, and *stroneme* to refer to distinctive units of tone, length, and stress respectively. The resulting theory is one that, whatever its practical merits in relation to language teaching and orthographic design, still addresses only a very limited range of the general issues involved in the study of sound structure.

J. R. Firth's life

However noteworthy the contributions of Sweet, Jones, and their students to phonetic research, there are few features of their views on strictly phonological topics which would warrant close independent attention in a work such as the present one. If British linguistics in the twentieth century has a clearly distinctive position vis-à-vis all other schools of phonology, this is largely due to the work of John Rupert Firth.

Firth was born in 1890, and studied history at Leeds University. After teaching history briefly in Leeds, he joined the Indian education service just before World War I. During the war years of 1914–18 he served in Afghanistan, Africa, and India; afterward, from 1920 to 1928, he was professor of English at the University of the Punjab in Lahore. He seems to have enjoyed his time there, and drew on material from Indian languages for examples throughout his subsequent career, but there is no record of any published work of Firth's during this period.

On returning to England in 1928, Firth was appointed senior lecturer under Daniel Jones in the department of phonetics at University College, London. Though he remained on the staff of Jones's department through 1938, he was increasingly occupied with part-time positions elsewhere as well. He served as assistant in the sociology of languages at the London School of Economics and Political Science; in the early 1930s, he participated in a series of seminars there with the anthropologist Bronislaw Malinowski, which had an important effect on his general view of language. He also served as special lecturer in the phonetics of Indian languages at the Indian Institute in Oxford.

London University's School of Oriental Studies (later renamed the School of Oriental and African Studies, largely as a result of the important work done there on African languages by linguists such as Ida Ward) had long been involved in work on language, and Firth was appointed a lecturer there in the late 1930s. After a year spent in India working on Gujarati and Telugu, Firth became a full-time senior lecturer in linguistics and Indian phonetics in the department of phonetics and linguistics at SOAS in 1938. To judge from his publications in the mid-1930s, Firth was already somewhat uncomfortable with the view of phonological structure held by Daniel Jones, and he was probably not displeased to find himself in another department.

In 1940, Firth was appointed to the position of reader, and in 1941 he succeeded the former head of the department of linguistics and phonetics. During World War II, Firth's department rapidly grew from a staff of two to fourteen, largely as a consequence of the responsibilities it undertook in the teaching of Oriental languages (particularly Japanese). This development was in stark contrast to that of Daniel Jones's department of phonetics at University College, which "after 1939 . . . was of necessity greatly reduced in staff and output of work" (Jones 1948). While "in the autumn of 1943 it was found pos-

sible to recommence courses on a limited scale" (ibid.), Jones's department
had clearly been eclipsed in importance by Firth's department at SOAS. It is
interesting to compare this effect of wartime language-teaching work on linguistics in Britain with the effect the army language program had in stimulating and consolidating the position of the 'neo-Bloomfieldian' linguists in the
United States (see chapter 11 below).

In 1944, the first chair of general linguistics in Britain was established at
the School of Oriental and African Studies, and Firth was named to it. This
position served as the basis for the general extension of his influence in British linguistics and phonetics until his retirement in 1956. In at least two areas,
phonology and semantics, his thought had developed into distinctive and
novel theories, which became the central topics of discussion during this period (and subsequently) among British linguists. In phonology, his 1948 paper
"Sounds and Prosodies" served to indicate, if hardly to codify, the characteristic features of a position radically at odds with any theory of sound structure
(such as that of Daniel Jones) that is based centrally on the phoneme. Many
commentators date the development of prosodic analysis from this paper; it is
fairly clear, though, that there is substantial continuity between the views expressed in the paper and that of his work in the middle and late 1930s.

Firth was certainly not unaware of linguistic work outside of Britain. He
refers to "several opportunities of exchanging views with colleagues of the
Prague School and other European linguists" (Firth 1935a); he had met Trubetzkoy on the occasion of a visit to London by the latter in the 1930s (Trubetzkoy described Firth to Jakobson in a letter at the time as the only scholar
he had met in Britain who could be called a linguist in the sense he and Jakobson had of the field). While he had little interest in Hjelmslev's work, he refers
to it occasionally (if only to reject its significance) and was evidently familiar
with it. He taught in the 1948 Linguistic Institute at the University of Michigan,
and refers often enough to American work to show that he was acquainted with
its main themes.

He devoted considerable energy to the study of the history of linguistics,
and his 1946 article "The English School of Phonetics" provides evidence for
the substantial accomplishments of English phoneticians well before the rise
of comparative Indo-European philology in Germany. In a 1949 paper, he discusses the relation between British and American linguistics—but devotes
much of his attention to eighteenth-century writings on language by Benjamin
Franklin, Noah Webster, and Lindley Murray. Firth clearly saw Sweet as his
major inspiration in the earlier tradition (and he certainly shared with Sweet at
least a caustic attitude toward German scholarship), though it is hard to find
substantial points of comparison between them. Despite his acquaintance both
with the history of the field and with contemporary work in linguistics being
done outside Britain, Firth's own theoretical position remained essentially *sui
generis*.

Firth's writings on general linguistics (and on phonology in particular) are nearly Delphic in character. Even the papers one might most expect to present systematic expositions of his theoretical position, such as Firth (1948a, 1957b), are full of obscure and allusive references and completely unclear on essential points. His students were perfectly aware of this characteristic of his writing: indeed, they often seem to take a perverse pride in Firth's very lack of clarity.

Firth's influence can hardly be attributed to his published work. Nonetheless, while this work does not come close to presenting a unified theory of linguistics (or even of some part of it, such as phonology), it is clear that he did at a minimum inspire the formation of a distinct position among his students. Although it would be a mistake to suggest that this represented a closed, definitive theory, one could plausibly ask what important and vital theoretical position ever attains to such a finished status. Certainly the papers represented in such volumes as *Studies in Linguistic Analysis* (1956) and Palmer (1970) represent as much of a substantive consensus as would be found in comparable collections of work within any other theoretical framework in twentieth-century linguistics. Firth and his coworkers were obviously in agreement about the goals, methods, and principles of a particular approach to phonological analysis; and it is an interesting problem to determine just how this picture emerged. We have very little evidence for the actual character or modality of Firth's influence on his associates. His published work is anything but a model of clarity, but he seems to have been personally a very charismatic figure. It is reasonable to surmise that the theory of prosodic analysis that developed around him in the 1950s at SOAS was worked out in the context of the study of practical analytic problems, rather than in any systematic lectures on theoretical topics. Indeed, it is much easier to arrive at some notion of what prosodic analysis is all about by studying representative examples than through the more explicitly theoretical literature.

In any event, Firth never wrote a definitive presentation of his theories in this (or any other) area. Though he seemed to have had it in mind to write a book to be entitled *Principles of Linguistics*, there is no evidence that any actual work was ever done on such a project. In his later years, his health was quite poor, and he did little writing between his retirement in 1956 and his death in 1960. The presentation of his views which follows, thus, is based only in part on his own expression of them: in order to form a coherent picture of his theory of phonology, it is necessary to infer the characteristics of such a theory from the descriptive work of his students. Since much of this body of literature was addressed more or less directly to the issue of justifying prosodic analysis (especially as opposed to phonemic theory), this procedure seems perfectly warranted.

The Firthian view of language and linguistics

Firth's distinctive views on language can probably be dated (as argued by Langendoen 1968) from his participation in Malinowski's seminars at the London School of Economics in the early 1930s. Malinowski at this time was concerned to develop an account of linguistic meaning as derived from the contexts in which utterances occur. The notion of the 'context of situation', in which linguistic events are situated, could be approached either narrowly (as a matter of the event immediately preceding, simultaneous with, and following the utterance) or more broadly (incorporating the whole cultural context of the utterance). Malinowski's own position evolved from the narrower interpretation in his early work in the 1920s to a broader one expressed around the time Firth was in contact with him, and it was this increasingly vague and non-operational concept of the 'context of situation' that Firth seems to have adopted.

Firth took the problem of meaning to be the central one in linguistic analysis—a position that seemed shocking to some commentators (see, e.g., Haugen's 1958 review of Firth's selected papers). In fact, his notion of meaning as applied in the normal sense of the term was not really very different from the conception held by American linguists like Bloomfield: the meaning of an utterance was equated with the function it has in a particular context, or with "the change produced by the sound on the behavior of people." This notion is effectively the same as Bloomfield's behaviorism (see chapter 10 below), with the principal difference being that Bloomfield felt meaning to be impossibly difficult to investigate in the state of science at the time, while Firth took such investigation to be central to the definition of the field. If language is meaningful activity, the analysis of language cannot avoid the analysis of meaning.

Pursuing the notion of meaning as 'function in context', Firth effectively extended the use of the term *meaning* to encompass not only semantic (or lexical) meaning, but also grammatical, phonological, and even phonetic meaning (as in his pronouncement that "part of the meaning of an American is to sound like an American"). Especially for American linguists in the 1930s, 1940s, and 1950s who were busy exorcising the notion of meaning from linguistics, such a move served mainly to raise hackles rather than to clarify Firth's views. Taken simply as 'function in context', however, this use of the word *meaning* is at most eccentric, and probably quite consistent with other schools' conception of the proper activity of linguists.

The 'grammatical meaning' of a morphological element, then, is on this definition simply the relation it bears to other morphological categories within particular contexts or, in other words, the position it occupies in a network of distinct morphological categories. Similarly, the 'phonological meaning' of a given piece of phonic material (e.g., a phonetic segment) is constituted by its function in context of being different from other possible material that could occur there. To call this relation the phonological meaning of the segment is terminologically unusual, but the relation itself is not very different in character from the fundamental relation of distinctiveness posited among phonemic elements by others.

A more important difference from most other theories, however, follows from the relativization of meaning (phonological, grammatical, lexical, etc.) to particular contexts. Since different ranges of possibilities might arise in different contexts, it follows that the meaning of a given element might change from context to context. The most concrete illustration of this point is to be found in phonology. Suppose a given language displays two phonetic nasal consonants ([m] and [n]) in word initial position, three ([m], [n] and [ŋ]) in word-final position, and four ([m], [n], [ɲ] and [ŋ]) medially before an obstruent, where the nasal appearing before a given obstruent is necessarily homorganic with the latter. In that case, the phonological meaning of any particular segment (say [n]) is different in the three contexts: initially, [n] is distinct from [m], but finally it is distinct from both [m] and [ŋ]; while medially in any particular context it is not distinct from any other nasal, since there is only one nasal that can appear before any given obstruent. Since the function of [n] in the three contexts differs, it follows that this phonetic material can take on any of three distinguishable phonological meanings depending on context.

Firth concluded from this interpretation of contextually relative meanings that different systems must be established for different positions, rather than having a single uniform system of phonological (or grammatical, lexical, etc.) elements which are instantiated everywhere (though perhaps subject to limitations on their distribution). The claim that an analysis must be *polysystemic* in this sense is a fundamental characteristic of the Firthian approach to linguistic problems.

Firth extends the claim of polysystematicity beyond the case of contextual limitations on distribution, however. He argues, for instance, that the linguist should start by providing analyses for quite limited parts of the language, considered in isolation. "Descriptive linguistics is at its best when it concentrates on what I call restricted languages. A restricted language serves a circumscribed field of experience or action and can be said to have its own grammar and dictionary" (Firth 1956). Particular restricted languages might be the language of buying and selling in a marketplace, or that of a particular poet's translations from Chinese, or the language of parents in speaking to small children. Crucially, the analysis of any one of these systems could be carried out on Firth's view without regard to the analysis of the others, and with no concern for consistency among the various analyses of restricted portions of the 'same' language.

Even within a given 'restricted language' in the above sense, analyses of different portions of the grammar might be completely independent of one another. Thus, the phonological system established for verb forms need not be the same as (or even consistent with) that established for nouns and adjectives.

Each aspect of a language is to be analyzed on its own terms, rather than in terms of a single system valid for the language as a whole. This polysystemic approach is explicitly presented as the denial of Meillet's claim that language is '*un* système *ou tout se tient*'. A language taken as a whole, for Firth, is the combination of a large number of heterogeneous systems which do not significantly hang together.

Most linguists find the implications of a polysystemic approach to language disconcerting and even antiscientific: surely there is such a thing as a language, including all of the disparate parts that Firth would analyze separately, and it must be the task of the linguist to discover the system underlying this language. But for Firth it was meaningless to speak of a single system of elements underlying a language, which exist in some sense that it is the linguist's task to discover. Structures and elements are not in any way present in a language independent of the linguist's analysis: they are merely abstractions the linguist makes from the phenomena of language use, and their goal is to provide a conceptual structure for understanding language use rather than to present some structure which has independent ontological status. There is no question of the linguist's finding (or failing to find) the 'right' set of structures and elements: only of some conceptual structure's being more or less insightful and appropriate than another for the presentation of some particular area of linguistic fact.

This attitude is not limited to the study of language but reflects a general philosophy of science. Such a nominalist approach, regarding the idealizations of scientific theories simply as names for the analytic categories of the scientist rather than as independently existing aspects of the phenomenon under study, has been consistently opposed to more realist views throughout the history of philosophy. Most empirical scientists, including linguists, tend to take a strongly realist attitude toward the essential elements of their theories. This difference in approach was characterized (or perhaps caricatured) by Householder (1952b) as that between 'God's truth' (or realist) linguistics and 'hocus-pocus' (or nominalist) linguistics: Firth is said to have claimed, indeed, that he was the originator of these terms, and that Householder had stolen them from him. Firth's polysystemic analysis, with its complete lack of connection among different parts of the same language, is undoubtedly the most extreme case to be found in linguistics of drawing the ultimate conclusions from the nominalist line.

While the linguist's description of a language is not, for Firth, a matter of the discovery of some antecedently given structure which exists independently of the analysis, it is of course not completely unrelated to external reality. Rather, the analysis must bear a direct relation to observable facts, a relation which has two sides. On the one hand, the categories of the analysis must have *exponents* in the data: that is, there must be identifiable aspects of concrete utterances which serve to instantiate the terms of the analysis in a well-defined way. This is hardly a very rigorous constraint on the analyst (it means in essence only that the analysis must be an analysis *of something*); but another requirement imposed by Firth is somewhat more interesting.

Not only must the data subjected to analysis provide exponents for the terms of the analysis, but the analysis must be one which 'renews connection' with the language. This means that it must be possible, given further data not originally taken into account in the analysis, to encompass such additional material within the original analysis as well. In other words, if the analysis is to be appropriate to the data, it must be predictive in that it also serves adequately for the potentially unbounded range of comparable speech material which could in principle be observed.

While such a predictive capacity was of course at least a *desideratum* for practically any linguist, elsewhere (notably in America—see chapter 11) much procedurally oriented theorizing took the line that the goal of an analysis was to provide as compact as possible a description of the distribution of elements within a given corpus. Of course, "to persons interested in linguistic results, the analysis of a particular corpus becomes of interest only if it is virtually identical with the analysis which would be obtained in like manner from any other sufficiently large corpus of material taken in the same dialect" (Harris 1951a), but the fact remains that a particular analysis could be validated, on that view, by its adequacy for a particular corpus. Firth's requirement that an adequate analysis must renew connection with the language was an explicit recognition of the unbounded nature of the object of study in linguistics—a point that would become a major issue in the rise of generative grammar in the late 1950s and early 1960s.

Systems and structures, sounds and prosodies

We turn now from consideration of Firth's general linguistic views to the specifics of his unique contribution to phonology proper, the theory of prosodic analysis. Analyses in the terms of this theory only appear, effectively, in the work of Firth and his students in the late 1940s—see in particular Firth (1948a), Henderson (1948, 1949), Scott (1948). In retrospect, however, we can identify its development with a period beginning in the mid-1930s.

It is hardly surprising that in Firth's papers from this early period (Firth 1934a, 1934b, 1935a), he adopts a view of phonological structure quite close to Daniel Jones's version of phonemic theory. He traces the origins of the word 'phoneme' to Kruszewski (not the entire story—see chapter 3 above), and gives as an example of his own understanding of the term a phoneme in Tamil whose 'alternant phones' include [k], [g], [c], [ç], [x], and [γ] according to context. The picture here is that of a phoneme as a set of variants, as suggested above for Jones (who cites this same example, crediting Firth, in various works of his own).

Already in early papers of Firth's (e.g., 1935a, 1936, 1937), however, his views began to change. In these papers he stresses not just the distinguishing function of phonemes, but the importance of relativizing this function to particular contexts. It is here that he argues most explicitly that when the range of contrasts in two given positions (e.g., syllable-initial and syllable-final) are not the same, the functional elements that appear in these positions cannot be identified even if they are phonetically the same. A syllable-initial [n] which contrasts only with [m] is not (for Firth) the same phonological element as a final [n] which contrasts both with [m] and with [ŋ]. These instances of [n] would all be members of the same phoneme for Jones, with some phonemes (e.g. [m] and [ŋ]) being subject to limitations on their occurrence in various positions. The polysystemic character of Firth's analysis (the need to establish independent, unrelated systems at positions in a structure where the contrasts are not the same) is urged quite forcefully, and can be considered a major point of these papers. The basic point is much the same as that made by Twaddell in the same year (see chapter 11 below), though Firth makes little reference to Twaddell in any of his publications.

Firth distinguishes two general aspects of the function of phonological elements. The *minor function* of an element is its simple distinctness from other possible phonological units, while it may also have the *major function* of marking a morphological category. He notes that many vowel oppositions in English have major function: thus, in *breed* vs. *bred*, the opposition between [i] and [e] serves to indicate not only the distinctness of these two words (the minor function of the difference), but also the distinction between present and past tense (a major function). The notion of major function is quite similar to that lying behind Kruszewski's 'alternations of the third category' and Baudouin's 'correlations': alternations linked directly to a morphological property. The importance of Firth's idea lies less in the discovery that some phonological differences may serve as minimal signs for morphological differences than in the fact that, from an early point, he assumed that nonphonetic factors (such as grammatical structure) were centrally relevant to the phonological analysis.

In papers such as "The Structure of the Chinese Monosyllable in a Hunanese Dialect" (1937), we find the emergence of another characteristic feature of Firth's later work. Here he proposes that certain properties of syllables in the language under investigation (a dialect of Chinese) are not properly associated with any individual segments but should be regarded as not 'placed': i.e., as properties of the syllable rather than of the segment. Of course, similar claims were made by linguists of all persuasions with regard to properties such as tone, stress, and other suprasegmental features (in the American sense); but Firth's innovation was in proposing such an analysis for properties normally considered strictly segmental. He identifies, for example, a property of *yotization* which is represented both by a y-offglide following the syllable-initial consonant and by distinctive variants of individual nuclear vowels.

Other (strictly phonemic) analyses might treat palatalization, for example, as a distinctive property of the consonant, and then characterize the vowel's quality as dependent on this; or perhaps take the vowel qualities as distinctive with palatalization conditioned by some of them. Firth maintains that the basic fact is the relation of co-occurrence between the two sets of properties, and this is best treated as a property of the entire syllable rather than localized phonologically in one place (to the exclusion of the other). A similar analysis is offered for a property of *labiovelarization*, which again is realized both as a modification of the initial consonant and as a set of distinctive variants for the vowels.

This notion that some phonological properties are not uniquely 'placed' with respect to particular segments within a larger unit is the beginning of the notion of *prosody* which plays such a central role in Firthian phonology. It represents the first substantial challenge within twentieth-century linguistics to the notion that division of the utterance into phonetic segments provides the essential basis for further analysis, and that the analysis can then proceed exclusively as a matter of assigning particular properties of the phonetic material to particular segments.

Indeed, Firth obviously had grave reservations about the validity of segmentation in general. In two postwar papers dealing with the techniques of phonetic analysis (1948b, 1950), he discusses the phenomenon of coarticulation (the mutual interleaving of the phonetic properties associated with distinct segments, so that no moment in time can be regarded as uniquely representing the properties of a single segment) and suggests that a segmental analysis both ignores the fine detail of articulation and paints a false picture by suggesting that speech is divided into discrete temporal units. He seems also to have been impressed by the possibility of certain phonetic techniques which appear to reveal properties of stretches of speech that are necessarily longer than a single segment. Palatography, for example, necessarily presents a unitary picture for an entire utterance (minimally, a single syllable): if the properties revealed in palatograms are relevant and interesting, he appears to be saying, they suggest something other than segmental analysis because of their intrinsically 'unplaced' character. A number of papers by Firth's students also appeal to palatographic evidence (as well as kymography, to the virtual exclusion of other instrumental phonetic techniques).

The central paper in the development of prosodic analysis is generally taken to be "Sounds and Prosodies" (1948a), though it would perhaps be difficult for the modern reader to see how this could be regarded as establishing a coherent program of research without the benefit of subsequent exegesis such as that provided by Robins (1957a, 1963), Lyons (1962), and Palmer (1970). The paper starts from the observation that we can recognize different domains within an utterance in which phonetic properties are distributed. Some occur over fairly long stretches: intonation, for example, characterizes an entire sentence (or at least an intonational phrase); stress patterns typically characterize an entire word; and tonal elements are generally distributed over an entire syllable. These properties are all of the sort often bracketed by phonologists as 'suprasegmental', but Firth suggests that if we take the possibility seriously, we will find the same phenomenon in more classically segmental domains, such as the properties of yotization and labiovelarization he had earlier proposed in his analysis of Hunan Chinese.

Recognizing this relation between properties and the structural domains within which they occur, we can distinguish two sorts of relations in linguistic structure (a division parallel to those made by Saussure, Hjelmslev, and others). On the one hand, some properties serve to organize or delimit stretches within an utterance. These *syntagmatic* relations between different subparts of the same utterance are what characterize (in Firth's usage) linguistic *structures* such as the organization of segments into syllables, syllables into higher units such as words, intonational phrases, etc. On the other hand, some properties serve as alternative (non-co-occurring) possibilities at some point in a structure, and function *paradigmatically* to contrast one linguistic form with another. An inventory of the paradigmatic possibilities available at a given position in a structure is the *system* operative at that position. The difference between structures and the systems which function within them is a central concept of Firthian phonology.

In providing an analysis of the phonological structure of a language, several different aspects can be distinguished. Essentially, we can identify three components of a phonologically analyzed form. First, its basic syllabic structure can be specified in terms of an abstract pattern of C and V (consonant and vowel) elements, without regard to the particular phonetic identities of these. In his description of Cairo colloquial Arabic, he notes that such a characterization must specify the number of syllables; their nature as open or closed; their quantity; and their sequential order. All of this information can be represented as a sequential arrangement of C's and V's.

Secondly, we can identify features which characterize or delimit particular aspects of this structure; a property with this function is called a *prosody*. A given property may be treated as a prosody because its manifestation extends over a number of positions within the structure, such as the properties of yotization or labiovelarization discussed earlier. Even if a property is only realized at a single position in a structure, however, it is treated as a prosody if its occurrence is specifically characteristic of that position. For instance, in a language which has both aspirated and plain consonants in syllable initial position, but only plain consonants elsewhere, it may be appropriate to establish a prosody of aspiration which is realized as aspiration specifically of the syllable-initial consonant (and whose absence implies non-aspiration), rather than positing both aspirated and plain consonants in the syllable-initial system. Such properties whose location is bound to a particular point in a structure serve to demarcate the structure, and not simply to characterize a paradigmatic element within it.

Finally, after the structure has been specified abstractly and the prosodies associated with it identified, the residual paradigmatic properties identifiable in particular positions can be organized into systems. The elements of these systems (each corresponding to a single structural position, and thus roughly segment-sized in their scope) constitute the *phonematic units* of the given position in the structure. These phonematic units can be called the *sounds* which co-occur in a structure with the various prosodies characteristic of that structure.

This, in outline, is the nature of a prosodic analysis: an apportioning of the phonic data of utterances among the elements of structure, prosodies associated with particular units of structure (phrase, word, syllable, or parts of syllables), which may form systems connected with those units, and the phonematic units which form systems at individual points of structure. To give any sort of feeling for the 'flavor' of a prosodic treatment of linguistic facts, it would clearly be necessary to go far beyond this mere sketch and present some substantive body of analyses, but this falls outside the scope of the present chapter. There are a few points we should make about the nature of this theory before proceeding to compare it with other phonological views, however.

We have presented the nature of a prosodic analysis above as a sort of deduction based on the phonetic material (and the regularities to be found in it) alone; but it should be stressed that Firth and his students did not at all maintain a separation of phonological from grammatical analysis. In fact, actual prosodic descriptions show extensive grammatical conditioning. This follows in part from the polysystemic nature of the analysis: the treatment of the phonology of verbs, for example, may be completely separate from that of nouns, and thus the statements in each part of the description are implicitly conditioned by the category under discussion.

The notion of 'major function', too, introduces the possibility that phonological differences may be directly linked (as in the case of Ablaut or Umlaut phenomena) to grammatical differences. Statements of particular elements in an analysis, too, could make use of as much grammatical information as necessary: in Robins's (1957b) description of nasality in Sundanese, for example, a prosody of nasalization is specifically defined to exclude a vowel which follows the plural infix marker from its scope. This element is not phonologically distinguishable from other sequences not involving the plural marker, and the phonological statement thus must make direct reference to the identity of particular morphemes.

Since a prosodic analysis was required merely to be 'appropriate' to the phonic data, and to 'renew connection' with the language in the sense of predicting data beyond the original corpus on which it was based, there is no reason to expect that it would be recoverable from the phonic data alone. That is, the analyst could perfectly well proceed in parallel on various aspects of the analysis, linking them up where possible and making use of one part of the analysis in another area where that seems useful. As a result, the grammatical and phonological analyses will typically be interdependent: the test of an adequate grammar is not whether (as for most American linguistics of the same period—see chapter 11) it is unambiguously recoverable from the data alone, but whether the entire grammar, once arrived at (perhaps by the application of rigorous procedures, perhaps by divine inspiration), satisifes the requirements that its terms have exponents in the phonic data and that it renews connection with the language.

It would be perfectly possible, for example, for phonetically identical material to have more than one phonological analysis: an example cited by Palmer (1970) is the nonequivalence of *banned* and *band* despite their phonetic identity. Such a rejection of the requirement that phonological and phonetic representations be mutually interconvertible in an unambiguous fashion is a point shared by Firth with Hjelmslev (see chapter 6 above), though Firth's opinion of Hjelmslev was that his writings were mere 'linguistic philosophy'.

It is obvious that the syntagmatic dependencies described in Firthian terms as prosodies are just the sort of regularity that generative descriptions would capture in terms of rules. The prosody of yotization, for example, might be represented by a rule (or set of rules) modifying the quality of vowels in syllables whose initial consonant is basically palatalized. Langendoen (1968) surveys a number of prosodic analyses and provides interpretations of their central features in terms of rules rather than prosodies. In his criticisms of this reanalysis, Robins (1969) appears to confuse two distinct issues: whether rules furnish a more appropriate format for description than (static) prosodies, and whether a description should be limited to the specification of only the distinctive features in a language. True, Langendoen's discussion appears to reject those aspects of a prosodic account which bring out the nondistinctive, subphonemic concomitants of distinctive properties; but this is a fact about the particular (heavily Jakobsonian) presuppositions of early generative work (see chapter 12 below) rather than a limitation inherent in description of syntagmatic regularities by means of rules.

By attempting to incorporate all of the syntagmatic regularities of language into an inventory of static representational elements (the prosodies), Firthian analysis makes certain implicit claims about the nature of these regularities in natural languages. In particular, since the relation between prosodies and their phonic realizations is the uniform one of exponence, it is impossible for one such prosody to interact significantly with another in the ways represented in a generative description by ordered application.

The essential content of the statement that 'rule A precedes rule B' is that information supplied by the operation of rule A is necessary to the correct application of rule B (and on the other hand, information which may be *destroyed* by the application of rule A is not available to rule B). If all rules are represented by prosodies, and these are defined as relations between a uniform level of structure and its phonetic instantiations, there is no analog of the notion of ordering. Therefore, any argument which tends to support the linguistic significance of ordered application is *a fortiori* an argument against this particular conception of prosodies (though not, of course, against the more general concept of phonological elements whose scope is not identifiable with a single segmental position).

In any event, it is quite clear that the Firthian prosodic analysis is entirely a theory of representations; indeed several Firthian papers cite as a virtue of their analysis the fact that it allows them to avoid the rule-related notions of 'assimilation', 'dissimilation', and 'action at a distance'. Regularities are incorporated into an analysis exclusively in the form of definitions of representational elements (structures, and the prosodic and phonematic elements that constitute systems at various points within them). The representations in question are quite different from those countenanced by phonemic theories, but they nonetheless have as their goal the interpretation of phonological regularities as elements of the representation of particular forms rather than as rule-governed relations among forms.

Relations between prosodic and other approaches to phonology

In order to gain any sort of sense of how different in character such analyses are from most other approaches to sound structure, the interested reader can only be urged to consult papers such as those in *Studies in Linguistic Analysis* and Palmer's *Prosodic Analysis* (1970). For the historical purposes of the present book, however, it is important to discuss the similarities and differences between prosodic analysis and some other theories. We make some comparisons below of the Firthian approach with (a) classical structuralist phonemic theory; (b) Harris's theory of *long components* in a phonemic analysis; and (c) the theories being developed at present of autosegmental, metrical, and skeletal phonology.

Comparisons between phonemic and prosodic analysis are fairly easy to make, since Firth (and his students) quite explicitly saw the prosodic theory as a more nearly adequate alternate to phonemics. Firth at least gave lip service to the idea that phonemic theory had a role to play in the design of orthographies and transcription systems: anyone who has read a prosodic description will have no trouble seeing that however valid it may be scientifically, such a theory is unlikely to serve as the basis of a practical writing system. Given his nominalist philosophy of science (and the principle of polysystemic analysis), there is no particular reason to doubt his sincerity in this regard, though he certainly rejected the idea that phonemic analysis had any scientific interest apart from such practical concerns.

Aside from the obvious difference in the nature of the representations posited, there are a number of other points distinguishing prosodic from phonemic analyses. While one might be tempted to compare the phonematic units of the former with the phonemes of the latter, for example, this would be a clear mistake. Both are essentially segment-sized units, it is true, and form systems of paradigmatic contrasts, but the similarities end there. In a phonemic analysis, all of the distinctive properties of an utterance are apportioned among the phonemes; while the phonematic units of a prosodic analysis neither exhaust nor are limited to the distinctive or phonologically relevant properties of a form. Prosodies too may represent distinctive properties: if aspirated stops are only possible in syllable-initial position, for example, this may motivate the positing of a syllable-prosody of aspiration, in which case the distinction between initial aspirated and plain stops is a matter of prosodic contrast rather a difference in phonematic units.

Another important difference between prosodic and phonemic analyses was alluded to above: the status of nondistinctive properties. Most schools of phonemic analysis (and at least early generative phonology as well) took the position that any property which does not serve to distinguish forms from one another should be excluded from the phonological description. At best, it is included in the definitions of the allophonic realizations of phonological units, but it certainly does not play a part in the definition of the primes of phonological structure. Prosodic analysis, in contrast, is concerned just as much with the nondistinctive as with the distinctive properties. Prosodies are defined in terms of *all* of the systematic syntagmatic regularities that are associated with one another in a given structure. In Sprigg's (1955) analysis of tone in Tibetan, for example, the exponents of either of the two tonal prosodies include (a) features of vowel pitch; (b) features of duration of the vowel; (c) features of aspiration, etc. in the initial consonant; and (d) features of voice quality in the vowel. Only one of these properties would need to be taken as distinctive, but all are included in the definition of the prosodies.

The polysystemic nature of the analysis, involving as it does a relativization of the system of contrasts established to particular subparts of the language, furnishes another difference between prosodic and phonemic approaches. In general, the goal of a phonemic analysis is to establish a system of phonemes for a given language: some writers recognized so-called 'coexistent phonemic systems' for limited subparts of the vocabulary (typically, the loanwords which would otherwise be problematic for the regularities characterizing the core or native vocabulary of a language), and at least Twaddell (1935) recognized the possibility of establishing different systems of contrast for different structural positions, but these were both marginal and controversial positions, and no phonemicist would have admitted different systems for nouns and verbs, or most of the other uses of grammatical conditioning made by prosodic analysts.

The issue might be stated as follows: phonemic analysts intended to generalize a single (phonetically based) system across as much of the language as possible, while Firthian treatments attempted to limit the focus of each part of an analysis as narrowly as possible so as to discover all of the existing syntagmatic regularities of sound structure—some of which may be restricted to very specific subparts of the language, perhaps to grammatically determined contexts. There was no need felt for all of these subparts of the analysis to be relatable to a single overall system.

A development in phonemic analysis which has obvious similarities with prosodic treatments was Harris's (1944b, 1951a) proposal to extend such an analysis by the extraction of certain *long components*. Essentially, this is a method for dealing with limitations on the distribution of certain units in the phonemic inventory. One may discover, for example, that in some language clusters of obstruents must always have the same value for voicing throughout, although voicing is generally independently contrastive: thus, /st/ and /zd/ are possible, but not /sd/ or /zt/. In such a case, one can say that voicing is a property which extends over an entire cluster, rather than being limited to a single segment. On this basis, a long component of voicing can be extracted and treated as an element of the phonemic system. The obstruents will now include only a single dental fricative /S/ and a single dental stop /T/, with [z] and [d] being treated as /S/ and /T/ combined with the long component phoneme of voicing.

Such an analysis bears an obvious similarity to the extraction of prosodies, but there are differences as well. One of these follows from the concentration of phonemic analysis on distinctive properties: only contrastive features are extracted as long components in Harris's analysis, while nondistinctive features are just as eligible for prosodic treatment as distinctive ones, if they display syntagmatic regularities of distribution. Further, if a property is extracted as a long component in one position (say voicing, in the example just mentioned), it is to be so treated in all positions: thus, all voiced obstruents in such a language are treated as combinations of a nonspecific obstruent with the component of voicing. A prosodic analysis, in contrast, may extract a given feature as prosodic in one position, but treat it as part of the definition of phonematic units in others. A final nasal consonant may be treated as part of a syllable-prosody of nasalization, for example, but serve as a phonematic unit in initial position, as suggested already in Firth's (1937) analysis of Hunan Chinese.

In his review of Langendoen's book on Firthian linguistics, Robins argues that another difference between long component analysis and prosodies is that "no particular structures are identified with the domains of long components, whereas it is cardinal for the abstraction of a prosody that the feature or features assigned to it as its exponent(s) should either characterize or demarcate a definite structure." Perhaps this is true in principle, but in practice Robins's claim is rather dubious.

If we examine Allen's (1951) treatment of retroflexion in Sanskrit, for example, it is indeed possible to say that the R-prosody he identifies is a property of the word; but its actual domain is only a particular consonant or cluster, or a stretch extending from an instance of *r* (syllabic or not) or *ṣ* (retroflex *s*) through as many following segments as possible until a dental or palatal consonant other than *n* is encountered. The actual domain demarcated by this prosody is in no interesting sense coextensive with an independently motivated structural unit. Similarly, vowel harmony in Turkish may (in the general case) extend from any arbitrary structural position to any other within the word. This prosody does not respect morpheme boundaries (the element *-Iyor-* 'progressive', for example, has an initial vowel that harmonizes with preceding vowels, but a second vowel which initiates a new span of back, rounded harmony); neither does it necessarily characterize an entire word, or have a scope whose boundaries necessarily coincide with the boundaries of a word.

Both in spirit and in execution, prosodic analysis is very different from phonemic analysis (with or without the addition of long components). It is, however, considerably closer to much recent generative work. The emphasis on enriched notions of phonological representation which has produced the theories of autosegmental, metrical, and skeletal phonology has resulted in analyses which are strikingly like prosodic treatments. It is interesting to read Palmer's (1970) comment on Firth's analysis of Arabic structure, which extracted as separate formal aspects (a) a set of properties of syllable structure, summarized as a sequence of C's and V's; (b) the sequence of consonants; (c) the sequence of vowels; (d) the position, nature, and quantity of the prominent; and (e) the clear or dark qualities of the syllables. Palmer calls this "quite a striking passage which may perhaps today no longer seem plausible," but the analysis proposed is virtually identical with that which an influential paper by McCarthy (1981) argues for Classical Arabic, with the exception of point *e*, which McCarthy does not discuss.

Similarly, a classic domain in which prosodic treatment is argued to be particularly appropriate is the description of vowel (and consonant) harmony systems, and here too the same systems have figured in arguments for extracting some features from the segmental core as 'autosegments'. Indeed, the same properties of vowel harmony systems have been used as arguments in both cases. Thus Sprigg (1961) argues that vowel harmony in Tibetan is better treated as prosodic than by rules of segmental assimilation, in part because the direction of the assimilation would be from right to left in some instances but from left to right in others. This is exactly parallel to an argument made by Clements (1976) that vowel harmony should be described in autosegmental terms because (in the general case) it is an essentially nondirectional process.

Autosegments in representations are closely similar to prosodies, and metrical and skeletal representations are quite close to Firthian 'structures' within which systems of phonematic units and prosodies operate. The notion of an autosegment's being linked lexically to a particular segment, for example, correspond closely to the Firthian notion that a prosody may have a 'focus'. There are some interesting differences as well, however. For example, a prosody may extend over several structural positions, just as an autosegment can, but there is no case in which more than one prosody from the same system can be associated with the same structural position, as in the autosegmental analysis of contour tones (which involve two or more independent tonal autosegments attached to the same vowel).

On the other hand, prosodic theory also allows a richer array of possibilities in some respects than autosegmental theory. A prosody, for example, may involve any arbitrary combination of phonetic properties, so long as they are systematically related to one another in a syntagmatic way: thus aspiration, tone, length, and voice quality (realized in different positions within the syllable) are all part of the same tonal prosodies in Sprigg's analysis of Tibetan. An autosegment, on the other hand, is simply a particular feature whose relation to structural positions in the skeletal structure is not one-to-one. It must thus be an individual, phonetically coherent feature (though several separate autosegments may be coordinated in their association with the segmental structure).

Another difference is that prosodies represent general syntagmatic dependencies, whatever their nature, while autosegments represent a particular property with scope greater (or less) than a single segment. Allen (1951) describes the phenomena associated with Grassman's law in Sanskrit by means of a prosody of aspiration, for example, which represents a *dis*-similatory relationship, and thus could not be encoded in a similar way within an autosegmental representation.

Aside from these points of detail, another major difference exists between the two theories. Prosodic analysis, as we noted above, is an attempt to encode the effects of rules exhaustively within a theory of static representations. Autosegmental and metrical formalisms, on the other hand, are simply theories of the representations that appear within a theory which contains significant rules as well. These rules may manipulate autosegmental and metrical structure in various ways, extending or contracting the scope of autosegmental associations, changing one metrical structure into another (as in processes of resyllabification, for example), etc. One consequence of this difference is that the extent of possible interrelation among 'prosodic' processes is much richer in this theory than in prosodic analysis, which has no analog of even simple cases of rule ordering. Other consequences of an enriched theory, in which representations not only are not limited to segmental ones but are subject to rule-governed manipulation, are only now being explored. A full understanding of these formalisms, however, would undoubtedly benefit from a study of the descriptive possibilities admitted by the rather more limited, exclusively representational theory of Firthian prosodic analysis.

8

Franz Boas and the
Beginnings of American Linguistics

In this chapter we return to the beginning of the period under consideration to consider the development of linguistic theory from a different perspective: its origins in the United States. Especially toward the end of the nineteenth century, the study of language in North America was to a great extent carried on in isolation from developments in Europe. This was true in part because of the natural limitations of scholarly communication at the time, but also because the motivations for such study were somewhat different in the 'old' and 'new' worlds. While of course never absolute, the separation of European and American linguistics remained sufficiently great at least until after the Second World War to warrant independent study of the two lines of development.

Linguistic study in the United States by the end of the nineteenth century was carried out within two rather different traditions. One of these determined regular academic studies in the major universities, especially those on the East Coast, and generally followed the historical and philological approach current in Europe at the time. Undoubtedly the best known representative of this sort of linguistics in America was Whitney.

William Dwight Whitney

Whitney was born in 1827 in Northhampton, Massachusetts, and grew up there; he graduated as a naturalist from Williams College in 1845. The fact that his brother was a geologist resulted in Whitney's participating in several geological survey expeditions during the next several years. The intellectual interest of geology at the time clearly made a significant impression on him as the foundations of this science underwent important changes in the nineteenth century, particularly with respect to the nature of the relation between contemporary observation and its historical interpretation. It was in geology that the notion was most clearly articulated that a genuine *explanation* of an observed state of affairs could be founded on a historical basis, provided one maintained a suitably rigorous theory of historical development.

The crux of this theory was the idea of *uniformitarianism* in historical change, or the view that the causes operating in the past were no different in principle from those that could be observed today. Uniformitarianism, that is, rejected exceptional or 'catastrophic' events (a common theme in earlier accounts of the earth's history) as the source of present natural features. Manifestly, the explanatory successes of nineteenth century geology had an important effect on the historical study of language at the same time. (For a discussion of the relation between the uniformitarian position in natural history and in linguistics, see Christy 1983.) Whitney's early exposure to this issue is surely relevant to an understanding of his linguistic views.

In 1849, Whitney's brother brought him a copy of Bopp's Sanskrit grammar from Europe, and this immediately became a source of fascination to him. He studied Sanskrit at Yale in 1849, and then went to Berlin to continue this study. He devoted particular attention to the Vedic texts, and prepared what became the definitive edition of one of these, the Atharva Veda. In 1854 he returned to Yale; the lack of salary for a professor of Sanskrit, however, required him to teach French and German as well in order to support his family. In 1870, he had become sufficiently eminent that Yale was concerned to prevent his moving to Harvard, and a chair was created for him.

Throughout his life, Whitney was active in the scholarly societies concerned with language (the American Oriental Society, the American Philological Society, the Modern Language Association, etc.). He published a number of papers on Indic and Indo-European topics as well as pedagogically motivated works on French and German. Undoubtedly his *Sanskrit Grammar* of 1879 is his single best-known work; this model descriptive study of the language retains significant interest for both the Sanskritist and the general linguist today, and is a major source of information for the details of Whitney's view of linguistic structure (see McCawley 1967b). At the time, it was well enough received to establish his credentials as a major figure in Indo-European studies.

In addition to his descriptive and historical linguistic work, Whitney also published two books on general linguistics: *Language and the Study of Language* in 1867, and *The Life and Growth of Language* in 1875. Both of these volumes were known to European scholars: Baudouin de Courtenay, de Saussure, and Fortunatov among others mention Whitney's general linguistic work as sound and interesting, and assigned it to their students to read. At Whitney's death in 1894, an international symposium was organized in his memory to which virtually every well-known figure in the linguistic world of the time contributed. Even Saussure wrote extensive notes for an appreciation of Whitney, though he never completed the article. At the time, Whitney was probably the one American scholar who was known and esteemed in world linguistic circles.

If we go beyond these biographical details to ask about Whitney's impact on the development of linguistics, however, it is difficult to identify much in the way of innovative propositions concerning the nature of language that originate with him, or major effects he had on the field. He was known less for revolutionary or even novel ideas than for the balance and common sense with which he confronted the often rather mystical excesses of much other nineteenth-century thought about language. He was particularly opposed to the views of Bopp, Schleicher, and others, who treated language as some sort of 'natural organism' subject to growth, evolution, and decay in an over-simplified biological way; and he devoted particular energy to combating the mechanistic views of Max Müller. To these opinions he opposed an emphasis on the social character of language, with the effect primarily of countering the prevalent metaphysical speculation concerning the 'organic' nature of language.

Whitney's main contribution to the field was thus probably in clearing the air of counterproductive, overly biological or mechanistic views of language, and in preparing the way for others to pursue more genuinely linguistic lines of thought. His own work was completely within the framework of the time, presaging in no important way the sort of structuralism that would soon dominate the field. For example, an essential preliminary to the 'structural' approach to language as it developed in the twentieth century is an appreciation of the separation between synchronic and diachronic study, and an abandonment of the view that explanation can be sought only in the history of an observed state of affairs. There is no evidence at all that Whitney was ready to make this move; indeed, his background in the study of geology undoubtedly predisposed him more than most to a historical view of explanation.

Even those who praised him most highly did so in terms other than those of strict originality: Saussure, for example, observes that "l'américain Whitney, que je révère, n'a jamais dit un seul mot, sur les mêmes sujets [i.e., the principles of the study of language] qui ne fût juste; mais comme tous les autres, il ne songe pas que la langue ait besoin d'une systématique" (quoted in Godel 1957:51). To the practice of linguistics in the United States at the end of the nineteenth century, Whitney must be considered to have brought an authoritative presentation of contemporary European work and a rather commonsense view of the nature of language within which more innovative theoretical understanding was possible (though not yet attained). These were anything but insignificant contributions; but their importance for the work of later linguists was preparatory rather than substantive.

Early work on American Indian languages

Aside from the sort of European-derived historical and comparative linguistics represented by Whitney, there was another quite distinct approach to the study of language in North America, which flourished largely outside of universities. For reasons that were by no means entirely academic, the languages of the indigenous peoples of the Americas excited great interest from the time of the first European contact. Explorers and missionaries, frequently encouraged and supported by various governments and private sources, accumulated large amounts of information about these languages dating at least from the sixteenth century. Though highly uneven in quality, much of this material preserves its interest today—at a minimum, for the obvious historical and archival reasons, but occasionally because it represents work of a high descriptive standard, as in the case of Roger Williams's *A Key into the Language of America*, a description of the Algonquian language Narragansett first published in 1643 and available in several modern editions.

Much of this work was conducted by missionaries who studied native languages for the specific, practical purpose of preaching to the 'heathen' and spreading European religion. Similar motivations persist into the twentieth century and down to the present in the work of such organizations as the American Bible Society and the Summer Institute of Linguistics, whose original missionary concerns have led to a great deal of basic descriptive research on otherwise little-known languages all over the world.

Study of the languages of the new world was also stimulated by the general enlightenment interest in the nature and diversity of humanity, given the obvious ethnographic fact that the native peoples of North (and South) America were in most ways very unlike average Europeans. Already in the early years of exploration of the Americas, it was recognized that language study was an important component of ethnography: at minimum as a tool for the practical purpose of communicating with the people under study, and for many investigators as an end in itself.

In the eighteenth century, much study of Amerindian languages was institutionalized under the guidance of Peter Duponceau at the American Philosophical Society (whose previous president, Thomas Jefferson, had also encouraged the collection of data on North American languages) and Albert Gallatin of the New York Historical Society. Both of these men were interested in collecting data from as many languages as possible, primarily for the purpose of establishing a classification. Gallatin's work in this area was further developed and extended in the nineteenth century by J. W. Powell, in connection with the U.S. Geological Survey. In 1879, the Bureau of Ethnology (later called the Bureau of American Ethnology) was established within the Smithsonian Institution, and under the direction of Powell this became the center of such studies in the United States.

Most of the research of the Bureau of American Ethnology during the nineteenth century consisted in the collection of word lists from native languages in a standard form established by Powell, resulting in classifications that were almost exclusively lexical in nature. More or less the high point of such research was Powell's *Indian Linguistic Families North of Mexico*, published in 1891. This work, though extensive, produced little information of a structural or grammatical nature. Such grammatical material as the Bureau's investigators collected was unrelated to the task of amassing word lists, and went largely unpublished.

The grammatical accounts (often from missionaries) that did appear were typically cast in the mold of Latin or other traditional grammar: the sort of description that identifies the nominative, accusative, dative, genitive, etc., in a language with no overt nominal inflection, the subjunctive in Chippewa or the ablative absolute in Siouxan, etc., while paying little or no attention to the major dissimilarities between these languages and those of Europe. It is of course potentially interesting to ask how the categories of one language, such as Latin, are expressed in another; but the naiveté of the work under discussion derives from the assumption that the grammatical categories of some particular model language (Latin) have a sort of logical primacy that converts such a comparison into an exhaustive treatment of the language under study.

Franz Boas

Major changes in the study of Amerindian languages came about as a result of the influence of Franz Boas, who was largely responsible for giving such work a more systematic and less anecdotal scientific basis. Out of this research was to grow a new and quite distinctively American approach to the study of language in general. 'Papa Franz', as he was referred to by some of his students, is generally regarded as the father of the authentically scientific study of language in North America, and this is undoubtedly an accurate picture; but in fact his influence on the development of the field was rather more complex than is usually assumed.

Boas was born in Germany in 1858, and studied natural sciences there. As a student, he was primarily interested in physics and geography and his training was in those areas rather than in linguistics or anthropology. In connection with his geographic studies, though, he became interested in the possibility of an influence of climate on language, and it was this proposition in part that he was examining when he first did fieldwork with the Eskimo people in 1883, as part of the work of the Jessup expedition. Over the following years he became familiar with a number of other peoples of the northwest coast of North America through his participation in various expeditions sponsored by German and British scientific societies.

Since Boas was completely untaught in the field of linguistics, he was at first unable to conduct research in this area himself. On his first field trips he had the services of another investigator, H. J. Rink, a Dane who had lived among the Eskimos for a number of years and who was in fact responsible for nearly all of the linguistic analysis of Eskimo material collected. As his interests became more clearly focused on general ethnographic questions, however, Boas developed the necessary skills for recording and analyzing the cultural materials he collected during a decade of work on the Northwest Coast. While it is clear that he had a general acquaintance (acquired through reading rather than formal study) with both the European philological tradition and American studies of the languages he worked on, it is also clear that his methods and the view of language they entailed were essentially worked out by him on his own as a consequence (and necessity) of the activity of doing fieldwork. Though his first work was in the tradition of collecting vocabulary lists and examining genetic relationships on this basis, he had become interested by around 1890 in deeper problems of the grammatical structures of the languages under investigation.

As Boas did more and more research on the ethnography of the northwest coast of North America, he developed a formal association with museums in the United States, and with the Bureau of American Ethnology under Powell. He had a position with the Field Museum in Chicago until 1894, when a BAE reorganization resulted in the loss of his job. A year and a half later he was offered a position in charge of the editorial work of the BAE, but accepted instead an offer to teach at Columbia. He settled in New York in 1896, and lived there (and taught at Columbia) until his death in 1942.

Though Boas was not working for the BAE, his influence there grew considerably as his competence as a fieldworker came to be recognized. At Columbia he made a major effort to train students to do fieldwork, and within a few years his students represented an important part of the field research personnel doing work on linguistic topics under the auspices of the BAE. With the development and final approval in 1903 of the project for the *Handbook of American Indian Languages* (designed to replace Powell's earlier handbook), Boas definitely assumed the leading role in the investigation of the native languages of North America.

Boas exercised in part an influence of a strictly intellectual nature, since his view of language was passed on to his students at Columbia and thus came to dominate field research in Amerindian linguistics. Through his connections with the BAE and other agencies, however, he came to control the major portion of what institutional support there was for linguistic research in the United States. He had little respect or tolerance for work he associated with earlier, more primitive approaches to language, and he saw it as a responsibility to control research support in such a way as to determine the kind of work that would be done in the future.

In particular, Boas completely rejected the efforts of missionary linguists, and as a result such work was not only not supported by agencies over which he had an influence, but was largely blocked from publication in channels under his control. His own students and close associates were the only ones whose work he trusted, and thus he was somewhat assertive about preventing others from working on languages on which one of his students was already occupied. When Boas had 'assigned' a given language to one of his students, it became virtually impossible for anyone else to find any support for studying it (or even in some cases to penetrate the native community) for an essentially indefinite length of time—even when the student in question was not in fact producing any results from the research intended.

The judgments of the preceding paragraphs on the exclusivity and proprietary attitude of Boas toward American Indian languages (as well as the power he exercised in this way) are undoubtedly overgeneralizations to some degree.

In any event, the demonstrated lack of sophistication of much other work and the limited resources available for support of linguistic investigation surely made many apparently harsh decisions necessary if research of importance was to be supported. The need to make such choices, combined with the extent (unequaled before or since) to which the power and responsibility related to them were concentrated in a single person, inevitably led to the effective exclusion from the field of many whose major failing was not belonging to the circle of those whose work Boas approved of.

As a result, it seems necessary to identify not only the (massive) positive aspects of Boas's contribution to American linguistics, which we will discuss at length below, but also a darker side of his legacy to Amerindian studies: an extreme degree of 'territoriality' among Americanists, which persists to the present. While there are of course many notable exceptions, a great many linguists working on these languages would much rather have a newcomer to the area work on somebody else's language or family than on their own, and feel that once a language has been undertaken by a given investigator with the approval of the scholarly power structure, it is inappropriate for others to encroach on the same linguistic territory—independent of the complexity of the language in question or the extent to which research on it is actually being made available to a larger public.

For Boas, such apparent protectionism was simply the only way to ensure that a reasonable scholarly standard replaced what he saw as the inadequacy and lack of sophistication of the then-existing descriptive tradition in American linguistics. He was concerned that the languages of North America be described in sufficient depth to allow meaningful conclusions about their structure, and also to allow for adequate interpretation of text material of ethnographic interest.

Indeed, these anthropological (as opposed to purely linguistic) considerations were generally uppermost in Boas's mind, and he stressed the accurate recording of extensive texts (often in the face of objections to the cost of publishing such material) as a central activity of the linguistic fieldworker. It is important to keep this ethnographic basis of his concern with language in mind in order to understand some features of his views.

Boas took up linguistic work originally as a necessary tool for the investigation of culture, language being a particularly revealing aspect of culture. Language for him provided a "window on the mind," whose special virtue is the largely unconscious character of the knowledge it represents. By virtue of this unconscious nature, language is not subject to the sort of ex post facto rationalization which distorts other expressions of culture, and an understanding of the structure of the language of a people thus provides a purer approach to their culture than the direct study of other institutions. The collection and study of texts in the native language was therefore both the only way to penetrate the nature of a society, and a particularly privileged way to approach the mind of those who live within the framework established by a given culture.

Historical linguistics also had a similar role to play, insofar as the study of language history furnishes clues to culture history.

Boas quickly discovered in his earliest fieldwork that his initial notion of an influence of climate on language was thoroughly misconceived (and he goes to the trouble of refuting any such connection in the Introduction to *Handbook*). His interests changed to a concern with genetic linguistics and the bases for establishing such relationships among languages. In 1888, and again later, he argued that Tlingit, Haida, and perhaps Athabaskan were related to one another—a relationship that rested on no particular vocabulary comparisons of the usual sort but, rather, on presumed structural similarities (see Levine 1979 for a critical review of the evidence that led Boas, and later Sapir, to this conclusion).

Based on his experience on the Northwest Coast, however, Boas gradually came to believe that effects such as borrowing, independent development of common features, and a general mutual assimilation of structural features within an area were so prevalent as to render significant historical classification of most North American languages impossible (or at least of limited interest) "in the present state of knowledge." He thus became increasingly skeptical of claims of genetic relationship between languages, and shifted his attention from historical to synchronic descriptions. As a partial replacement for the apparent inadequacies of historical comparison, typological studies based on such accounts might provide a valid method for comparing languages. Indeed, it has been suggested (by Voegelin 1952 and Stocking 1974) that much of the uniformity in the presentation of various languages in the *Handbook of American Indian Languages* is due not so much to a coherent and uniform theory of language as to the desire to provide a common expository format that would facilitate such typological comparison.

Linguistic theory and Boas's *Handbook*

The *Handbook of American Indian Languages* marks a major turning point in the study of linguistics in America. Originally conceived as a series of sketches which would replace Powell's earlier survey with a presentation of Amerindian language structures in greater depth, the work came to have a much wider significance than this. Even disregarding the actual content of the *Handbook* sketches, the choices that were made in organizing this first large-scale effort to describe these languages had lasting consequences. On the one hand, the selection of authors had the effect of establishing a relative uniformity with regard to the 'linguistic politics' of the developing field; and, on the other, the comparatively uniform format and style of presentation of the *Handbook* descriptions served as a model for the organization of grammar which was highly influential in determining the topics investigated by later workers.

More central, however, was the overt, substantive contribution made by the

Handbook to the formation of American linguists' views. Boas's Introduction argues persuasively, in concise and highly readable form, for a general approach to language that stresses the sufficiency and internal consistency of each individual language without regard to its adherence to the grammatical or conceptual system of another. Boas's point was that each language should be studied in its own terms rather than examined only through the optic of some other (presumptively 'ideally logical') system; this seems so obvious today as hardly to be a possible source of major revolution, but it suffices to read a few eighteenth- and nineteenth-century descriptions of North American (or other 'exotic') languages to convince oneself of the major change it represented.

Boas's insistence on approaching each language in terms of its individual features would become (as argued by Teeter 1964) the basis for the characteristic position of later American structuralism "that languages could differ from each other without limit and in unpredictable ways" (Joos 1957:96). Actually, though, there are subtle but important differences between the view expressed in the Introduction to the *Handbook* and the interpretation given it in later work. Boas did indeed stress that languages are not all variants of the same basic scheme which could be found in nearly pure form in some one model language; but to say that comparison between languages does not reveal all of their structure is not to say that they are incomparable.

The requirement that a new language be approached without a particular set of preconceptions about its structure did not entail that there is no universal framework encompassing language structures, or that differences among languages can be arbitrarily great. Rather, Boas's point was that no universally adequate conceptual framework existed at the time and, more importantly, that no particular language could furnish in itself an adequate framework for the understanding of all others. Boas's views in fact presuppose (and to some extent, argue for) an underlying system of linguistic universals which determine the range of possible structures of human languages, and which is itself the proper object of investigation for general linguistics.

In relation to sound structure, for example, he discusses the range of articulatory capacities of the human vocal apparatus. He concludes that "the number of sounds that may be produced in this manner is unlimited" (1911: 15), which has the consequence that the set of sounds used by one language does not suffice to categorize those used by another. Nonetheless, "each dialect has its own characteristic phonetic system, in which each sound is nearly fixed, although subject to slight modifications which are due to accidents or to the effect of surrounding sounds. . . . One of the most important facts relating to the phonetics of human speech is, that every single language has a definite and limited group of sounds, and that the number of those used in any particular dialect is never excessively large" (1911:16).

The thrust of this observation is that, while the *number* of sound types available to natural languages may be unlimited, the sorts of things that are possible as sound systems are not unlimited at all. Rather, an inventory of possible sounds can be specified in advance, as a function of human articulatory capacities, and each language makes its own particular, distinctive, and limited selection from this antecedently given class of possible sounds. There is a perfectly good universal theory of the sounds of language to be found in such a characterization; but such a theory cannot be equated with the particular sound inventory of any specific language or group of languages.

A similar observation is made with respect to the range of "groups of ideas that find expression in fixed phonetic groups" (1911:24). Again there is an inventory of possible ideas which can be so expressed; this inventory, like that of possible sounds, is not limited to some finite number, but this does not mean that no theory of the range of possible ideas could exist. There exists no obvious and direct basis for a theory of this sort, such as is provided for a theory of sound structure by the facts of the articulatory capacities of man, but this hardly precludes the claim that linguistically expressed ideas are taken from some universally available set.

Of course, as in the case of sound systems, each language makes its own selection from this set, and the selection made by one language is quite independent of that made by another. The finiteness of this selection is argued to follow as a theorem from the finiteness of the expressive range of the phonetic system, with the further result that "since the total range of personal experience which language serves to express is infinitely varied, and its whole scope must be expressed by a limited number of phonetic groups, it is obvious that an extended classification of experience must underlie all articulate speech" (1911:24). While we will never understand the grammatical classification imposed by a given language if we limit ourselves to the categories available in some other language, this does not at all entail that there could be no general understanding of the range of ideas systematically expressible in language.

The system of grammatical categories in any particular language is not simply an inventory of ideas which that language *can* express in determinate ways, but also a range of concepts which *must* be expressed in that language. Since these systems differ from language to language, important differences between systems may rest less on what is possible than on what is obligatory. In English, for example, noun phrases necessarily indicate the number (singular or plural) of their referent, and the category of definiteness; verbs are necessarily marked to indicate tense. By comparison, Kwakwala ("Kwakiutl") noun phrases contain no necessary mark of the distinction between singular and plural, or of definiteness; and Kwakwala verbs have no necessary indication of tense. On the other hand, Kwakwala noun phrases must indicate the deictic relation between the speaker and the referent, and Kwakwala verbs must indicate whether the action referred to was actually witnessed, learned about by hearsay, or took place in a dream.

The point is not that the categories of one language cannot be expressed in the other: Kwakwala speakers have perfectly good ways of indicating number, tense, etc., when these categories are essential to an understanding of the situation described, just as English speakers can indicate how an object is located with respect to the speaker, or the fact that something described took place in a dream. The fundamental influence of a particular grammatical system lies not in a limitation on expressive power but in differences in the range of categories with respect to which a speaker is required to commit himself (like it or not) in any utterance in the language in question.

A given language is characterized by its own selection from the range of possible sound systems, then, and also by its selection from the range of possible ideas which may (or must) be expressed as grammatical categories. Furthermore, "in the languages of the world, the number of processes which are utilized to express the relations of terms is limited. . . . The only methods that are available for expressing the relations between definite phonetic groups are their composition in definite order, which may be combined with a mutual phonetic influence of the component elements upon one another, and inner modification of the phonetic groups themselves" (1911:27). The range of morphological devices available for systematic exploitation, then, is subject to very strict substantive limitation—much narrower, in fact, than the limitations on sound systems and on semantic/grammatical systems.

This picture, then, does not at all entail a rejection of the notion of universals of linguistic structure, though that was the interpretation often given to Boas's views (at least rhetorically) by his successors in seeking to distance themselves from what they saw as the excesses of traditional approaches to language. In part, no doubt, there was a component of simple chauvinism in this: an attempt to identify a distinctively 'American' linguistics. By founding their methods on a radical and eye-catching exaggeration of a fundamentally commonsense principle, later investigators sought to stress the special and independent character of linguistics in America. In essence, however, Boas's insight (while fundamental) was not quite so dramatic as advertised, and consisted essentially of the observation that an adequate universal theory of language could not be founded exclusively on the facts of a single 'model' language or group of languages.

Boas's views of phonology

When we seek to understand Boas's own picture of sound structure, it is necessary to rely on indirect evidence to supplement his limited explicit treatments of the subject. The discussions of phonetics (broadly construed to include everything from the details of articulation through comparatively abstract morphophonemic alternations) in the Introduction to *The Handbook of American Indian Languages* and in individual descriptive studies of particular languages are not really concerned with developing a general *theory* of such structure; what they seek to establish is an adequate and consistent practice. Given Boas's central interest in ethnography rather than in the study of language per se, it is natural that morphology and syntax (the formal correlates of the domain of meaning) occupied much more of his attention.

Nonetheless, it is worth making the effort to reconstruct as complete a picture as possible of Boas's views. In part, of course, this enterprise is interesting in its own right: the conception of linguistic structure held by anyone with Boas's enormous experience of unusual languages could hardly fail to be worthy of attention. But for historical purposes, it is especially important to know what Boas thought about the organization of sound systems in natural languages. An obvious reason for this is that his views were communicated (whether explicitly or implicitly) to his students, and thus constituted the foundation of their work. Somewhat less directly, we can note that his notion of sound structure was formed in the context of practical fieldwork and more or less informal reading rather than as a matter of concentrated theory-building. These factors lead to the conclusion that the 'theory' of phonology which we may attribute to him actually represents a sort of pre-*linguistic* consensus about the way in which languages are organized. Both historically and logically, then, Boas's position represents the starting point from which later theorizing about phonology in America would proceed.

If Boas was primarily interested in studying the conceptual organization of language for ethnographic purposes, he still felt that an essential preliminary to such study must be the phonetic recording of texts (and of individual linguistic forms). This first step of representing *accurately* the material the linguist collects, then, is of fundamental importance for the analysis of a language's structure. Without a method of recording textual material with sufficient accuracy to allow its faithful reproduction, the linguistic (or ethnographic) fieldworker is not in a position to confirm any conclusions that may be drawn from an analysis. This concern for phonetic accuracy is absolutely essential to Boas's projects, and overrides all other considerations in determining the proper way to represent linguistic material. An understanding of this point is the key to a number of aspects of Boas's views.

For example, it is quite clear that the question of whether or not two sounds are in contrast within a given language plays little or no role for him in determining whether or not they should be recorded with distinct symbols. Insofar as two sounds are distinguishable phonetically, it is necessary to reproduce this distinction in a faithful rendition of texts in which they occur; and thus the difference should be recorded where it appears, regardless of whether the analysis seems to indicate that it is a predictable one. This interpretation is overwhelmingly supported by the evidence of Boas's practice in recording and presenting phonetic systems for descriptive purposes. The inventories of segments which are enumerated in his various grammars include large numbers of noncontrastive elements which are quite consistently distinguished in texts and in example forms.

A good instance of this practice is provided by Boas's treatment of the vowel system of Kwakwala, the language to which he devoted more of his attention than any other. In his posthumously published grammar (Boas 1947), he regularly distinguishes some seventeen separate vowels. These distinctions are marked both in the forms cited in the grammar and in the vast amount of textual material he published during nearly fifty years of work on the language. Of these, however, at most seven (and more likely six) vowels are actually in contrast with one another. This difference does not in the least represent a failure on Boas's part to notice the regularities of distribution in the language: as Swadesh (1948) points out in a review, the 'phonemicization' of the vowel system is quite clear from his description, and he states plainly the predictabilities that there are among the vowels; nonetheless, he goes right on writing all of the predictable variants with distinct symbols.

The question of whether a difference between two sounds is predictable (or, on the other hand, contrastive) was thus not a matter of indifference to Boas: if a description were to provide an accurate and comprehensive analysis, it must state such regularities as characterize the language in question, including predictabilities in the distribution of phonetic segments. Still, the fact that such regularities form part of the descriptive analysis does not for Boas entail the conclusion that they determine the nature of a linguistically significant representation. Stating the relevant rules as part of the grammar is quite sufficient; if the linguist proceeds from there to reduce certain predictably distributed segments to a uniform representation, nothing of significance is gained to compensate for the resulting potential loss in immediacy and phonetic accuracy of the transcription. Boas's practice thus corresponds quite closely (insofar as it is appropriate to interpret it as a theory) to the 'fully specified surface variant' view of phonological structure described above in chapter 2.

In the 1920s and 1930s, the notion of a 'phonemic' representation was being articulated—and hailed as a major insight into the nature of human language. Boas certainly did not disappear personally from the American linguistic scene during this period; after the publication of the *Handbook* and the grammars associated with it, he played a prominent and forceful role in the development of the field in the years between the two world wars. There is no reason to doubt his complete familiarity with 'phonemic' views, but he remained at least unreceptive (if not outright hostile) to the replacement of phonetic by phonemic transcriptions as phonemic theory gradually took prominence as the cornerstone of a 'scientific' approach to language.

As noted by the last of his students during this period (see Schultz 1977), he was willing to acknowledge the potential interest of phonemics; after all, the basic insight of all phonemic views is simply the proposition that a linguistic description must express the fact that some phonetic differences can correspond to differences of linguistic signs, while others cannot. He did not, however, encourage his students to make use of phonemic representations, claiming "that the difference between phonemic and phonetic writing is only a practical one. I prefer phonetic writing which does not prejudge the phonemic interpretation. The latter is given in the phonetic rules which may be verified from the phonetic writing while they cannot be verified from the phonemic writing. The more complex the phonetic changes controlled by purely mechanical conditions the more difficult it is to read phonemic writing" (from a letter of 3 August, 1939, cited by Schultz 1977:56).

Indeed, Boas even rejected a more or less phonemic representation in cases where it clearly corresponded to the intuition of a native speaker. A striking instance of this is provided by his treatment of textual material in Kwakwala. A native speaker of this language, George Hunt, learned from Boas how to write it, and during many years when Boas was not himself in the field, he employed Hunt to collect texts for him. In fact, the bulk of Boas's published Kwakwala texts were written down directly by Hunt; Boas would then go through them and make certain editorial emendations before sending them for publication. Among these changes were some more or less systematic ways in which Boas corrected "the defect[s] of [Hunt's] writing" (as discussed in Boas 1930:xi ff.), in effect so as to make it more phonetically accurate by restoring noncontrastive differences eliminated by Hunt.

An important change is introduced by Boas in the treatment of the variants of /ə/. He notes explicitly that this appears as the vowel he writes ⟨î⟩ when following palatals, as ⟨ŭ⟩ following labialized consonants, and as ⟨ă⟩ after laryngeals and uvulars. Hunt (usually) wrote all of these in the same way: as ⟨E⟩ (=[ə]). He also wrote phonetic [u] after nonlabialized consonants as ⟨wE⟩—expressing the fact that this sound is a contextually conditioned variant of [ə]. Boas, however, went through all of Hunt's material and 'corrected' these interpretations by restoring the phonetic variants. In *The Religion of the Kwakiutl Indians* (1930:xiv–xviii) he presents a sample text in both Hunt's and his own, emended, form. Every case of Hunt's ⟨E⟩ after the appropriate consonants has been replaced by ⟨î⟩, ⟨ŭ⟩, or ⟨ă⟩; and ⟨wE⟩ has been rewritten as ⟨ŭ⟩. It is obvious here that phonetic literalness not only dominates the linguist's analysis, but even overrules the native speaker's intuitions in determining the proper way to represent the sound structure of utterances.

In order to achieve the necessary degree of phonetic accuracy in recording a strange language, Boas insisted that the investigator must first of all be free of those predispositions about linguistic sounds that derive from his own native language and those similar to it. Given the phonetic capacities of the human vocal apparatus, the number of actual different sounds that can be produced (and perceived) is infinite. As noted above, Boas pictured each language as making its own idiosyncratic selection from among these, a selection which is in principle completely independent of the selection made by any other language, and which need not overlap with the sounds used in some such other language. As a result, the unfamiliar sounds which an investigator encounters in, for example, Tlingit must be regarded in their own right, and not as imperfect attempts to produce sounds familiar from English, French, German, etc.

This might well seem so obvious as not even to bear stating, but in fact

Boas was combating an actual and even pervasive impression in the literature of his time. Missionaries and other early fieldworkers had observed that when working on a strange language they often encountered sound types which presented them with real difficulties for consistent recording. For instance, in Pawnee a sound type was found which sounded sometimes like [d], sometimes [n], sometimes [l] or [r]. It had been claimed on the basis of such experiences that 'primitive languages' were in part characterized by such a phenomenon: they were asserted to contain so-called *alternating sounds*, whose essence was that they were not articulatorily well defined but mixed or fluctuating in character.

In an early paper (one of his few explicit discussions of phonological issues), Boas (1889) attacked this notion, claiming that it was completely illusory. The so-called "alternating sounds" are not, he urged, fundamentally different in their degree of articulatory constancy from those found in familiar languages, but simply *different* from those with which the investigator is familiar. In attempting to perceive them in terms of sounds from his own native language, the fact that they are not fully identical with any of these leads to an unclear and vacillating perception; but this is a fact about perception and not about the sound itself. A perceptual system founded on the sounds of some particular language (perhaps supplemented by exposure to a few others) will inevitably be ill equipped to respond to sounds that fall outside its predisposed inventory; but that fact results from the effects on perception of learning a particular language and not from any fundamental difference in character between the sounds of, for example, German and Pawnee.

Boas argues for this conclusion from two sorts of fact. On one hand, sounds of the same language can be shown to be recorded in different ways by investigators whose own language backgrounds differ. He suggests that in some cases, it is even possible to determine the native language of the linguist by looking at the way unfamiliar sound types are transcribed. On the other hand, the exact same phenomenon is experienced by speakers of American Indian languages when confronted with sounds of English, German, French, etc., which are unfamiliar to them on the basis of their own languages. To a speaker of Tlingit, for instance, certain sounds (or sound groups) in English appear as 'alternating sounds', since their nonoccurrence in Tlingit leads to a vacillating and inconsistent perception of them (at least at first—but it is exactly first impressions that matter here, since the sort of fieldwork on which the 'alternating sounds' doctrine was based was largely a matter of rather superficial exposure for the purposes of collecting word lists). These two lines of argument converge on the same conclusion: that the phenomenon of 'alternating sounds' is a fact about perception, and not a characteristic of certain ('primitive') languages.

Representations and rules in Boas's descriptions

Boas's position on the question of 'alternating sounds' implies that particular languages classify phonetic segments in such a way that any sound which fails to contrast with a given unit is treated as in some sense equivalent to it. At least, this is one way of approaching the phenomenon: if an unfamiliar sound in Pawnee does not occur in English, it obviously does not contrast with such English sounds as [n], [d], [r], and [l], and so could be assigned to the same category as any of these, indifferently. We might interpret this as at least a precursor of later 'phonemic' theories, which have in common the assignment to the same category of sounds that do not contrast with one another.

Actually, however, just the opposite is true, and Boas's position represents a consistent view that phonetic substance in its most literal sense is the only linguistically significant kind of representation of sound. The phenomenon of alternation or perceptual vacillation is founded, according to him, on the fact that the concrete sound in question does not occur at all in the language of the observer, and thus is not identical—in strictly *phonetic* terms—with any sound that does occur in that language. When forced to categorize it, the observer can only do so in terms of another system which is the only one familiar to him: that of his native language. Since there is no phonetic identity between the sound in question and any element of that system, the resulting categorization can only be vacillating and inconsistent. This has nothing to do with the fact that the sound does not *contrast* with sounds in the observer's language, but only with the fact that it does not occur among them. The only surprising thing about the phenomenon of 'alternating sounds' on this view is that it does not arise more pervasively, given the actual diversity of phonetic differences among the world's languages. If it does not, this can only be because human linguistic perception is able (at least *in extremis*) to make some use of raw phonetic similarity (quite independent of any notion of contrast).

Boas's notion of a linguistically significant representation of the sound structure of utterances, then, is strictly and concretely a phonetic one. This does not at all preclude the statement of regularities of distribution and alternation, but does require that such regularities be the subject of a system of "phonetic rules" which form part of the grammar without in themselves determining a special mode of representation of forms. As far as the structure of such a grammar is concerned, Boas's general statements and his actual descriptive practice are quite consistent in assuming a division into three separate (though not unrelated) components: (a) an inventory of the sounds which occur in the language (whether contrastively or not); (b) a description of their possibilities of combination (including limitations on consonant clusters, initial or final consonants, co-occurrence of individual vowel and consonant sounds, etc.); and (c) a system of "euphonic laws" that specify modifications in the shape of linguistic elements when they appear in combination with others.

In this scheme, there is little to say about the role played by the inventory of occurring segments, beyond the fact that (in principle) it includes all phonetic variants—though in practice much phonetic detail is actually ignored in these lists. With regard to the "possibilities of combination," these are typically specified by formulas or lists detailing the range of consonants and clusters that appear in various positions (initially, intervocalically, finally), as well as remarks about the possibility of vowel sequences, initial or final vowels, etc. This is of course the domain that would later come to be called *phonotactics* within American structuralist theory; since the terms of such statements in a Boasian grammar are phonetic segments (and not 'phonemes'), however, they also include a certain amount of the information about the occurrence of particular phonetic variants in particular positions that would later be coded in the definitions of phonemes.

It is perhaps the class of "euphonic laws" which is most important to investigate further. These are "laws by which, automatically, one sound in a sequence requires certain other sounds either to precede or follow it" (Boas 1911:79). The notion of "automatic" here should not be confused with the sense in which some later writers have spoken of "automatic alternations": Boas intends simply 'under the conditions specified in the rule', and not necessarily 'under the requirements of phonotactically motivated conditions' or the like. Indeed, in various places a division is made between euphonic laws that are "phonetic" (i.e., which serve to eliminate prohibited sequences or otherwise enforce the conditions on possible sound combinations) and those that are not. The latter, of course, are exactly the processes that would be treated as *non*automatic by later theories: rules that are conditioned by grammatical, morphological, or purely lexical factors.

The presentation of euphonic laws in most of the grammars in the *Handbook of American Indian Languages* seems to presume a sort of substantive theory about the range of possible phonetically motivated processes in natural languages. Euphonic laws are discussed under a series of headings: consonantal changes versus vocalic changes; retroactive versus anteactive versus reciprocal changes; contraction, apocope, epenthesis, vocalic harmony, etc. Most of these categories are those of traditional phonetics and historical linguistics, of course, but it would be interesting to know more about the role such classification played in the conception of sound systems held by Boas and his coworkers.

The strongest sort of theory seems to be implied by statements such as: "*Vocalic Harmony.* The tendency toward vocalic harmony is so inconsistent in Siuslaw, that one is almost tempted to deny the presence of such a process. The two examples I have been able to find are extremely unsatisfactory and do not permit the formulation of any clearly defined rules" (Frachtenberg 1922:452). We could interpret this as an indication that (at least in principle) universal phonetic theory provides an inventory of substantively defined phonetic processes which may form the bases of particular euphonic laws; and that the job of the investigator is to verify, for each of these processes, how and where it is instantiated in the language in question.

There is undoubtedly at least a component of this sort of thinking in the *Handbook* and related grammars, but it is certainly not easy to document as a theoretical assumption. It seems more likely that the motivation for the classifications of processes which appear is the simple desire to impose some sort of expository organization on the presentation, as well as a wish to make the grammars comparable with one another. Given the extent to which different grammars make use of rather different classificatory schemes, however, not even this end can be said to be successfully attained.

Among the nonphonetic euphonic laws, some appear as "grammatical processes" in that they serve directly to express meaning. For example, in (Nass) Tsimshian, some forms show "modifications of length and accent of stem syllables" which serve to distinguish singular from plural (e.g., *halai't* 'ceremonial dance', pl. *hā'lait*; *hanā'q* 'woman', pl. *hā'naq*). These changes are obviously not phonetic, but they are also not conditioned by any other overt element of the form beyond the component of its meaning which they serve to express. Such laws are quite comparable to the class of *correlations* in the theories of Kruszewski and Baudouin de Courtenay (see above, chapter 3).

Not all nonphonetic euphonic laws are of this sort, however. Many instances of such laws are simply morphologically conditioned alternations: changes conditioned by the presence of a member of some particular class of morphemes in the environment of the sound in question, regardless of the phonetic admissibility of the segment sequence that would result if the change were not performed. An example of this sort is furnished by Kwakwala: in this language, every suffix which is added to a form can be classified as *neutral*, *hardening*, or *weakening*. Neutral suffixes have no effect on the stem to which they are added (aside from any necessary phonetically conditioned ones, of course). Hardening and weakening suffixes, on the other hand, result in certain systematic modifications of the final consonant of stems to which they are attached: roughly, the hardening suffixes cause glottalization and the weakening suffixes voicing. It is not possible to give a phonetic definition of these classes of suffixes, and the changes involved can in no way be related to phonetic requirements. It is simply an arbitrary property of individual suffix morphemes that they harden, weaken, or leave the stem unchanged.

Boas seems in various places to assume that euphonic laws operate on natural classes of segments (i.e., classes defined by some unitary, independently motivated phonetic parameter) and replace them by members of some other natural class. For example, in the case of the Kwakwala hardening and weakening processes just cited, we find not only straightforward replacements of plain stops by glottalized or voiced ones, respectively, but also "a number of unexpected relations of sounds." Perhaps the most unusual of these is the fact that the palatal fricative ⟨x·⟩ is replaced by [n] before hardening suffixes and by (glottalized) ['n] before weakening suffixes. Boas concludes that "[t]he change of $x\cdot$ into n suggests that the n may belong rather to the anterior palatal series than to the alveolar series" (Boas 1911:430), a claim which has no basis in articulatory phonetic facts, but which must refer to some other notion of what it means for a segment to "belong to a series." Such a reliance of euphonic laws on natural classes would of course be perfectly consistent with the view suggested above that a class of possible processes is specified in a language-independent way by phonetic theory; but there is too little further support for such a position in Boas's works to go beyond these observations.

The relations between forms specified by euphonic laws are in some cases cumulative, in a way we would now represent by ordering the rules so that one may apply to the output of another. Again referring to an example from Kwakwala, we can note that the effect of "weakening" suffixes on terminal -s is to change this either to y or to dz (the choice being determined lexically by the root). Such a y, in turn, is vocalized to $\langle\bar{e}\rangle$ ([i:]) when it occurs between two consonants, by an independently motivated rule. Thus, the stem $x\cdot\hat{i}s$ 'disappear' (actually /$x\cdot s$/ morphophonemically, with the vowel inserted by rule where necessary), when followed by the weakening suffix -'$nak\breve{u}la$, yields $x\bar{e}'nak\breve{u}la$ 'to disappear gradually', by change of s to y and subsequent vocalization of y between consonants. On the other hand, if the weakening of s to y yields a sequence ay, this is changed by another (independently necessary) rule to the vowel $\ddot{a}$: e.g., qas 'walk' with the same suffix yields $q\ddot{a}'nak\breve{u}la$. In both cases, one rule (vocalization of y, or coalescence of ay to $\ddot{a}$) must be assumed to apply to the result of applying another (here, weakening of s to y before certain suffixes). The composite nature of such changes is made quite explicit in Boas' descriptions.

Typically, the instances of 'ordering' found in Boas's grammars have the character of the example just illustrated: one rule establishes conditions on which another rule operates (a 'feeding order' in today's terminology). In a few cases, though, we find Boas explicitly stipulating that such an interaction of rules does *not* obtain. In his description of Dakota, for example, he establishes that the position of the accent in this language is generally on the second syllable. However, "when an unaccented initial vowel or syllable ending in a vowel is contracted with a following vowel, accented or unaccented, the initial syllable carries the accent. This is due to the fact that the second vowel, on account of its position would take the accent, if the syllables were not contracted" (Boas & Deloria 1939:21). Such a description implies that the accent rule applies 'before' the contraction rule, and perhaps more importantly, that it does not apply after this latter. It would only be necessary to mention this fact, of course, if the basic assumption about the interaction of euphonic laws were that they apply wherever their conditions are satisfied—unless explicitly prohibited from doing so.

Abstractness in Boas's phonological practice

The "euphonic laws" thus appear to constitute a class of derivational rules, applying in some sort of sequence to an underlying representation and converting it by stages to a concrete phonetic form. This impression is certainly reinforced by the relatively free use of locutions such as "becomes," "is transformed into," "is replaced by," etc.; and by the explicit presentation of base forms as the source of occurring surface forms. It is on this basis that, as discussed briefly in the Introduction above, Postal (1964) claimed that Boas actually had a notion of morphophonemic (or 'systematic phonemic') representation, and rules of derivation to convert this into a ('systematic') phonetic representation along essentially the same lines as generative phonology.

We have argued above, however, that Boas accorded no real status to any representation other than a phonetic one: how is this to be reconciled with his apparent appeal to underlying forms and complex systems of rules relating the one to the other? It seems most accurate to think of the role of 'base forms' (a term which Boas does not use) and "euphonic laws" as simply a system for computing the shapes of surface forms. It is only the surface forms themselves that have any significance; but in some instances the specification of what surface forms are possible, or of the surface form in which some given combination of meaningful elements appears, requires a sort of inferential calculation making use of other (virtually always surface) forms and the "euphonic laws" of the language. On this view, "x becomes y in the environment C" should be interpreted as "where, on the basis of other forms, you would expect to find x, but condition C obtains, form y is actually found."

This is, of course, simply the terminology of most traditional grammars. To some extent the dynamic, process-oriented nature of this terminology is almost inevitable: it is hard to say "under conditions C, x does not occur, but y occurs as a substitute" without at least the metaphor of a process of replacement. By no means negligible in forming such a manner of speaking, however, was the influence exerted by nineteenth-century historical linguistics, which served as the background for the grammars of Greek, Latin, German, and other languages with which Boas (and for that matter, most subsequent students of these languages) might have been familiar.

Long after the point at which general linguists responded to Saussure by asserting the independence of synchrony and diachrony, such traditional grammars maintained (at least covertly) the conception that the explanation of a synchronic state of language lies in the sequence of historical changes from which it arose. The role of this historical factor is evident in Boas's use of the expression "etymological form" for what modern phonologists would call a "base" or "underlying" form. This locution can, in fact, be interpreted as support for the claim that for Boas, these representations do not actually correspond to any part of the synchronic linguistic system at all; and that any

reality they (and the computations based on them) may have is strictly historical in nature.

When we look at the "etymological" (or base) forms Boas cites in his descriptive practice, we find that these are typically the forms in which the linguistic elements in question appear in isolation. For example, "in Pawnee:
ta'tuk "*t* 'I have cut it for thee', and *rīks* 'arrow', combine into *tatu'riksk* "*t* 'I
cut thy arrow'. . . . the elements *ta-t-ru*ᵉ*n* combine into *ta'hu*ᵉ*n* 'I make' (because *tr* in a word changes to *h*); and *ta-t-rīks-ru*ᵉ*n* becomes *tahīkstu*ᵉ*n* 'I
make an arrow' (because *r* after *s* changes to *t*). At the same time *rīks* 'arrow'
occurs as an independent word" (Boas 1911:31–32). In such a description,
the elements posited as base forms are usually explicitly justified by citing a
form in which they occur without change, preferably in isolation.

Sometimes, however, the isolation form itself is subject to some sort of
modification; and in such a case, Boas takes that (occurring surface) alternant
as basic which has the greatest predictive value as far as the other alternants
are concerned. For example, in Dakota the great majority of verbs whose stem
has the shape CVC end in a suffix -*a*. This suffix does not occur, however,
when the verb is compounded, reduplicated, or used in a subordinate form.
These latter cases, then, present the stem in isolation. When the terminal -*a*
suffix does not appear, however, the final consonant of the stem undergoes
certain changes. Among these changes, both *t* and (the affricate) *c* "are
changed to a weak, almost voiceless *l*." Examples of these alternations include *ši'ca* 'bad', which becomes *šil*; and *ška'ta* 'to play', which becomes
škal. The final consonants of both 't-stems' and 'c-stems', then, appear as *l* in
their isolation form. Boas argues, however, that "on account of the lack of
differentiation in the shortened forms of stems ending in *t* and *c*, both of
which take the form *l*, it seems that the forms with terminal *a* should be considered as more fundamental' (Boas & Deloria 1939:12).

Boas's "euphonic laws", then, express relations between the shapes of (surface) forms, rather than a synchronic derivation of such forms from some
more abstract representation. The distinction is perhaps a subtle one but nonetheless real. The point is that any given form has only a single significant representation (a surface phonetic one). To predict the shape in which a particular
combination of meaningful elements will appear, it may well be necessary to
take several other forms (as well as the relevant euphonic laws) into account;
but the regularities involved are expressed through a network of rules relating one form to another rather than through a different representation of the
form itself, which is more abstract and 'morphophonemic' than phonetic in
character.

We have already argued above that Boas also did not maintain a significant
level of morphophonemic representation for forms, since the euphonic laws
are primarily expressions of regularities in the relations between (surface)
forms rather than between different representations of the same form. We can
note further in this connection that the euphonic laws are not exploited in such

a way as to reduce the elements of representations to a minimum by extracting all possible predictabilities.

An example of this is furnished by the treatment of vowels in Kwakwala: both in the *Handbook* sketch of this language and in his posthumous grammar, he observes that the vowels written ⟨ä⟩ and ⟨â⟩ "are evidently secondary phonemes. In almost every case it can be shown that *ä* is derived from *ea* or *ya*, *â* from *aw* or *wa*" (Boas 1947:207). An extensive system of explicit rules is presented (ibid. pp. 212ff) to describe the alternations among these vowels (including also cases in which *ä* is apparently derived from a sequence of two *a*'s); by means of these rules, every instance of the vowels *ä* and *â* in the language could be represented in terms of otherwise occurring elements with no loss of information. Nonetheless the "derivation" of these vowels from sources such as *ae*, *ay*, *aw*, etc. only comes into play in the case of explicit alternations. Only when the same element shows up in some forms with *a* or *e*, in others with *ä* is the relation between *ä* and *ae*, etc., invoked. Intramorphemic or other nonalternating instances are represented simply as *ä* (or *â*) without comment. Boas adheres to this sort of practice in numerous cases, because the role of euphonic laws in his grammars is to express systematic relations between distinct but related forms, and not to extract the underlying, irreducibly distinctive content of the individual forms themselves.

On the whole, then, attempts to interpret Boas's views on phonology in terms of later theories that posit significant levels of phonemic or morphophonemic representation do not seem to be warranted. The notion that any representation in Boas's work is like a (structuralist) phonemic one is directly controverted by his explicit and resolute rejection of phonemic reinterpretation of surface phonetic forms. It has been said "that Boasian grammars 'itemize' but 'on the whole they do not structure'" (quoted by Stocking 1974:478 from Hymes 1961). This is true in the sense that the paramount consideration in linguistic analysis for Boas is accuracy and completeness in recording; reinterpretation of phonetically recorded material in terms of which elements are distinctively opposed to one another (the essence of 'structural' phonemic analyses) is regarded as at best unnecessary and potentially a source of loss of information.

On the other hand, Boas's descriptions (and those influenced directly by him) are thoroughly explicit in bringing out, through a system of rules for the composition of forms (including both 'phonotactics' and 'euphonic laws'), just what the limits are on the range of different forms in the language. That these descriptions "itemize" in the sense of recording as wide a range of forms as possible as accurately as possible is of course true. We could only conclude that they do not "structure" the languages with which they deal, however, if we were to accept the notion that the only way to elucidate the structure of a language is in terms of an alternate representation of its forms, which makes exactly the distinctive oppositions explicit.

We conclude, therefore, that Boas's phonology falls rather straightforwardly within the 'fully specified surface variant' view sketched above in chapter 2. That is, the only significant representation of utterances is a surface-phonetic form—but a complete grammar also contains, in addition to such representations, a system of rules which describe predictabilities of various sorts in (a) the range of shapes of possible utterances, and (b) the systematic relations in shape that arise between distinct but related utterances.

Boas's view of phonological form, then, is rather similar to that of Saussure. Of course, Boas attributes much less theoretical importance to the fact of *distinctness* of forms than did Saussure, but the rules of a grammar constructed according to his views nonetheless express quite rigorously those variations in shape that are possible within the 'same' linguistic element, as opposed to those which must correspond to an opposition between different elements. Saussure's interest was largely theoretical, and it is thus necessary to infer most of the practical consequences of his views (as discussed in chapters 1 and 2 above), while the situation is almost exactly reversed in Boas's case. Nonetheless, if the interpretations we have given here are correct, the actual substance of the conception of phonological structure held by the pioneers of European and of American linguistics in the twentieth century was strikingly similar.

9

Edward Sapir

As observed in the preceding chapter, Boas continued to play a leading role in the development of American linguistics right up until his death in 1942. His influence was exerted through his direction of various funding agencies and organs of publication and, more generally, by his approving and encouraging (or withholding such support from) the work of other scholars. It was, for example, partly because of Boas's 'patronage' that Roman Jakobson was able to establish himself in the United States within a relatively short time after his arrival.

In substantive terms, however, Boas's influence on the development of linguistic theory in America was rather indirect in the years following the publication of the first volume of the *Handbook of American Indian Languages*. Though his basic tenets continued to define the orientation of linguistic research and to form the basis of a developing American approach to the science of language, he did not himself play a leading role in the formation of linguistic *theory*. This was not at all because (as has sometimes been suggested) he was averse to theory but, rather, because his own interests were largely elsewhere: in the more general field of ethnography, not only linguistics; and within linguistics, in the description of the native languages of North America. It thus fell largely to Boas's students, proceeding from his general views, to develop a more specific and articulated theory of linguistic structure. By far the most important among Boas's students in this respect was Sapir, who had substantially eclipsed Boas as a theoretician of language by the mid-1920s.

Sapir's life

Edward Sapir was born in 1884 in Lauenburg, Germany. When he was five, his parents emigrated to the United States, where he attended school in New York. He received a BA from Columbia in 1904, and went on to earn a master's degree there in Germanics. While at Columbia he met and began to study with Boas; in the years immediately following his MA he did fieldwork in the state of Washington on the Wishram dialect of Chinook, and in Oregon on Takelma, under Boas's guidance. In 1907–8 he was a research associate in anthropology at the University of California (Berkeley), where he worked on

Yana. This was followed by two years' appointment at the University of Pennsylvania in Philadelphia, as a fellow and subsequently as instructor. During this period (with the support of the University of Pennsylvania Museum) he had a Southern Paiute student to work with in Philadelphia, and did fieldwork with the Utes. In later years he seems, like many others, to have somewhat idealized his graduate student days in Berkeley and Philadelphia, and to have rather resented the administrative and other job-related duties that interfered with the conduct of research in the professional positions he occupied.

In 1909 he had submitted his description of Takelma as a dissertation to Boas at Columbia, and was awarded a doctorate. In 1910 he was hired to head the newly established division of anthropology within the Geological Survey of the Canadian National Museum (the forerunner of the present Museum of Man) in Ottawa, where he was to "establish a thorough and scientific investigation of the native races of Canada, their distribution, languages, cultures, etc., and to collect and preserve records of the same" (quoted by Murray 1981:64 from a 1910 letter to Sapir from his new superior, the deputy minister of mines).

Though initially enthusiastic about this opportunity (which made him virtually Boas's Canadian equivalent), he soon became disheartened and complained about the bleakness and isolation of his life in Ottawa. In fact during these years he did fieldwork on a large number of languages (including Nootka, as well as Sarcee, the first work he did on a language of the Athabaskan family which was to occupy him off and on for much of his life), and published a great deal in a number of areas. His Takelma grammar (essentially his 1909 dissertation) was published in 1922 in volume 2 of the *Handbook of American Indian Languages*. This work is truly incredible in its comprehensiveness and insight when one considers that it was based on only a month and a half of fieldwork. Around 1917 he wrote his description of Southern Paiute (which was not published until 1930); in 1921 he published his popular outline *Language*. These three items were essentially the only book-length works Sapir produced in his entire career, but together with a large number of shorter articles on linguistic and more general cultural topics, as well as nonlinguistic writings, they make the list of his publications during his Canadian years impressive indeed.

While he was in Ottawa, Sapir's first wife suffered a series of mental and physical illnesses from which she eventually died. An added disappointment was the fact that his efforts to develop anthropological research on the native peoples of Canada were largely halted by the financial and other exigencies of the First World War. Coupled with his perception of the contrast between the freedom of his student days and the amount of comparatively unrewarding responsibility incumbent on him as an administrator, these frustrations increased his feelings of isolation and alienation.

In this period Sapir began to devote a considerable amount of time to artistic expression—poetry and music, as well as the writing of quite a number of (literary) reviews. From 1917 through the early 1930s, he was a major contributor to *The Dial* (one of the most important American literary journals of the time) as well as a reviewer and writer for other journals such as *The Freeman*, *Poetry*, *The New Republic*, *The Nation*, and others far from professional linguistics and ethnography. Many of the same concerns that dominate his nonacademic writing, however, also appear in connection with his work in anthropology. He became increasingly interested in questions of psychiatry and the nature of personality, and particularly in the relation between personality and culture.

While his linguistic work always constituted a sort of foundation for the exploration of such issues, he was generally more interested in expanding the relation between the study of language and other domains than in the development of specifically linguistic methodology. As the field became increasingly self-aware and professionalized in later years (recall that, in the 1920s, there really was no such distinct discipline as linguistics at any American university), this would put his work rather at odds with the tendency of most other linguists to emphasize the uniqueness of the object of their research and the methods appropriate to it.

In 1925 Sapir was offered a position at the University of Chicago, which he was happy to accept. At Chicago he had a great many students (many of whom, with a few exceptions such as Hoijer, later followed him in his move to Yale); and within a short time he was a major figure in American anthropology. He continued to do fieldwork on several languages (including Navajo and Hupa) and had the opportunity to do many of the things whose absence he had regretted in Ottawa. For a time he continued to write poetry (and to participate in the University of Chicago poetry club); but eventually the pressure of other work left him little time for anything but his professional obligations.

Gradually becoming disillusioned with the amount of administrative effort demanded of him at Chicago, he accepted the very attractive offer of a Sterling Professorship at Yale in 1931. At Yale he again attracted a number of students (including most of those later associated with his name, such as Stanley Newman, Morris Swadesh, Mary Haas, Benjamin Whorf, and others), though he had very few beginning students, in contrast to his years at Chicago. He was still by no means free of administrative obligations, and also encountered a certain amount of anti-Semitic feeling (for example, he was apparently blackballed from the Yale faculty club). In 1937–38, these irritations were exacerbated by a series of heart attacks, and he died of heart disease in 1939.

Sapir's background as a student of Boas obviously had a great deal of influence on his later views. His first work (such as his Takelma grammar) is clearly within that tradition, though it also shows a great amount of originality and independence. In fact, more of Sapir's apparently distinctive position can be traced to its Boasian roots than is sometimes recognized: the stress he put on the psychological foundations of linguistic knowledge, the extent to which a language can be studied in order to analyze the unconscious categorization that underlies the worldview of its speakers—these basic goals are a direct working out of Boas's view of language as "a window on the soul." Sapir's original contributions to the development of a comprehensive theoretical view of language and its structure are not in any way to be minimized, but it should also be recognized that both in general and in many of its specifics, the resulting systematization has a great deal in common with the position sketched (and to some extent practiced) by Boas.

This approach to language as a profoundly internal mental phenomenon must be contrasted (as of course it usually is) with the behaviorist, positivist, and mechanist climate of research which grew up during the 1930s and 1940s. The central figure in the rise of such an approach to linguistics was Leonard Bloomfield, whose work will be the subject of the following chapter. Typically, presentations of the history of American linguistics associate Sapir's views with the 1920s and early 1930s, and treat Bloomfield as succeeding Sapir. As stressed by Hymes and Fought (1981), however, the actual chronology is somewhat more complicated.

In fact, Bloomfield and Sapir were essentially contemporaries; and if Sapir was clearly a prominent figure in anthropology in the 1920s before Bloomfield became well known, the 1930s were a time in which both were active and influential. Certainly Sapir was more prominent in the relations between American and European linguists in the development of phonology; he corresponded extensively with Trubetzkoy in the early 1930s (though these letters were destroyed before his death, and cannot now be examined), and the latter spoke positively of him on many occasions. When the International Phonological Association was established under the influence of the Prague school linguists in 1932, it was Sapir who was elected as the sole American member of its board, and he continued to be the primary link between European and American phonologists until his death.

Sapir and Bloomfield of course knew and interacted with one another to a considerable extent (they were colleagues at Chicago, and in part in competition for students there between 1927 and 1931), though it seems they were anything but fast friends. Sapir's own style of research was based much more on brilliance and intuition, searching for dramatic insights whose foundation might (or might not) be confirmed by later systematic investigation. Bloomfield was much more methodical in the way he felt theoretical propositions ought to be worked out, and while admiring Sapir's more virtuosic approach, he referred to him (at least in matters outside of language) as a "medicine man" (Hockett 1970:540). Sapir, for his part, "admired Bloomfield's ability patiently to excerpt data and to file and collate slips until the patterns of the language emerged, but spoke deprecatingly of Bloomfield's sophomoric psychology" (ibid., pp. 539–40). Such a contrast in styles cannot have made for an easy cooperation; nor were their relations improved, one imagines, by the fact that most of the best students at Chicago left to follow Sapir to Yale in 1931. Overall, if one had to bet in the early 1930s on the likely outcome of the inevitable rivalry between the two, one would surely have had to predict the continued ascendancy of Sapir.

While Sapir did indeed continue to exert an important influence on linguistics throughout the 1930s, 1940s and 1950s through his own work and that of a series of students (and their students in turn), his was increasingly a peripheral, even eccentric position in relation to the main stream of development of the field. Sapir was thus gradually eclipsed by Bloomfield, for a number of rather superficial (but nonetheless important) reasons.

Among these is surely the fact that Sapir died in 1939 and was thus unable to exercise the influence of his undeniably attractive abilities in the years during and right after World War II. Further, his students and closest associates were, after the war, either dead (Whorf), unemployed (and subject to political persecution, in the case of Swadesh), or employed in universities on the West Coast (Haas, Hoijer, Newman) where their influence on academic politics was almost negligible. In addition to these factors, there was the fact that Bloomfield had written a major textbook (Bloomfield 1933) which had a formative influence on virtually all the immediately following generations of students in linguistics, while Sapir had not; and also the fact that Sapir taught only once at the (summer) Linguistic Institute (a major institution in the formation and training of a new generation of scholars who saw themselves professionally as linguists), while Bloomfield taught there several times.

Finally, one must not neglect the fact that Bloomfield's appeal to a positivist, mechanist philosophy of science was completely in tune with the 'ideological' climate of academic research at the time. If linguists saw a major part of their task as the establishment of a distinct discipline of linguistics which was not simply a part of Germanics, Romance, Semitics, comparative philology, anthropology, etc., it seemed that the way to achieve this goal was by stressing the status of linguistics as a *science*; and here Bloomfield's approach seemed much more appropriate than Sapir's mentalism and flashes of intuition. The appeal of research which takes on at least the trappings of 'science' has of course not disappeared; one can argue about the extent to which such considerations distort scholarly judgments in particular cases, but there is no question that they contributed to the relegation of the 'Sapir school' to a marginal position in American linguistics in the late 1930s and subsequently.

Sapir's view of the nature of language

It is on the basis of his conception of the object of study in linguistics that Sapir differs most fundamentally from the approach to language which arose during the 1930s and came to dominate research in America, especially after World War II. In contrast to these later developments, Sapir believed in the importance of a rich and highly structured domain of interior mental phenomena, including in particular virtually all of what is essential to the nature of language. In chapter 10 and 11, we will trace the development by which, for many linguists, language came to be considered as exhaustively studiable in terms of its external manifestations: sounds, and patterns of observable behavior to which 'meaning' could be reduced (at least programmatically, in principle). For Sapir, in contrast, these physical aspects of language were ·merely peripheal (almost incidental) concomitants of a reality which is to be sought in the mind, and whose study provides invaluable information about the nature and structure of human cognitive activity.

The consequences of this difference are quite clear in the domain of interest to us here, the study of phonology. For nearly all theoreticians of the time, certainly including Sapir, a central role is played in phonological structure by a basic segmentlike element: the *phoneme*. Linguists who approached language strictly in terms of its external manifestations, however, founded this notion on the study of the physical sounds of speech: through extracting the acoustic or auditory properties which distinguish one speech sound from another, or through an analysis of the distribution of various physical segment types. Sapir's conception is quite different, since the physical implementation of a phoneme is among its least interesting properties. True, phonemes are realized in the sounds of speech; but their essence is rather something in the mind whose most important features may be unrelated (or even in direct contradiction) to measurable aspects of a physical event. In a much-quoted passage, the central reality of sound structure is likened to "an ideal flow of phonetic elements . . . heard, inadequately from a purely objective standpoint, as the intention of the actual rumble of speech" (Sapir 1921:56).

The claim that language is primarily a psychological rather than a physical activity does not at all imply that the structure of this activity is given in advance by the innate, biologically controlled organization of the human brain. On the contrary, Sapir stresses in the introductory chapters of his book *Language* his view that "speech is a human activity that varies without assignable limit as we pass from social group to social group, because it is a purely historical heritage of the group, the product of long continued social usage." He specifically contrasts walking, which "is an organic, an instinctive function (not, of course, itself an instinct)" with speech, which "is a non-instinctive, acquired, 'cultural' function" (ibid., p. 4). Language, like the rest of culture, is something that we learn more or less as we find it, and because it is there, rather than because we are in some way inherently predisposed to acquire a system of a particular nature.

Sapir's stress on the cultural (rather than biological) basis of language can be traced rather directly to the views of Boas. In American anthropology in the twentieth century, this stress on the social environment rather than biological background as the source of cultural institutions affects many more domains of study than just language; and Boas is often cited as the dominant figure championing such a position in anthropological studies as a whole. His student Margaret Mead, for example, is generally felt to have been urging a fundamentally Boasian view in her enormously important study of Samoan society in 1928, which argued for a cultural rather than biological foundation for many human attitudes (aggressivity, jealousy, the turmoil of adolescence, etc.).

In the social and political context of the 1920s and 1930s (and subsequently), this stress on environment rather than heredity as a determinant of human cognitive functions and attitudes was generally felt to be an important contribution of the social sciences, useful in supporting 'liberal' positions on desirable social change. Recent controversy about Mead's work, in fact, has centered on the claim that she misrepresented (or at least misperceived) the facts of Samoan society in order to exaggerate the importance of such social factors at the expense of inherited ones—a predisposition she is presumed to have acquired from Boas.

Boas's stress on diversity (as opposed to some sort of biologically inherited uniformity) played an essential role in forcing the recognition that languages (or cultures) very different from those of Europe had to be approached in their own terms, rather than as imperfect or primitive approaches to some uniform ideal system. Obviously, this position has general cultural and political implications for many issues beyond the narrow question of how a particular science (linguistics or anthropology) should be organized. In urging a nonbiological view of the essential nature of language, Sapir was supporting the same point in what seemed the only logically possible way; for if human language is actually determined in its structure by innate, biologically inherited factors, it would appear that it should tend toward a uniform evolution and final state (at least within a genetically uniform sampling of humanity). The observed diversity of human language and its historical change, however, seems to contradict this view rather directly. Based as they were on such an 'organic' determinism, the typologies of language and its evolution that were proposed in the nineteenth century could be shown to be hopelessly inadequate as a characterization of linguistic reality: a result which Sapir felt was not at all an accident but a direct consequence of their inadequate underlying conception of the nature of language.

A number of factors thus led Sapir to stress the social as opposed to biological basis of linguistic structure: his education with Boas, the developing climate of opinion in academic anthropology in the 1920s and 1930s in conjunction with liberal political views during the same period, and the apparent necessity to make such an assumption in order to explain the evident diversity of human languages and their failure to follow the same evolutionary sequence. In seeing the structure of language as strictly an accidental consequence of cultural environment, however, free of any sort of necessity, this view leads logically to a major problem for linguistics. In the passage quoted above, language is argued to be "a human activity that varies without assignable limit"; but this implies that there are absolutely no (nonaccidental) universals of linguistic structure—a finding at variance with the manifest fact that, if languages may be very different from one another in many ways, we still have no difficulty at all in knowing what sort of activity and system in a society to call 'language', and in fact no difficulty in finding many ways in which languages resemble one another.

Sapir was of course well aware of the fact that languages do not actually differ from one another in absolutely arbitrary ways, and that there are at least some generalizations that are valid across languages. Identifying specific dimensions along which languages may in fact differ from one another (and thus by implication, properties in terms of which they are comparable), through the development of an explicit typological scheme applicable in principle to any language, occupied a considerable amount of his efforts. To be coherent, the position that any comprehensive typology is possible must rest on the assumption that there are some universals of human language; and once he asserted that these do not have a biological basis, it was logically incumbent on Sapir either to propose some other foundation for them or to deny their existence.

The denial that there are any significant linguistic universals was the path often taken by American structuralists (see Joos's famous statement about the arbitrary differences possible among languages, cited in the previous chapter), but not by Sapir: "It would be too easy to relieve ourselves of the burden of constructive thinking and to take the standpoint that each language has its unique history, therefore its unique structure. Such a standpoint expresses only a half truth" (Sapir 1921:121). In fact, we observe that languages show similarities in structure despite being unrelated to one another (at least in the time frame relevant to the development of the features in question). He suggests that these similarities may have their origin in the fact that "a language changes not only gradually but consistently, that it moves unconsciously from one type towards another, and that analogous trends are observable in remote quarters of the globe" (ibid.); but, whatever their source, it is important for the linguist to develop a framework in which both the similarities and the differences among languages can be adequately represented. This he attempts to do in his book *Language*.

He observes first of all that previous classificatory schemes were much too limited to encompass the actual variety of human language. There are several reasons for this: they usually involved too few categories (e.g., 'isolating' vs. 'agglutinating' vs. 'inflecting'); they were established with regard to only a single aspect of linguistic structure (typically the formal mechanism of word formation); they were based on a sample of too few languages; and (most importantly), they were guided by the aim of arriving at a uniform evolutionary sequence culminating in some particular ltype—often the language of the investigator, or perhaps classical Greek and Latin—as the manifestation of the ultimate stage of the evolution of civilized expression.

Sapir's own scheme is certainly more ramified than any other proposed up to the time. It would take us much too far afield here to explore it in detail, but we can note that it is based on three quite different dimensions. One of these (the most innovative aspect of his framework) is the type of *concepts* expressed in a given language. He assumes that every language must express a range of basic (concrete) concepts corresponding to the reference of simple lexical items, especially nouns and verbs. In addition, every language must express a certain range of *pure relational* concepts, which "serve to relate the concrete elements of the proposition to each other, thus giving it definite syntactic form." The positing of such categories as *necessary* ones is already a significant departure from the strong view that languages are in principle arbitrarily different from one another.

In addition to these minimal requirements, corresponding essentially to lexical roots in the one case and to purely syntactic inflectional categories in the other, languages may allow for two sorts of interpenetration of referential and relational constructs. As one possibility, languages may express *derivational* concepts, by which the meanings of radical items are modified to form new lexical items (e.g., an agentive operator which takes basic concrete verbs and produces nouns with the sense 'one who typically or often [verb]s'); and as another, they may allow for certain *concrete relational* categories. The latter are categories such as agreement in person, or in 'natural' (as opposed to purely arbitrary) gender: categories that play a role in inflection and the organization of syntactic structure, but which nonetheless have a sort of semantic or referential basis as well. He arrives at four general categories of language, depending on whether one, the other, both, or neither of these possibilities is realized in a given language. It can be seen that Sapir assumes a division between syntax and lexicon as the basis for a distinction between inflectional and derivational morphology; that such a point of view furnishes the only satisfactory foundation for this traditional opposition is argued in generative terms by Anderson (1982a).

Sapir's second dimension of linguistic contrast is the traditional one of the formal means by which those concepts which find expression in a given language are realized: isolating (where each concept is expressed in a separate word), agglutinating (where distinct concepts are expressed by distinct, nonoverlapping parts of words), fusional (where some amalgamation of distinct concepts into single or overlapping parts of a word is found), and symbolic (where some concepts are expressed not by a separable part of the word, but rather by the structural relation between one word and another, as in cases of Ablaut like *sing/sang/sung/song*). Employing such a classification in addition to that distinguishing types of concept allows Sapir to characterize a language in which concepts of one type (e.g. derivational ones) are expressed in one way (e.g. symbolically), while those of another (perhaps pure relational ones) are expressed in another (e.g. by agglutinating affixes). Finally, Sapir allows for the classification of languages along a third dimension, that of "degree of synthesis" or typical conceptual complexity of individual words—an essentially continuous scale ranging from *analytic* through *synthetic* to the extreme of *polysynthetic*.

Sapir's overall classificatory framework is much more complex, and accordingly more delicate than any of the traditional nineteenth-century schemes. One may still question whether it provides dimensions that are adequate to characterize the significant differences and similarities among the world's languages; but that is not our purpose here. Rather, what is interesting is the role which Sapir thought a typology plays in a theory of language. Precisely because it provides a number of potentially independent dimensions, rather than a single unidirectional scale like most of those that preceded it, it serves a fundamentally synchronic, descriptive purpose. It is intended, that is, to describe what the structure of a language is, rather than how far along a presumed evolutionary scale it has progressed.

It is reasonably clear also that a primary goal of typological research today is *not* intended to be served by Sapir's framework. Current typological work (at its best, at least) seeks to establish necessary connections among phenomena: for example, Greenberg's celebrated typology of SOV, SVO, and VSO languages was intended not simply to specify the range of freedom available to the languages of the world with respect to the major constituents of the sentence, but also to bring out connections between that relative order and other features, such as the relative order of nouns and modifying adjectives, the choice of prepositions or postpositions, etc. Precisely because Sapir's schema provides nothing beyond a range of mutually independent categories, it lacks such a logical structure, and in fact there is little evidence Sapir looked for implicational relationships among typological parameters provided by his system.

On the other hand, Sapir did think there were profound relationships which might eventually be discovered between the categories of linguistic structure in his terms and basic aspects of culture and of mental life. Together with Benjamin Whorf, he was largely responsible for bringing to prominence in anthropological discussion the claim that the structure of our language determines many aspects of the way in which we see and structure the world. In other words, the categorizations imposed by language channel and structure our thought, leading us to see some connections among phenomena while ignoring others—differing connections for the speakers of differing languages. This is of course a natural development of Boas's ideas about the importance of differences in the categories languages treat as obligatory, optional, or unexpressed; but Sapir and Whorf pursued the psychological implications of this position much further than Boas. While he did not claim to be able to demonstrate actual connections between the categories of his typology and language-specific cognitive differences, Sapir did feel that the elucidation of such connections was a role typology should be able to play.

We should also mention two other potential applications of a typological schema according to Sapir, both in the sphere of historical linguistics. First, there is his celebrated theory of linguistic "drift." This notion is intended to represent the fact that, even after a language has divided into several distinct, separated speech communities, the evolution of the several individual descendants of that language may well continue to pursue very similar lines. This leads to a state in which several members of a family make the same innovation quite independently of one another (or at least without any necessary contact between them)—which of course makes the historical linguist's task that much harder in determining which features of the daughter languages should be attributed to their common ancestor. Often presented as something quite mystical, the most straightforward way to interpret Sapir's notion of linguistic drift is simply as the claim that change is motivated by structural factors, and that such structural factors, present in the ancestor of a group of related languages, may persist and continue to influence their later evolution even after their separation. Ideally, a typology ought to provide categories in terms of which to identify such structural factors and clarify their influence on change.

Additionally, typology played a role in Sapir's own concrete historical work. He did extensive research of this sort, including historical studies in Indo-European (especially Tocharian) and Semitic, but especially in the classification of American Indian languages. One of his best-known theoretical claims, in fact, was his far-reaching proposal for a genetic classification of the languages of North and Central America into six large groups. This classification was based on a large number of rather remote linguistic relationships, many of which could not be proved or even significantly supported by standard comparative evidence; and one naturally asks what Sapir based his assertions on.

It is fairly clear that most of those claimed genetic connections which Sapir posited without support from common vocabulary rested on presumed similarities in structure—just the sort of parallels that a typological framework ought to be able to make explicit. The evidential role of such structural similarities is particularly strong within Sapir's general perspective on language as culturally based, but otherwise largely arbitrary; if the role of factors other than cultural transmission in determining the structure of a language is comparatively small, it should follow that structural similarity is strong presumptive evidence of a genetic relationship, since the preservation of such factors over the period of evolution from a common ancestor is virtually the only (nonaccidental) explanation for their presence. The role of typology here is to provide an instrument sensitive enough to identify such similarities; once identified, such a *prima facie* case for genetic unity must eventually be supported by standard comparative evidence, but typology ought to show the historical linguist where to begin looking.

If we have devoted so much space to a consideration of Sapir's views on typology, it is not because of the interest his specific proposals hold for the modern reader. Rather, it seems important to understand the central role which the general notion of a typological characterization of linguistic structure played in Sapir's view of a theory of language. An understanding of that role, in turn, makes clearer the sense in which Sapir construed language as a psychological phenomenon. As an aspect of human mental and cognitive life rather than merely an external system of interpersonal signals, language plays a profound role in determining the way we see and organize the world, but its own structure is in turn determined culturally, in an external and contingent fashion that allows little or no role for innate or other biological factors. For Sapir, the fundamental problem of linguistics was thus not the construction of a 'theory of grammar' but the elucidation of the relationship between language on one hand and culture and personality on the other.

Sapir's conception of phonological structure

In discussing the role of sounds in language, Sapir starts from a perspicuous comparison of an articulatory gesture as it functions linguistically, and what is effectively the same gesture as it might be used nonlinguistically. Though physically identical in all relevant respects, these differ dramatically in their integration with other similar gestures, both syntagmatically and paradigmatically—i.e., both in terms of their place in a sequence of human activities, and in their relation to other, alternative gestures. They also differ in what counts as an accurate performance of the gesture in question, but, most importantly, they differ in the intention underlying the gesture in question. Nonspeech gestures have directly functional significance, while the same gestures when used linguistically serve simply as a "link in the construction of a symbol." This sort of distinction between a physical act and its linguistic uses is highly reminiscent of Saussure: it should be noted that Sapir never refers to Saussure in his theoretical writing.

It follows, then, that the essential nature of a sound as used in speech lies in this special character of the intentionality underlying it: in the fact of what a speaker has in mind in producing it, not the physical details of the production itself. Sapir draws a useful analogy between sounds in speech and other tools used by humans: a club is a club not because it has a particular physical form but because it is put to a particular use. Phenomenological philosophers such as Heidegger make a similar point in arguing that the logically prior reality of a tool such as a hammer is its "readiness to hand" (i.e., its suitability for fulfilling particular intentions of a conscious user), and that its "presence at hand" (i.e., its specific character as a physical object with certain dimensions, weight, etc.) is an aspect that arises only secondarily, when we step back from its basic being as a hammer to regard it as a mere object.

The fundamental nature of a speech sound is thus to be sought in the uses to which it is put in the intentions of a speaker. This reality is a mental rather than a physical one, and it is exactly this 'mentalism' that is generally taken to characterize Sapir's view. To say that the basic unit of sound structure (the phoneme) has a psychological basis, however, is to tell only part of the story. Even if the physical properties by which the speaker's phonemic intention is realized are logically secondary from a linguistic point of view, that does not mean they are unreal, irrelevant, or completely arbitrary. Even if "a club is not defined for us when it is said to be made of wood and to have such and such a shape and such and such dimensions" (Sapir 1933[1949]:46) since the essence of "club-ness" lies in the use to which we put it rather than in these properties, we still could not choose any arbitrary physical object (an apartment building, say, or a pool of water) and decide to think of it as a 'club'. Similarly, we could not choose to regard any arbitrary vocal event (a Bronx cheer, for example) as filling the role of the English phoneme /d/. A complete conception of either clubs or phonemes can only be reached when we regard them as physical objects (or events) of a particular sort, invested with a particular intentional value.

A concentration on the mental reality of phonemes to the complete exclusion of their physical properties has led some interpreters of Sapir to suggest that he rejected or ignored their phonetic properties. This is quite at variance with his practice; in his descriptive work, not only does he describe phonemes in standard articulatory terms, presenting charts of phonemes classified by traditional phonetic dimensions, but he often appeals to phonetic properties as having an explanatory role in the operation of phonological processes. In his "Glottalized Continuants" article (Sapir 1938), for example, he notes that in Navajo the phoneme /ỵ/ (glottalized [y]) only exists in alternation with unglottalized /y/, where it is produced as a result of the "d-modification" rule. As he observes, the reflex one would expect in Navajo for "d-modified" /y/ is /ẓ/; and this is in fact found in most cases. However, the regular "d-modified" forms of /m/ and /n/ are (glottalized) /m̓/ and /n̓/; and he suggests that the (otherwise nonexistent) glottalized /ỵ/ arose by analogy with these segments. The 'analogy' involved can only be based on the notion that (at least for sonorants), "d-modification" involves an alternation between segments with and without the phonetic property of glottalization.

Recall also that he speaks of the phonemic reality of language for a speaker/hearer as "an ideal flow of *phonetic* elements" (emphasis supplied). Sapir's phonemes are thus 'ideal' in the sense of constituting a mental reality which may correspond only indirectly to physical events—but not in the sense of having no phonetic properties. The phonemic properties of a segment are those a speaker/hearer assigns to it in his mind, but the result is still something that can be regarded as an ideal *sound* rather than a complete abstraction.

Reinforcing this interpretation is an important constraint noted by McCawley (1967c) on Sapir's phonemic analyses. These are quite consistently presented in the form of charts of the phonetic segments that occur in a language, in which some elements are enclosed in parentheses. The parenthesized segments are those that are regarded not as phonemes but as variants of other, phonemic segments. As a result of this way of conceiving of phonemes, it is clear (as McCawley argues) that the set of phonemes for Sapir is always a subset of the set of occurring phonetic types. He did not, thus, allow for analyses in which some phonemes are phonetically abstract in the sense of

230 / Edward Sapir

combining a collection of phonetic properties that never occur together in any surface segment—a type of analysis proposed for several languages in the early years of generative phonology, and the basis for a part of the so-called 'abstractness' controversy.

We will suggest below that Sapir's constraint on the segments that can occur in phonemic forms is simply one part of a larger limitation on the extent to which phonemic representations can deviate from the regularities that characterize phonetic forms. What is of interest to us here is the following: Sapir's presentation of phonemic elements as the nonparenthesized subset of a language's segment inventory shows that phonemes cannot be abstract in the sense of 'phonetically nonoccurring'; but it also shows that they are quite concrete in the sense of being homogeneous with phonetically complete (i.e., fully specified) segments. They thus have phonetic properties, even if (a) these properties alone do not constitute the primary reality of the phoneme, since it is its 'use' within the system of the language that primarily determines its linguistic essence; and (b) the properties of the phoneme corresponding to a given phonetic segment may not be determinable by direct physical measurement (for reasons that we will explore below).

McCawley (1967c) also notes that Sapir seems to have conceived of phonemes not as collections of properties but rather as unitary individuals: as he puts it, logically similar to proper rather than common nouns. It is interesting to observe that this point of view would have allowed Sapir to respond to an objection made by Bloomfield concerning the linguistic significance of phonetic representations (had he addressed the question). The issue will be dealt with in more detail in the following chapter: if one thinks of the segments in such a representation as characterized by the phonetic properties which are observed and recorded in them, then any (humanly accessible) phonetic transcription must be incomplete due to the possibility that additional properties not noted explicitly in it could in principle be distinguished as well. If one thinks of a phonetic segment as a unitary whole, however, as Sapir apparently did, then a possible response to this charge of necessary incompleteness would be that simply to name an individual is sufficient to provide a unique identification, even if all of its properties are not known. For further discussion of Bloomfield's point, see the following chapter.

Even though Sapir did not conceive of a phoneme as defined by a collection of phonetic properties, there is another sense in which a phoneme's linguistic identity is decomposable into a number of individual factors. An essential characteristic of a phoneme is that it forms part of a small finite inventory of comparable elements, which together constitute a system. Indeed, a phoneme is described as "a functionally significant unit in the rigidly defined pattern or configuration of sounds peculiar to a language" (Sapir 1933[1949]:46). Individual phonemes are thus sounds which are located in an "inner configuration of the sound system of the language" (Sapir 1925[1949]:41f.), and the place of a (phonemic) sound in such a structure is given not by its objective phonetic properties, but rather by "a general feeling of its phonetic relationship resulting from all the specific phonetic relationships (such as parallelism, contrast, combination, imperviousness to combination, and so on) to all other sounds" (ibid., p. 42).

"Parallelism" here may well be based on the phonetic properties sounds have in common, but this is only part of the story. Sounds are also close to one another in the pattern of a language if they share aspects of distribution. For instance, the English phonemes /p, t, k/ belong together not only because they constitute the voiceless stops of the language but also because (a) they occur initially, medially, and finally; (b) they may be preceded by *s* in all positions; (c) they may be followed by *r* initially and medially; (d) they may be preceded by *s* and followed by *r* initially and medially; (e) each has a voiced correspondent. Proximity of sounds in a language's pattern may also be shown by the alternations they enter into: thus, in English /f/ and /v/, /s/ and /z/, /θ/ and /ð/ are related because they alternate (*wife/wives*, [a] *house/* [to] *house*, *bath/bathe*, etc.), while /p, t, k/ are not grouped by such a relationship with /b, d, g/ (though they are in German).

The full system of language's phonemic pattern is thus given not by phonetic factors alone (though these are not irrelevant), but also by a wide range of distributional, morphological, and other nonphonetic properties in terms of which sounds may be similar or different. It follows from this that what is the same inventory of phonemes from a phonetic point of view could be organized into more than one distinct system; and Sapir makes this conclusion explicit in his papers on phonological structure. He notes, for example, that essentially the same pair of phonemes (/θ/ and /ð/) can be found in both English and Spanish, but that the structural connection between them is much closer in English (where they are related by alternations) than in Spanish (where they are not, and where on the contrary /θ/ alternates with velar /k/ instead). The converse of this, that the same "inner configuration of the sound system of the language" could be built on phonetically distinct segment inventories is also argued, thus establishing the essential role of nonphonetic factors in determining the character of a phonological system.

It is not clear that Sapir ever actually worked out the entire phonology of a language on the basis of the sort of property he argued was fundamental in determining phonological structure, but he did include in his descriptive work numerous references to affinities between sounds that were established on this basis. The importance of this point of view was that, while it is primarily a theory of the nature of elements occurring in a class of representations, the elements themselves and their relations to one another are defined in terms of the rules of the language: rules governing distribution, on the one hand, and rules describing alternations on the other.

The resulting theory is a theory of phonemic representations that we can characterize as a 'fully specified basic variant view' in the terms of chapter 2 above, similar in that respect to the early views of Baudouin de Courtenay and the first works of Trubetzkoy. Subsequent work, especially that influenced by Bloomfield, would depart from this position on many points: by abandoning Sapir's psychological approach for an external one, by reducing the content of phonemic elements to the minimum of properties necessary to specify their distinctive function, and by sharply reducing the abstractness of the relation between phonemic and phonetic form. In all of these respects, American phonology followed a course of development similar to that found between the early views of Baudouin and the later position of Trubetzkoy and Jakobson's work.

Another difference between Sapir's conception of phonemic structure and that of later American structuralists bears some relation to all of these points. The range of nonphonetic regularities (stated in a grammar by rules) which were considered as relevant to establishing a phonemic system soon came to be restricted to questions of the surface distribution of phonetic segments alone. Sapir's position accords a crucial role to the study of rules in establishing the nature of phonemic elements, where the class of rules involved is a rather comprehensive one. An exclusive focus on regularities of surface distribution would gradually result in a theory that only accorded theoretical status to the representations themselves.

Sapir's descriptive practice in phonology

Most of Sapir's theoretical writing in phonology (e.g. Sapir 1921, 1925, and 1933) was devoted to establishing the notion of 'phonemes' and the difference between a linguistically significant representation of sound structure and a phonetic representation of speech as a physical reality. This is true even of Sapir 1921, where the word *phoneme* is not used as such, although there is nonetheless an obvious continuity of views with later work. Much valuable evidence concerning Sapir's conception of phonological structure can also be obtained from a consideration of his practice in describing particular linguistic facts (most comprehensively, in complete grammars such as Sapir 1922 and 1930). It is worth exploring these issues further, aside from whatever intrinsic interest the question may have, since Sapir was highly regarded during his lifetime as an insightful descriptivist, and it was on the model of his work that his students and others sought to continue a 'Sapir tradition' (for some discussion, see Harris 1944a, 1945, 1951b, as well as Hymes & Fought 1981).

A prominent regard in which Sapir's practice differed from that of most subsequent American structuralists was the degree of abstractness of the relation between phonetic and phonemic form. This was argued explicitly and exemplified in theoretical papers such as "La réalité psychologique du phonème" (1933), and can be illustrated from virtually any of his descriptive works. It is convenient to discuss this abstractness in terms of the degree of deviation Sapir permitted from the principle that would later be taken to define "the practical requirements of phonemics (i.e., given the phoneme in an environment, we know what sound it represents; and given the sound in an environment, we know what phoneme it represents)" (Harris 1945:239).

It is quite clear (and often remarked) that Sapir allowed for many descriptions in which the phonemic representation of a form cannot be determined from its phonetic form alone. Most of the examples in his "psychological reality" paper (1933) are intended to make exactly this point, and it pervades his descriptive work. As one example, in his Takelma description (Sapir 1922) he cites an instance in which as many as four different phonemic forms (the stem $sā^ag$ followed by nothing, by glottal stop, by t' or by k') all converge on exactly the same phonetic representation ($sāk'$).

Such a possibility arises because phonemic elements are construed not as recodings of phonetic forms but as an inner psychological reality that corresponds to the physical event of speech, where the correspondence is mediated by a system of (possibly quite complex) rules. Among their effects, some of these rules might describe neutralizations of multiple phonemic forms in a single phonetic form—by specifying that under given conditions two different phonemes have the same variant, by deleting certain phonemic elements from the phonetic representation under given conditions, or by directly replacing one phoneme by another in the environment in question. Sapir was not concerned to state a procedure by which one representation could be recovered from the other without appealing to any other information: for him the relation between phonemic and phonetic realities might be mediated by any and all aspects of human cognitive abilities, and such phenomena as neutralization were not seen as posing any problems of principle whatsoever.

The possibility of having nonunique phonemic forms that correspond to the same phonetic representation was a point on which later linguists explicitly separated themselves from Sapir. The kind of phonemic-to-phonetic relationship he envisioned would later be explicitly distinguished from phonemics and characterized as 'morphophonemic'. It appears that Sapir accepted this terminology at least in his last years, and in fact an important source of morphophonemic theory in American linguistics was Sapir's collaboration with Swadesh, Newman, and Voegelin (among others of his students) around 1933–36. Sapir uses the term *morphophonemic* in such late works as his 'Glottalized Continuants' paper (Sapir 1938), and his students devoted much attention to morphophonemic as opposed to phonemic description (at least in the sense that term came to have for others). The absence of any systematic theoretical statement from Sapir on the matter, however, leaves us in some doubt as to the role of a distinction between morphophonemics and phonemics in his thinking.

Less commonly remarked than the difficulty of recovering Sapir's phonemic forms from phonetic information alone was the fact that he does not appear to have required unique translatability in the other direction, either. That is, in some instances more than one variant may be assigned to the same phoneme, without its necessarily being possible to determine in terms of phonological factors alone which variant will occur in a particular form.

In his Southern Paiute description, for example, he discusses at length (Sapir 1930:47–48) the distribution of the alveolar and palatal spirants and affricates (*s* and *c* = [š], *ts* and *tc* = [č]). He finds that the distribution of the alveolar and palatal segments is largely complementary (determined by the qualities of the surrounding vowels), and on this basis *c* is described as a variant of *s* and *tc* as a variant of *ts*. The rule distributing *tc* and *ts* is straightforward: *ts* appears before *i* and *tc* elsewhere. The distribution of *c* and *s* is more complicated, and depends on an interplay of preceding and following vowel. However, there is a small residue of cases in which one of the two appears in the environment characteristic of the other, including a few near-minimal contrasts: cf. *ɔsɔrɔɲwi-* 'to snore' vs. *qɔc·ɔvï-* 'tinder', or *ta-na'c·iχa* 'cleft in hoof' vs. *pi-na's·iχa* 'between one's legs'. Some surface contrasts of this sort may be due to the operation of a set of assimilation rules (ibid., pp. 54ff.) when more than one spirant or affricate appear in a word, and some may result from morphologically governed 'analogies'. Nonetheless, there is also a class of instances in which the distribution of alveolar vs. palatal articulation is simply not predictable.

Here, as elsewhere, what is important to Sapir is that in the overwhelming majority of cases these two phonetically similar types are not in contrast, and there are frequent interchanges between them depending on the vocalic environment. On this basis, Sapir treats them as phonemically identifiable: in the dictionary accompanying the Southern Paiute grammar, he describes *c* as a "mere" variant of *s*, and thus not a "primary sound," even though their complementarity is not quite absolute. This is a sort of violation of the principle quoted above from Harris that later phonemicists, more concerned with methodological rigor than with representing their intuitions about a language under discussion, would certainly not countenance. Nonetheless, it is a sort of situation which we might well find fairly often in natural languages if we were to look closely for it.

Consider the following situation, for example. In Danish, the (short) vowel *a* shows considerable variation in quality depending on a following consonant, ranging from a rather back vowel before *r* to a rather front vowel before dentals. Before velars and labials, however, there is some difference across dialects: in some, *a* before these segments is roughly as front as before dentals, but for other (especially conservative) dialects, *a* in such positions has an intermediate degree of backness. In general, each individual dialect has a predictable distribution of such phonetic variants, though the principles involved differ slightly from one to another.

Now imagine a speaker of Danish who has been exposed in early childhood to two distinct dialects; suppose, for example, that the child was brought up in part by a nursemaid speaking a dialect different from that of his parents. In a few words the nursemaid's pronunciation may be retained, even though the parents' dialect is acquired as a whole. As a result, the speaker's lexicon may contain apparent contrasts between a relatively front *a* and a further back quality before labials or velars: *bamse* 'teddy-bear' with front [a], but *hamstre* 'hoard, accumulate' with further back [*a*], reflecting the source of the former word in one dialect and the source of the latter in a slightly different one.

When such a situation is encountered, it is usual to dismiss its significance for synchronic phonologies by saying that it involves two (or even more) coexistent systems, each of which is valid for a distinct portion of the vocabulary. Even if we admit that such an account somehow solves the descriptive problem as far as our hypothetical Danish speaker is concerned, that is not the end of the matter: this speaker's children may well learn their language from him, preserving the minute vowel distinctions within his vocabulary, and in their speech there is no longer a question of nonhomogeneous sources or distinct coexistent systems. Though explicit descriptions of such a situation are rare in the literature, a certain amount of anecdotal evidence and unsystematic personal observation suggests that it may well arise with some frequency in real speech communities.

One way to characterize this state of affairs, of course, is to say that for the speakers in question, the result of the (original) dialect mixture is the creation of a new contrast between two short *a* phonemes. This suggests, however, that the difference is one which is capable of differentiating words by itself: i.e., that a form like *bamse* pronounced with the back vowel of *hamstre* would constitute a potential new word of Danish. Alternatively, however, one might adopt a solution similar to that of Sapir's description of alveolars and palatals in Southern Paiute: treat both of the *a*'s as corresponding to the same phonemic entity, but allow for the realization of that entity to differ slightly from word to word as a lexical property of individual items which is not completely governed by rule. In that case, *bamse* pronounced with a back *a* would not be a *new* word of Danish but, rather, a different (possibly incorrect) pronunciation of 'teddy-bear'.

Such allowance for lexically idiosyncratic variation within the realization of a single phonological category might be described in several ways. In Sapir's case, an individual lexical entry for a form contains (as we will note below) both the phonological representation and a list of its principal occurring surface variants. Thus all forms with either *s* or *c* are listed together under *s* in his Southern Paiute dictionary, but those which show phonetic *c* (generally for completely predictable reasons) have the phonological unit in question represented in this way. In such a framework the state of affairs under discussion here is described by allowing different phonetic subentries to be associated with the same phonemic form. Alternatively, if one distinguishes in representations between numerically specified 'detail values' for features and the binary valued categorial interpretation imposed on them (as sketched, e.g., in Anderson 1974), one might simply allow lexical representations corresponding to a given category to vary slightly within the range of that category.

The point to be made here is not that such a minor insouciance on Sapir's part toward the precise distribution of variants as is shown by his description of Southern Paiute alveolars and palatals corresponds to some deep insight which was buried by the hostile attitudes of later phonologists. There is no reason to believe that Sapir intended to make systematic use of the sort of descriptive possibility just raised. What is important, however, is the recognition that explicit attempts to make phonemic theory as rigorous as possible in subsequent years involved the claim that any phonetic difference between forms necessarily corresponded to one of three possibilities: (a) a contrastive distinction between two phonemes; (b) a completely predictable difference between two variants ('allophones') of the same phoneme; or (c) free variation between variants of the same phoneme, with no phonological role.

In fact, a fourth possibility was implicit in Sapir's practice: a difference between variants of the same phoneme, which thus does not correspond to a contrast between two potentially distinctive phonological units, yet is not 'free variation' either, since it is distributed idiosyncratically in particular lexical items. We have only hinted above at an answer to the question of exactly what phonological functions such a description could serve, and what situations it might be appropriate for, but it perhaps warrants further examination—which is only possible if the methodological assumptions of phonemicists since Sapir are reexamined.

Rules and their interactions in Sapir's phonology

We have noted above in passing that Sapir imagines a phonemic representation to be related to phonetic form by the operation of a system of rules. In his descriptions (most of which, it should be recalled, were actually written at a relatively early stage of his professional career) he typically refers to the elements of a phonemic representation as 'organic'; it is in terms of whether a given element is organic or not that it may differ from a merely phonetic segment—and, as we have emphasized here, not in terms of its nature as a relatively complete specification of a (possible) articulatory segment.

Organic elements of a form are also referred to sometimes as 'morphological'—by which it is not meant that they serve individually as the realization of morphemes, but rather that in the form in question they are present in the phonological representation of some morpheme (rather than being introduced by rule). From this fact and others, it is easy to see that the difference between 'organic' and 'inorganic' segments is a function of the status of a particular *token* of a segment, not of an entire segment *type*: the same segment type may be organic in some occurrences and inorganic in others. Some segment types may be variants (rather than phonemes), however, in which case the phonetic identity of the segment in question is always introduced by rule.

The rules stated in Sapir's descriptions may be distinguished in various ways, though whether any of these classifications had any systematic status for Sapir is open to question. One difference which he appeals to more or less explicitly in his typology, however, is that between phonetic processes which by themselves serve to mark some grammatical category ('symbolic' processes, like vowel ablaut in Germanic for example) and those which either serve simply as accessory marks of some category or are determined by phonological factors alone.

A particularly important difference is that between rules which state regularities of distribution and rules that describe actual alterations in the (ideal, or phonemic) form of words. Sapir follows roughly the outline of Boas in stating as many general distributional regularities as possible that hold over the entire inventory of surface forms in a language—restrictions on possible consonant clusters, vowel sequences, adjacent or other multiple stresses within the same word, co-occurrence of particular vowels and consonants or accentual elements and syllable types, etc. These are formulated as generalizations about the range of surface forms in the language, and subsequent statements of rules that alter the form of linguistic elements are, whenever possible, motivated by (or at least related to) such restrictions and generalizations.

We can also distinguish rules which describe the distribution of properties (or variants) whose occurrence is completely predictable from those that relate independently occurring segment types. In Southern Paiute, for example, Sapir treats such properties as stress and the devoiced variants of vowels as predictable, while other segment types are potential phonemes. In consequence, since variants are everywhere predictable, their appearance is completely abstracted away from in giving lexical (or phonemic) representations. Other elements which may be introduced by rule, in contrast, also have an independent status in the language as phonemes: in Southern Paiute a nasal consonant may be phonemic or it may be introduced by rule (after a 'nasalizing' stem); long and short vowels are phonemically distinct, but rules lengthen short vowels or shorten long ones in various positions; *tc* (a variant of *ts*) is an independent phoneme from *t*, but it is also the result of the palatalization of *t* after *i*, etc.

In cases where the presence of a phonemic element within a morpheme is predictable by some rule affecting sequences of morphemes, it is nonetheless written as such in phonemic forms: thus, intramorphemic *tc* after *i* is always written as such, and never as *t*. As a result of this practice, we may well find two distinct statements of what is apparently the same regularity: in Southern Paiute the statement that only spirantized forms of the (nongeminated) stops appear when they are intervocalic is quite separate from the rule of spirantization that affects single prevocalic stops after vowel-final stems. With regard to the t/tc alternation, a statement that within morphemes only tc (and not t) appears after i is needed in addition to the palatalization rule which replaces t by tc when i precedes. The relation between the two is generally made overt, however: the rule governing the alternation will be explicitly motivated by the need to maintain the overall regularity (tc but not t appears after i) where it would otherwise be violated in the juxtaposition of independent elements.

Relations between 'organic' (or phonemic) forms and phonetic structure may be quite complex, and the rules which establish the relation are not necessarily independent of one another. Sapir's generalizations are quite uniformly formulated as processes which replace one representation with another ('item and process' descriptions, as Hockett 1954 would later christen them), as opposed to the static statements of distributional regularities ('item and arrangement') which were the norm in most later American phonemic theories. Sapir manifestly intended such replacements to represent a part of the synchronic grammar of the language, and not simply a fact of its history: in several places in both the Takelma and the Southern Paiute descriptions, as well as in his account of Wakashan in the 'Glottalized Continuants' paper, he explicitly contrasts "living" processes in a language with those changes which have only "etymological" value.

The mechanism of rules which replace one representation with another lends itself naturally to a particular expression of rule interrelations. When one rule presupposes information that is provided by another in order to operate correctly, we normally formalize this situation by ordering that rule after all others whose operation it presupposes; and Sapir employs ordering at least as a metaphor in the same way (again, as a synchronic descriptive device rather than exclusively a historical account).

Kenstowicz (1975) explores the assumptions of Sapir and others in this regard, and establishes a number of properties of the ordering relation as employed by Sapir. He notes, for example, that the role of ordering is in general limited to the description of 'feeding' situations (cases, that is, in which one rule has the effect of creating new instances for another rule to apply to). Whenever a rule creates a situation to which another rule could apply, Sapir assumes that the natural state of affairs is for this subsequent modification to take place. He does sometimes observe explicitly that this is the case—for example, "an original γ is sometimes weakened to a glide$^\gamma$ or even entirely lost before or after an u-vowel, more often after an ï-vowel. *Vocalic contractions may then result*" (Sapir 1930:52; emphasis supplied). More often, however, he lets this sort of situation go unremarked.

In the case of 'bleeding' orders (cases in which a rule is prevented from applying to a form that would otherwise undergo it by the intervention of a second rule) or 'counterfeeding' orders (where a possible feeding relationships does not obtain), the failure of a rule to apply is stated explicitly. In Southern Paiute there is a general rule by which "when an initial w comes, by derivation or compounding, to stand after a vowel, it regularly becomes nasalized to '*ŋw-*"; we are also told that "[t]his rule does not operate, however, when *w* becomes intervocalic by reduplication" (Sapir 1930:49). A possible alternative descriptive account would simply order the rule nasalizing *w* after processes of derivation and compounding, but before reduplication; however, Sapir employs order only to describe (realized) feeding relationships rather than in the more general fashion of many later theorists.

Another particularly important descriptive device in Sapir's work, supplanting order in many instances, is a direct appeal to the difference between organic and inorganic elements. In describing the stress system of Southern Paiute, he states a general principle of stress on alternate moras to which (he makes clear) there are numerous apparent exceptions. These exceptions are all due, however, to the operation of rules shortening, lengthening, or diphthongizing vowels, or coalescing them, or inserting glide vowels in certain cases. The overall generalization is "that all inorganic increments and losses have no effect on the mora-construction of the word" (Sapir 1930:38). One might formulate this simply by ordering the stress rule before any of the other processes, but apparently the nonfeeding nature of the relationship in question makes it preferable for Sapir to state it in terms of the difference between organic and inorganic elements.

It is worth noting that there is actually one class of exceptions to the generalization that stress is assigned to alternate *organic* moras: Sapir notes that "long vowels resulting from contraction of long + short vowels, however, count as ordinary long vowels. . . . Similarly, vowel plus diphthong results in a two-moraed diphthong. . . . In other words, no three-moraed syllables are found" (ibid.). This would imply that (in a description based entirely on ordering) the stress rule should apply after vowel coalescence, but before other shortening, lengthening, etc., rules. Again, since the generalization is not one involving a feeding relationship, Sapir chooses to describe it in terms of the nature of the representations involved rather than in terms of the interaction of rules.

The relation between rules and representations

We turn finally to a feature of Sapir's work which has been responsible (at least indirectly) for a considerable amount of comment in the recent literature: his conception of the lexical structure of individual linguistic elements within a comprehensive description. Though he never specifically discusses this question in theoretical terms, relevant information is to be found scattered throughout his work. Most importantly, we have the example of his Southern Paiute dictionary (part 3 of Sapir 1930) to go by.

A dictionary representation must, of course, specify all of the information about an element which is 'morphological' in character—i.e., its organic phonological shape and any additional idiosyncratic properties which distinguish it from other elements in the language. The format of entries in the

Southern Paiute dictionary is rather interesting, however. Each item is presented in (a) an approximation to its organic (or 'phonologic') form; and (b) the surface form of representative words in which it appears. The latter are of course predictable from the former by rule. We can observe that any alternants which differ from the organic form (or from one another) in terms of some phonemic segment are generally given; alternants which differ in terms of variants (i.e., completely predictable segment types, the parenthesized elements in a chart of the occurring phonetic segments) are not necessarily made explicit. Thus, stress and vowel or sonorant devoicing, for example, are always predictable in Southern Paiute for Sapir, and so stress is not marked and all vowels and sonorants are shown as voiced in lexical entries (though these properties are of course marked in the surface full-word forms given to exemplify lexical items).

The presence of *both* phonemic and (more nearly) phonetic forms in a lexical entry could have allowed Sapir to describe exceptional lexical items: thus, if some item fails to undergo a rule, he might simply not list the variant of it that would be produced by this rule, with the implication that the operation of the rule is blocked for this item. We can observe that this practice of giving both phonetic and phonemic forms would also allow Sapir to describe lexically idiosyncratic phonetic realizations of a single phoneme, as in the case of Southern Paiute *s* discussed above.

In addition to the basic and variant forms of an item, a lexical entry may also contain information about its effect on other items. This is in the form of arbitrary markers (i.e., ones that are not interpretable as any phonological segment) which trigger certain morphologically conditioned rules in the grammar. The most celebrated example of this is the marking of every stem (and most affixes) in Southern Paiute with respect to which of three arbitrary classes it belongs to: 'spirantizing', 'geminating', or 'nasalizing'. "Here the deciding factor is the nature of the preceding stem or suffix, which, as far as a descriptive analysis of Paiute is concerned, must be credited, as part of its inner form, with an inherent spirantizing, geminating, or nasalizing power" (Sapir 1930:63). The inclusion of such arbitrary morphological properties in lexical items represents an implicit claim that purely phonological accounts of alternations are not always possible: i.e., that it is not possible in such a case to reduce the characterization of an element as spirantizing, etc., to other aspects of its phonologically motivated form.

This is a conclusion of Sapir's which, at least in this particular case, has been contested by a number of writers. Discussions by Harms (1966), McCawley (1967c), Chomsky and Halle (1968:344ff.) (as well as untold numbers of student homework assignments and term papers) have suggested phonological characterizations of the difference among Sapir's three classes of Southern Paiute stems and suffixes. Typically it is observed, for example, that the effect of spirantizing morphemes is exactly what would be predicted if the items in question simply ended in a vowel (since intervocalic single consonants always appear in spirantized form), provided 'geminating' and 'nasalizing' morphemes ended in something else. It is usually suggested that nasalizing elements end phonologically in a nasal consonant, while geminating ones end in a voiceless vowel (Harms) or an unspecified obstruent (Chomsky & Halle). On the basis of this characterization, a set of purely phonological rules can be formulated to derive the three variants of following elements, eliminating the morphological operators 'spirantizing', etc.

There is no reason to imagine that Sapir simply missed the possibility of such a solution: his descriptive insight into the language was clearly quite sufficient to see this analysis, and in fact many of its ingredients are present explicitly in his description (see, e.g., the remarks on spirantization as the normal case in Sapir 1930:63–64). If he chose to describe this situation by means of morphological and not phonological properties of elements, it is likely that some systematic reasoning lay behind the decision. In fact, it is possible to show that the solutions in the subsequent literature were not available to Sapir in principle. Furthermore, it can be shown that his description is in fact more accurate on empirical grounds than the phonological alternatives that have been proposed.

We can see immediately that one of these possibilities would not have been open to Sapir: Harms's proposal to identify geminating stems by a final voiceless vowel, as opposed to final voiced vowels in the spirantizing class. For Sapir, voicing of vowels was a property that was completely predictable, and voiceless vowels were variants (rather than phonemes). Since an organic representation consists only of phonemes, it could not contain voiceless vowels, and so Harms's solution is excluded. Note that it will not do to say that the geminating class of morphemes in itself establishes the phonemic status of voiceless vowels: it remains the case that voiceless vowels only exist in surface forms under specific, predictable conditions, and since this generalization remains valid regardless of the morphological alternation in question, voiceless vowels are excluded in principle from organic representations.

We confine our attention, therefore, to Chomsky and Halle's proposal that geminating elements end in an obstruent consonant (which they suggest is actually t, though that is irrelevant to the present discussion) and nasalizing ones in a nasal consonant. From Sapir's point of view this solution would not have been unacceptable in the way Harms's would be, since both obstruents and nasal consonants of course appear in phonemic forms; but there is a different problem.

This is that Southern Paiute forms always end in a vowel, and positing stems and suffixes that end in consonants (obstruents or nasals) would violate what is otherwise an absolutely valid generalization about the language. This generalization is not true of phonetic forms directly, since apparently consonant-final words are created by rules of vowel devoicing and subsequent reduction of voiceless vowels or their absorption into a preceding spirant, or by elision of final short vowels before a word beginning with a vowel. It is also

true that words may end with a glottal stop; but Sapir argues in his phonological description that an organic glottal stop is actually associated with a
syllable as a whole, and not with a specific sequential position within it. It
may be realized syllable-finally, but more often is found somewhere within
the vowel articulation—or even in a neighboring syllable. When these predictable effects are abstracted away from, however, the generalization remains
that Southern Paiute words end in open syllables, and Sapir quite evidently
interprets the same generalization as applying to individual lexical elements.
Morpheme-final obstruents and nasals, then, could not be posited in phonological forms without violating a canonical pattern of the language.

The issue which we suggest Sapir implicitly resolved on this basis has only
recently been raised explicitly. Hale (1973) argues that in several languages,
the assumption that a completely general phonological account should be
given for a morphologically limited phonological pattern leads to incorrect
consequences for reasons quite close to those that apparently motivated Sapir.
Strictly speaking, the discussion of these examples falls outside of the historical purposes of the present work. Since the issue is one of current relevance, however, and since it can be shown that Sapir's solution is actually validated by the evidence from Southern Paiute along the same lines as those
argued by Hale, an appendix to the present chapter contains a further elaboration of these points.

It appears, in fact, that the generalization at work here is of a piece with
other constraints imposed in effect on Sapir's phonological analyses. The fact
noted by McCawley that the set of phonemes constitutes a subset of the set of
surface phonetic segments is clearly of the same order, since a posited phoneme which did not meet this requirement would violate an obvious generalization about surface forms. Another instance of the same respect for surface regularities is to be found in the fact that "any characteristic common to
all the alternants of a morpheme will appear in Sapir's phonologic representation of it" (McCawley 1967c:110). This does not mean that the phonologic representation is necessarily one of the occurring surface alternants, of
course, or even that all of the components of such a representation show up in
some surface alternant (e.g., the absolutive suffix in Southern Paiute is assigned the representation *pi*, despite the fact that the initial consonant always
shows up as spirantized *v*, geminated *p:*, or nasalized *mp*). It does entail,
however, that any valid generalization about the surface form of an element
will be reflected in its underlying representation.

In Sapir's phonology, then, generalizations induced from surface representation play an essential role in constraining the set of underlying ('phonemic',
'phonologic', 'organic') representations. Even though the relation between
the two in any particular case may be quite complex, the two are unified on a
global basis across a language by a single set of regularities of distribution
and canonical structure.

Importantly, we should recall that the same set of regularities plays a significant role in determining the class of phonological rules. These are in general assumed to operate so as to affect morphologically complex representations in which some generalization would otherwise be violated, so as to make them conform to the generalization. For example, a language allowing only two-consonant clusters may insert an epenthetic vowel in the environment CC_C *so as to avoid a cluster of three consonants*. This rationale for the existence of phonological rules, taken over largely from Boas, serves as the basis of a distinction between genuinely phonological and (at least partially) morphologized rules for Sapir.

The features of Sapir's practice which are most often noted are the distance between his underlying representations and surface phonetics, and the role played by rules of alternation (formulated as replacement processes) in his grammars. To understand the central points of his analyses, however, it is important to see that both of these components of an analysis are construed by him as organized by the regularities obtaining in surface forms. The elements of phonological representations are determined by reference to rules of the language: as observed above, the natural classes and linguistically significant affinities among phonemic elements are given by the regularities of distribution and alternation that they participate in. Conversely, the phonological rules of the language function primarily to maintain a regularity determinable from the canonical form of surface representations. Few linguists, historically, have held as unified a view as Sapir of the interrelationship of considerations of rules and representations in a single structure within natural languages.

APPENDIX: Abstractness and Sapir's analysis of Southern Paiute

A central feature of Sapir's analysis of Southern Paiute is his claim that the spirantizing, nasalizing, or geminating effect of stems (and affixes) on a following affix is to be stated as a morphological property of individual elements, rather than in terms of phonologically derived consequences of the elements' underlying shape. As suggested above, such an analysis would be required for Sapir if he were to avoid positing underlying shapes that violate an otherwise valid generalization about the language—that words (and thus stems) do not end in consonants. A set of similar cases are discussed by Hale (1973), including a particularly clear example furnished by the phonology of several languages of the Polynesian family. Hale's discussion is based on Maori, but we take our examples below from Samoan, where the facts are entirely parallel.

In Samoan there are no consonant clusters, and no final consonants; i.e., all syllables are open. There is very little inflectional morphology in the language, but most verbs have a so-called 'passive' form, and many have a plural and/or a reciprocal in addition. The passive is almost always formed by the addition of a suffix which is the reflex of proto-Polynesian *-Cia*, where the particular consonant that appears differs from one verb to another: thus, *o'o* 'arrive, reach', passive *o'otia*, but *oso* 'jump', passive *osofia*, *ula* 'make fun of', passive *ulagia*, *inu* 'drink', passive *inumia*, etc. Since the consonant that appears in the suffix depends on the root that is involved, the lexical entry for a root must contain some indication of which form the suffix takes when added to it.

There are evidently two basic alternatives open for the description of these facts. We might follow Sapir's example in his Southern Paiute and characterize each stem with an abstract morphological operator: thus, the phonological representation of *o'o* would be simply /o'o/, with the additional indication that it is a '*t*-stem' (as opposed to /oso/, which is an '*f*-stem', etc.). In this case, the suffix itself would have several morphologically determined forms: /-tia/ with some verbs, /-fia/ with others, etc.

Alternatively, we might incorporate the suffix consonant into the representation of the stem itself, giving underlying representations such as /o'ot/, /osof/, etc. In this case, the suffix could be given a unitary underlying form /-ia/; and the correct forms could be derived simply by the application of a rule deleting final consonants when no suffix follows. On that basis /o'ot/ would yield surface [o'o], but /o'ot+ia/ would give [o'otia] since the truncation rule would not apply in this form. This second solution involves no arbitrary morphological features, and only a single completely automatic phonological rule (final consonant truncation). It is evidently simpler from a purely formal point of view than the morphological account; and it is noteworthy that Bloomfield, in his discussion of this example (Bloomfield 1933:219), adopts it without further comment, as obvious. This is also an example frequently used in elementary linguistics classes, since the phonological account of the variation is so easy to arrive at.

Nonetheless, there are some problems for this solution. From a purely phonological point of view, the fact that some suffix variants are not simply *-Cia* poses a slight problem: the forms *-ina* (e.g. *salu* 'sweep', passive *saluina*), *-a* (e.g. *ave* 'take', passive *avea*), and *-na* (e.g. *'ai* 'eat', passive *'aina*) are not obviously derivable from some stem form plus /-ia/. Assuming we ignore these as simply suppletive forms of the suffix, there still remain more serious difficulties. For instance, the causative form of verbs is made with the prefix *fa'a-*, sometimes with reduplication of the root. Interestingly, virtually all such causatives take the passive suffix /-ina/, regardless of the suffix taken by the noncausative: e.g., *pa'u* 'fall' has the passive *pa'utia* indicating that its stem-final consonant (on the phonological solution) should be /t/, but its causative *fa'apa'u* has the passive *fa'apa'uina*. Similarly, *manatu* 'remember' has the passive *manatua*, but its causative *fa'amanatu* 'remind' has the passive *fa'amanatuina*. The stem *oso* 'jump' apparently ends in /-f/, if this is what is indicated by the passive *osofia*; but in that case the causative *fa'aosooso* is doubly problematic: first because the supposed final /-f/ is not preserved before the reduplicated copy (i.e., the causative is not **fa'aosofoso*); and second because its passive is *fa'aosoosoina* (not **fa'aosoosofina*).

One might claim that the causative morphology involves truncating the final consonant and thus replacing the passive ending appropriate to the root with another; but aside from the fact that this seriously weakens the explanatory force of the proposed final consonant in the phonological form, it will still not resolve all difficulties. In addition to the passive, Samoan also has another suffix (the reciprocal), which usually takes the form -*C(a')i* with different consonants depending on the root. Forms such as *fe-ita-ga'i*, reciprocal of *ita* 'be angry', appear to lend support to the final consonant solution, since the passive of this stem is *ita-gia*: the two show the same idiosyncratic consonant, a fact which is immediately explained if this consonant is part of the stem. But in that case, forms such as *alofa* 'love' pose a problem: its passive is *alofa-gia*, but its reciprocal is *fe-alofa-ni*. In such a case there is apparently no single form of the stem which can account for all variants.

Hale cites similar facts, together with a number of generalizations about the direction of regularization through historical change, to argue that despite the simplicity of the phonological solution, the descriptively adequate account of this variation is actually the morphological one. Most importantly for our purposes, he argues that in this case (and in other unrelated ones which he examines), the morphological solution is to be preferred for a principled reason: because the phonological solution posits underlying forms (with final consonants) which violate an important surface generalization about the language (all syllables are open), this disparity between the canonical forms of deep and surface representations excludes the phonological solution altogether. We argued above that it is exactly this consideration which (at least in part) led Sapir to prefer a morphological account in Southern Paiute: phonological (near-)surface forms always end in vowels, so it is not possible to posit underlying forms that violate this generalization by ending in obstruent or nasal consonants.

If Sapir was thus led to a morphological analysis of the consonant alternations in Southern Paiute by considerations like those noted by Hale, this would constitute only a theory-internal argument for his solution, and it is especially important (if we are interested in the correctness of the theory) to ask whether there is additional evidence bearing in the same direction. In fact, when we examine the phonology and morphology of Southern Paiute (and Sapir's description of it) more closely, there turn out to be important problems for the phonological view which also argue in favor of the morphological account.

In his discussion of why he adopts the morphological position, Sapir notes that there is no independently motivated difference in the phonological shape of spirantizing, geminating, and nasalizing stems to which their differential behavior could be related. Of course, that is just what is in question; and the claim of the phonological account is precisely that there is such a difference, but that it is neutralized if no suffix which would manifest it follows the stem. Sapir argues on the basis of comparative data that there is no consistent etymological difference either, which would not of course bear directly on the synchronic descriptive issue (though it is strongly suggestive of a non-phonological account if one believes phonological alternations are usually, if not always, the reflex of historical change).

Much more significant than the sort of plausibility argument one might found on historical considerations, however, are the purely descriptive problems which a phonological account must face. Recall that on that view, suffixes are uniformly represented with simple consonants, and the spirantized, geminated, and nasalized alternants arise by virtue of the effect of a stem-final vowel, obstruent, or nasal on this segment. This assumes that the suffix shapes appearing with particular stems are exclusively a function of a unitary underlying phonological property of stems.

There are a number of suffixes, however, which have invariant forms, regardless of the character of the stem they are attached to. Some of these are consistently nasalized (e.g., -ŋqï- 'Indirective, to, for'); some geminated (e.g. -q:u- 'numeral objective'), and some invariably spirantized (e.g., -γa- 'durative'). On one version of a strictly morphological account, all that would need to be said about these items is that their lexical entries have only a single phonetic form corresponding to their organic form: this has the effect of blocking the morphologically conditioned selection of nonoccurring variants. On the phonological account, however, one must introduce additional rules: for example, to eliminate a posited underlying stem-final nasal or obstruent consonant before a suffix which is invariantly spirantized.

A number of other suffixes appear in two of the three possible forms, but not in the third. In general, these appear either spirantized or nasalized but not geminated. After geminating stems these elements occur spirantized: for example, the agentive suffix -vi/-mpi has no geminate form, and thus appears spirantized after the geminating stem nɔ:- 'to carry on one's back' (in e.g. nïŋwï'nɔɸı 'man-carrier'). Sapir traces the nasalized variants of these suffixes to an independent phonological rule of nasalization applying after a nasal in the preceding syllable (as in the future suffix -vania, appearing as -mpania in iviŋumpania 'will take a drink'). This process is distinct from morphological nasalization, which does not require a nasal consonant in a nasalizing element: for example, the stem pa'a- 'to be high' and the suffix -vi 'agentive', among others, are nasalizing despite the lack of a nasal consonant in their phonological form. Sapir thus treats the nasalization of the 'two-shape' suffixes as extraneous, and reduces the issue to a difference between forms that undergo the morphological processes of consonant alternation and those that do not. A problem is posed for this account, however, by the fact that such suffixes appear nasalized after even those nasalizing stems that contain no nasal consonant: payimpani 'I shall go', from nasalizing payi- 'go, walk' plus the future suffix -va/mpa-.

In order to describe the exceptional items on the purely phonological account, it must be assumed either that they undergo spirantization even after obstruents or that they trigger exceptional deletion of a preceding obstruent (but not of a nasal). One interpretation of Sapir's morphological account, in contrast, simply involves omitting a geminated alternant from the lexical entry: the nasalized form will be chosen correctly where appropriate, with the spirantized form treated as the 'elsewhere' case.

Some of these exceptional suffixes simply represent specialized uses of one of the variants of a regular, alternating suffix. The suffixes -γi 'to come in order to' and -$\gamma wa'ai$ 'to go in order to', for example, are invariantly spirantized. They are clearly related, however, to the alternating suffixes $\gamma i/k:i/\eta ki$ 'to come while ——ing' and $\gamma wa'ai/k:wa'ai/\eta kwa'ai$ 'to go while ——ing'. To describe this phonologically, we must assume the suffix acquired a special sense together with the necessary exception features to enforce spirantization even after consonant-final stems; but if we take Sapir's account, we need only say (as he does) that one of the existing variants of the regular suffix acquires a special sense.

Just as the description of the suffixes poses problems for the phonological account, a consistent description of the stems also seems difficult on that view. For example, the same stem may well appear with one suffix variant in some cases but with another in others: e.g., $wa'a$ 'cedar' is normally geminating, as shown by $wa'ap:\ddot{i}$ 'cedar tree', but sometimes takes nasal suffixes as in $wa'ampi$ 'cedar berry'. To describe such cases, we would have to assume the stem has two distinct phonological shapes, distributed on a morphologically determined basis.

In this same vein, there is an interesting semisystematic tendency for spirantizing stems to be treated as geminating when they are compounded with other independent stems: e.g., $a\eta qa$- 'red' is normally spirantizing, as shown by $a\eta qa\gamma a$ 'to be red', but often appears as geminating in compounds like $a\eta qap:a\gamma\ddot{i}$ 'red fish, trout' or $a\eta qa$-$q:ani$ 'red house'. Sapir notes that the tendency to use geminate variants of stems in compounds may be due to the greater phonetic similarity between this form and the (initial, thus unspirantized) consonant of the simplex form; for discussion, see Darden (1984). For our purposes, the interesting point is that Sapir sees this restructuring as "the first step towards the dulling of a consciousness of consonantal alternations and toward their development into mere historical survivals" (Sapir 1930:70). He envisions a developmental sequence similar to that posited by Baudouin de Courtenay and Kruszewski (see above, chapter 3), by which a process which may once have been phonological has become morphological, and is on its way to becoming a merely lexical relic. If we assume the phonological view, we must claim that the unusual behavior resides not in the second element of such compounds, where Sapir plausibly localizes it, but rather in the development of irregular obstruent-final variants of the *first* elements—variants which only appear compounded.

None of this evidence demonstrates conclusively that a phonological account of the Southern Paiute suffix alternation is *impossible*; rather (like

Hale's evidence from Maori and the similar facts reviewed above from Samoan), the evidence indicates that it is less appropriate than the morphological analysis pursued by Sapir. Further evidence derived from the facts of reduplication makes this case even clearer. Reduplication normally copies the initial CV of an element; e.g., *sivai* 'whittles' reduplicates as *sisivai* 'whittles many times'. The stem consonant following the reduplicated syllable, being no longer word-initial, is subject to change, and the changes it undergoes are the same three as those found in suffix alternation: spirantization, gemination, or nasalization. Since the shape of the stem is more self-evident than the identity of a hypothetical stem-final consonant, the facts of reduplication ought to provide clear evidence for whether or not phonological structure is the essential determinant of these alternations.

Cases in which reduplication results in nasalization appear to provide some evidence in favor of the phonological account, because most of these are stems of the shape /CVNX/ (e.g., *qani* 'house', which reduplicates as *qaŋqani* 'houses'). If we allowed the reduplication rule to copy CV(N), instead of only CV, and treated nasalization as resulting from a sequence of nasal consonant plus stop, this result would follow directly. Unfortunately, however, there are some instances in which nasalizing reduplication arises without a nasal consonant in the stem (Sapir cites *pɔmpɔtsats-* 'lizard'), which suggest that nasalization in reduplication (though largely predictable) is in part morphologized.

The case of geminating reduplication is much more difficult to explain phonologically. The class of stems that geminate when they reduplicate seems completely unpredictable: thus, *tava'c:up:ï* 'dry' reduplicates as *tʌta'ɸʌcupï*: 'all dry' with a geminate, but *tavin'na* 'put out one's breast, strut' reduplicates as *tara'vin'naai* 'keeps putting out (his) breast' with a spirantized form. It should be emphasized that there is no consistent correlation between the form CVCX where the second C is an obstruent (or a geminate) and geminating, rather than spirantizing reduplication. Further, the gemination may affect a stem-internal consonant, rather than a stem initial one: e.g., *ivi* 'drink' reduplicates as *i'ip:i* 'drinks repeatedly' with a geminate, or *tïvʷïn:aɣai* 'leads', as *tï'tïp:ïnaq:ai* 'leads away several times'. Finally, the same stem may appear with more than one kind of reduplication, in different morphological categories. The stem *qwïï-* 'take' forms a distributive *qwïywïï* 'several take (one object)' with spirantizing reduplication, but also an iterative *qwïqwïï* 'to take one object several times'. All of these facts indicate that morphological factors and not phonological structure determine the applicability of the process of 'gemination'.

We conclude, then, that a variety of evidence suggests that Sapir was right in treating the spirantizing, geminating, and nasalizing processes in Southern Paiute as morphologically rather than phonologically conditioned. This result is of some interest in itself, but we have pursued it at such length here not simply as a matter of descriptive linguistics. Rather, the point to be made is that a phonological solution (if correct) would have been perfectly available to Sapir, if systematic considerations had not led him to prefer the morphological account. These systematic factors, we suggest, are the same as those recently discussed by Hale: a desire to avoid positing underlying forms which would violate a basic generalization about the structure of surface forms in the language.

IO

Leonard Bloomfield

Few figures in the history of linguistics stand out as dramatically as incarnations of their time and place as does Leonard Bloomfield, the symbol of theoretical thought about language in North America from the 1930s through the 1950s. Most of the development of linguistic theory in America during this period is usually attributed either to his own work or to the work which his students and followers carried out in the name of his views. As we will see in chapter 11, a good deal of what went on in the self-consciously 'post-Bloomfieldian' period was not particularly close to Bloomfield's own views; but many nonetheless felt that a scientific approach to language could be largely identified with the task of working out Bloomfield's theoretical notions. Especially from the point of view of those elsewhere, American linguistics in this period basically *was* Bloomfieldian linguistics.

Of course, Bloomfield was by no means the only linguist of note in North America during this period: we remarked in the previous chapter that his activity during the 1930s overlapped with that of Sapir, who was a major figure before Bloomfield's work was generally known; for that matter, Boas was still alive when Bloomfield was working. Some of the reasons for Bloomfield's gradual ascendancy have already been noted: probably a central consideration was his identification with the growth of linguistics as an autonomous scientific discipline. Boas and Sapir had established an independent position identified with the study of language in North America, but their work was largely thought of as a tradition within the field of anthropology. Bloomfield, on the other hand, was closely identified with the rise of a distinct professional field of linguistics.

One factor in this identification was his prominence in the development of the distinctive institutions of the new field. He was one of those (together with George Bolling and Edgar Sturtevant) who wrote the "Call" for the formation of a linguistic society in the United States, as well as the author of the lead article "Why a Linguistic Society?" in the first issue of *Language*. He participated enthusiastically in the activities of the society, and was its president in 1935. He taught several times at the Linguistic Institute, including introductory courses that served as the focus of attention at this annual event. To appreciate this, we must recall that the institute served a much more important service function in its early days, before linguistics was taught per se in more than a very few universities; and its introductory course constituted virtually the only way for many to gain an idea of the content of the discipline.

Another relevant factor was the constant stress in Bloomfield's writing on the independence of linguistics from other fields, and the consequent necessity to develop its autonomous assumptions in a rigorous way from minimal basic principles. This he felt to be essential to the scientific status of the study of language; and the alignment of these views with the philosophical and scientific tenor of the times made him a natural candidate for the status of theoretical spokesman for the new discipline. As early as 1926, when he published his "Set of Postulates for the Science of Language," Bloomfield had staked out the issue of 'scientific rigor' as peculiarly his own.

Subsequently, his text *Language* served as the introduction to the field for more than one generation of students, and this impact was reinforced by his popular and effective teaching at the LSA's summer Linguistic Institutes. Though he had few students himself, his role in the organization of the army's Intensive Language Program during World War II further reinforced his influence on the most active and aggressive of younger scholars, who would dominate the emerging field after the war. Taken together with the genuine novelty of his theoretical views, these factors help to explain why, as linguistics took on a clearer professional identity in the United States during the 1930s and 1940s, a large part of that identity was based explicitly on the work of Bloomfield.

Bloomfield's life and career

Bloomfield was born in Chicago in 1887, and grew up there and in Elkhart Lake, Wisconsin. In 1903 he went to Harvard, where, by virtue of some extra credit awarded on entrance, he was able to earn a BA by 1906. He then went to the University of Wisconsin, where his meeting with Eduard Prokosch apparently helped him to settle on Germanic and linguistics as a career. In 1908 he left Wisconsin for the University of Chicago, from which institution he received his doctorate in 1909 for his thesis "A Semasiological Differentiation in Germanic Secondary Ablaut."

This work is essentially a series of 249 families of words within Germanic, each of which shows a pattern of (innovated) Ablautlike vocalic variation which is utilized for essentially sound-symbolic purposes. These sets are preceded by an introduction to the nature of the phenomenon and some remarks on the correlation between particular vocalisms and their gross semantic spheres. Though this work clearly addresses issues of some generality, it is also an excellent example of the detailed investigation of particular topics which marked Bloomfield's research in Germanic and, later, his study of Algonquian languages.

In 1909, he began his teaching career at the University of Cincinnati, and in

1910 went to the University of Illinois. In those years (and in fact for most of his academic life) his major teaching responsibility was German—often the most basic courses. This occupation with elementary language teaching was by no means just a painful necessity for Bloomfield: he concerned himself with problems of language pedagogy throughout his life, and spent much energy on bitter criticism of the attitudes of 'educationists' whose methods he found sadly wanting in light of modern linguistic understanding. Among his less-known writings are to be found a *First German Book* from 1923, as well as an English reader for elementary schools, which was organized to minimize the trauma of the idiosyncrasies of English orthography for beginning readers. The strictly linguistic interest of these works, alas, is not as great as the commitment they show on his part to problems of linguistic pedagogy.

He spent 1913–14 in Leipzig and Göttingen, improving his background in Indo-European, Sanskrit, and related studies. His preparation in these areas was already quite substantial thanks to work with Prokosch and others at Wisconsin, and to his year at Chicago; it is also probably not irrelevant that his uncle Maurice Bloomfield was a distinguished Sanskritist (and the second president of the Linguistic Society of America). During this year he studied with Leskien and Brugmann among others. It seems that such study in Germany was a necessary rite of passage for those who wanted to advance in the academic profession of Germanic studies; but Bloomfield chose an unfortunate time to pursue this field. The outbreak of the first World War radically reduced interest in German in the United States, and although statistics are not available, he probably found himself with a greatly reduced number of students. The resulting spare time may have something to do with the fact that in 1915–16 he took up his first real fieldwork—on Tagalog, with a native speaker who was a student at Illinois.

In 1914 Bloomfield published his first major work, *An Introduction to the Study of Language*. This book, based on Wundt's views on the psychological basis of language, was fairly well received, and (though not particularly revolutionary) furnishes an excellently organized and presented view of the state of general linguistics at the time. In connection with this book, it is interesting to note something that was already becoming a particularly American trait in writing about language. More than one of his reviewers found Bloomfield's examples from a wide variety of 'exotic' languages unconvincing (because unfamiliar), and took him to task for appealing to these rather than sticking to the well-known members of the Indo-European family.

In 1921, he was offered a promotion from assistant professor at Illinois (where unconfirmed rumor has it that he was in fact denied tenure) to full professor at Ohio State University. He naturally accepted, and finally had the opportunity to teach some linguistics, but his primary responsibility was still in German. A more important aspect of his years at Ohio State than his actual teaching there, though, was probably his association with the psychologist

Alfred P. Weiss, whose behaviorist views (in conjunction with more general scientific influences of the times) quickly came to replace completely Bloomfield's earlier acceptance of Wundt.

Bloomfield was invited to the University of Chicago in 1927. It was during this period that he and Sapir were colleagues (albeit somewhat uneasy acquaintances). Most of the students in linguistics at Chicago were working with Sapir; although Bloomfield again taught some linguistics, his main responsibilities were still in Germanic philology. During his period at Chicago, he became increasingly well known as a general linguist. Though he continued to work in Germanic, he had begun fieldwork (as early as 1920) on languages of the Algonquian family. His field work was supported for one summer (in 1925, working with Sweet Grass Cree in Saskatchewan) by Sapir and the Canadian Department of Mines; it is perhaps interesting to note that Sapir, who did not know Bloomfield at all directly, was initially hesitant about this appointment, fearing that Bloomfield might be too much of a philologist to make a good fieldworker.

His Algonquian work was to occupy much of his attention for the rest of his scholarly life, covering a number of the languages of the family in considerable depth. It also served as the basis of what would become a paradigmatic demonstration of the power of the comparative method, and of its applicability to unwritten languages as well as to those with a long period of attestation: a consonant cluster reconstructed by Bloomfield for proto-Algonquian on the basis of a single set of cognates was subsequently confirmed by the discovery of unique reflexes in other, previously unstudied (or poorly described) dialects of the family. As a validation of the general assumptions of neogrammarian theories about historical change, this result took on nearly the same value as did the discovery of Hittite for Saussure's posited abstract *coefficients sonantiques* (the 'laryngeals').

Especially after the publication of his 1933 book *Language*, Bloomfield became a truly major figure in American linguistics. In 1940 he was made Sterling Professor of Linguistics at Yale, where it was expected that he would be able to devote all of his attention to general linguistics; but unfortunately he never really settled in at Yale. His wife was unwell at the time he arrived there, which contributed to his unhappiness about his general circumstances. The outbreak of the second World War disrupted normal academic life, and much of Bloomfield's energy from 1942 to 1945 was devoted to the practical problems of the army's Intensive Language Program. Then, in 1946, he suffered a disastrous stroke, from which he never really recovered. Though he lived until 1949, he was essentially unable to do further scholarly work during this period; and at his death left a number of projects (including his major grammar of Menomini, as well as a lexicon of the language, and a grammar of Eastern Ojibwa) unfinished. Much of this material has since been prepared for publication, largely through the efforts of Charles Hockett.

Bloomfield's view of language, linguistics, and psychology

Bloomfield's opinions about the nature of language and the procedure by which it should be investigated marked a major reorientation in American linguistics, but we cannot examine here all of the issues raised by his position. A substantial literature already exists in this area (see, e.g., Hockett 1970; Esper 1968; Teeter 1969; Stark 1972; Hymes & Fought 1981, and numerous references cited there), and a survey of it would take us far afield. On the other hand, one central issue is directly relevant to establishing the bases of Bloomfield's specifically phonological views and must be at least sketched. This is the question of his attitude toward psychology, and especially the role of 'meaning' in linguistic structure. In this connection we treat briefly some aspects of the philosophy of science that are dealt with explicitly in his writings.

Bloomfield's first work in general linguistics (his 1914 *Introduction*) starts from two general sets of premises: those of Wundt's *Völkerpsychologie* with respect to the central part played by psychological considerations in understanding the nature of language; and those of his neogrammarian teachers concerning the mechanical nature of linguistic change and the possibility of a rigorous account of its operation. His enthusiasm for neogrammarian theories never weakened, and in fact he saw as one of the advantages of the overall position that he later developed the extent to which it allowed him to rationalize the underlying assumptions of the neogrammarians.

Within a fairly short time, however, whatever doubts he may earlier have had about the explanatory value of Wundtian psychology were replaced by an ardent commitment to behaviorist (or "mechanist," as he preferred to put it) assumptions about the nature of the human mind. This change in outlook appears quite clearly in his 1926 "Postulates," where he attempted to state the foundational assumptions of linguistic study in as explicit a way as possible. The influence of his acquaintance with Weiss at Ohio State is clearly evident here, at least on the surface: the "Postulates" are intended to be modeled on Weiss' set of postulates for psychology, though in fact the resemblance is not very close (Bloomfield's postulates in fact resemble the axiomatization of linguistics attempted in Pāṇini's grammar more than they do Weiss's postulates for psychology). More importantly, no doubt, the terminology of reference to psychological factors is wholeheartedly behaviorist in orientation (as when the *meanings* of utterances are defined as their "corresponding stimulus-reaction features").

The central factor underlying both his maintenance of neogrammarian assumptions about change and the shift in his point of view on psychology was undoubtedly Bloomfield's passion, a product of the times, for scientific explanation based solely on propositions relating observable factors and influences by principles of logic and mathematics alone. Throughout his career, he would again and again ridicule appeals in the supposedly scientific linguistic literature to 'mentalistic' explanations. It is important to understand that, by this term, he did not mean (as often understood by subsequent commentators) to deny the existence of human mental life. Rather, he intended to reject the notion that a deterministic, causative role is played in shaping linguistic (or other) phenomena by a mysterious and unobservable entity ("mind"), whose principal property is its nonobedience to the normal laws of physical structure or to any other discoverable system.

There are, of course, conceptions of the nature of mental and cognitive activity that allow such systems to be taken seriously as the objects of non-mystical investigation, but without requiring (as early behaviorists did) that they be reduced to special cases of the activity of other physical organs. Bloomfield, however, saw appeals to a distinctive mental structure underlying language not as attempts to elucidate the special nature of this cognitive system but, rather, as an attempt to evade any rational explanation for the facts of language. Considering the excesses along such lines that had earlier been committed in the name of a romanticist philosophy of language and mind, this concern was by no means totally illusory. For Bloomfield, however, the obvious (and only) alternative to antirationalist speculation about the mysteries of the human soul was to deny scientific existence to anything other than the material embodiment of mind in a system of nerves and related tissue supporting systematic patterns of electrical activity.

Bloomfield's account of mind (and particularly the nature of meaning, a linguistic aspect of mind) in his later work such as *Language* is thus intended to be founded on factors that are (at least in theory) observable. The description he gives of meaning is entirely in terms of situation, context, and the disposition of a speaker to respond in particular ways to particular stimuli. If we knew every detail of a speaker's history, he suggests, from a complete description of the composition of his nervous system, internal organs, etc., at birth through a comprehensive history of all stimuli to which he was ever exposed, we could in principle know how he would respond to any particular linguistic stimulus—and the combination of such a stimulus with its response in a given situation was all Bloomfield recognized as coherent in the notion of the meaning of a linguistic form. To assume that in addition the form corresponded to an unobservable 'concept' internal to the speaker was for Bloomfield simply antiscientific mysticism.

Bloomfield thus did not (as he is often portrayed as doing) reject the notion that linguistic forms have meanings. He did believe, though, that a satisfactory account of meaning would involve an encyclopedic knowledge of the world and its laws in the most minute detail—a task obviously going far beyond the scope of linguistics, and in fact constituting the subject matter of the nonlinguistic sciences of physics, physiology, etc.

It is quite clear that if we examine this account of meaning in detail (without Bloomfield's *a priori* commitment to purely 'mechanist' foundations for theoretical constructs), it is no more defensible than the 'mystical' view he was attacking. He does not in fact attempt to give the required description of the meaning of any particular utterance (and more importantly, to go beyond the treatment of particular utterances on particular occasions to the meaning of a sentence in general, independent of its particular situational context), but there is every reason to believe that, if he had, he would have found it essentially a matter of faith to maintain that, at a sufficiently minute level, there are observable factors which completely explicate sentence meaning. Most of the internal neurological events and material consequences of previous stimuli that Bloomfield's view depends on for its account of mind are as much a matter of faith on his part as the 'mentalist' picture is for others.

In fact, the choice between 'mentalism' and 'mechanism' as paths to the understanding of meaning is one between research programs rather than between concrete propositions or theories. Both views assume that there is something linguistically relevant (the 'meanings' of linguistic forms and their parts) which must be accounted for; they differ in the assumptions they make about where to look for a suitable foundation for this construct. Bloomfield himself considered that only the mechanistic approach could be defended as scientific; but interestingly enough, he maintained repeatedly that the choice between them was, strictly speaking, irrelevant to linguistics.

The reason for this is that linguistics is concerned with the study of languages as systems that pair sound and meaning, and he felt that the structure of such associations could be investigated even in the absence of a precise knowledge of just what the sounds and the meanings are that are paired. Sound and meaning enter the construction of linguistic theories at an absolutely basic level: the "fundamental assumption of linguistics," first presented in his 1926 paper and subsequently developed in several other places (including *Language*), is that "in every speech community some utterances are alike in form and meaning" (Bloomfield 1933:78). Nonetheless, just what the meanings of those utterances are (as well as the phonetic details of their production) need not be known in order to get on with the business of analyzing the system in which they have meaning.

Somewhat paradoxically, then, Bloomfield introduces his view of linguistic meaning only to exorcise the details of it from the investigation: to claim not that linguistic analysis disregards meaning but that the concrete nature of meaning can be reduced to a postulate, something external to language itself. Strictly speaking, then (as he argued on various occasions), the issue of mentalist versus mechanist theories of meaning is one that is external to the development of a theoretical account of the structural properties of language. In a provocative (if somewhat overstated) image, he likened the circumstances of his 'anti-mentalism' to "a community where nearly everyone believed that the moon is made of green cheese, [in which] students who constructed nautical almanacs without reference to cheese, would have to be designated by some special term, such as *non-cheesists*" (Bloomfield 1944; reprinted in Hockett 1970:417).

Meaning, like the moon, is an essential term of theories in the relevant domain, but the concrete content of either is strictly speaking an orthogonal issue. Admittedly, Bloomfield felt compelled (and entitled) to push his own opinions about what meaning is and how it should (and should not) be investigated; but it is noteworthy that the specific details of his reductionist account play little or no role in his discussion of other areas of linguistic structure. What remains is the assumption that utterances (and their parts) have meaning; that linguists as a practical matter know a great deal about what these meanings are, when they are alike or different, etc.; and that even if they cannot give a complete scientific account of individual meanings, their practical knowledge still allows them to get on with the task of analyzing language, since meaning enters the analysis only in the form of a posited external property of linguistic forms.

Whether meanings can be successfully treated as outside the scope of linguistics is an issue quite parallel to that raised by efforts to exclude phonetics in a similar way as an external discipline. This attempt on Bloomfield's part will be discussed below, where it is argued that, while the issue is a substantive one, there are good empirical reasons for including the study of linguistic phonetics within the science of language (and not only as a branch of physics or physiology). In the case of the study of meaning, however, it must be admitted that our actual substantive understanding of this area is sufficiently meager that we are far from being able to develop the corresponding argument. Fortunately, in a work devoted to phonology, this issue can be left unresolved.

The independence of linguistics from any particular psychological assumptions seemed to Bloomfield to be recommended not only by general methodological considerations but by substantive ones as well. Thus, psychology is fundamentally the study of the workings of individual minds; and Bloomfield found it difficult to accept that this could provide an adequate basis for explaining the workings of an essentially social phenomenon like language.

More importantly, the posited independence of linguistic mechanisms provided a basis for an explanatory theory of language change. For Bloomfield, the overwhelming accomplishment of previous study of language was the body of results achieved by nineteenth- and early twentieth-century comparativists concerning the history and development of languages. These results, in his view, were inseparable from the assumption of the regularity of sound change. In numerous articles and reviews, he criticized scholars who would admit even as a marginal possibility the existence of sporadic or incomplete sound changes, the inhibition of sound change by factors such as onomatopoeia or specialized meaning, and other such nonphonetic influences. Even a single clear instance of such a limitation on the operation of sound change would, he felt, essentially evacuate the explanatory power of the notion itself, since it would lay open the possibility that any observed change was due to the operation of sporadic factors, and not to a clear regularity at all.

This does not mean that Bloomfield recognized only blind phonetic change as a mechanism of linguistic development. In *Language* he gives one of the clearest accounts available in the literature of the workings of mechanisms such as analogy and a variety of sorts of borrowing. The point is that each of these other mechanisms can be distinguished from sound change per se, and when these manifestly distinct categories are set aside, what remains is simply "sound change"—a fully determinate process, which does not fall into "sporadic" and "regular" types. A shift which is validly considered "sound change" may of course take place only in some specifiable set of phonetic environments; but this simply indicates that in the general case, sound change consists in the replacement of certain sound *sequences* by other sound sequences. In particular, it does not mean that sound changes can affect only a portion of the vocabulary determined by some extraphonetic criterion.

Having argued that sound change (strictly construed) is an essentially regular process, Bloomfield finds the explanation of that fact in the autonomy of linguistic structure. His reformulation of the classic neogrammarian principle ("Sound laws have no exceptions") is simply that "phonemes change": i.e., that it is possible that the articulatory implementations of phonemes or their structural interrelations may be changed, but that when this happens it affects in identical ways every linguistic form in which the changed phoneme occurs. Since the role of phonemes in particular forms is dependent only on the nature of the phonemes in question, and not on the meaning, frequency, etc., of the forms themselves, there is no way that such factors could possibly influence the working of a change affecting the phonemes. A correct understanding of the independence of linguistic structure from factors that are properly extralinguistic allows for the deymystification of the traditional doctrine, and for its understanding as a genuinely explanatory principle.

It can certainly be argued (as of course it has been) that Bloomfield's views on the nature of mental and cognitive organization were excessively simplistic, and that they cannot form the basis of a genuinely adequate theory of language. We definitely have no intention of maintaining the contrary here. Nonetheless, his repeated insistence that linguistics is independent of his or any other particular psychological assumptions should be taken at face value. His radical deterministic behaviorism certainly had much less influence on his theories in such central areas of linguistic structure as phonology and morphology than his pronouncements would later have on his students and successors.

In practice, Bloomfield's appeal to notions such as 'meaning' in developing his picture of linguistic organization is not significantly different from that of the "mentalists" he often caricatured. This observation is illustrated, somewhat ironically perhaps, by the quotation from a review in the *New Statesman* which appears on the dust jacket of the British edition of his book *Language*. "Most palatable of all," the reviewer finds, "are Chapters 24, Semantic Change, and 25, Cultural Borrowing, in which we get right away from the mechanics of language and can follow the play of the human mind." It is doubtful that Bloomfield agreed that this judgment accurately picked out the best side of his work, but it is clear that his psychological assumptions did not bar him from making insightful observations about "the play of the human mind," or from making use of "mental" data as well as physical ones in elaborating a theory of language.

Bloomfield's conception of the phoneme

The specifically phonological side of Bloomfield's theory of language is presented primarily in his comprehensive survey *Language* (1933); citations below are from this source unless otherwise indicated.

Discussion of phonemic structure starts from a consideration of the *gross acoustic features* of utterances. Bloomfield observes that from the standpoint of the physicist or physiologist, there are an unlimited number of properties of utterances that could be registered, but of these "only a part are connected with meanings and essential to communication (*distinctive*)," (ibid., p. 77). It is with these that the linguist is fundamentally concerned, since the essential task of linguistics is to work out the consequences of the basic postulate that "*in every speech community some utterances are alike in form and meaning*" (ibid., p. 78; italics in original). With respect to the sound side of utterances, this implies an analysis of the system by which similarities and differences in form are utilized to signal similarities and differences of meaning.

Of course, this analytic task cannot be performed with reference to phonetic data alone. "To recognize the distinctive features of a language, we must leave the ground of pure phonetics and act as though science had progressed far enough to identify all the situations and responses that make up the meaning of speech-forms" (ibid., p. 77). Making use of our everyday knowledge of linguistic meanings, we can thus explore which differences in phonetic properties correspond to differences in meanings, and which do not. Essentially, then, "phonology involves the consideration of meanings" (ibid., p. 78). There would hardly be any need to point this out, except that subsequent work within a paradigm professing to follow Bloomfield's lead attempted to develop techniques of phonological analysis that could proceed on the basis of a corpus of raw phonetic data alone, without reference to its interpretation.

In analyzing the differences in sound that correspond to differences in meaning, it soon becomes evident that these are limited in number. We find, according to Bloomfield, that linguistic forms can be divided into parts (corresponding in size to phonetic segments); and that these parts can be isolated and recombined into other forms. On this basis, he defines a *phoneme* as "a minimal unit of distinctive sound feature" (ibid., p. 79). This notion separates those phonetic properties internal to a given segment-sized stretch of an utterance that are (potentially) distinctive from those that are not. Only the former belong to the phoneme itself, while the nondistinctive features that accompany these in actual realizations of the phoneme are not significant for the linguistic study of speech. In the familiar case of English voiceless stops, for example, the properties distinguishing one place of articulation from another would form part of the phonemes /p, t, k/, while the property of aspiration would be absent from the phonemes altogether.

Bloomfield's conception can thus be identified (in the terms of chapter 2 above) as a theory of 'incompletely specified' phonemes: the phoneme is made up of only some of the identifiable phonetic properties of the segment, and the nondistinctive properties play no essential role in the linguistic system. This point of view, of course, differs fundamentally from, for example, Sapir's 'fully-specified basic variant' theory. Bloomfield's phoneme is a proper subset of the phonetic properties that are actually realized in a given portion of a speech event: it is thus neither an abstract 'mental image' of a segment nor a complete phonetic segment of any sort, in contrast to Sapir's conception.

Bloomfield's phoneme is a cluster of exactly the distinctive properties of a segment, and on the basis of his particular phrasing it has sometimes been suggested that he considered phonemes to be analyzable into constituent distinctive features along lines similar to those followed by Trubetzkoy, Jakobson, and others. There is little or no support for such a conception in Bloomfield's own writing, however. Rather clearly, the "minimal unit of sound feature" that is a phoneme was considered by him to form a unitary *Gestalt*, whose further componential analysis was not linguistically relevant. Despite the use of the word *feature*, which would later come to have great theoretical importance, there is every reason to believe that Bloomfield meant only to oppose the distinctive properties (taken as a whole) of a segment to their nondistinctive accompaniments.

One sort of argument (*ex silentio*) for this interpretation follows from the observation that Bloomfield never appeals systematically to constituent subproperties of phonemes as playing a linguistically significant role in descriptions. In common with all linguists of his generation and others, he makes unsystematic use of traditional phonetic terms to designate classes of segments in stating particular generalizations, but this terminology functions simply as a framework of reference and not as a theoretical analysis in itself (as the distinctive feature system did for Trubetzkoy and Jakobson, for instance).

More interestingly, though, Bloomfield gives a different account of the organization of a set of phonemes into a system—one which plays a role essentially similar to that assigned by others to a set of phonetically defined features, but which is not at all based on the phonetic components of phonemes. The starting point for interpreting the role of particular phonemes in the system of a language is indeed a traditional chart based on "practical-phonetic" (i.e., articulatory) classifications. He then observes, however, that such schematic ways of organizing the phonemes of a language, "even when they exclude nondistinctive features, are nevertheless irrelevant to the structure of the language, because they group the phonemes according to the linguist's notion of their physiologic character, and not according to the parts which the several phonemes play in the working of the language." To remedy this deficiency, he offers an alternative basis for the organization of phonemic systems.

The sort of presentation of the "structural facts" of a phonemic system which Bloomfield proposes obviously owes much to the ideas of Sapir (see chapter 9 above), and also shows similarities to the account provided (later) by Hjelmslev (see chapter 6). His classification of the phonemes of English begins with their role in the structure of syllables, a notion which he takes to be definable in terms of peaks of sonority. On this basis he arrives at a division of phonemes into vowels (sounds that are always syllabic) and consonants (sounds that are always or sometimes nonsyllabic). The latter class includes the two subclasses of mutes (always nonsyllabic) and sonants; the subclass of sonants is further subdivided depending on the conditions that determine whether particular segments are syllabic or not.

One might well ask why syllabicity, an apparently phonetic property (given Bloomfield's definition of it in terms of sonority peaks) should play a role in defining the systematic structure of the set of phonemes in a language, while other phonetic properties (such as place and manner of articulation) are treated as unsystematic. The answer to this is apparently that syllabicity (in contrast to other properties of a segment) relates not simply to the segment itself but to the way in which it is integrated with other segments into larger structural units. In fact, all of the properties Bloomfield recognizes as determining "the parts which the several phonemes play in the working of the language" have this character.

This becomes clearer when we move on to the other set of criterial properties he discusses. Besides their role in syllable structure, phonemes are also classified in terms of their specific distributional properties: whether they appear initially, finally, in given positions within clusters, etc. A large number of specific distributional classes are thereby adduced, and Bloomfield claims that such a classification will provide a unique definition for every phoneme in the language. The combination of syllabic and distributional properties thus serves (to the exclusion of purely local phonetic properties) to define the system of phonemes in a language.

It will be recalled that both Hjelmslev and Sapir proposed similar distributional bases for determining the phonological system of a language, and that both of these authors also emphasized the independence of such classifications from purely phonetic considerations. We can note an interesting difference between Bloomfield and these other writers, however: while they recognized the pattern of alternations into which a given segment enters as contributing to its linguistic identification, Bloomfield makes no provision for such properties. Thus, both Sapir and Hjelmslev would recognize the fact of alternations such as *bath* versus *bathe* in English as establishing a connection between [θ] and [ð] in this language; while (Castillian) Spanish *dice* [diθe] 'says' versus *digo* [diɣo] '(I) say' and *dije* [dixe] '(I) said' shows a connection between [θ] in this language and velars. Evidence of this kind is not treated by Bloomfield as relevant to the establishment of phonemic systems.

This follows from the fact that Bloomfield apparently considered a phonological theory of a particular language to be essentially (and perhaps exclusively) a theory of the representations to be assigned to each particular linguistic form in the language, independent of all other forms. As we will see in a later section, he certainly expected the linguist to describe the facts of alternation; but this description, in contrast to the phonemic representation of utterances, is a reality only for the linguist and not for the speaker. For the speaker, what is essential about each form is the way in which it is composed out of elementary units of linguistic sound structure (the phonemes); and the ways in which these combine with one another into larger units thus constitute their essential structural properties. Systematic relations between one form and other, distinct forms (through alternation, for example) are to be assigned quite a different status: their reality, if any, is a part of the morphology (or syntax) of the language, not of its phonology.

Patterns of alternation thus do not enter into defining the place of phonemes in the structure of a language; neither do local phonetic properties of segments. The only things that are relevant are the distinctness of phonemes from one another, as shown by their ability to distinguish meanings, and the idiosyncrasies they show in combining into larger units. But although these are the bases on which a phoneme's structural role is based, its identity is also phonetic: it *is* a "minimal unit of distinctive sound-feature."

It is "lumps or bundles" of "gross acoustic features" that constitute the units "each one of which we call a phoneme": importantly, the "phoneme-features [are] present in the sound-waves," and have their linguistic significance by virtue of the fact that the speaker has been trained to produce and respond to only these features, while "ignor[ing] the rest of the gross acoustic mass that reaches his ears" (Bloomfield 1933 : 79). Even though in their realization the distinctive features (phonemes) are necessarily accompanied by nondistinctive ones, only the former have linguistic significance. Bloomfield's phoneme is a thoroughly concrete aspect of the speech signal; only the system within which it finds its place is abstract, in the sense that phonetic analysis alone cannot tell us which "sound-features" have a distinctive function, or what possibilities of combination are available to any one of them.

Representations in Bloomfield's phonology

Given the system of phonemes of a language, we are in a position to record utterances in it. To do that, we need to establish a "system of symbols which provides one symbol for each phoneme of the language we are recording"; but it makes no difference what these symbols are, as long as we define their implementation. In particular, there is no reason to represent the fact that the phonetic manifestation of similar phonemes varies from one language to another by using different symbols in transcribing different languages. This may seem a point of hardly any importance; after all, it is quite a familiar observation that the terms of a phonemic description derive their significance from the fact that they differ from one another (internal to the language in question), and not from their absolute identity. On that basis, any set of distinct symbols would serve equally well to represent phonemic forms. Aside from this rationale, however, Bloomfield offers further motivations for his decisions about concrete matters of transcription that are worth noting.

On one hand, Bloomfield was concerned about a purely practical matter: the cost of printing scholarly works making extensive use of special typography. Bloomfield and Bolling (1927) urge that the expense of printing complex linguistic material for the limited and esoteric audience constituted by linguists might actually have the effect of limiting publication opportunities and reducing the flow of relevant scholarship. If linguists would content themselves with transcriptions which deviated as little as possible from the standard symbols of the alphabet plus a few common diacritics, they could avoid a potential economic problem. Since such a minimally exotic transcription could always be linguistically adequate, there is no reason to complicate matters beyond it. Trivial as this may seem, Bloomfield returns to it elsewhere, as he feels there is absolutely no principled justification for incurring the extra expense of highly detailed transcriptions.

Of much more theoretical significance, however, is the question of why one would want to use a detailed transcription system in the first place. Clearly specialized symbols and combinations of diacritics are intended to capture not simply the inventory of phonemes of a language but their phonetic manifestation as well: to serve as a phonetic rather than a phonemic representation of the language. Here Bloomfield raises an objection that is quite startling to the modern reader: he asserts that such phonetic transcriptions can never have any sort of systematic status in linguistic description.

Virtually all views of sound structure have assumed that utterances can be represented in (at least) two distinct ways, each with its own importance. One of these is a phonemic (or phonological) representation, which indicates the properties of the form that differentiate it from other forms in the same language; and another is a phonetic representation, which indicates in an objective, language-independent way how the form is pronounced. Disagreement arises about the conditions to be imposed on the relation between the two, or the possible existence of other, distinct representations (e.g., a morphophonemic one), etc.; but few have questioned the position that these two are an irreducible minimum in an adequate phonological theory. Bloomfield, however, states quite clearly that, for him, only the phonemic representation has any systematic significance, and the phonetic transcription should be dispensed with.

His motivation for this claim is an interesting one, and should be attended to. In actuality, the properties transcribed in a phonetic representation are as much a consequence of the scholarly biography of the transcriber as they are of anything else. Individual linguists, that is, learn to hear certain distinctions and to mark them in certain ways; and the distinctions they learn are a product of the phonetic phenomena manifested in the languages they (and their teachers) have worked on. No matter how many such properties they indicate in their transcription, there is always a limitless set of additional phonetic facts about the utterance that *could* be indicated, had the transcriber the experience (and the patience) to hear and mark them.

Clearly a complete record of the physical implementation of sound sequences would be of interest to a linguist; but for that, a phonographic (or tape) recording of the utterance is needed, perhaps supplemented by a cineradiographic record, EMG recordings, and the like. For Bloomfield, any particular phonetic transcription is simply an imperfect approximation to this complete physical record; and as such without theoretical significance. The phonemic transcription, on the other hand, represents in a complete way the content of an utterance in terms of its distinctive components (since the phonemes of a language are relatively few in number); and so attains scientific significance.

Bloomfield's objection is in fact a serious one (rather more serious scientifically, perhaps, than his point about the cost of typesetting!), and one which phoneticians have not always taken pains to answer. After all, any phonetic transcription represents some of the properties of an utterance while omitting others; what is the theoretical justification for such choices? If none can be provided, we must conclude that (except in the context of specialized phonetic discussions of particular phonetic details) any representation which falls short of physical completeness is a mere approximation to the truth, and thus not linguistically significant because it is imperfect (in a way phonological representations need not be).

There is a natural extension of this point about transcriptions which goes to the heart of the status of phonetics as a discipline within linguistics. If phoneticians are occupied with simply recording and measuring any physical property of utterances they can detect, their activity is surely defensible as a subfield of physics or physiology; but there is no evidence that the resultant accumulation of (seemingly endless and anecdotal) numbers tells us anything about language. Some speech scientists, indeed, appear to accept this conclusion implicitly: they assume that the lowest level of representation provided by a language-particular grammar is roughly equivalent to an autonomous phonemic transcription, and that this is related directly to physical speech by the general properties of the articulatory apparatus (including, e.g., 'coarticulation' effects) and its acoustic consequences. On this view, nothing between a phonemic representation and its physical implementation properly belongs to the description of utterances internal to a particular language. Phonetics could then be said to be strictly external to linguistics, in the sense that its subject matter does not belong in the grammars of particular languages.

Those who believe in the linguistic relevance of phonetic investigation must eventually address this issue. Research based on the 'phonemic principle'— the observation that within a given language some phonetic differences serve to distinguish meanings while others do not—has over and over again been held to yield the conclusion that this insight relegates phonetics to a status strictly outside of linguistics. Bloomfield's claim about the linguistic nonsignificance of a phonetic transcription is simply a particular articulation of the expulsion of phonetics from linguistics which was also asserted by Baudouin de Courtenay, Trubetzkoy, Hjelmslev, and others.

Of course, an empirical demonstration that all phonetic properties below the 'phonemic' level are in fact governed entirely by language-independent properties would serve to establish this conclusion. Since no such demonstration has ever been given, however (or even explicitly claimed), other grounds for the assumption must be sought. The position of Bloomfield (and many others) on this issue, we submit, rests fundamentally on the conception of language as a system of communication alone: as exclusively a set of efficient principles for encoding information. If the nature of language is simply that of a system for communicating meanings, then only those of its features that serve that end can be called essentially linguistic—which implies that only distinctive (or 'phonemic') properties of sound structure are really a part of the system.

Yet when we compare languages with one another, we see quickly that the system of distinctive sound features is by no means the only way in which language organizes sound structure. It is an empirical fact that the distribution of nondistinctive features is just as essentially governed by the grammar of a particular language as is the range of contrasts that serve to distinguish meanings. It is just as much a fact about English that stops are aspirated in certain positions and not others, or that vowels are longer before some consonants than before others, etc., as it is that voicing in stops can distinguish, for example, *pat*, *bat*, *pad*, and *bad*; and a speaker has failed to acquire the system of English if these nondistinctive properties are not correctly distributed, just as if he produces both *bat* and *bad* with final voiceless stops.

It is only in comparatively recent years (especially through the research of Ladefoged and his coworkers—see, e.g., Ladefoged 1980) that the range of systematic phonetic differences within and between languages has come to be seriously studied and appreciated. A wide range of phonetic parameters are apparently governed in quite systematic—but different—ways by principles particular to individual languages. If linguistics is to provide a comprehensive framework for the description of natural languages, it must provide for the linguistically controlled manipulation of parameters that are not distinctive within a particular language, or not even distinctive within any language, such

266 / LEONARD BLOOMFIELD

as the release of stops (see Anderson 1974), the differences among types of 'glottalized' stops, and a host of others.

Development of a descriptive framework that accommodates *all* of the properties systematically determined by language-particular regularities (in any language) is of course the subject matter of phonetics—but *linguistic* phonetics, and not a branch of physics, physiology, or some other auxiliary discipline. Such a study is essentially a matter of describing the systems of natural languages, and not the physical world. Distinguishing the range of variation in phonetic properties that can come under linguistic control from that which is always mechanically determined (such as, perhaps, the position of the epiglottis in speech), always freely variable under the control of the individual (e.g., loudness of the voice), or otherwise linguistically non-systematic is precisely the task of the linguistic discipline of phonetics. The criterion of whether or not a parameter distinguishes meanings within a particular language does not serve by itself to delimit the linguistic from the non-linguistic properties of speech.

Discussion among phoneticians has not, in general, attempted specifically to respond to Bloomfield's objection. Work such as Ladefoged's in developing a cross-linguistically adequate theory of linguistic phonetics, however, implicitly supplies a rejoinder. A phonetic transcription can be said to have linguistic significance insofar as it indicates all and only those physical properties of an utterance that are potentially under linguistic control, in the sense that their distribution can constitute a component of the difference between one language and another. Phoneticians can go on measuring any discoverable parameter of speech signals; the demonstration that a particular property is linguistically relevant, however, depends on showing that its distribution is determined as a matter of the difference between one linguistic system and another, and not that it serves as the basis of a meaning-differentiating contrast—or, on the other hand, simply that it can be measured.

There is thus a principled basis for positing a level of representation of utterances which is neither a complete physical record nor confined to the distinctive features of the language in question. This is exactly a phonetic representation in the traditional sense; the fact that such representations may turn out to be incomplete in particular cases is a reflection of the present state of our knowledge, not of their theoretical status. To appreciate the linguistic significance of this representation, however, it is necessary to recognize that the system of a language has properties other than those of a minimal code for distinguishing and conveying meanings in communication.

The 'abstractness' of phonemic representations

Although Bloomfield did not believe in the linguistic significance of a phonetic representation, his phonology does not reduce to the description of a single, phonemic level. The phonemic representation is related to physical reality (as represented by a laboratory record, for instance), at a minimum, and the description of this relation constitutes a definition of the phonemes involved. As we have noted above, the phonemes of a language are identified with the distinctive component of a segment's 'gross acoustic features', and so we would expect the phonemic representation to be related to its realization in a formally simple way, as a subset of the phonetic properties of the latter.

In particular, we would expect from Bloomfield's theoretical premises that, given an adequate definition of the phonemes of a language, we could translate mechanically beween physical implementation and phonemic form (by simply identifying the relevant features, a task that must surely have a unique solution in particular cases), and vice versa (by supplying, to whatever extent necessary, the redundant or nondistinctive correlates of the distinctive articulations). This two-way translatability would correspond to the condition later labeled 'bi-uniqueness', which played a central role in postwar discussions of the nature of the phoneme. In actual practice, however, Bloomfield's analyses do not meet this condition. Notably, he often provides phonemic representations that are not uniquely recoverable from phonetic data alone. This fact was the subject of considerable disagreement between Bloomfield and his students and colleagues, and the circumstances are worth examining in a bit more detail.

One instance in which Bloomfield's phonemic representation was not necessarily recoverable from phonetic information involved the role of grammatical structure, and especially the boundaries between words. In a paper that appeared in 1930 in *Le maître phonétique*, Bloomfield argued that the segments [x] and [ç] in German could be regarded as variants of the same phoneme. Superficially, this proposal is contradicted by apparent minimal pairs such as *kuchen* [ku:xən] 'to cook' vs. *Kuhchen* [ku:çən] 'little cow', where the two segments contrast. Bloomfield argues, however, that the latter is in fact a compound, and that the diminutive suffix -*chen* should be treated phonologically as a separate word. Given the rule '[x] occurs only after *a, o, u, aw* of the same word', with [ç] occurring elsewhere, the form *Kuhchen* will show [ç] and not [x]: although the segment in question follows *u*, this vowel is not part of the same word.

The problem, of course, is that there is nothing in the phonetic form of *kuchen* or *Kuhchen* which corresponds to the posited boundary between two words in *Kuh-chen*, aside from the difference between [x] and [ç]. Bloomfield, however, believed in the reality of words as linguistic units, and thus in the availability of such grammatical boundaries as potential conditioning factors for subphonemic differences. Hockett (1970:542) reports a revealing anecdote: "Bloomfield, Hoijer, and Hockett lunching together in Chicago. Hockett proposed that when it is impossible to hear word-boundary there is no justification for representing it by a space (or otherwise) in a phonemic transcription. Hoijer, with Bloomfield's obvious approval, says that that is just where the space is most needed. Subject changed."

The phonological role of boundaries (under the name of 'grammatical pre-requisites to phonemic analysis') would later become a major point of contention in discussion of the nature of the phoneme, thanks largely to the arguments of Pike. It is clear, however, that there was little or no issue for Bloomfield: the status of the word was provided for in his set of basic linguistic constructs ("A minimum free form is a *word*"—Bloomfield 1926, def. 10), and thus he assumed that words could be delimited where necessary. Insofar as the distribution of phonetic alternants of a phoneme showed sensitivity to the boundaries between words, this was perfectly admissible. Note that in the German case, the sequence of phonemes is perfectly recoverable from the phonetics (since both [x] and [ç] correspond to the same phoneme), and the phonemic form is translatable uniquely into the phonetic, given that word boundaries can be referred to. Even where the relevant boundaries are not directly attested in the speech signal, a phonemic representation is assumed to have some grammatical structure: minimally, an organization into words.

An issue which occasioned even more discussion concerned the consequences for phonemic representations of certain contextually determined neutralizations. The concrete problem was posed most directly by Bloomfield's treatment of vowels in unstressed syllables, especially in English. Phonetically, such vowels are commonly reduced to a uniform quality, representable as schwa (we ignore here those dialects which distinguish between a relatively high and a relatively nonhigh reduced vowel, [ɨ] versus [ə]). Bloomfield, however, in his transcriptions of American English forms never uses a schwa, but rather writes symbols in unstressed syllables that correspond to full vowels in stressed syllables.

Sometimes, Bloomfield assigns these reduced vowels a quality similar or identical to that appearing in the corresponding syllable of a related form with a different stress pattern. Thus, he writes *protest* (verb) as [pro'test], with a first syllable which is similar to that of *protest* (noun), written ['prowtest]. But vowels in related forms are not by any means always represented by the same symbol: the reduced initial syllable of *convict* (verb) is written with [o] as [kon'vikt], while the unreduced initial in the corresponding noun is written with [a] as ['kanvikt]. He writes a wide variety of vowel symbols in unstressed syllables: at least [o], [e], [i] and [ɛ] (Bloomfield's symbol for the first vowel in *atom* and *atomic*), without these differences' corresponding to any consistent phonetic distinction. The sequence of a reduced vowel followed by one of the sonants [r], [l], [m], or [n] is usually written as a syllabic resonant (e.g., *pickerel* ['pikṛl]), but otherwise no special symbols are used to represent the obscure quality of unstressed vowels.

The result is a phonemic transcription which cannot be recovered from phonetic data alone, since no phonetic cue tells which reduced vowel is involved. For Bloomfield, the important point seemed to be the possibility of prediction in the opposite direction: given an indication of the vowel, together with a

marking of stress, it is always possible to determine which vowels are phonetically schwas. As Bolling put it in a note appended to Kent's review of *Language*, "reductions in unstressed syllables may lead either to a change of phonemes, as in *isn't* ['izn̩t]; or to the nondistinctive modification of a sound, as
in *business* ['biznes]. The former must, of course, be recorded; the latter
is sufficiently indicated by the stress-mark. To write ['biznəs] would be like
the meaningless underlining of a schoolgirl. Bloomfield refuses to do this"
(quoted in Hockett 1970:275). In other words, when the phonetic form is adequately indicated by a nonreduced vowel together with the position of the
stress, there is no need to introduce a special additional symbol.

A problem with this analysis is that there is no indication of how Bloomfield actually arrived at his phonemic forms. He often writes [o] in unstressed
syllables, corresponding to his use of that symbol (in a way condemned by
most of his reviewers) for the vowel in *son*, *but*, etc. On the other hand, he
also writes [e] for many reduced vowels, without there being any obvious motivation for his choice of that symbol over [o], or over one of the other occurring unstressed vowel symbols. He may well have had some criterion in mind,
but it is far from clear what it was.

The corresponding situation in other languages is more straightforward,
however. In Russian, Bloomfield writes ['gorot] for the word *gorod* 'city',
phonetically ['gorət], because the form alternates with others in which the
reduced vowel appears as [o] (or with the prestress reduced variant of [o],
i.e. [a]). In discussing Russian, and also in an exchange with Hockett about a
very similar problem in Ojibwa, Bloomfield makes it clear that he prefers a
transcription which (a) indicates the pronunciation unambiguously (even if
circuitously), and (b) "tells the reader what unreduced vowel is involved"
(Hockett 1970:375). This leaves another question unanswered: what to do
when reduction is predictable but no alternant exists to show what the corresponding unreduced vowel should be. Bloomfield saw this as a problem, but
seems to have assumed that even in these cases it is appropriate to set up some
unreduced vowel, while he acknowledged that he had no real answer (cf.
Hockett 1970:373).

At least in the case of vowel reduction, then, Bloomfield clearly recognized
phonemic representations that were not uniquely recoverable from phonetic
data alone: a limited variant of Hjelmslev's ideal notation with resolved syncretisms (see chapter 6 above). It is natural to ask how far this reconstruction
of an underlying unit in positions of neutralization could be allowed to go
in Bloomfield's conception. Why, for example, does he does not write a
final voiced stop in Russian ['gorot], given the fact that devoicing is predictable here, and the form [goro'da] would show what underlying segment is
involved?

An interesting citation by Kent in his review of *Language* (quoted in
Hockett 1970:271), from private correspondence with Bloomfield, furnishes
the answer: final [t] is transcribed in ['gorot] (and similarly in the case of Ger-

man words with predictably devoiced finals) "because in these languages [d] and [t] are distinct phonemes," while in the case of reduced vowels, the product of neutralization is not an independently occurring phoneme. Formulating this in other terms, an archiphoneme (in the Praguian sense—see chapter 4 above) is represented by a full phoneme when its phonetic realization occurs independently as that phoneme, but by a special symbol when the product of neutralization is an otherwise nonoccurring segment type. In the terminology introduced by Hjelmslev (see chapter 6 above), Bloomfield allows for the resolution of *fusions* but not of *implications*.

Confirmation of this interpretation is provided not only by Kent's cited remark, but also in an interesting way from Bloomfield's analysis of English. In his book *Language*, Bloomfield never writes schwa in transcriptions of reduced vowels in the Chicago dialect of English he describes there. When we examine the 1934 British edition of this book, however, we find that the reduced vowels are practically everywhere written as schwa—a change Bloomfield evidently made himself.

The reason for this was not that Bloomfield had a change of heart about how to represent reduced vowels, but rather that the transcriptions of English were systematically altered in the new edition to conform to Southern British rather than Chicago pronunciation (except in the few cases where specific dialect forms are under discussion). Interestingly, the Southern British dialect has a phoneme which Bloomfield represents as schwa: the last vowel of *bitter*. While he could probably have treated this as the syllabic variant of [r], parallel to his analysis of American English, he does not; in any event, 'syllabic *r*' is phonetically distinct from the reduced vowels in Chicago English, but not in Southern British. Once a phonemic schwa is established for this latter dialect, the status of the reduction of unstressed vowels changes: to maintain the glossematic terminology, reduction is an implication in British English, while it is a fusion in American English. As a result, underlying full vowels are presented in unstressed syllables in phonemic representations of Chicago speech, but the corresponding vowels of Southern British are written as schwas.

It is by no means clear what theoretical justification Bloomfield thought may have existed for resolving the one kind of syncretism but not the other (he expresses some doubt about the matter in the quotation cited by Kent), but it is clear that he maintained the principle under a variety of analytic circumstances. As a result of this fact (and also of the appeal to inaudible word boundaries in conditioning phonemic statements), his phonemic representations were actually rather more abstract than those of most other linguists (apart from Hjelmslev) who used the term.

Morphophonemics and the description of alternations

Besides his phonemic representations, Bloomfield also made descriptive use of more abstract, 'morphophonemic' representations. These have a rather different status in the grammar, only in part as a consequence of their greater distance from what is directly recoverable from the facts of speech alone. It is to his practice in this regard that we now turn.

The word *morphophonemic* does not appear at all in Bloomfield's 1933 book, where he speaks simply of *phonetic modification* ("a change in the primary phonemes of a form" associated with its grammatical combination with other forms). The first use of "morphophonemic" that we find is in his 1939 contribution to the Trubetzkoy festschrift, where it is probably motivated by the usage of the honoree. Though their contacts were not particularly close in later years, Bloomfield had shared a bench with Trubetzkoy in 1913 at Leskien and Brugmann's lectures in Leipzig. The relevant chapter of the posthumous Menomini grammar is also entitled "Morphophonemics," though it is not possible to determine with certainty just when that title was assigned.

More important than the word, of course, is the sort of linguistic variation it refers to, and Bloomfield's attitude toward this. 'Phonetic change' clearly appears in the 1933 book as a category of linguistic variation distinct from that found among the alternants of a single phoneme: such "change in the primary phonemes of a form" is put on a par with other concomitants of "the meaningful arrangements of forms in a language," i.e., "its *grammar*": *order* (the sequence in which the constituents of a complex form are arranged); *modulation* (the use of secondary phonemes of stress, pitch, etc.); and *selection* (the simple choice of one form rather than another). Bloomfield's discussion of morphology in *Language* treats a great deal of the variation that would be called morphophonemic by later writers. It is clear that this variation is dealt with as alternation between distinct phonemic forms, and not as alternation between distinct realizations of the same phonemic form.

The first systematic treatment of morphophonemics in Bloomfield's work is his classic 1939 paper on Menomini. Here the fundamental methodology of such descriptions is described with clarity:

> The process of description leads us to set up each morphological element in a theoretical *basic* form, and then to state the deviations from this basic form which appear when the element is combined with other elements. If one starts with the basic forms and applies our statements . . . in the order in which we give them, one will arrive finally at the forms of words as they are actually spoken. Our basic forms are not ancient forms, say of the Proto-Algonquian parent language, and our statements of internal sandhi are not historical but descriptive, and apply in a purely *descriptive order*. However, our basic forms do bear some resemblance to those which would appear in a description of Proto-Algonquian, some of our statements of alternation . . . resemble those which would appear in a description of Proto-Algonquian, and the rest . . . , as to content and order, approximate the historical development from Proto-Algonquian to present-day Menomini. (Bloomfield 1939: 105–6)

A morphophonemic description, then, starts from a "theoretical basic form," and applies to this a series of rules modifying its shape. "The forms now arrived at are *phonemic* forms of the actual Menomini language. Menomini phonetics, however, allows a great deal of latitude to some of its phonemes, and of some overlapping between phonemes" (ibid., p. 115). The description of this subphonemic variation is the responsibility of a different part of the grammar, namely, the principles defining the phonetic realizations of phonemes.

These "theoretical basic forms" are made up largely of phonemic elements, but also include some additional abstract units. For example, in Menomini there is a rule by which *n* is replaced by *s* under certain circumstances. A large number of *n*'s are not subject to this change, however, and these Bloomfield writes *N* in basic forms. The morphophonemic element *N* is everywhere replaced by *n*; it corresponds not to a distinct phoneme, but rather to instances of *n* whose behavior with respect to the alternation in question is unusual. Several other distinct morphophonemic symbols are introduced in the Menomini description for vowels whose behavior with respect to one or another alternation is not the usual one; these are all converted to normal phonemic vowels before the end of the derivation.

This overall technique of morphophonemic description was clearly derived from that of Pāṇini's grammar of Sanskrit. Bloomfield was well acquainted with Pāṇini's work from his early education in Indo-European; he described it in a 1929 review as "one of the greatest monuments of human intelligence and (what concerns us more) an indispensable model for the description of languages" (Hockett 1970:219). As we remarked above, it is possible to suggest that the *saṁjña* rules of Pāṇini's *Aṣṭādhyāyī* (cf. Kiparsky 1979, chapter 6, for a description of these), and not Weiss's postulates for psychology, furnished the actual substantive inspiration for Bloomfield's (1926) attempted axiomatization of linguistics.

The rules of a morphophonemic description are motivated by the need to treat alternations among phonemically distinct forms of the same grammatical element in a systematic way. A language with no alternations would have no morphophonemic rules, and there would be no reason to establish a theoretical base form for any grammatical element that differed from its surface phonemic form.

Internal to the set of rules, Bloomfield (1933:210–11) also assumes at least the outline of a classification. Alternations can be *phonetic* if they relate alternants that differ in terms of phonetic modification (change in a limited number of phonetic properties, as with the variants [-s], [-z], and [-ez] of the English regular plural) rather than wholesale replacement (e.g., the alternation between the regular plural endings and [-en] in *oxen*). They may independently be classified as *regular*, when some linguistically recognizable characteristic of the environment conditions the alternation, as opposed to alternations conditioned by an arbitrary set of forms; again, the plural ending of *oxen* serves as an example of an irregular alternation, since there is no linguistically relevant property of *ox* that conditions the ending [-en]. Finally, an alternation is *automatic* if it is regular and conditioned by the phonological structure of the environment as opposed to grammatically conditioned alternations.

The bulk of the rules in Bloomfield's morphophonemic descriptions represent automatic alternations. Though these may well have some specified (arbitrary) exceptions, they are regularly conditioned in terms of the morphophonemic environment. In fact, the use of distinct symbols for morphophonemes is motivated by the desire to render as many alternations as possible automatic in this sense.

To this end also, many items are set up in theoretical shapes that differ from the form they take in isolation. Thus, final consonant clusters are set up in Menomini forms despite the fact that all such clusters are reduced to a single consonant phonetically in final position, in order to account for the shape stems show when followed by further endings. Some sequences of segments are established underlyingly which cannot ever occur in surface forms. For instance, -w- is always lost in the semivowel sequence -wy- after a consonant; this representation is used to describe those instances of -y- that do not cause palatalization of a preceding consonant. Such analyses (including also his positing of underlying stem-final consonants in Samoan verbs) show that Bloomfield definitely did not adhere to the constraint discussed in the previous chapter and its appendix on Sapir's underlying forms. Purely diacritic distinctions are also set up, in which two or more underlying forms have the same surface realization but different phonological behavior.

In addition to formulating the description so that as many rules as possible will be automatic alternations, Bloomfield also formulates individual rules in as general as possible a fashion, rather than limiting himself to attested instances of their application. For example, he states a rule by which all sequences of postconsonantal semivowels contract with a following vowel other than a or ā. Statements of the particular contraction products are subordinated to this general rule, and he also notes that no instances of the contraction of y with ō, o are attested—showing that the rule is actually more general than necessary.

In at least one instance, this desire to maximize the generality of particular rules even leads Bloomfield to violate the basic principle that phonemic analysis should show all *and only* the distinctive properties of segments. In Menomini, there is a rule by which long and short *e* and *o* are raised to *i* and *u*, respectively, when a high vowel or semivowel follows later in the word (with some added complications that are irrelevant here). Interestingly, this rule is the only source of phonetic ū in the language. Properly speaking, then, ū should not be treated as a phoneme in Menomini but as a variant of ō. If this were done, however, the rule in question could not be stated in its full generality, since the output of the morphophonemic rules is supposed to be a sequence of phonemes, not variants. The morphophonemic rule should thus be stated so as to apply to e, ē, and o, but not ō; and then a distinct rule should be stated to convert phonemic ō to phonetic ū under the identical conditions.

This is of course a perfect example of the argument Halle later adduced against the linguistic appropriateness of a 'taxonomic' phonemic level, which we have already mentioned in chapter 4 above and to which we will return in chapter 12 below. Bloomfield quite recognized the problem presented by this example and took two different lines of approach toward it. In his 1939 presentation of Menomini, he states (on this basis) that since ū occurs only in this alternation, it "is not a full phoneme." In his presentation of "actual Menomini phonemes," he includes ū but puts it in parentheses (a unique status) and refers to it (without further explanation) as a "semi-phoneme."

By contrast, in *The Menomini Language* Bloomfield includes ū in the list of phonemes without comment or parentheses. Later, he discusses its special status, but argues that it should be treated as a phoneme anyway: "In this alternation, however, the difference of o: and u: is parallel with that of e: and i:, two sounds which unmistakably figure as separate phonemes. Moreover, this difference of o: and u: is maintained by persons in whose speech the alternation has lost its regularity. Also, there are a few interjections in which u: (and never o:) is used: *capu:q* 'splash!', *ku:h* 'stop it!'. A contrast of o: and u: appears in the foreign words *co:h* 'Joe' and *cu:h* 'Jew'" (Bloomfield 1962:5). The arguments thus reduce to: (a) the generality of the alternation, which would be destroyed if ū were treated as it otherwise should be, i.e., as nonphonemic; (b) the probable phonemic status of the vowel in marginal idiolects which have lost the regular morphophonemic rule; and (c) the appearance of unconditioned ū in a few expressive forms and foreign borrowings. Clearly none of these arguments (except possibly the last) really bear on the phonemic status of ū, which would undoubtedly have been treated as a mere variant if it were not for the necessity to state the alternation as a unitary generalization.

Numerous other aspects of morphophonemic description would have to be explored in order to arrive at a complete understanding of Bloomfield's practice. The chapter in *Language* devoted to morphology, for example, treats at considerable length the issue of how underlying forms are to be arrived at. As one would imagine from the importance he attaches to generality of rules, the primary consideration is to choose a representation from which all alternating variants can be produced by means of rules of automatic alternation. Often this is one of the occurring variants of the alternating form, though perhaps not the one that appears in isolation. For example, he indicates a distinction in Russian between voiced and voiceless final obstruents which is neutralized in the unextended form; he posits Samoan verb stems with underlying final consonants which are always deleted when no suffix follows, and similarly he sets up Menomini forms with final clusters that are generally simplified unless suffixed.

Frequently, it is not considerations internal to the alternating form that motivate the decision on a basic shape but, rather, aspects of the rules involved. For example, Bloomfield considers the forms of the regular plural in English, and concludes that [ez] should be taken as basic (rather than [s] or [z]) because a rule is necessary in any case to delete the vowel in contracted forms of the copula *is* (e.g., *Jack's coming*), and the same rule can be extended to the plural (for criticism of this argument, see Anderson 1973). Considerations of rule generality sometimes lead Bloomfield to take as underlying a shape that is not usually thought to be 'basic' in some other sense: thus, he takes the basic form of French adjectives to be the feminine, since the masculine can be derived from that by a simple rule of final consonant deletion.

Other principles can also be found behind Bloomfield's practice which determine the way his descriptions are organized. For example, Kenstowicz (1975) finds reasons, developed in greater detail by Miner (1981), to believe that Bloomfield's rules are stated so as to lead to derivations that minimize the 'opacity' of forms in roughly the sense of Kiparsky (1973b). Miner also argues that Bloomfield's rules are sometimes more complex than they would otherwise need to be in order to minimize the need for artificial intermediate stages of a derivation.

We do not go further into these issues here, however, because they have little or no bearing on Bloomfield's actual theory of the phonological structure of language. This may seem contradictory, but in fact there is good reason to believe that such principles as one can uncover in his morphophonemic practice would have been attributed by Bloomfield to the activity of linguists, rather than to the nature of language. This of course is quite contrary to the practice in phonology today, where claims about the organization of linguist's grammars are intended to be interpreted as claims (in some sense) about the structure of natural language.

Bloomfield clearly believed that phonemic representations, and the relation between them and phonetic realization, correspond to something 'real' about a language. The status of alternations and their description in morphophonemic terms, however, is somewhat different. Bloomfield was certainly of the opinion that the relation between alternating forms was a real one: alternating forms that differ phonemically are still variants of the same grammatical element. The status of the morphophonemic rules that describe the relation is nonetheless dubious. "What is here involved is not merely our convenience, but the speakers' habit of correlating morphological complexes. To be sure, we take the liberty of inventing a basic (morphophonemic) formula and then telling how it is to be modified to produce the actual (phonemic) utterance, but this is merely a descriptive device" (Hockett 1970: 371). The correlation of actual phonemic forms in alternation here is 'real,' but this is a matter of morphology rather than of phonology. As for the morphophonemic mechanics by which we describe that correlation, "this is not a question about the language: it is a question about the clearest and most convenient way of telling about the language" (Hockett 1970:375).

While Bloomfield was certainly one of the most noteworthy early practitioners of the morphophonemic method of description, (which he had learned from Pāṇini's grammar), we should not therefore make the anachronistic assumption that he understood such descriptions in the same way linguists do today. In particular, he seems clearly to have considered them in the same light as he did Pāṇini's description: an elegant artifact, providing a uniform and concise account of a complex set of facts, but not to be confused with the actual language capacity of speakers. Only the phonemic forms, and the morphological fact of relations between them, could be considered to have that status. For Bloomfield, the beginning and the end of a theory of phonological structure in natural language was a theory of phonemic representations.

II

American Structuralist Phonology

The present chapter discusses phonology in America between the appearance of Bloomfield's *Language* and roughly the late 1950s. In contrast with previous chapters, this development cannot be presented adequately from the point of view of any one individual, for a variety of linguists contributed in important ways to the theoretical position which characterized these years. The spectrum of opinion on fundamental issues which is represented by these various scholars is interesting for its breadth, but also, in certain essential respects, for its relatively narrow focus.

Some prominent American structuralists

Bloomfield himself was of course still active at least until his stroke in 1946; yet he took surprisingly little part after 1933 in the development of the linguistic theories that were associated with his name. Few contributions came from Bloomfield to the increasingly lively theoretical discussions of phonological topics, with the exception of his "Menomini morphophonemics"; and it could be argued that even that paper had primarily descriptive rather than theoretical goals as far as Bloomfield himself was concerned. His attention seemed more on general issues in the philosophy of science, his Algonquian work, and such practical problems as those of the wartime language teaching program.

There was no central figure, then, in the postwar years in North American linguistics; instead, a variety of individuals developed issues whose roots (if not their details) can be found in Bloomfield's earlier statements (especially the "Postulates" of 1926, and *Language*). Though they often disagreed among themselves on particular points, these linguists were in general agreement at least on an agenda and also, importantly, on a common way of talking about those issues that interested them. We find a rather rapid development of a distinctive vocabulary, idiom of expression, and style of presentation which marks a clear break with previous work.

It is impossible not to associate this distinct scholarly style and the consensus of attitudes that went along with it with the changes that had taken place in the professional status of linguistics. "The significance of the Bloomfieldian generation is that it is the first to be employed (or seek employment) as *lin-*

guists; that is, to claim a place in academic life in virtue, not of knowledge of a language or language family, but of knowledge of a methodology for the study of any language, of language in general" (Hymes & Fought 1981 : 117). The establishment of this new discipline as a distinctive (and respectable) one required, in the minds of many, an accentuation of those characteristics which differentiated it from the study of particular languages, and from philology. Central in this regard was the claim of linguistics to a uniquely 'scientific' approach to the study of language, a claim that rested on its methodological underpinnings in the empiricist, logical-positivist views of contemporary philosophers of science.

Most of the contributors to this developing theory identified its origins with the ideas of Bloomfield (though, to a lesser extent, Boas and Sapir were seen to have played important roles in the rise of a distinctively 'American' linguistics). What came later was usually claimed to have arisen out of Bloomfield's work (though it often differed in fundamental ways from Bloomfield's actual views); and indeed the period is typically identified as that of 'neo-' or 'post-Bloomfieldian' linguistics. We prefer to refer to it here simply as that of 'American structuralism', so as not to imply an identification with Bloomfield's own writing.

The label 'American' does not refer only to the geographical location of the research in question. True, few linguists outside of the United States had any role in its development, though some of these, such as Trubetzkoy and, later, Hjelmslev, were often cited as relevant (even if not completely sound). Perhaps more importantly, the name also emphasizes the extreme sense of national identity, indeed chauvinism, that characterizes much of the period. Feelings of antagonism toward foreign scholarship and scholars became particularly unpleasant during and immediately after the war; but even when the attitudes involved were considerably more benign, one finds rather often an attitude of pride in things American that reflects the attitude of complacency in American society as a whole in the postwar period.

Several of the central figures in the 'Bloomfieldian' mainstream were identified (both in their own view and in that of others) as the direct heirs of Bloomfield's theoretical positions. Bernard Bloch's papers on problems of phonemic analysis (as well as his influence as editor of the journal *Language* between 1939 and 1965) contributed significantly to establishing the basic position which American linguists presupposed (even if only to disagree with it). Charles Hockett, often considered the most individually creative and wide-ranging of the major American structuralists, also contributed to the basic theoretical consensus in many areas. As not only Bloomfield's student, but an Algonquianist as well (and Bloomfield's scholarly executor), his place in the 'succession' was clearly established.

George Trager was perhaps the most radical of those claiming to develop Bloomfield's thought directly, especially regarding the rigor (and vigor) with which he rejected any role for considerations of meaning in linguistic analysis or description. Henry Lee Smith made linguistics visible (or audible) to the public at large through a popular radio program dealing with dialect differences in American English. He later collaborated with Trager to produce a standard, if controversial, codification of phonemic analysis as applied to English (Trager & Smith 1951). Other figures whose work was accepted as contributing to what became the established position in the field included Archibald Hill, Martin Joos, and Rulon Wells.

The association among these figures was not merely that of scholars pursuing the same lines of academic research; it also involved a sense of personal solidarity and community of interest. Reading the papers of the time (as well as the commentary in Joos 1957, a political as much as a scholarly statement), it becomes clear that they felt themselves to be a group of crusaders with a common mission. This is of course a perfectly standard state of affairs in academic life, but it becomes particularly important under the conditions of American linguistics in the 1940s and early 1950s when there was no single, dominant personality in the field and when responsibility for scientific judgment was therefore more than usually diffused.

A figure whose work was clearly central to the dominant theoretical trend but who was somewhat outside it in more personal terms, was Zellig Harris. Harris's rigorous and purely distributional methods in linguistic analysis must be regarded as the intellectual highpoint of the attempts to develop the logical consequences of the 'Bloomfieldian' position. His papers in phonology and morphology, and his attempt to extend structuralist methods to syntax, were widely read, attended to, and cited; but he himself seems to have been less close personally to the community of American linguists than others mentioned above. In part, this may result from the fact that he came to linguistics from a background in Semitic rather than in Indo-European (especially Germanic or English) or Amerindian studies. It may also result from his frequently expressed outspoken admiration for Sapir's methods, even if he devoted much of his attention to developing a very different alternative. Finally, factors of personality (possibly including his intense interest in Zionist political questions) must have played a role in setting him apart.

Somewhat more marginal was a group of scholars identified as the successors of Sapir rather than of Bloomfield. These included Morris Swadesh, Mary Haas, Stanley Newman, Carl Voegelin, and others with interests oriented more toward anthropological and Amerindian studies than toward 'theoretical linguistics' in the sense that notion came to have. Those whose sympathies went with Sapir were evidently more interested in finding accommodation with the Bloomfieldians than vice versa. There is little attempt on these scholars' part to downgrade Bloomfield's work, while Sapir's views (especially on the psychological basis of language) were often attacked or even derided from the orthodox 'Bloomfieldian' perspective, lumped together with other examples of now démodé 'mentalism'.

Finally, one can identify a group of linguists whose main contribution to the theoretical debates of American structuralism was as critics. Two of these, Eugene Nida and Kenneth Pike, were involved primarily in the development of practical methods for investigating unfamiliar languages: in both cases, this concern arose from their association with the work of Bible translation groups. Another figure, Charles Fries, shared with Pike a location at the University of Michigan, but was primarily interested in English. All three were identified as antagonistic toward certain aspects of 'Bloomfieldian' practice—especially the (often overstated) rejection of appeals to meaning in any form.

It is quite interesting to note not only the points on which they attacked other American structuralists, but also the extent to which even these critics of the theory shared many of its basic assumptions. Undoubtedly their position outside the main currents of the time (as indicated by the freedom with which their views are attacked or simply rejected by other, more central figures) resulted from their critical stance, but the more social factor of the lack of prestige of religiously motivated fieldwork cannot be ignored, at least in the case of Pike and Nida. The exclusion of any of Pike's work from Joos (1957) is particularly striking, and impossible to account for in terms either of its intellectual quality or its relevance to the dominant issues in American structuralist discussions.

The American structuralist view of language

Given the number and diversity of the participants in the development of American structuralism, one would hardly expect a single uniform and homogeneous theoretical position to have resulted from their work. In hindsight, however, it is also easy to exaggerate the diversity of this group. While their views naturally evolved over time, it is impossible to deny the existence of a fundamental community of opinion among them. Sources for their opinions on foundational issues are to be sought in the relation they felt existed between their work and that of earlier traditions, especially in America.

An important study of the bases of American structuralism in previous work (as it was perceived) is provided by Teeter (1964), who points out some important basic assumptions and their sources. First, from Boas's stress on the individuality of linguistic systems, and the necessity to consider each system in its own right, the notion was taken over that there are no universally valid structural principles in language. As we have seen above (chapter 8), Boas did not at all deny the existence of linguistic universals: indeed, his notion of language structure was based on rather strong assumptions not only about the form of grammars, but also about the substantive content of both semantics and phonetics. Nonetheless, his emphasis on diversity (intended to combat the traditional Latin-based grammatical model) was interpreted as a demonstration that "languages could differ from each other without limit and in unpredictable ways," in the much-cited formulation of Joos (1957:96).

Joos's remark was aimed specifically at the sort of phonological theory developed by Trubetzkoy and Jakobson, based as it was on the assumption of a universal set of phonological features and the search for far-reaching universal principles of phonological systems. Nonetheless, the scope of the objection is broader than this. Boas is also cited, for instance, as the ultimate source of potential skepticism about the validity of even a phonetic segmentation of the speech signal: from him, the "practicing linguist, in the American sense" had learned that in this respect too "languages can differ without limit as to extent and direction" (ibid., p. 228).

The claim that linguistics could not successfully be based on a search for valid universals of language was considered by Joos as a conclusion from Boas's work that might have to be reexamined. "The abandonment of deduction in favor of induction has never been reversed. At first it left the science stripped of general doctrines about all languages. Favorable at the start, this state of opinion could be, and in many older workers actually was, maintained past its function and could become a hindrance to further development. Once a number of unprejudiced descriptions had resulted from it, induction could be applied to those new descriptions too, and general doctrines about all languages could emerge again" (ibid., p. v). The problem with a program such as that of the Prague school, then, was not the simple fact of looking for universals but the attempt to present a deductive, explanatory system. Universals should, rather, be discovered as purely inductive generalizations.

This is a point with profound implications for the sort of work linguists should do. If they believe there is a general set of explanatory principles underlying language, and that it is their goal to find and understand these principles, they ought presumably to organize their work by formulating tentative systems with a rich deductive structure, and then look for evidence of the fit between such systems and the properties of actual natural languages. Joos indeed attributes a related motivation to Boas as well: "A general truth about language, to Boas' way of thinking (or perhaps feeling), would have to be based on nothing less than the biological or even the physiological character of man (he was a physical anthropologist too)" (ibid.). One wonders at the omission of the psychological character of man, as well, given Boas's intense interest in human mental life; but in any event Joos's objection to Boas's presumed deduction of the properties of natural languages from a limited set of foundational assumptions is that while an explanatory system of principles might be possible, it would have to be based on factors outside of language, and any "such theories still lay far in the future" (ibid.).

Recognition of the limitations on how far linguistics could go in making connections with the only apparently possible bases for an explanatory theory (i.e., with extralinguistic factors) was attributed to Bloomfield. Bloomfield was generally held to have insisted that linguistics must proceed without reference to the mind, a restriction that not only prevented theorizing about the psychological implementation of linguistic structure but, indeed, eliminated all serious work in semantics. It will be recalled (from chapter 10 above) that what Bloomfield actually maintained was not so much the nonexistence of mind as its nonaccessibility to a physicalist theory in the absence of comprehensive, encyclopedic knowledge from other domains; but in practice the two were the same. While Boas had clearly believed that psychological explanations would be forthcoming for many aspects of linguistic structure, the narrow interpretation of Bloomfield's views about psychology ruled out the possibility that such a basis could be found for explanatory principles underlying the nature of language.

Similarly, Bloomfield had argued that phonetic data (aside from the implementation of phonemic contrasts) were simply irrelevant to linguistic structure. This view was based on the claim that, from the perspective of a given language, phonetic facts other than contrastive ones were more or less accidental concomitants of the distinctive properties. Of course, fieldworkers no more abstained in practice from the use of phonetic representations and assumptions than Bloomfield had done in his own fieldwork; but his rejection of theoretical status for phonetics within linguistics was widely quoted with approval.

In the absence of a serious notion of universal phonetics (apart from physics and physiology, nonlinguistic disciplines treating the facts of language without distinguishing them from others), there was simply no way for phonetic data to serve as the foundation of linguistic explanations. Interestingly, both Pike (1943) and Hockett (1955) wrote full-scale treatments of phonetics, and Joos (1948) presented the first systematic exposition of the application of the techniques of acoustic analysis to linguistic phonetics. Nonetheless, in the theoretical literature the status of phonetics remained (in principle) that of an auxiliary discipline. Though it was Trubetzkoy who was responsible for the aphorism that "phonetics is to linguistics as numismatics is to economics," the attitude was the same among American structuralists. Linguistics was thus cut off on both sides (semantics and phonetics) from any access to principles that could have a possible explanatory role.

Since the only valid roads to a deductive theory of language were thus (at least temporarily) foreclosed, the only acceptable activity for linguists in the meantime was the neutral gathering of facts about as many languages as possible; and the only acceptable 'general principles' of language were inductive generalizations based on the available corpus of such descriptions. This reasoning led to a widespread replacement of *structural* as an epithet for linguistics in America by *descriptive*, to emphasize the fact that the primary task was conceived of as the gathering of unbiased information rather than the supposedly premature search for explanatory principles.

In the work of American structuralist (or, as they preferred to call themselves, descriptive) linguists, these general principles led to a number of rather well-marked characteristics. For example, it is obvious that these notions would further emphasize the tendency in American linguistics (already strong, as a result of its anthropological and Amerindianist origins) to concentrate on extensive fieldwork. In the absence of deductive explanatory principles, the only scientifically respectable activity for linguists was to go on looking at as many languages as possible. Of course, linguists other than American structuralists also made it a point to seek out data from a wide range of languages; Trubetzkoy and Jakobson, for example, can hardly be faulted for not paying attention to such considerations. Nowhere else, however, did description for its own sake acquire the prestige among linguistic scholars that it had in America during the structuralist period.

This bias hardly prevented the writing of papers whose primary thrust was theoretical in nature; but it did contribute to the establishment of a 'standard form' for such papers, in which the theoretical point is presented in the context of a discussion of specific facts and how to 'handle' them, rather than exclusively on its own account. This is a characteristic of American linguistic writing which continues unabated today, and which still distinguishes it from much European work in linguistic theory.

Another observable emphasis in American descriptive work was the concern to remain within the bounds of what was considered 'scientific'. In the context of the positivist, mechanist, operationalist, etc., views current in the philosophy of science, this meant avoiding appeals to unobservable factors ('mind', 'intuitions', etc.) in description. Especially important was the requirement that analyses had to be replicable, in the sense that any observer, given the same data and a mechanical statement of the way analyses were to be arrived at, would be able to come up with the same account. Analyses based on the investigator's intuitions about the structure of the language, unless these could be translated into manipulations of observable data, were thus invalid.

A natural consequence of this need to make the description sufficiently explicit to be replicable was a tremendous concentration (at least on the part of 'orthodox Bloomfieldians' such as Bloch, Harris, and their close associates) on specifying procedures of analysis. This concern might also be seen as arising from the fact that in the absence of underlying explanatory systems, the procedures by which linguists reduced data to descriptions of language were virtually the only subject matter of linguistics that remained to talk about; but this would not be at all the entire story.

Many subsequent writers on the period have suggested that it was characterized by a general lack of 'theory'; but that is to miss the importance of the description of analytic procedures. Some fieldworkers, of course, were primarily interested in describing actual, practical procedures to be followed by a linguist working on an unfamiliar language from scratch; but such concerns were not really what was meant by the concern with analytic procedures in the literature of the period. Most theoreticians realized (generally from firsthand experience) that fieldwork involved repeated access to intuitions, guesses, shortcuts, appeals to meaning, etc.; but it was still required that an analysis be validated by specifying a mechanical procedure that could, in principle, have been followed so as to lead inexorably from observations to the resulting description without the intervention of unsystematic factors. Such a 'gedanken-experimental' reconstruction of the connection between data and analysis, no matter how tortured and impractical under real conditions, served to establish the point of principle that no unobservable or unreplicable factors were involved in an essential way.

It is difficult to exaggerate the extent to which this concern with the explicit formulation of (at least theoretically applicable) procedures dominated the style of linguistic work in the American structuralist period. The present writer, whose initial studies in linguistics were with representatives of this approach, recalls vividly a succession of arguments whose essential point was: "I don't care if it *is* the 'right' answer; how do you justify having found it?" Linguistic theory, in the absence of universals or an appeal to underlying explanatory principles, was by no means nonexistent; but it did reduce largely to the specification of what connection existed between facts of language and their analysis. This connection was to be formulated in terms of a set of procedures (most extensively, by Harris; but the aim was shared by most workers in the field). As a result, linguistics found itself in the curious position of having much more to say about the activities of linguists than of speakers of natural languages.

This seemed perfectly natural at the time, however, especially in the context of available theories of the learning that was presumed to underlie language acquisition. If we assume that the child comes to the language-learning task with the same absence of presuppositions that the linguist was trying strenuously to achieve, it is natural to imagine that their paths to language are much the same. If language-learning proceeds without recourse to assumptions or unobservable factors, the same sort of procedures followed (at least in principle) by the hypothetical field linguist ought to specify what happens. But in that case, the class of languages accessible to the child (the class of possible natural languages) is adequately and accurately specified by the description of the procedures that could possibly be involved in their acquisition from primary linguistic data.

In a paper considered at the time to be an outspoken defense of the 'reality' of linguistic structure as opposed to the notion that linguistic analysis is simply a matter of playing games with language data, Hockett (1948, in Joos 1957:279–80) made it clear that he saw an essential similarity between the activities of the linguist and of the child: "The analytical process thus parallels what goes on in the nervous system of a language-learner, particularly, perhaps, that of a child learning his first language. . . . The essential difference between the process in the child and the procedure of the linguist is this: the linguist has to make his analysis overtly, in communicable form, in the shape of a set of statements which can be understood by any properly trained person, who in turn can predict utterances not yet observed with the same degree of accuracy as can the original analyst. The child's 'analysis' consists, on the other hand, of a mass of varying synaptic potentials in his central nervous system. The child in time comes to *behave* the language; the linguist must come to *state* it." Though such a strongly 'realist' position on the nature of linguistic structure was definitely a minority one, for those who took it, such a presumed parallel between the linguist and the child could be seen to validate the formulation of analytic procedures as a genuine theory of natural language.

Another, related assumption should also be mentioned as relevant to an understanding of the specific linguistic theories developed by American structuralists. It was generally assumed that, like the learning system, the perceptual system of human speakers of natural languages operated with little or no access to facts beyond the immediately observable. In particular, it was generally taken for granted that the 'outer layer' of speech perception was a system roughly analogous to a voice-operated typewriter: something that takes an acoustic waveform as input, and on the basis of nothing but a specification of the phonemic system of the language, yields as output an interpretation of that waveform in the form of a sequence of phonemes. After this initial processing has been performed, 'higher' levels of the speech-understanding system can operate on the string of phonemes to yield an interpretation in terms of morphemes, and so on up through higher level structures.

If speech perception involves such a 'bootstrapping' interpreter, whose operation consists of little or nothing but the segmentation and consequent classification of raw acoustic input, a number of essential properties of the linguistic system follow. In particular, it must be the case that language involves an essential intermediate level of structure which is directly recoverable from the speech signal, and which contains all (and perhaps only) the information relevant for higher-level interpretation. If only this sort of phonemic level is accessible in principle to the perceptual system, it follows (at least on moderately 'realist' assumptions about linguistic structure) that phonemic analyses not meeting such a condition should be excluded in the description of natural languages. This led to another of the important slogans of the period: the prohibition against 'mixing levels', or allowing considerations from higher levels of structure to play an essential role in determining the relation between phonemic and phonetic representations.

Given the premise that the actual speech signal is much too complex to be directly manipulated by higher levels in speech processing, and that some sort of phonological representation mediates between the signal and the analysis of its linguistically relevant properties, it seemed self-evident that the phonological representation could only have properties that were recoverable from the bare signal itself. Only much later, with the development of rather richer and more highly structured views of perception as an active rather than purely passive process (along the lines of the 'analysis by synthesis' view, for example: see Halle & Stevens 1962 for an early proposal), did it become possible to imagine a coherent picture of phonological structure that transcended these limitations. Until then, however, it seemed clear to linguists that what could be assumed with confidence about the process of perception provided further motivation for a rather minimal theory of linguistic structure, along the lines of American structuralist phonemics.

Initial formulations of the notion of 'phoneme'

In the context of this general background, we turn now to the specifically phonological aspects of American structuralist linguistic theory. On the basis of the claim by Bloomfield and others that a representation of the significant sound properties of utterances should take the form of a sequence of phonemes, the fundamental task for a theory of phonology was clearly to provide an adequate definition of what phonemes were.

Bloomfield had given a definition ("minimal same of vocal feature") which located phonemes in the external phonetic form of the utterance as a subset of its identifiable acoustic properties. This concrete physical definition did not satisfy all analysts, however. Furthermore, many examples of phonemic analyses in Bloomfield's own practice did not seem to be easily reconciled with his definition, and attempts were made either to reformulate the notion of phoneme so as to be consistent with those analyses, or else to defend more consistent ones. In this discussion, the type case (as indicated in the previous chapter) was Bloomfield's treatment of reduced vowels—and, by implication, other instances of phonologically conditioned neutralization. The central issue in this discussion gradually crystallized as the extent to which phonemic representations should be unambiguously recoverable from phonetic data alone.

Discussion of the nature of the phoneme became a major topic in the journals of American structuralism. Indeed, Bloomfield is said once to have suggested to Bloch, as editor of the journal *Language*, that the number of papers on phonemics was getting to be excessive and should be reduced. The starting point for many of these discussions was Bloomfield's own definition, but virtually none of the subsequent writers on the topic accepted in detail his notion of the nature of the phoneme. A number of alternative conceptions emerged, gradually converging on a consensus view by the late 1940s. By that time, the problem shifted from what phonemes were to how to define operational procedures that would yield them.

Shortly after the publication of Bloomfield's 1933 book, the issue of reduced vowels and their implication for phonemics was addressed in an article 'The Phonemes of Russian' by George Trager (1934). He summarizes the issues raised between Bloomfield and Kent (in his review of *Language*) noted above in chapter 10, and in particular the difference between Bloomfield's treatment of vowel reduction and that of final consonants in Russian. Trager finds the disparity between these two parts of the analysis unsatisfactory, and proposes that an adequate phonemic analysis should be based on the uniform principle of "avoid[ing] the use of more than one symbol for the same sound (except where differing structure permits the distinction into two phonemes)" (Trager 1934:339).

Subject to the qualification in parentheses, this would prevent the analyst from representing the same phonetic segment (in the same environment) differently in different words. In the relevant instance, Russian final [t] could not be identified as /t/ in some words (e.g., rot 'mouth') but as /d/ in others (e.g., rod 'kind'). However, the issue turns entirely on when "differing structure permits the distinction into two phonemes." Trager argues that when there exists an alternation between two otherwise distinct phonemes, conditioned entirely by their phonological environment, and internal to a paradigm, then "since the paradigm exists in the mind of the speaker as a psychological reality, there exists a psychological difference in the sounds," found in the position of neutralization as well (ibid., p. 341).

In contrast, when there is no intraparadigmatic alternation, the only available phonemic interpretation is "complete psychological identification of the original voiced sound with the new, voiceless sound, and their merging into the voiceless phoneme, despite the presence of the voiced sound in the original of the derivative, or in some other derivative" (ibid., p. 342). The similarity of this condition to one proposed by Kiparsky (1973a) in the context of the debate over abstractness in generative phonology will not be missed.

It should be noted that the criterion of phonological conditioning is intended by Trager to be a necessary one. Where two phonemes alternate under conditions that are at least partially morphological in nature, he treats the difference as 'morphonemic', and argues that it does not affect the phonemic representation directly.

It is somewhat ironic that Trager, who would later become one of the most extreme 'antimentalists' among the main stream American structuralists, takes a stand in this article much closer to that of Sapir than to that of Bloomfield—indeed, he refers explicitly to Sapir (1925) for the notion of a psychological difference between 'ideal' sounds that happen to be phonetically identical. This is a reflection of the fact that Trager was a student of Sapir as well as of Bloomfield. As noted in chapters 9 and 10 above, Sapir's influence (and indeed priority with regard to the notion of the phoneme) was still clearly recognized during the 1930s. Bloomfield's *Language* did not immediately upon publication supersede all other work.

The irony is compounded by the fact that a linguist much more closely identified as Sapir's student, Morris Swadesh (1934), presented in the same volume of *Language* a formulation of the basic principles of phonemic analysis which is much closer to the orthodox 'Bloomfieldian' view. Though Swadesh starts from a position that could be construed as basically Sapirian (characterizing phonemes as "percepts," and thus psychological in character), his actual development of the position is much more external in conception than Sapir's own discussions.

According to Swadesh (1934, in Joos 1958:34), the "inductive procedure," which is the only way in which "the phonemes of a language can be discovered," begins naturally enough with the phonetic facts. First, it is necessary to normalize the phonetic material somewhat, by abstracting away from free variation so as to arrive at a consistent representation for each word. One then performs a phonetic segmentation, looking for substretches of words that establish partial identities between them, and treating as units sets of phonetic properties that are found in constant association. Two or more of the resulting phonetic segments can then be treated as "subtypes of the same phoneme" if they are in complementary distribution (i.e., "only one of them normally occurs in certain phonetic surroundings, and . . . only the other normally occurs in certain other phonetic surroundings" (ibid., p. 35)). When complementary distribution would allow the assignment of a given segment type to either of two possible phonemes, "it is to be identified with one rather than the other if there is a more definite phonetic similarity in that direction" (ibid., p. 35). Here, in essence, is the procedure whose refinement as a definition of 'phoneme' would constitute the core of American structuralist phonology.

In only one major respect does Swadesh differ from the majority of later writers: this is the issue of the phonetic substance of phonemes. As noted above, he considers phonemes to be "percepts" identifiable with a phonetic type, where "it is possible to define the type in terms of a [phonetic] norm and of deviations from the norm" (ibid., p. 33). When more than one phonetic type is assigned to the same phoneme (by virtue of their complementarity of distribution), "instead of one norm, there may be two or more. Such variant norms are ordinarily conditional, depending on the phonetic surroundings in which the phoneme occurs" (ibid., p. 33). The phoneme itself is thus defined by an ideal phonetic segment type, as for Sapir; Swadesh's notion of phonological representation is fundamentally a 'completely specified basic variant' theory as defined in chapter 2 above, but differs from, for example, Sapir's version of this position by allowing more than one 'basic variant' for the same phoneme. Others would take this one step further, by identifying the phoneme not with any of its phonetic variants ('ideal' or not), but rather with the *class* constituted by their union.

It is important to note that Swadesh's procedure (which is said to "follow from the nature of the phoneme", p. 34) allows no possibility of phonemic differences that are not recoverable from the phonetic facts. In fact, he does not discuss any such potential examples, and we do not have direct evidence in this paper for the way he would have treated them. Given his association with the tradition of Sapir, and his practice in later work, we can presume that he would have wanted to recognize 'psychological' differences in the phonemic value of the same phonetic segment as it appears in different words (depending on such evidence as alternations); but his actual statements make no provision for this situation, and therefore appear to preclude it. The general circulation and accessibility of Swadesh's paper may thus have contributed to reinforcing in practice an attitude toward phonemics which was more physicalist than he in fact intended.

Swadesh also discusses, in treating the establishment of the phonemes of a language, the ways in which a set of phonemes are organized into a system. Indeed, he establishes a requirement that phonemic analyses should be established so as to maximize 'pattern congruity'. This notion was to be interpreted as the integration of particular details into "the general phonemic pattern of the given language" (ibid., p. 35).

The establishment of *systems* (rather than simply *inventories*) of the phonemes of a language was a task which most American structuralists recognized as part of the task of phonological theory, though such a goal is somewhat difficult to understand on purely internal grounds. For most, the role of phonemes in linguistic structure was the purely differentiating one of identifying the distinctive function of sound units, and little else. Internal relations (beyond mere mutual distinctness) among the phonemes of a given language were the subject of much discussion, but it is hard to see what role these relations played, once established. American structuralists did not, for example, attempt to establish general structural laws of phonological systems based on their internal organization, as did Trubetzkoy and Jakobson. One must apparently assume that the attribution of structure to phoneme systems in this view was simply unconnected with other aspects of the theory.

Sapir and Bloomfield, it may be recalled, had also discussed the bases for assigning a structure to the system of phonemes in a language. Both had denied a constitutive role in such structures to phonetic similarity per se; Swadesh, however, in line with the more physicalist form of his theory, admits phonetic properties as at least contributory to phonemic structure. Likewise, many would add as a desideratum for phonological systems a tendency to symmetry along the phonetic dimensions of contrast. This can also be expressed as the claim that it is most natural for the various features which serve to distinguish one phoneme from another within a language to be independently distributed among the phonemes.

In addition to these factors, however, Swadesh and other writers admit further criteria under the notion of 'pattern congruity'. Some are common to earlier work: segments that share distributional properties are assumed to be ipso facto similar, for example, as claimed by both Sapir and Bloomfield. In addition, phonemes whose internal distribution of phonetic variants follow similar principles (e.g., all of the voiceless stops in English have aspirated, unaspirated, and unreleased variants under essentially the same conditions) were considered to be thereby related. Further, segments which were related by alternation were considered by some (following Sapir, but not Bloomfield) to be related to each other within the system by virtue of this fact. 'Pattern congruity' involved maximizing all of these forms of relatedness among phonemes.

All of these factors contributing to the internal structure of phonemic systems correspond to regularities that, on other theories, would be treated as rules rather than as part of the definition of units. The character of American structuralist discussion, however, was such that the burden of such regularities was displaced onto the ontological status of the phonemes themselves. Of course, linguists stated regularities of distribution when they found them. Such statements were construed, however, not as having independent importance but as defining the phonemic units. Actual statements of distribution quite often took the form of mere lists of the occurring consonant clusters in various positions, arranged perhaps in tabular fashion for ease of reference but with little or no attempt to extract generalizations. The regularities themselves, and the forms they might take if construed as rules of the language, were of only incidental interest: the focus of attention was on the phonemes and their definitions, which were assumed to constitute the essence of a language's phonological system. We return to this issue and some of its effects in a later section.

Twaddell's "On Defining the Phoneme"

Already by the mid-1930s, then, two distinct conceptions of the nature of the phoneme had emerged within American linguistics. According to one of these, associated in America with the tradition of Sapir and elsewhere with such writers as Baudouin de Courtenay and Trubetzkoy (at least in his early work), phonemes were fundamentally psychological in nature: 'ideal sounds', 'the mental equivalent of a speech sound', 'percepts', etc. In contrast, an opposing view identifiable with Bloomfield's definition and also with those proposed by writers in the British tradition such as Daniel Jones, considered phonemes to be overt aspects of the physical speech event: either some constant fraction of the phonetic properties of sounds identified as functionally equivalent; or as classes of actual, fully specified sounds that are so identified. In 1935, a monograph by W. Freeman Twaddell challenged both of these positions and suggested that 'phonemes' are simply fictitious units used in order to express an analysis of the contrasts in a language as a system for transcribing utterances in that language.

Twaddell first attacks the psychological view of the phoneme, in terms heavily dependent on Bloomfield's view of psychology. Since on that view we know nothing at all about the 'mind' except what we can observe externally in terms of stimuli and responses, it is a conceptual and logical error to say that phonemes are a 'mental' reality. For Twaddell, as for Bloomfield, such descriptions simply assign a name to the unobservable: "they identify an entity which is inaccessible to scientific methods within the frame of linguistic study" (Twaddell 1935, in Joos 1957:57).

Twaddell considers the arguments of Sapir (1925, 1933) in some detail. He reviews the several examples reported by Sapir in which speakers characterized objectively different sounds in the same way (from which he had argued that the sounds in question corresponded to the same 'mental reality'), as well as those in which speakers characterized as different sounds that are phonetically the same. In the former cases, Twaddell argues that all that is involved is the informant's failure to make some distinction which a trained phonetician might make, and that the examples thus provide no evidence at all for a nonovert, 'mental' reality. In the second group of Sapir's examples, Twaddell argues that the differences being characterized are morphological rather than phonological in character. While they attest to a speaker's ability to distinguish morphological or lexical classes, they do not therefore bear on the claim of a 'mental' difference in phonemic representations, because there is no evidence that the distinction in question is fundamentally phonological and not simply a matter of differential responses given to different morphological categories.

The position Twaddell defends in the face of Sapir's examples is difficult to argue against on empirical grounds. On the one hand, he claims that where speakers fail to distinguish phonetically distinct sounds, that is simply a fact to be registered (rather than attempting to explain why some distinctions, and not others, are made). On the other hand, when speakers find a difference between forms that the phonetician cannot distinguish, either there is no other factor correlated with the difference in question (in which case, there is no confirmation of the claim of a difference), or there is such another factor, in which case Twaddell claims that it is this nonphonological factor, rather than a mentally real phonological difference, that is at issue. This position, that "what you see is all you get," might be argued to yield a less-than-satisfying account of many phenomena, but it is at least internally consistent. Until fundamental critiques of various forms of behaviorist psychology were developed (in particular Chomsky 1959, with regard to language), there were few specific arguments available which would convince such 'antimentalists' of the utility of abandoning that stand.

Having excluded (on his assumptions) the psychological view of phonemes, Twaddell moves on to attack the physicalist views. He considers first the position maintained by Bloomfield, that phonemes correspond to invariant subportions of the phonetic signal. Now a major advance of early twentieth-century science (including, of course, phonetics) had been the recognition that the physical world is essentially continuous, and that no two events are identical in the sense that no degree of precision in measurement could fail to find a difference between them. As a result of this pervasive nonidentity of phenomena, the problem of discovering actual invariants across classes of events is a nontrivial one. Certainly phoneticians had not succeeded in isolating such invariants in the acoustic (or physiological) record of speech, and Twaddell suggests that Bloomfield was in error in assuming that these would eventually be found. He concludes, then, that this first version of the physical theory of phonemes is at best a program of research for phoneticians, and not a satisfactory basis for a theory of phonology.

He then moves on to consider the other common variant of the physicalist view, that of Daniel Jones, that a phoneme is "a family of sounds in a given language, which are related in character and are such that no one of them ever occurs in the same surroundings as any other in words" (quoted by Twaddell 1935:64). Against this view, he argues not that the notions involved are ill defined but, rather, that the procedure of grouping sounds together on the basis of complementary distribution is arbitrary.

In positions where certain distinctions are neutralized, that is, it is required to assign the sounds that *do* occur to phonemes that also occur elsewhere; and there is no available criterion to validate one assignment over another. He considers the case of English stops after [s] as an example, where Swadesh had argued for assignment to the voiceless phonemes /p/, /t/, /k/ on the basis of complementary distribution and phonetic similarity. Twaddell suggests that there are as many phonetic properties warranting an assignment to /b/, /d/, /g/ as to /p/, /t/, /k/; and that there is accordingly no reason to prefer one analysis over the other. In the absence of some constant characteristic distinguishing the sounds of one family from those of another (which brings us back to the problem with Bloomfield's view), the families involved have no unique identifiability and thus no demonstrable reality.

Having argued that phonemes could not be adequately defined either in psychological or in purely physical terms, Twaddell suggests that the appropriate conclusion to draw is that 'phonemes' in the sense of minimal units of distinctive sound function, forming a unitary inventory within a language and concatenated with one another in an additive way to form words, are at most a fictional byproduct of an analysis of the distinctive relations within a language. He proceeds to develop this alternative view, starting from the observation that words (not segments) are the minimal free forms of a language which stand in contrast. While we can localize the various aspects of a contrast between words in distinguishable segments, we have no *a priori* right to identify the contrasts we find in one location with those found in another. He suggests that a similar view can be attributed to Jespersen as the basis of that linguist's lack of enthusiasm for phonemic theories.

Twaddell's procedure begins by registering the minimal contrasts in every possible environment. The vocalic contrasts among *beet, bit, bait, bet, bat*, for example, constitute one such set; those among *seek, sick, sake, sec*, and *sack* constitute another, etc. In each set, the primary fact is the array of *differences* between the forms taken pairwise; secondarily, we can identify the terms of these relations of difference—i.e., the phonetic segments which are different—and call these *microphonemes*. We can then, in each such set, arrange the differences in some order corresponding to the phonetic distinctions involved. The sets just mentioned, for instance, could be ordered by the difference in tongue height in their medial segments. The order assigned to each such class is effectively arbitrary, so long as its phonetic basis is stated.

Such ordered classes of minimal differences can then be compared with each other. In some cases, it is possible to assign orders to two classes and align them with one another so that "the qualitative articulatory differences among the corresponding phonetic events are similar and in a one-to-one relation" (ibid., p. 69). For example, the two sets cited above, ordered by tongue height as suggested, can be so aligned. Given such a correspondence, "the sum of all similarly ordered terms (micro-phonemes) of similar minimum phonological differences among forms is called a *macro-phoneme*" (ibid.). This process does not rest on a claim of phonetic identity (even partial) among the micro-phonemes that are summed in a single macro-phoneme, but rather on the fact that the *differences* between corresponding members are parallel to one another.

The set of macro-phonemes of a language will in general be much larger than the set of 'phonemes' in traditional terms, because whenever there is a different number of contrasts in one position than in another, the contrast sets cannot be put into one-to-one correspondence, and consequently their micro-phonemes cannot be identified under macro-phonemes. For Twaddell this was not a particularly unfortunate result, since it has the merit of not falsifying the facts. If it is the relations between forms that are phonologically primary, and there are fewer contrasts in one position than in another, it is a distortion to make any identification of the terms of the one set of contrasts with those of the other. His position here is essentially the same as that of Firth (see chapter 7 above) on the same issue.

Twaddell's view thus is fundamentally similar to that which we attributed to Saussure in chapter 2 above: a phonological theory based on 'fully specified surface variants', in which the substance of the phonology consists in a direct analysis of the contrasts among surface phonetic segments in various positions, and not in defining some more abstract unit (the phoneme) which lies behind them—either as a partial specification of their 'core' phonological properties or as an ideal mental entity or sound intention. Twaddell is quite explicit about the identification of his view with Saussure's, though this in itself means little, since many phonologists have invoked Saussure's name with no particular justification. The present analysis can be seen, however, as substantiating Twaddell's claim to continue Saussure's approach as opposed to most other theorists. For what it is worth, Saussure and Twaddell are among the very few to take seriously the claim that analysis of differential relations is not only the foundation of phonological analysis but its end as well.

(Macro-)phonemes are fictions on this view because the phonological description in substance stops at the elucidation of the network of differences among forms. "It follows, therefore, that it is meaningless to speak of 'the third phoneme (micro- or macro-) of the form *sudden*', or to speak of 'an occurrence of a phoneme'. What occurs is not a phoneme, for the phoneme is defined as the term of a recurrent differential relation. What occurs is a phonetic fraction or a differentiated articulatory complex correlated to a micro-phoneme. A phoneme, accordingly, does not occur; it 'exists' in the somewhat peculiar sense of existence that a brother, qua brother, 'exists'—as a term of a relation" (ibid., p. 74).

Twaddell intends to resist the natural temptation, noted in the introduction to the present book, to move from the fact that some forms are alike and some different in certain ways to the assumption that there is an inventory of 'real' positive entities that themselves embody these contrasts, and that can be added to one another to constitute linguistic forms. For him such formulations are not ultimately meaningful (since we have no warrant for going from the fact of difference between words to the claim that there are 'atoms' of difference, or phonemes), and they "are at all events dangerous, as leading all too readily to a kind of mythology in which the hypostasized 'phonemes' play their roles, or an equally mythologic view of the linguistic process according to which a speaker reaches into his store of phonemes, selects the proper number of them, arranges them tastefully, and then produces an utterance" (ibid., p. 75).

It is important to note that Twaddell's goal here is to suggest a more ontologically conservative notion of phonological structure than either the psychological or the physical views he opposed to his. Interpretations of his claim that the phoneme is a descriptive fiction have more commonly centered on the association of his views with the distinction between 'hocus-pocus' and 'God's-truth' approaches to linguistic structure (see chapter 7 above for some discussion of this terminology). He does indeed associate himself clearly with the 'hocus-pocus' position: "The sum of [differential] relations among the elements is the phonological system of the language. This phonological system is of course nothing objectively existent: it is not definable as a mental pattern in the minds of the speakers of the language; it is not even a 'platonic idea' which the language actualizes. It is quite simply the sum of all the phonological relations among the forms of a language, as those relations are determined by objective study. The phonological system is the phonetician's and the phonologist's summarized formulation of the relations: it is not a phenomenon, nor an intuition" (ibid., p. 76). There are few clearer statements of the view that linguistic structure is the creation of the analyst rather than something which exists in nature for him to find. This is by no means the only or even the most important point to be drawn from his work, however.

Twaddell's point should not be reduced to a claim of 'hocus-pocus' status for phonemic analysis, because this issue is largely orthogonal to the one he primarily addresses. One can perfectly consistently maintain either a 'hocus-pocus' or a 'God's-truth' view of the status of one's analysis, while presenting that analysis in any of the forms we have surveyed above (incorporating, i.e., partially specified, fully specified basic, or surface-variant notions of phonologically significant representation). The central claim of Twaddell's paper is not that the analysis is a creation of the analyst but that the analysis should be limited to presenting a system of differentiating relations without presuming in addition to establish a set of positive additive entities that lie behind these contrasts.

Twaddell's view should also not be reduced to a plea for philosophical nominalism—the claim that scientific constructs are simply names for the terms of a theory and do not have ontological status beyond the role they play in stating the theory. Again, one can hold either nominalist or realist views about the 'entities' referred to by scientific theories, quite independently of one's views on what sort of theory is appropriate to a particular domain (in this case, which sort of representation might be phonologically relevant).

Whether one agrees or not with the premises on which Twaddell bases his rejection of alternative views of phonemics, it is hard to deny that his is by far the most sophisticated discussion in the American structuralist literature of the status of 'phonemes' in linguistic analysis. Nonetheless, as Joose notes somewhat laconically, "the macro-phoneme was not adopted; but phonological discussion was noticeably more cautious for a few years after" (Joos 1957:80). In fact, though Twaddell's monograph was much cited, American structuralists continued to be more interested in what phonemes were than in the rather subtle notion that phonology should talk about systems of relations and not sets of related elements.

In the occurrence, consensus rapidly formed around a notion of the phoneme that was quite close to that of Jones. For most subsequent writers in the American structuralist mainstream, phonemes would be conceived of as classes of segments that were phonetically similar and in complementary distribution. Since these classes were carefully distinguished from the actual segments that were their members (a number of linguists of the period having learned at least the rudiments of set theory), the resulting representations cannot be identified with any of the specific theories distinguished in chapter 2 above.

One can speculate that, had Twaddell's lead been followed, subsequent discussion would have concentrated much more on the nature of the regularities of relation among linguistic forms and less on questions of how to represent forms in terms of elements of contrast. In fact, however, the main impact of Twaddell's work was effectively to banish both Sapir's 'ideal flow of phonetic elements' and Bloomfield's 'minimal same of vocal feature' from serious contention as definitions of the phoneme. As the notion of phonemes as classes gained ground, discussion turned to other issues: in particular, the conditions which could be relevant in identifying the phonemic classification of any given phonetic segment.

Subsequent developments in structuralist phonemics

Most of the discussion of the nature of the phoneme in the American structuralist literature was concerned less with its ontological status (the problem addressed by Twaddell), than with the conditions governing the relation between phonemic and phonetic representations. This issue had been raised by Trager and other commentators on Bloomfield's analyses of reduced vowels and similar cases of neutralization. It was posed in general terms by Chao (1934), a paper noted mostly for its demonstration that multiple alternative phonemic analyses might exist for the same phonetic data, depending on choices made by the analyst with no necessary motivation in the structure of the language itself. Chao also noted, however, that "given a phonemic symbol, the range of sounds is determined, and the choice within the range is usually further determined by phonetic conditions. It would also be a desirable thing to make this reversible, so as to include the aspect of writing; that is, given any sound in the language, its phonemic symbol is also determined" (Chao 1934, in Joos 1957:49).

General practice in the period, following that of both Sapir and Bloomfield, certainly did not provide for this "desirable thing," but it was not until 1941 that the issue was made into a major point of principle. Bloch's paper in that year, "Phonemic Overlapping," distinguished two different senses in which the phonemic symbol corresponding to a given sound might not be directly determined by its phonetic character. One is relatively benign: it may be that the same sound is assigned as a variant of two distinct phonemes, but in such a way that its phonemic value is still uniquely determinate given the phonetic context. This situation, called "partial overlapping," is exemplified by the flap occurring medially in American English *butter*. Bloch suggests that a phonetically identical flap occurs for some speakers after [θ] in words like *throw*. In the former case the flap is assigned to the /t/ phoneme, while in the latter it is assigned to /r/, "but the intersection is only partial and never leads to uncertainty or confusion: every such flap between vowels belongs to the [t] phoneme, every flap after a dental spirant belongs to the [r] phoneme" (Bloch 1941, in Joos 1957:94).

Much more pernicious, however, is the state of affairs characterized by Bloch as "complete overlapping," where the same sound occurs as a variant of more than one phoneme in the same phonetic environment. Several examples of this have arisen earlier in the present book. The paradigm case is perhaps the assignment of final voiceless obstruents in German, Russian, and other languages to voiced phonemes in some forms but to voiceless ones in others; Bloch cites Bloomfield's analysis of reduced vowels in the same connection. He argues that such analyses must be consistently excluded, for "a system in which successive occurrences of a given sound x under the same conditions must be assigned to different phonemes necessarily breaks down, because there can be nothing in the facts of pronunciation—the only data relevant to phonemic analysis—to tell us which kind of x we are dealing with in any particular utterance" (ibid., p. 95).

Bloch's paper was enormously influential, and his position was quite generally accepted by subsequent workers. The argument is that cases of 'complete overlapping' must logically be excluded; but, as pointed out by Kilbury (1976:75), the logic is less that of demonstration than of definition. Bloch defines phonemic analysis in such a way that only "the facts of pronunciation" can be relevant to it, and this does indeed entail the incoherence of analyses involving complete overlapping.

Given the climate of assumptions outlined in earlier sections above (including an implicit theory of perception shared by most linguists, and the denial of significance to any sort of 'mental' constructs in linguistic structure), the limitation proposed by Bloch really did seem to follow quite necessarily. This opinion could only be revised in a rather different climate, in which there figured a notably richer view of the process of perception, and in which language was once again assumed to involve aspects of human cognitive organization rather than merely a network of directly corresponding stimuli and responses.

Bloch showed plainly that the condition he had presented was more than a slogan; it had serious consequences for the range of possible analyses. He illustrates this with facts concerning American English vowels, which generally have longer variants when followed by voiced sounds than by voiceless ones: for example, *bid*, *bed*, and *bad* have phonetically longer vowels than *bit*, *bet*, and *bat*. This also applies to the vowel [a]: *pod* has a longer vowel than *pot*. Now in Bloch's dialect there are a few words in which a long and a short [a] contrast: *balm*, *father*, and *starry* for example have longer vowels than those of *bomb*, *bother*, and *sorry*. He suggests that the long member of this pair also appears in the word *pa*. Now suppose that we wanted to treat the distribution of vowel length as nonphonemic (i.e., to assign both long and short vowels to the same phonemes) where it is determined by a following segment. In that case, however, we would confront the problem that *pa'd* (in *pa'd go if he could*) is phonetically identical with *pod*; and thus the assignment of the vowel of *pod* to the 'short-[a]' phoneme while that of *pa'd* is assigned to 'long-[a]' would result in complete overlapping. This analysis must thus be rejected.

Bloch concludes from this that "the neat parallelism" of the facts of vowel length in vowels other than [a] with those affecting [a] must thus be destroyed. In order to avoid complete overlapping, the relation between the vowels of *pot* and *pod* must be treated as a relation between phonemes, while that between *bit* and *bid*, for example, is a relation between variants of the same phoneme. He recognizes that this is an unfortunate conclusion, but argues that it is the only scientifically valid one. The explicit recognition of such unpalatable consequences of the general principles of American structuralist phonemic theory is one of the most striking features of Bloch's work; indeed, it is carried considerably further in his discussion of Japanese (Bloch 1950).

There are alternatives to Bloch's analysis of English vowel length which would have allowed him to preserve "the neat parallelism" among the vowels largely unimpaired, even on his assumptions. For example, if the [a:] of *pa*, though phonetically long, is nonetheless taken as a variant (in final position) of the short /a/ phoneme, the situation reduces to one of partial overlapping. This is beside the point, however. What is important is that, beginning with this paper, American linguists thereafter accepted the exclusion of complete overlapping as a necessary condition on phonemic analysis—regardless of the consequences for the coherence of the resulting description. The necessity followed implicitly, as suggested above, from more general assumptions about the nature of language. The condition that phonemic representations be uniquely recoverable from phonetic data alone (together with its converse, that phonemic representations be uniquely translatable into phonetic form up to the level of free variation) was later given the name *bi-uniqueness* by Harris (1944a).

The essential motivation for the biuniqueness requirement on the relation between phonemic representations and phonetic form was the assumption that only "the facts of pronunciation" could possibly be relevant to phonemic analysis. Another aspect of this same claim was the explicit restriction that "no grammatical fact of any kind is used in making phonological analysis" (Hockett 1942, in Joos 1957:107). 'Grammatical' (i.e., morphological or syntactic) analysis is based on a phonemic representation; and if circularity is to be avoided in the resulting description, facts from such 'higher levels' cannot play a role in arriving at this representation. The point was sometimes presented in this way, as a methodological one, and sometimes as a consequence of biuniqueness (following from the need to exclude nonphonetic factors); but its substance was the general prohibition of analyses which 'mixed levels'.

Of course, most analysts admitted the possibility that, after arriving at a phonemic analysis, and then proceeding to analyze the morphology, one might go back and revise the initial phonemic system in light of the morphology so as to make the latter more coherent. After all, it was known (Chao 1934) that phonetic data typically support more than one possible valid phonemicization, and there was no reason not to choose that analysis which yielded the most satisfactory system at all levels. It was argued explicitly (e.g., by Hockett 1947) that such a procedure was defensible—provided that the phonemic system chosen was one that, considered apart, satisfied the condition of biuniqueness and did not involve essential reference to other levels of analysis. 'Mixing levels' was a perfectly satisfactory expedient as a field procedure, as long as it left no traces in the resultant grammar. This possibility follows from (and also illustrates) the separateness of actual field procedures and the abstract, idealized procedures that constituted the definition of constructs such as 'phonemic representation' within the linguistic theory of American structuralism.

Some linguists rejected the prohibition against mixing levels, however. The best-known arguments against this requirement were those of Pike (1947b, 1952), under the heading of "grammatical prerequisites to phonemic analysis." Pike argued that a satisfactory phonemic analysis might require access to information about the grammatical structure of forms, and he provided a number of cases in which such information seemed clearly relevant. Pike's examples all fall into the same class with one presented earlier by Bloomfield in his analysis of [x]/[ç] in German: all involve the role of grammatical boundaries in conditioning the appearance of particular variants of phonemic units. The indication of boundaries of course constitutes a rather limited use of grammatical information: much less radical, for example, then would become common in early generative work, where it was assumed that phonological rules could have access to a complete, structured phrase marker with hierarchical information, identification of morphological categories, etc.

Pike's arguments were not in general accepted by the mainstream of American structuralist phonemicists, since the admission of inaudible grammatical factors in a phonemic description would have dealt too severe a blow to the conception of 'phonemic representation' they assumed. An alternative was quickly found, however, which allowed for most of Pike's cases while maintaining at least the semblance of independence from 'grammatical prerequisites'. This was the positing of additional phonemic elements, called 'junctures', whose realization generally consisted not in some actual segmental element, but rather in their distinctive conditioning effect on other phonemes.

Moulton (1947), for example, posits an element /+/ of "open juncture" (a notion going back to suggestions of Trager & Bloch 1941) in his analysis of German. "This phoneme has two allophones: at the beginning or end of an utterance it appears as a pause of indefinite duration; within an utterance it appears as a brief pause or, in free variation, as zero" (ibid., p. 223). The extent to which internal instances of /+/ in German (such as those posited before the diminutive element -*chen*) actually can be realized by an overt pause is unclear, but this is not of course their main function. What is important is the fact that "we may assume this element wherever we find a pause (of whatever duration) and, in addition, wherever we find (1) aspirated /p t k/; (2) a glottal stop; and (3) the sound [ç] following (phonetically) a central or back vowel or semivowel" (ibid.).

Moulton is thus able to achieve Bloomfield's reduction of [x] and [ç] to a single phoneme, but without referring directly to grammatical structure, by referring instead to a phonemic element which is defined in (superficially) phonetic terms as potential pause alternating with zero. Of course, he observes somewhat disingenuously, "the places where /+/ occurs usually coincide with syntactic and morphological boundaries" (ibid., p. 224); but this is not a problem, since the definition of the element does not refer to such boundaries. For further support of the independence of /+/ from grammatical structure, he cites a few borrowings with exceptional stress in which internal instances of /+/ might be posited for reasons unrelated to boundaries.

Ingenious uses of 'juncture phonemes' allowed descriptions to maintain the letter of the prohibition against the appearance of grammatical information in phonemic analyses, while evading some of the worst consequences of a restriction to "the facts of pronunciation." The consequence, however, was a considerable enrichment of the notion of 'phoneme': when the phonetic manifestation of a 'phoneme' of 'close juncture' (aside from its effect on adjacent phonemes) could be defined precisely as an *absence* of potential pause, it is clear that analyses had come a long way from the notion of phonemes as discrete, additive signaling units. Further enrichment of the phonemic concept came with the attempt (especially in the mid- to late 1950s) to accommodate the facts of stress, distinctive pitch, and intonation—together with junctural phenomena—into a unitary inventory of phonemic units homogeneous in their linguistic status with segmental phonemes. Since the phoneme was taken as the 'atomic' building block of contrast, however, there was little alternative, whenever new dimensions of contrast were noticed, to incorporating these facts into an ever-widening conception of the phoneme.

The concentration of attention in American structuralism on the nature of the phoneme continued to characterize theoretical discussion throughout the 1950s, leaving the status of rule-governed relations *between* phonemes in a somewhat ambiguous position. On the one hand, analysts considered such regularities (especially those expressing distributional facts) important enough to warrant a place in descriptions and to influence (if not completely determine) phonemic analyses in the name of 'pattern congruity'. On the other hand, since a phonological description was conceived first and foremost as a theory of phonemic representations in a particular language, the only way such considerations could enter the picture was as part of the definition of individual phonemes.

Recall that the theory itself was presented in the form of a set of analytic procedures, which if followed were supposed to lead to objects of the intended sort. This entailed that phonological 'rules' only had status insofar as they could be incorporated in procedures. As opposed to the (static) representations that are arrived at by applying them, no particular 'reality' was attributed to the procedures themselves; and thus it was not really possible to sustain rational arguments about the form of possible rule-governed regularities that might occur in natural languages. In the absence of any sort of independent criterion that might decide which regularities were linguistically relevant and which accidental (or simply nonlinguistic), discussion tended to be quite anecdotal and aprioristic.

The concentration of phonological attention on questions of the nature of representations, with the consequent marginality assigned to rule-governed regularities in linguistic structure, has by no means been confined to American structuralists among theorists of natural language. However, some of the characteristic features of this theory reinforced this tendency here more than in other theories. Among these are the rigorous attention to the 'separation of levels', and the concomitant exclusion of most alternations from phonological relevance, together with the general requirement that phonemic representations be bi-uniquely related to phonetic data, which excludes even phonologically conditioned alternations between phonemes from relevance. Neither situation was considered wholly satisfactory by the linguists involved, but on the basis of their overall principles no alternative seemed to present itself. Excluded from a central position in the theory, regularities other than simple matters of distribution were either relegated to the nonsystematic status of 'pattern congruity', or else treated in twilight zone of morphophonemics. It is to this aspect of American structuralist theory that we turn next.

American structuralist morphophonemics

The history of morphophonemic description within American structuralism is a somewhat uneasy one. Facts regarding all but the most superficial alternations between related forms are intrinsically beyond the scope of such a theory of phonology, since 'relatedness' between forms is not deducible from "the facts of pronunciation alone." Any sort of description that attempts to reduce related elements to an underlying unity, so long as the elements themselves involve distinct phonemes (in the biunique sense of American structuralism), must therefore necessarily lie outside of phonology.

As a result, American structuralists had recognized more or less from the beginning a discipline of 'morpho(pho)nology' or 'morphophonemics'. According to Swadesh (1934:37), this part of linguistics dealt with two things: "the study of the phonemic structure of morphemes," and also "the study of interchange between phonemes as a morphological process." Definitions of the scope of morphophonemics offered by subsequent writers (including Bloch, Harris, Hockett, Wells, and others) varied somewhat as to whether both of these were to be handled in the same part of the grammar. Everyone was agreed that "interchange between phonemes," or the study of systematic relations in shape of related forms, was a part of morphophonemics (assuming there was such a field); the differences hung on whether the statement of regularities of morpheme shape (what would later be called 'morpheme-structure rules' within generative grammar) belonged there too. The issue seems largely terminological, however, since no one ever claimed that anything much depended on the decision. Our interest here is primarily in the treatment of regularities in the shapes of related (rather than individual) morphemes, and we will use the term 'morphophonemics' in that sense.

The earliest American phonemic work assimilated many facts of morphophonemic alternation to the rest of the phonology. This was certainly true for Sapir, and to a limited extent (as we have discussed above) for Bloomfield as well. At least by 1939, though, Bloomfield also distinguished a separate treatment of morphophonemics (in the specific, restricted sense of internal sandhi alternations) from phonemics. As discussed in the previous chapter, Bloomfield's technique for morphophonemic description was derived from Pāṇini: it consisted in the setting up of 'base forms', to which a set of ordered rules applied one at a time to derive eventually the surface (phonemic) form.

We can say, in fact, that while Bloomfield held a 'partially specified surface variant' view of phonemic structure, he took a 'basic variant' view of morphophonemic structure—extending the terminology of chapter 2 to this new domain.

A combination of phonological and morphophonemic facts also appears in Trager's paper on Russian, as noted above. Interestingly, this paper stimulated Trubetzkoy to write to Jakobson that although Trager's analysis of Russian was completely off the mark, his descriptive framework and terminology seemed to be an attempt to imitate morphophonemic work of the Prague school phonologists. Swadesh's paper in the same year, which explicitly distinguishes phonology from morphophonology in much the same way Trubetzkoy did, also seemed part of an American attempt to imitate the Praguians. In retrospect, although there is some clear borrowing of Praguian terminology, the notion that Trager and Swadesh were trying to be like Trubetzkoy and Jakobson seems somewhat far-fetched. The distinctions between phonology and morphophonemics were still blurred, however, just as they had been in the work of Baudouin de Courtenay—and American phonologists, like those in Prague, were attempting to draw lines in accord with their understanding of the nature of phonemic structure.

As 'pure' phonemic doctrine developed, it came to exclude the treatment of morphophonemic alternations more and more definitively (both in America and in Europe). This did not, of course, prevent linguists from recognizing that there were indeed systematic relationships of this sort whose description belonged in a comprehensive account of language structures. But since these relationships could not be accommodated within the phonology (*sensu stricto*), the only place for them was in the description of morphology. As a result, the subsequent history of morphophonemics (at least in America) is entangled with the emergence of a distinctive view of the nature of morphemes.

Bloomfield's approach to morphophonemic description in terms of basic variants and ordered rules came in for a certain amount of criticism from the 'post-Bloomfieldian' generation. To them, despite Bloomfield's specific disclaimers, such a description looked suspiciously like a historical account. What, after all, could such a sequential application correspond to *except* the sequence of historical changes that had given rise to a present-day alternation? Linguists such as Wells, Lounsbury, and others in their methodological discussions of morphophonemics felt that it was necessary to maintain a strict exclusion of anything of the sort from synchronic grammars, and thus rejected Bloomfield's descriptive technique. In general, this formed part of a more general tendency in American linguistics to eliminate dynamic, processlike statements deriving forms from one another or from more basic forms, in favor of static descriptive accounts which directly characterized the range of occurring forms. This preference results, of course, from the underlying assumption that it is only the representations of individual forms that linguistics should focus on, since only the forms themselves are observable and thus 'real'.

The alternative to process-type descriptions which developed centered around the method of 'morpheme alternants'. This was first discussed in detail by Harris (1942), and arises as an answer to a problem concerning the nature of the morpheme. Following Bloomfield, Harris starts from the definition that "every sequence of phonemes which has meaning, and which is not composed of smaller sequences having meaning, is a morpheme" (Harris 1942, in Joos 1957:109). Morphemes are thus identified with particular sequences of phonemes; but this has the unfortunate result of "dissociat[ing] certain morphemes which we wish, because of the grammatical structure, to unite" (ibid.). In the simplest case, the three forms /-əz/, /-z/, and /-s/ of the English regular plural ending constitute three different phoneme sequences, and thus three different morphemes on this definition. From the point of view of the syntax, we obviously want to treat these as the same morpheme; which means we must revise our notion of 'morpheme'.

Harris's procedure is first to isolate the minimal meaningful sequences of phonemes, as before, but to call them "morpheme alternants" instead of morphemes. He then groups together as a single "morpheme unit" any set of morpheme alternants that have the same meaning and which are in complementary distribution. The model is obviously the same as the phonological one: a morpheme on this view (Harris's "morpheme unit") is a set, which is related to its members or allomorphs (a term introduced by Nida to replace Harris's "morpheme alternant") just as a phoneme is a set consisting of its allophones.

Having organized morpheme alternants into morphemic units, we can now examine the differences among the alternants of individual morphemic units. "If we find another morpheme unit having an identical difference between its alternants, we can describe both units together. Thus between *knife* and *knive-*, which make up one unit, the difference is identical with the difference between *wife* and *wive-*, which make up another, and with the difference between *leaf* and *leave-*, and so on. Instead of listing both members of each unit, we now list only one representative of each unit with a general statement of the difference which applies to all of them: Each of the units *knife, wife, . . . ,* has an alternant with /v/ instead of /f/ before /z/ 'plural'" (ibid., p. 111).

This method of description is not dramatically different at first sight from an analysis with base forms and rules to convert them into surface forms, but there are important distinctions nonetheless. Note that Harris does not actually *derive* the form *knive-* from *knife* by a rule turning /f/ into /v/: rather the representation *knife*, together with the fact that this morpheme appears on the relevant list, serves as an abbreviation for the two alternants *knife* and *knive-*, with one alternant appearing in a particular environment and the other appearing elsewhere. As far as the language is concerned, the morpheme simply has two alternants, with the same status: one is not derived with respect to the other.

Alternants are grouped together into morpheme units in the same way regardless of whether the differences among them are systematic or not: *am, are, is,* etc. are grouped together in the same way as the alternants of the regular plural or *knife/ knive-*. Where the variation is recurrent, we can state it in a descriptive formula, and then summarize the allomorphs of a given morpheme by a representation which is not in itself a morpheme alternant, but which in conjunction with the formula allows us to determine the actual morpheme alternants.

Later in the paper, Harris makes clearer the static, formulaic character of the representations which are provided for individual morpheme units. He also introduces a minor revision. Instead of writing /nayf/ for 'knife', and then including this element on a list of those to which the descriptive statement of the f/v alternation applies, we can write such elements with a special morphophonemic symbol /F/: thus, /nayF/ is subject to the alternation, but /fayf/ is not. It is important to be clear about the status of the elements such as this /F/. They are clearly *not* intended to be additional phonemes of the system, or to have a direct phonetic interpretation at all. Rather, /F/ is an abbreviation for the formula: (phonemic) /v/ before the plural /-z/, (phonemic) /f/ elsewhere. In this way, morphemes are provided with unitary representations insofar as their alternants are systematically related, but the role of these representations is to abbreviate the list of occurring phonemic alternants, and nothing more. Morphemes are units; they are sets, composed of alternants which are also (as phonemic sequences) units. A unitary representation is simply a convenient abbreviation for the set of alternants united in a given morpheme, employed where possible, but having no other systematic status.

Morphophonemic symbols such as /F/, which serve as abbreviations for a set of alternating phonemes under various conditions, are parallel to the morpho(pho)nemes posited by Trubetzkoy (see chapter 4 above). In both cases, the only condition on the formation of a morphophoneme is that the conditions of occurrence of the various alternating phonemes subsumed under it be stable and recurrent. No requirement at all is imposed that the alternation be phonetically coherent or 'natural': the morphophonemic symbol simply replaces a list of individual phonemes, each of which has some particular environment in which it occurs.

We can contrast this sort of abstract morphophonemic symbol with another usage, which is found in Bloomfield's work. In his description of Menomini, Bloomfield represents morphological elements as abstract base forms, which are composed for the most part of phonemic elements. Their interpretation is such that, if no rule applies to change a given phoneme into some other, it is realized as such. Certain symbols, however, do not have a direct phonemic interpretation but are abstract: these *must* be replaced by some phonemic symbol (or, of course, deleted) if the resultant representation is to be well formed. Such abstract symbols are typified by the element /N/ used (in Bloomfield 1962) to represent an /n/ which fails to undergo palatalization: after the palatalization rule applies, changing /n/ to /s/ in certain environments, all instances of /N/ are replaced by /n/, thus merging with remaining instances of this phoneme.

In every case, Bloomfield uses abstract (i.e., nonphonemic) symbols in base forms to represent the fact that certain elements which are otherwise phonemically unitary show two distinct types of behavior with respect to particular rules. Thus, /n/ and /N/ are both realized as phonemic /n/, and differ only in that /n/ is subject to a palatalization which /N/ does not undergo. We can distinguish this sort of abstract symbol from that represented by Harris's /F/, in that Bloomfield's /N/ (and other such symbols in his grammar) is simply used to indicate an /n/ which behaves unusually. In generative terms, the difference between /N/ and /n/ is that one bears an exception feature which the other does not. Harris's /F/, on the other hand, represents a completely arbitrary collection of elements related only in that they occur in corresponding places in related allomorphs of the same morphemes under the conditions of an alternation.

Naturally, it is possible to express the 'Bloomfieldian' sort of morphophoneme in terms of the other type. We can say that Menomini /N/ is represented by simple phonemic /n/ in all environments, while /n/ is a morphophoneme represented by phonemic /s/ in some environments, and by phonemic /n/ in others. Interestingly, Bloomfield (1939) uses the special symbol /N/ for the alternating segment, and /n/ for the nonalternating. This usage is more nearly in line with that of other writers on morphophonemics, and with the conception of morphophonemes as formulas for alternations; perhaps the reversal of usage between Bloomfield (1939) and Bloomfield (1962) reflects a difference in conception.

One of the most important early American structuralist papers on morphophonemics, that of Swadesh and Voegelin (1939), illustrates both of these usages for morphophonemic symbols simultaneously. On the one hand, in discussing the role of abstract morphophonemic symbols in descriptions, Swadesh and Voegelin treat the same English example (*wife/wives, leaf/leaves*, etc.) that Harris would discuss three years later, and propose the same account: a morphophoneme /F/, which serves as an abbreviation for the alternation 'phoneme /v/ before plural /z/, phoneme /f/ elsewhere'. On the other hand, in their discussion of Tübatulabal, they use morphophonemes in the way Bloomfield had: that is, to represent two variants of the same surface phoneme which differ in their behavior with respect to particular rules of the grammar.

Tübatulabal exhibits an extensive network of alternations between long and short vowels. Swadesh and Voegelin show that in a number of cases, vowels that would otherwise be long appear short when followed by a voiceless obstruent, while either a long or a short vowel may be followed by a voiced obstruent. This suggests a rule shortening vowels before voiceless (but not voiced) obstruents. Unlike the obstruents, the nasals, semivowels, liquid /l/, and laryngeals (/h/ and /ʔ/) do not show a distinction between phonetically voiced and voiceless forms. In some instances, however, vowels are shortened before members of this class, while in others they are not. Among the non-obstruents, then, we have two sorts of morphophonemic behavior: some segments trigger shortening, while others do not, although there is no phonetic (or, *a fortiori*, phonemic) difference between the two.

An obvious morphophonemic solution would be to set up two classes of nonobstruents—underlyingly voiced versus voiceless—in parallel with the two (phonetically motivated) classes of obstruents. It could then be stated that vowels are shortened before voiceless segments but not before voiced; and, subsequently, voiced and voiceless nonobstruents could be merged (as phonetically voiced segments in the case of the nasals, and /l/, and as voiceless for the laryngeals). Interestingly, Swadesh and Voegelin do not propose this solution. They do indeed set up two classes of nonobstruents, but instead of treating the difference as a matter of voicing, they simply call one class "shortening consonants", and the other class "neutral" or "nonshortening". A phonetic interpretation is almost ostentatiously avoided.

A similar analysis is provided for the vowels. Some vowels in Tübatulabal show up as long unless affected by a shortening rule; while others show up short unless affected by a (positional) lengthening rule. Again, the obvious analysis would seem to be to distinguish the two classes phonetically, as underlying long versus short vowels. Instead, Swadesh and Voegelin distinguish 'heavy' from 'light' vowels, and use a different diacritic to mark 'heavy' vowels in morphophonemic representations from that used to mark long vowels in phonemic forms. Both in this case and in that of the consonants, the interpretation is clear: differences between morphophonemic symbols do not correspond directly to phonetic or phonemic differences but to differences between two sorts of behavior that may be shown by the 'same' surface phonemic segment type—exactly as in Bloomfield's usage. This variety of abstract morphophonemic symbol can be distinguished from that of the /F/ in *leaf*/*leaves*, but both sorts of morphophoneme are quite distinct from phonetic/phonemic elements.

Rule interactions and the nature of descriptions

In addition to the status of elements in morphophonemic representations, other issues of importance which can be identified in the morphophonemic theories of American structuralist writers include their treatment of rule interaction or ordering. Recall that, in Bloomfield's method of description, the rules of a morphophonemic analysis are applied in a sequence (or "descriptive order"), with each rule applying to the result of the application of the previous rule. The precise order of application of the rules of a grammar is a matter to be specified in the grammar itself. To say that one rule 'precedes' another in a description means more precisely that the results of the first rule's application are presupposed by the second, and, furthermore, that any information destroyed by the first rule is not accessible to the second (see Anderson 1974 for discussion). For Bloomfield, as for generative phonologists (at least until about 1970), such relations of presupposition among rules were to be specified in the grammars of individual languages just like any other aspect of the rules themselves. Other writers on morphophonemics, however, while they assume something like a relevant applicational sequence for the rules of the grammar, make assumptions that are rather different from Bloomfield's.

It would take us too far afield here to examine in detail the alternatives to a specified descriptive order which can be found in American structuralist morphophonemic descriptions (see Kenstowicz 1975 for extensive discussion), but one important tradition can be noted, which Kenstowicz traces to the work of Sapir. We noted in chapter 9 above that Sapir assumed that rules applied in a sequence, but a sequence which was predictable from general principles rather than specified in the grammar. In addition, Sapir allowed rules to refer to the difference between 'organic' elements (those present in underlying forms), and 'inorganic' ones (those produced by the operation of a rule). Since the reference to 'organic' vs. 'inorganic' elements is a distinction available to any rule of the grammar, it allows rules to have access to information which previous rules have in fact destroyed. This possibility arises in the case of an 'organic' segment which has been altered by a rule, but whose underlying source is still accessible to subsequent rules.

References of this sort to the underlying value of a segment which has in fact been altered by a rule are found in a number of papers in the 1930s, 1940s, and 1950s, (including Swadesh & Voegelin 1939, in particular) as documented by Kenstowicz (1975). In general, the assumptions underlying rule interactions within particular grammars went undiscussed in the theoretical literature, and it is not always clear how much significance to attribute to the assumptions which can be shown ex post facto to be necessary in order to get a particular description to yield the correct results. In at least one case, however, the particular issue of reference to basic versus derived forms is specifically addressed.

Harris (1951a), dealing with the nature of morphophonemic description, raises the question of the role of descriptive order. He cites rules of Bloomfield's from Menomini, where (a) morpheme-final /n/ is replaced by /s/ before /e/ or /y/; and (b) final vowels are dropped. "When we now meet /ōs/ 'canoe', /ōnan/ 'canoes', we recognize that this alternation can be stated as the sum of the previous two. However, this can only be done if we set up a morphophonemic /ōn-e/ and then apply our two alternations in the order in which they are stated above; if we first drop the /e/, we will have lost the condition for then replacing the /n/ by /s/" (Harris 1951a:237).

On the face of it, Harris here commits a logical error which is in fact rather common in the subsequent literature (including some generative discussions). He seems to argue that this example demonstrates a need for descriptive order, when in fact it simply shows that if the rules involved are applied in an order, it makes a difference which order. (For some discussion of such cases, see Anderson 1974, chapter 5.) True, applying the rules in the reverse of the order presented above yields an incorrect form (/ōn/); but it is also true that if both rules apply to the *same* representation (the underlying form) independently of one another (i.e., if the rules apply simultaneously), the correct result is also obtained. What is necessary is simply to ensure that when the rule replacing /n/ by /s/ applies, the presence of a final /e/ is still accessible. This can be achieved either by (a) having the rule dropping final vowels apply only after the rule of /n/ to /s/; or (b) allowing the /n/ to /s/ rule to examine the underlying representation, regardless of whether final vowel loss also eliminates the /e/ from the surface form.

Despite the apparent implication of his statement quoted above, Harris is well aware of this possibility, and in the next paragraph suggests that an alternative to descriptive order is precisely that of allowing rules to be stated so as to refer either to morphophonemic (i.e., 'organic' or underlying) environments or to phonemic (or surface) environments. His proposal, then, is similar to that implied in the practice of Sapir and others; it differs in that he intends reference to the morphophonemic/phonemic distinction to replace all significant order. Note that rules might still have to apply in (an implicit) sequence: if a rule is so stated as to have a crucially phonemic environment, it cannot apply until after some other rule has converted the relevant morphophonemic elements into phonemes (since Harris assumes that even a morphophoneme with a uniform phonemic realization is distinct from the corresponding phoneme). However, there are some situations which are clearly ruled out on this view: in particular, it is impossible for an intermediate representation, distinct both from underlying and from surface form, to play a significant role in conditioning alternations.

Other differences in the consequences that follow from the theories of Sapir, Bloomfield, and Harris concerning rule interaction could easily be adduced, but we limit our remarks in this connection to those above. With the exception of Bloomfield's general statement of his practice in Bloomfield (1939, 1962), and Harris's discussion just referred to, very few linguists of the period addressed such issues directly, despite the need for substantial assumptions about rule interaction in all serious morphophonemic descriptions. Wells (1949) provides what is probably the most structured and sophisticated discussion of the theoretical problem of how rules of alternation interact with one another—and the very extent to which this paper was generally ignored by others at the time probably illustrates well just how marginal such concerns were in the context of American structuralist theoretical discussion.

This marginality results from the larger fact that, within American structuralist theory, morphophonemics had no real status other than as a 'technique' for describing in a compact way the sets of allomorphs belonging to individual morphemes. Morphophonemics deals with regularities in the relations between forms, but since only the forms themselves are directly observable, in terms of the American structuralists' limited view of the nature of language, only the forms are 'real'. Regularities are not facts of the same order, to be accorded the same status in the grammar: rather they are something the linguist finds in the relation between forms. Of course, it is incumbent on him to describe these relations, but how he goes about it is his own business and not a matter of linguistic fact.

It is true that Bloomfield (among others) discussed the existence of alternative descriptions of the same sets of facts, and proposed choices among these. More specifically, Bloomfield in several places urges that the analyst should always choose the 'simplest' available solution. In the light of subsequent linguistic theory, one might therefore be tempted to attribute to him a notion of evaluation applicable to the comparison of grammatical descriptions, in the domain of morphophonemics as well as elsewhere; but this would fairly clearly be an error. When Bloomfield talks about one description as 'simpler' than another, he does not mean this in the technical sense of generative grammar (cf. chapter 12 below), but simply in the presystematic sense that one description might be shorter, less complicated, less redundant, neater, etc. than another. Naturally, linguists should strive to maximize readability, and also conciseness. Beyond this, however, and as a question of a 'correct' linguistic analysis, any description was potentially correct if it got the forms right, and presented an accurate account of the phonemic, morphemic, etc. systems of the language.

For the American structuralists, as for Bloomfield, a language was basically a hierarchy of inventories: an inventory of phonemes, which could be concatenated to form morpheme alternants; an inventory of morphemes, which could be combined to form words and syntactic constructions which themselves formed further inventories. A description of a language was fundamentally a definition and enumeration of the elements that made up these inventories.

Only when this conception was replaced by the notion that a language is a structured cognitive system was it possible to take seriously the idea that a description had to comprehend something other than the set of forms (at various levels of analysis). In describing such a cognitive system, not only the forms but also the rules which express regular relations among them (and further, the principles which determine the interpretation and application of the rules) correspond to something 'real'. In those terms, it is possible to raise the issue of whether a particular description, or a particular format for descriptions in general, is right or wrong. For American structuralists, however, morphophonemics fell entirely into the area of 'regularities' rather than that of 'items', since their principles excluded such facts from phonemics, and thus this aspect of linguistic description occupied only the nonsystematic status of a descriptive technique that was not really part of the language itself.

12

Generative Phonology and Its Origins

In this chapter, we consider the background and initial progress of generative phonology from the mid-1950s to about the time Chomsky and Halle's *The Sound Pattern of English* appeared in 1968. There are two distinct aspects to the issue of how generative phonology developed during this period, both related to its antecedents. On the one hand, there is the question of how generative phonology both built on and replaced other traditions; and, on the other hand, it is worth examining how generative phonologists dealt with these questions of origins. This second question is of some interest in the case of this particular theory, because so much of the early literature of the field was a conscious attempt to interpret the past—in part to break with it and in part to renew connections with supposedly forgotten insights of previous research. The question of the actual (as opposed to perceived) historical origins of the theory has obvious importance if we hope to identify those aspects of it that have been taken over unexamined from other views and maintained well after the basic assumptions underlying them had been abandoned.

Generative phonology, in particular the work of Noam Chomsky and Morris Halle, brings together the two principal lines of development we have been concerned with in earlier chapters. As a student originally of Zellig Harris, Chomsky's background was in the most rigorously formal, procedural, distributional sort of American structuralism. Halle, on the other hand, was a student of Roman Jakobson, and thus trained in a much different, 'European' tradition. Their collaboration resulted in a theory radically different from either source, but with essential roots in both.

We make no attempt in this chapter to present the principles of the theory of generative phonology. Other works exist for this purpose (e.g., Anderson 1974; Hyman 1975; Kenstowicz & Kisserberth 1975; Sommerstein 1977—not to mention Chomsky & Halle 1968), and the sort of sketch that could be given in a few pages here would be of little use. Instead, our main concern here is to sketch the historical development of the first years of generative phonology, with particular reference to the factors that differentiated this new approach to the field from previous work, and which resulted in the widespread abandonment of structuralist theory (at least in the United States) in its favor.

The decline and fall of American structuralism

The history of the rise of generative grammar (and of generative phonology in particular) is in large part that of the abandonment of American structuralism. To many nonlinguists, the theory of generative phonology may seem 'structuralist' in its essence because it is based on the premise that structure (and not simply inventory) is paramount in language; but the particular sense that the term had taken on in linguistics by the 1950s (both in America and in Europe) was much more specific, and the replacement of that view by the generative one was a genuinely fundamental one in numerous ways. The appearance of any new theory inevitably involves the replacement of older views; but the relation between American structuralist and generative views was particularly confrontational. In this section we discuss the early course of that confrontation, following largely the excellent account given by Newmeyer (1980).

By the 1950s, linguistics was no longer a marginal field studied as a part-time interest by scholars whose major responsibility was to some other discipline. Particularly in the United States, it had become a thriving subject in its own right, with a substantial number of faculty and students working in well-established departments of linguistics specifically on linguistic problems. This new body of linguists had a strong sense of professional identity, reinforced by the apparatus of an orthodox academic discipline (a professional society, annual meetings, the summer Linguistic Institutes, several journals clearly dedicated to their work, etc.); to a significant extent, that identity was based on the specific claims of structuralist theory to a uniquely privileged and scientific view of an important object of study, human language. Any new theory questioning basic structuralist assumptions would naturally have encountered a certain amount of intellectual resistance, but the resistance in this case was also to what many saw as a threat to the very foundations of the field.

To outsiders, American structuralist linguistics in the mid-1950s seemed to be something of a model science: so well organized, indeed, that it threatened to find itself out of a job by virtue of having solved all of its major problems. The basic principles of phonemics and morphemics had been more or less clarified along lines sketched in the previous chapter, and the extension of essentially the same conceptual structure to syntax seemed possible at least in principle. Given this structure, the main problem for linguistics was posed as that of developing procedures of analysis applicable to the data of arbitrary languages, which would yield descriptions of the desired form. It was generally felt that the bases of these procedures were already well understood, and that all that remained before linguistic analysis would be effectively reduced to a mechanical task (which might even be automated) were refinements in certain relatively minor details.

Seen from within the field, however, the situation was not quite so optimistic. From several sides, challenges had arisen which seemed to undermine important basic assumptions. There was certainly no overall doubt about the essential correctness of the lines of research being pursued; but there were nevertheless a number of points on which the foundations of structuralism were potentially vulnerable to a concerted and coherent attack.

One of these was the set of issues in the philosophy of science which had furnished such powerful motivation to Bloomfield and the immediately following generation. In the period between the two world wars, the operationalist, verificationist assumptions of logical empiricism had been so dominant as almost to establish the limits of 'scientific inquiry'. Much of the appeal of American structuralist linguistics was based on its roots in this approach to research, and the consequent validation of structuralist theory as uniquely 'scientific' in the history of research on language.

By the 1950s, though, philosophers of science were increasingly questioning the validity of the sort of empiricism to which linguists had hitched their wagon. It became clear that fundamental scientific concepts in many fields simply did not have the kind of operational definition required by the logical empiricists, without thereby being rendered meaningless. Science in general was becoming more concerned with the extent to which theories taken as a whole have explanatory and predictive power within a given domain, bringing coherence and clarity to it, rather than with the manner in which individual statements within a theory can be operationally verified. With this turn, much of the philosophical rationale for the specific conceptual foundations of structuralism crumbled.

In a related development, the approach of radical behaviorists in psychology was also being questioned. The link between behaviorism and more general issues in the philosophy of science is clear; but it was specific studies showing the need to posit psychological mechanisms with more complexity and structure than stimulus-response chains, rather than the attitude of philosophers, that had begun seriously to reduce the appeal of behaviorism by the mid-1950s. Chomsky's (1959) review of Skinner's *Verbal Behavior* provided a more or less definitive blow to these views in the specific area of language, but the process of reevaluation of their explanatory power was already well along.

Of course, with the decline of acceptance of behaviorism came a willingness to consider more structured and less simplistic psychological theories in important areas such as perception and learning. We suggested in the previous chapter that acceptance of a particularly limited view of perception seemed to provide a powerful argument in favor of bi-unique phonemic representations; and the notion that (first) language learning takes place by simple induction against the same assumptionless background as linguistic fieldwork seemed to validate the procedural approach to the definition of fundamental linguistic constructs. With the discrediting of behaviorist assumptions in both areas came further weakening of the support for American structuralist theory and methods that had appeared to come from considerations going beyond linguistics.

Strictly within the field, however, there were also problems to be noted. An increasing amount of evidence had developed by the mid 1950s that the strict requirements of a bi-unique phonemic analysis (the cornerstone of structuralist linguistics) often led to descriptions that were seriously counterintuitive.

Bloch had first discussed this problem in his 1941 paper "Phonemic Overlapping" in which, as discussed in the previous chapter, he showed that the requirement of biuniqueness had the consequence of breaking up the "neat parallelism" of the vowels of American English with respect to the distribution of vowel length. In this case, he argued that a proper understanding of the theoretical construct of the phoneme actually led to an advance: the discovery that the facts were not so parallel after all. Similarly, in the revision of his analysis of Japanese phonemics between his treatment in 1946 and that in 1950, apparently simple and elegant principles disappear into a welter of particularities. Again, this was hailed as an advance in understanding that came from the strict application of biunique phonemic analysis; but structuralist phonemics could really stand only a certain number of such 'advances'. As they accumulated, it became less and less clear that a theory with such consequences was actually improving linguists' understanding of the structure of language.

A particular area in which numerous analytic difficulties arose was the treatment of suprasegmentals: stress, pitch, and juncture. Considerable energy, both descriptive and theoretical, was lavished on these phenomena during the 1950s. Trager and Smith's (1951) analysis of English, with several distinct levels of phonemic stress and pitch and a set of junctural elements, was the center of much discussion. As facts in this domain became clearer (if not clear), two conclusions seemed ineluctable: first, that the description of suprasegmental phenomena (at least in English, the most extensively studied case) required extensive reference to grammatical structure if it was to be coherent; and, second, that the contrasts involved were in no serious sense recoverable directly from the phonetic data alone. It was only in 1965 that Lieberman showed experimentally that without access to other information, even highly trained phoneticians could not judge stress accurately; but this conclusion had long since begun to force itself on those who worked in the area. The facts of stress (as well as pitch and juncture) seemed absolutely intractable within a theory that required bi-uniqueness and that denied the phonology access to grammatical information.

In fact, the first significant impact of generative work on the assumptions of American structuralism came arguably not from work in transformational syntax but from the phonological proposals made by Chomsky, Halle, and Lukoff in a 1956 paper "On Accent and Juncture in English." They provided an analysis of English stress which required only a simple accented/unaccented distinction in phonological representations in place of the four degrees of stress of the Trager-Smith system. The description was manifestly more elegant than any previous treatment—but it depended essentially on rules that were sensitive to grammatical structure, applying in cyclic fashion to successively higher levels of constituents in order to derive the complex surface facts from a simple and straightforward phonemic form.

Chomsky, Halle, and Lukoff's paper established a powerful *prima facie* case for the necessity of abandoning structuralist assumptions in order to arrive at a coherent analysis of English suprasegmentals, but the defenders of those assumptions hardly rushed to embrace the new proposals. In 1957, at the Second Texas Conference on Problems of Linguistic Analysis in English, the analysis was vigorously attacked and (in the opinions of the participants in the conference), conclusively demolished. Explicit rebuttal of this attack did not come until Chomsky's lectures at the Linguistic Institute in 1964 (subsequently published as Chomsky 1966), but the issues involved were discussed in various places in the meantime, and the appeal of the analysis spoke for itself.

In the following year (1958), the organizers of the Third Texas Conference invited Chomsky to present his work in person. The idea seems to have been to bring all of the 'big guns' of structuralist linguistics to bear on the new theory, so as to stamp it out before it went too far. The actual consequences were rather otherwise, however, as a reading of the transcript of the conference (Hill 1962) makes fascinatingly clear. As Newmeyer (1980:35) says, it shows "Chomsky, the *enfant terrible*, taking on some of the giants of the field and making them look like rather confused students in a beginning linguistics course." By this time, the emerging challenge of generative grammar to the assumptions of American structuralism had become serious indeed. Even a few structuralists were beginning to be convinced themselves.

The ascendancy of generative phonology

By the late 1950s, then, the conceptual underpinnings of American structuralism were seriously weakened, and the alternative presented by a developing theory of generative grammar was beginning to make an impression on the field. The impression should not be given, however, that structuralist linguistics simply melted away in 1957 or 1958.

Noam Chomsky was well placed to expose the weaknesses of American structural linguistics. Born in 1928, his interest in language was developed as early as the age of ten, when he read the proofs of a book by his father (the Hebrew philologist William Chomsky) on Hebrew grammar. At the University of Pennsylvania, Chomsky met Zellig Harris (whose political views attracted him initially as much as his scholarship). It was through reading the proofs of Harris's (1951a) *Methods in Structural Linguistics* that Chomsky first learned linguistics. At Penn, he wrote an undergraduate thesis and subsequently a master's thesis on the morphophonemics of modern Hebrew (Chomsky 1951; published 1979). This work has the goals of a generative grammar, and deals not simply with morphophonemics but with the entire grammar of the language from syntax through phonology. In its form a system of ordered rules intended to characterize the range of grammatical sentences in the language, it more nearly resembled the historical studies of his father than it did the sort of work Harris was doing. There is little evidence that Harris noticed this, however, or that he even read Chomsky's thesis. Interestingly, the only linguists who did show any interest in this work were the Indo-Europeanist Henry Hoenigswald at Penn and Bernard Bloch at Yale.

Through the recommendation of the philosopher Nelson Goodman, Chomsky was appointed a junior fellow at Harvard from 1951 to 1955. This position gave him essentially complete freedom to work on whatever he wanted, and at first he pursued the development of the procedural methods he had learned from Harris. In Cambridge, however, he met Morris Halle (then a graduate student at Harvard), with whom he spent a great deal of time in discussion. By 1953, both Chomsky and Halle had become thoroughly disillusioned with the refinement of structuralist procedures as a theory of language; and, with Halle's encouragement, Chomsky began to work out the ideas underlying his master's thesis. The result was a volume of about a thousand pages, *The Logical Structure of Linguistic Theory* (Chomsky 1955; published 1975) in which most of the fundamental ideas of generative grammar are laid out and explored.

Though the book was rejected by the only publisher to whom he sent it, Chomsky also submitted one chapter of it as a dissertation at the University of Pennsylvania. Thanks to the influence of Halle and Jakobson, he had a research position at MIT, where he also taught scientific French and German and some undergraduate courses in logic and philosophy. More importantly, he had the freedom to continue developing his ideas about the foundations of linguistics in a stimulating and unrestricted atmosphere, with the collaboration of Halle and others at Harvard and MIT.

In 1957, a volume of Chomsky's notes for an undergraduate course at MIT was published in a new series which had been started with Jakobson and Halle's (1956) *Fundamentals of Language*. This was *Syntactic Structures*, a work which might have gone essentially unnoticed had it not been for a review by Robert Lees that was published by Bloch in *Language*. Lees's (1957) review forcefully brought generative grammar to the attention of the American linguistic community, and can be said to have initiated the process of change that eventually led to the replacement of structuralism by generative grammar in American linguistics.

As a result of his training with Harris, and the amount of attention he had himself given to the task of defining linguistic structure in the form of a set of rigorously explicit procedures, Chomsky well understood the fundamental problems that plagued this approach. On the other hand, his own education had been thoroughly independent, and his first substantial results (in *The Morphophonemics of Modern Hebrew*) were achieved without substantial reference to structuralist assumptions. When he became convinced that the effort was necessary, he was thus in a better position to strike out in a radically different direction than were those with a personal commitment to structuralism.

One of the strongest points of American structuralism was its concern for formal analysis and explicit statement. Thanks in large part to Chomsky, this continued to play a central role in generative grammar, even though most of the substance of the structuralist position was replaced. However, given his talent for devastatingly rigorous argument and analysis, the effect when he did attack the established view was dramatic.

Chomsky's proposals quickly became the center of syntactic discussion, after the appearance of *Syntactic Structures* and Lees's review of this book. To a considerable extent, however, the impact of *Syntactic Structures* can be attributed to the fact that structuralist linguistics simply didn't have a serious 'theory' of syntax. There was general optimism that one was possible as 'an extension of morphology by other means' (to paraphrase von Clausewitz), but little of substance can really be said to have been accomplished. Some linguists were quite ready to see transformational syntax, in fact, as an approach that could be directly incorporated into structuralist descriptions in the form of a new analytic technique requiring only minimal modifications in the basic assumptions of the theory.

The situation was completely different in phonology, however. Here there was no sort of theoretical vacuum to be filled: this was territory that structuralism was generally felt to have conquered for scientific study, and where it was felt to be strongest. Chomsky, Halle, and Lukoff's (1956) paper had seriously questioned the tenability of the basic proposition that phonological structure was independent of grammar, but the Texas conferences of the following two years showed that the established figures in the field were largely unwilling to accept this result—even in the absence of a genuine alternative in the description of English stress. At the 1959 Texas conference, Chomsky was again invited, and this time presented a paper on English phonology which extended the arguments of Chomsky, Halle, and Lukoff (1956); it is probably significant (and no accident) that the proceedings of this conference were never published. In 1959 also, Halle's *Sound Pattern of Russian* extended the attack to the bases of the biuniqueness condition, but again acceptance of this critique by the main stream of American linguistics was anything but immediate.

In 1962, the International Congress of Linguists was held in Cambridge, Massachusetts. Zellig Harris had been asked to give one of five plenary session papers but turned down the invitation; the organizers of the Congress (including Morris Halle) then asked Chomsky instead. Chomsky devoted a large portion of his paper "The Logical Basis of Linguistic Theory" (subsequently published in various versions, eventually as Chomsky 1964) to an extended criticism of the assumptions of structuralist (or 'taxonomic') phonemics. The aggressive tone and forceful argumentation of this paper were set in a context which made it clear that the problems it raised were by no means matters of mechanics, to be solved by a further refinement of structuralist procedures, but rested on the same basic issues that were being challenged by transformational theories in syntax. Such a linking of the two was essential if the philosophical impact of generative grammar was not to be trivialized by being restricted to those parts of language that structuralists just hadn't gotten around to yet. Those who would attempt to treat transformational syntax as a technique to be grafted onto a structuralist phonology and morphology were forced to face the fact that those areas were equally challenged—which many were unwilling to do.

Two other short papers by Halle (1962, 1964) further presented the case for a generative approach to phonology; but while many younger scholars had become convinced of the importance of the theory by this time, the field (and its institutions, such as the annual meetings of the LSA) continued to be dominated by structuralist studies. Nonetheless, generative grammarians were increasingly on the attack, at meetings and in articles and reviews in the principal journals.

The climax of this confrontation can probably be marked as 1965. In that year, Fred Householder published a long, strongly worded attack on generative phonology in the first number of the new *Journal of Linguistics*, an article which summarized virtually all of the objections and grievances against the new theory that were current in the field. The editor of the journal, John Lyons, asked Chomsky and Halle in advance of the appearance of Householder's paper whether they would like to reply. Chomsky and Halle were then at work on *The Sound Pattern of English*; and Lyons's invitation presented them with an opportunity to deal with the polemic issues surrounding generative phonology in isolation from the positive statement that the book would make. They therefore agreed, and the resulting reply (Chomsky and Halle 1965), which appeared in the immediately following issue, provided a detailed and— for most—conclusive response to the structuralist criticisms.

After 1965 there were still attacks from the structuralist side (e.g., Hockett 1968; Lamb 1966), but with the exception of a vigorous counterattack by Postal (1968, a manuscript which had been circulating in prepublication versions for at least three years before), generative phonologists simply failed to pursue the question after that. As far as the determination of the major direction of subsequent research was concerned, the issue was settled. Chomsky's effective lectures on phonology and syntax (on alternating days) formed the primary focus of the 1966 Linguistic Institute at UCLA, and consolidated the central position of generative grammar (including phonology) in American linguistics. A number of new departments were created more or less *ex nihilo* during the 1960s, largely as a result of the tremendously increased interest in the field which the new theory of generative grammar brought about. With the exception of these (and MIT), it would be difficult to find a major linguistics department in the United States (at least through the early 1970s) without a certain core of (often vocal) structuralist opponents of the new trend, but these figures found themselves increasingly isolated and unattended to by the great majority.

Morris Halle and the bases of generative phonology

Morris Halle, born in Latvia in 1923, had a rather different background from Chomsky's. After emigrating to the United States in 1940, he studied engineering in New York until he was drafted in 1943. After the war, he attended the University of Chicago, where he received a degree in linguistics; in 1948, he went to Columbia to study with Jakobson, and came with Jakobson to Harvard the next year. He was thus a part of the circle of talented young Slavicists around Jakobson during these years, and collaborated with Jakobson on a number of influential works. His Harvard Ph.D. thesis in 1955 was entitled "The Russian Consonants: A Phonemic and Acoustical Study."

On the basis in part of his engineering background, Halle held an appointment in the Research Laboratory of Electronics at MIT while he was a student at Harvard. He was subsequently (in 1951) hired by the MIT department of modern languages to teach German and Russian. A part of his research on acoustics at MIT while he was still a student involved collaboration with Jakobson and Gunnar Fant, and resulted in *Preliminaries to Speech Analysis* (Jakobson, Fant, and Halle 1952), a formulation of the Jakobsonian distinctive-feature framework in simultaneous acoustic and articulatory terms. His initial reputation was earned as an acoustic phonetician, and only secondarily (through his association with Jakobson) as a phonologist.

Although Jakobson was particularly interested during the early 1950s in providing an explicit acoustic basis for the distinctive features, he had also done some particularly elegant work on the morphophonemics of Slavic languages (particularly his article "Russian Conjugation," Jakobson 1948)— work which was virtually ignored by American linguists other than Slavicists at the time. Halle was greatly impressed and attracted by this work, but also struck by the difficulty of relating anything like an adequate morphophonemic representation of utterances directly to the acoustic facts. The morphophonemic analysis had such obvious coherence and explanatory value that it seemed inconceivable to deny its importance in the structure of language, as most American phonemicists attempted to do; but on the other hand, if this analysis did indeed have a real role in linguistic structure, its relation to the physical signal must be much less direct than was posited for a structuralist phonemic representation.

In 1959, Halle published *The Sound Pattern of Russian*, in which the several aspects of this problem are addressed. Indeed, the many distinct areas which this book deals with in combination make it rather strange reading today: we are unused to finding a combination of general linguistic theory and detailed analysis of the phonology of a specific language together in a single volume with an introduction to the physical acoustics of speech and detailed acoustic description of the surface segments of the language. All of these are central to Halle's project, however. He had decided that morphophonemic representation was extremely important to the structure of language; but (reflecting another influence from Jakobson) he believed that a representation which was perceptually recoverable from acoustic data was important as well. His goal was to show how these two levels of description were related to each other, and what characteristics each level had. Since linguists were not generally acquainted with the results of the rapidly developing theory of the acoustics of speech, it was necessary to give an introductory sketch of this area in order to make his results comprehensible.

Though it is not, perhaps, the most readable part of this book, the section for which it is primarily remembered is the introduction to the first chapter, "A Theory of Phonology." Here Halle lays out a number of assumptions claimed to be necessary to an adequate phonological theory; but, most importantly, he argues that a level of representation meeting the specific conditions of structuralist phonemics (in particular, the bi-uniqueness condition) cannot naturally be incorporated into such a theory.

In order to account for "ambiguities due to homophony" (Halle 1959:23), a morphophonemic representation is indispensable; and a universal phonetic representation is similarly necessary to express the facts of speech. The latter is, for Halle, one in which all of the features in a universal inventory—for example, the Jakobsonian system—are specified in a way that has a direct acoustic and articulatory interpretation. In contrast to both of these, a structuralist phonemic representation has the property of specifying all and only the distinctive sound properties of an utterance, while still being recoverable from phonetic data alone (i.e., it meets the condition of bi-uniqueness). Halle's argument was that such a representation can not in general be incorporated in an analysis without resulting in "an unwarranted complication which has no place in a scientific description of language" (ibid., p. 24).

We have already had several occasions in previous chapters to refer to this argument, which in important ways represents the cornerstone of early generative phonology. Halle first presented it in a paper read at the 1957 winter meeting of the LSA, but it only took on its full force when embedded in the more comprehensive context of *The Sound Pattern of Russian*.

There the argument appears in a discussion of one of "six formal conditions which phonological descriptions must satisfy" (ibid. p. 19). The first two of these require that representations be organized into sequences of segments and boundaries, where the segments are further specified in terms of a system of properties called the *distinctive features*. The third condition then addresses the way in which the phonological representation is related to "the observable data, i.e. to the actual speech events" (ibid. p. 20). Halle notes that all phonologists would accept the requirement that it should be possible to

infer the (linguistically relevant) properties of the utterance from the phonological representation (his "condition (3)"), but that there is less unanimity
about the additional requirement ("condition (3a)") that it be possible to "infer . . . the proper phonological representation of any speech event, without
recourse to any information not contained in the physical signal" (ibid. p. 21).

The basis for Halle's rejecting "condition (3a)" (i.e., the bi-uniqueness requirement) is as follows:

> In Russian, voicing is distinctive for all obstruents except /c/, /č/,
> and /x/, which do not possess voiced cognates. These three obstruents
> are voiceless unless followed by a voiced obstruent, in which case
> they are voiced. At the end of the word, however, this is true of all
> Russian obstruents: they are voiceless, unless the following word be-
> gins with a voiced obstruent, in which case they are voiced. E.g.,
> [m'ok 1,i] 'was (he) getting wet?', but [m'og bi̊] 'were (he) getting
> wet'; [ž'eč 1,i] 'should one burn?', but [ž'eǯ bi̊] 'were one to burn'.
> In a phonological representation which satisfies both condition (3)
> and (3a), the quoted utterances would be symbolized as follows:
> /m'ok 1,i/, /m'og bi/, /ž'eč 1,i/, /ž'eč bi/. Moreover, a rule would be
> required stating that obstruents lacking voiced cognates—i.e., /c/,
> /č/ and /x/—are voiced in position before voiced obstruents. Since
> this, however, is true of all obstruents, the net effect of the attempt to
> meet both condition (3) and (3a) would be a splitting up of the
> obstruents into two classes and the addition of a special rule. If con-
> dition (3a) is dropped, the four utterances would be symbolized as
> follows: {m'ok 1,i}, {m'ok bi}, {ž'eč 1,i}, {ž'eč bi}, and the above rule
> could be generalized to cover all obstruents, instead of only {č} {c}
> and {x}. It is evident that condition (3a) involves a significant in-
> crease in the complexity of the representation." (Ibid. pp. 22–23)

The nature of this argument is quite interesting to consider. Importantly, it
does not at all consist in bringing linguistic facts of a novel sort into consideration: similar facts had already been noted by researchers within the American structuralist tradition without provoking a rejection of the bi-uniqueness
principle. The situation described by Halle arises any time a single rule (here,
voicing assimilation) results in a change of phonemic identity for some segments (e.g., the change from {k} to /g/ in {m'ok bi} → /m'og bi/), but simply a
subphonemic variant for others (e.g. {ž'eč bi} → [ž'eǯ bi̊]).

We have already noted that Bloomfield's Menomini contains a similar example in the treatment of the "semi-phoneme" ū, which is produced by the
operation of a phonologically conditioned raising rule, and which thus should
not be accorded phonemic status, but which must be treated as a phoneme if
the output of the morphophonemic rules is a string of phonemes. Bloch's discussion of American English vowel length would support a similar conclusion, as he implicitly admits. Hamp (1953), in discussing the processes of
initial mutation in Celtic, cites facts of the same nature and even adduces

them specifically as evidence against the validity of a biunique phonemic representation. Yet none of these (or other) arguments resulted in the elimination of the biuniqueness condition, while Halle's argument based on the same sort of example did undeniably persuade many who had remained unconvinced before.

In part, we can probably attribute the persuasiveness of Halle's demonstration to its timeliness. As we have summarized in the preceding sections, many American structuralists by 1959 already had doubts about the conceptual soundness of the theory. The biuniqueness principle was a fundamental part of structuralist phonemics, but one that seemed both to follow from its underlying (and now compromised) premises, and to lead in many cases to unappealing and counterintuitive analyses. Thus, the field may simply have been ready for a concerted attack on this principle.

It should also not be ignored that Halle's argument was embedded in a comprehensive theory of phonology, whose elegance was illustrated by the accompanying analysis of highly complex patterns of phonological relationships in Russian. One might well have been willing to accept even rather radical theoretical premises in order to arrive at comparably satisfying results. In addition, the Jakobsonian framework of distinctive features, by its close association with the most sophisticated work being done on speech acoustics, had acquired an image of technological advancement that made it the natural successor to the 'scientific' image American structuralism had previously cultivated. Here too, a predisposition to take the theory seriously may have contributed to the acceptance of its basic premises.

Whatever the role of such factors in assuring the effectiveness of Halle's argument, however, its most important role lay in the emphasis it put on the centrality of *rules* in a phonological description. Note that the entire argument rests on the observation that, in certain situations, a level meeting the conditions of bi-uniqueness requires some unitary regularity of the language (here, voicing assimilation) to be split up into two effectively unrelated rules. Now in a theory (such as American structuralist phonemics) in which only the representations of forms have 'real' status, such an argument is nonsensical or at best irrelevant: the principles relating one representation to another (the rules) are simply parts of the definitions of individual elements of representations, and have no independent status whatsoever in the grammar. If they can be formulated in a simple and concise way, so much the better; but the notion that the elements of representations themselves should be chosen for the convenience of the rules was inconceivable.

The immediate consequence of Halle's discussion was a change in phonology in the direction of much more abstract representations than those permitted within a theory which concentrated on biunique phonemics. But it must be emphasized that this move was, in an important sense, an ancillary consequence of a more fundamental reorientation in phonological research: a shift from a concentration on the properties of phonological representations and their elements to a much greater stress on the rules of a grammar. Naturally, concern with questions of representations and their nature did not disappear overnight. Nonetheless, the recognition was dawning that rules as well had to be taken seriously as part of a grammar if language was to be examined as a complex cognitive system rather than an inventory of phonemes, morphemes, words, and constructions. Since the study of rules, their properties, and their organization into linguistic systems was virtually unexplored territory, this reorientation had a much more important effect on the nature of phonological research than the mere fact that generative underlying representations are more abstract than biunique phonemic ones.

The antecedents of generative phonological theory

Almost from the beginning, both Chomsky and Halle invoked the names of figures from the prestructuralist past as precursors of the sort of work they were doing. With reference to phonology, Sapir is referred to in these terms on numerous occasions, as is Bloomfield (in his practice—e.g., Bloomfield 1939—though not with regard to his theoretical writings). Chomsky (1962) also cites de Saussure as having a picture of phonological representation rather similar to that of generative phonology, though this is a rather isolated reference. Subsequently, Chomsky further emphasized connections between generative grammar and the rationalist philosophy of the Port-Royal grammar, Descartes, Humboldt, and others (cf. Chomsky 1966).

Claims that this earlier work (whether philosophical or linguistic) was in some way the source or origin of notions in generative grammar would have to be qualified as mere rationalization ex post facto. Chomsky's ideas were developed largely in isolation from the linguistic tradition. He has emphasized himself (e.g., in Chomsky 1979) the extent to which his early work was done completely outside the framework of any particular sort of linguistics and with little awareness of its specific antecedents. Similarly, his explorations of early rationalist philosophy were largely conducted after the essential program of generative grammar was already formulated and well underway.

Chomsky's discussions of the early rationalists have provoked strong reactions from historians of science and philosophy, who accuse him of rewriting the history of ideas as a grand conspiracy to develop the notion of a generative grammar. In fact, however, a more reasonable assessment is available: the point of his historical interpretations is that earlier thinkers about language had some very similar insights to those that motivate work in generative grammar, but their point of view was subsequently replaced by very different ones, and those insights thus were lost—in the sense that they did not guide subsequent work. One attempts to explore the attitudes toward language of earlier philosophical writers not in order to see them as generative grammarians manqués, or to associate the prestige of their names with current theory, but because, insofar as their work was based on similar premises, it may well be of considerable current relevance. Generative grammar can only stand or fall as a theory of natural language on the basis of its own explanatory value, but it may still be quite worthwhile to examine the place of its underlying assumptions within other, larger philosophical contexts.

The conception of a language as a system of rules (rather than a set of representations) which lies at the heart of Halle's *Sound Pattern of Russian* and his arguments against structuralist phonemics was naturally quite consistent with Chomsky's notions. *The Morphophonemics of Modern Hebrew* had already presented a similar picture, and discussions between Chomsky and Halle during the 1950s had resulted in essential agreement between them around a program represented by these works and Chomsky (1955). The analysis of English proposed by Chomsky, Halle, and Lukoff (1956) is similarly in line with this conception of a grammar, though that paper addressed primarily the question of how to represent stress.

Some aspects of this theoretical program for phonology have clear antecedents in the work of the Prague school, as is only natural given Halle's association with Jakobson. One such part of the theory is the weight given to the system of distinctive features as a theory of universal phonetics. For various reasons, American structuralists had never really taken to distinctive feature analyses (with the exception of a few works such as Hockett 1955), but this representation was essential to the new theory of generative phonology. A major point of contention between American structuralist and early generative theories, in fact, was the insistence of the former that phonemes should be attended to as unitary elements of contrast, while generative phonology maintained that the contrastive value of phonemic segments was a byproduct of contrasts in features. The consequent claim that segments were merely 'unsystematic abbreviations' for complexes of features served as a major irritant in the new theory for older workers in the field.

A primary reason for the attention to features was the prominence within the theory of the notion of evaluation of grammars. Grammars were to be formulated in a uniform notation which would make it possible to compare alternative descriptions of the same facts, and it was intended that such a comparison would form the basis of a notion of explanation in linguistics. An appropriate evaluation measure would designate one of a class of alternative grammars as preferred over other available possibilities, and in this way questions concerning the structural properties of language could be posed in terms of appropriate characteristics to assign to such a measure. The use of a feature notation played a central role in early proposals for an evaluation measure over phonological descriptions.

An aspect of language structure which was assumed to be highly valued was the extent to which rules of grammar express 'linguistically significant generalizations' (though it has often been claimed that a weakness in the theory is the absence of any independent notion of what these are). Formulating rules and representations in terms of features contributes to the assessment of generality, Halle (1962, 1964) argued, because it reflects in the form of length of statement the generality or naturalness of the classes of segments which an expression refers to: in an adequate universal feature system, it takes fewer features to characterize more general natural classes than less general ones. If grammars are systematically expressed in a notation based on features, they can be compared in a straightforward way which will reflect the degree of generalization captured by a given formulation. The role of features in the theory was thus quite different from that which it served in Prague school work, but the emphasis on the decomposition of segments into constituent dimensions of contrast is a point of similarity between the two.

Another Praguian theme in generative grammar was a basic concern for explanation in linguistics, and the concomitant search for universal properties and laws of linguistic structure. As we have seen, both universals and explanatory principles were considered by American structuralists to be either nonexistent or beyond the scope of possible research. American linguists sought maximally explicit and comprehensive descriptions of particular languages, but generally felt that the only sort of universals that could be maintained were inductive generalizations about the corpus of languages described to date. This was directly contrary to European practice—which was generally stigmatized in America as vague and impressionistic. Generative grammar restored explanation and the search for universals of language to a central place in linguistics, in the context of a concern for explicitness and formal statement which could hardly be confused with 'mere philosophy'.

In contrast with its relation to European linguistics (specifically, the positions associated with Jakobson) the notion that there is continuity between early generative phonology and its American structuralist predecessors is far from obvious, at least to judge by the rhetoric employed on both sides. There are, nonetheless some important assumptions of structuralist work which were taken over into generative phonology with little or no reexamination. One such area is that of morphological structure.

Structuralism had developed a picture of words as exhaustively analyzable into sequences of concatenated morphemes: minimal units of meaningful sound structure. Discussion of this conception had uncovered a large number of important problems: 'zero' morphemes, 'portmanteau' morphemes (e.g., French *au* for *à* + *le*), meaningless 'morphemes' (such as connectives and thematic vowels), 'morphemes' of replacement (e.g., the plural marker in *man/men*), subtraction, etc. Since no real alternative existed within structuralism to the notion of morphemes as units of form linked inseparably with units of meaning, this picture persisted even in the face of the unfortunate consequences noted by Hockett (1947), Nida (1948) and others.

The history of this problem is insightfully presented by Matthews (1972). As he notes, generative grammar simply took over unchanged as part of its notion of underlying representation the conception of morphological structure as a "fictitious agglutinating analog" of the actual forms of a language

(Lounsbury 1953, in Joos 1957:380). Only rather recent work (e.g., Matthews 1972; Anderson 1982a) has proceeded to reexamine the appropriateness of this model of word structure within a generative theory of grammar; the bulk of generative descriptions have been (and continue to be) based on essentially (American) structuralist assumptions.

As we have argued above, the emphasis of generative phonology broke with previous work from the beginning by emphasizing the centrality of rules in a theory of language. The focus of early work (which continues today; though see later in this chapter and chapter 13) was on the nature and formulation of rules, with questions of representation subordinated to these in the sense that the representations were arranged so as to maximize the generality of the rules. It was taken as at least a goal to reduce any state of affairs in which two or more phonologically diverse forms existed for related elements to a description in which a common underlying form appears, and the divergence in surface form is accounted for by the operation of maximally general rules. A rule was presumed to exist wherever related forms differed in shape, with only a few irreducible exceptions such as the verb *be* in English—but even here some made a noble attempt to state apparently suppletive paradigms as governed by rule (e.g., Foley 1965b). The underlying forms that were posited were whatever was necessary to maximize the generality of the rules involved.

The emphasis on rules, however, is not the only prominent goal of early generative descriptions. Another is the effort to provide underlying representations from which the last drop of redundancy has been wrung: representations which specify the absolute minimum of information in order to distinguish one morpheme from another within the system of a given language. In part, this is simply the continuation of the project which most phonologists since Saussure have set for themselves. If one conceives of a 'phonological' representation as one which specifies all and only the distinctive or signalling properties of forms, it follows that all other (predictable, or redundant) information should be excised from this representation. More specifically, however, the form in which this effort was implemented in early generative descriptions derives from Jakobson's concerns with information theory and the mathematical theory of communication.

At least in early generative descriptions, this appears particularly in the way the phonological system of a language is presented in the form of a 'branching diagram'. Such a diagram is an arrangement of the segments of a language into a sequence of successive choices (each corresponding to a particular feature), such that at each point the number of elements representing one possible choice (or feature value) is roughly equal to that represented by the opposite choice. The overall set of distinctions among segments is thus organized so as to minimize not simply predictable specifications, but more particularly the number of actual specifications necessary to identify uniquely any given (underlying) segment.

Superficially, at least, the motivation for branching diagrams of phonological segment inventories seemed to follow from the more general task of evaluation of grammars: if the evaluation metric for grammars is to be based on the measure of length of expression when descriptions are formulated in a standard notation, and if feature notation is an appropriate way to represent segments and classes of segments, then it follows that a grammar should be organized so as to minimize the number of features necessary to characterize any individual segment.

There is an important flaw in this argument, however. The claim of short-ness of expression as an appropriate evaluation procedure is not really an empirical proposal about the nature of language; it is, rather, a framework within which such proposals can be made. Any expression can trivially be made to be shorter than any other by the choice of an appropriate set of abbreviatory conventions: proposals that one formally characterized type of rule rather than another is more natural in human languages are then made in the form of proposals for the set of such abbreviatory conventions. Much of generative phonology up through the appearance of Chomsky and Halle (1968) and work immediately deriving therefrom was explicitly devoted to just this task. The assumption that, given a set of notational conventions for rules, length as a function of the number of specified features can be taken as an appropriate measure of generality for rules, however, does not at all entail the conclusion that the number of feature specifications in the lexicon should be similarly minimized. In fact, there is little if any connection between the notion that rules should be formulated in maximally general terms and a requirement that the lexicon should be specified with as few features as possible.

Especially during the 1960s, generative grammars were concerned with various aspects of the problem of eliminating as many features as possible from underlying representations. This was done by optimizing the distribution of contrasts, in association with a set of morpheme structure rules which filled in the redundant features. In part, this project of extracting as much redun-dancy as possible followed from the considerations of evaluation discussed above, but it was also simply assumed (as part of generative phonology's Jakobsonian heritage) that this was part of what one did when one described the phonology of a language. The requirement of redundancy-free underlying representations, however, and the status of morpheme structure rules (vis-à-vis ordinary phonological rules) raised a number of strictly mechanical prob-lems (some of which are reviewed by Stanley 1967). These problems are not reviewed in detail here, since they are well treated in the existing literature.

In is interesting to note that a concern for morpheme structure rules and the elimination of redundancy gradually disappeared from generative descrip-tions, without ever being effectively renounced as a theoretical concern. The presentation of 'branching diagrams' for the segments of a language is a prac-tice which fell out of use by the mid-1960s, and concern for the statement of redundancy rules more or less disappears by the end of the decade. It might be possible to attribute this change to proposals such as that of Stanley (ibid.)

and the last chapter of Chomsky and Halle (1968), both of which argued (for somewhat different reasons) that lexical representations should after all be fully specified, and that redundancy should be treated in other ways. This does not seem to be the entire story, however.

Early concern for evaluation procedures, in the form of specific arguments that (in an appropriate notation) shorter descriptions could be empirically validated as correct, turned out to be something of a dead end. Virtually the only actual argument of this form in the literature is Chomsky and Halle's often repeated citation of the differences among *brick* (an occurring word in English), *bnick* (an impossible word in English) and *blick* (a possible, but nonoccurring word in English; it is amusing to note that, apparently unknown to Chomsky and Halle, *blick* had been employed some years before as a nonce word by the philosopher R. M. Hare to designate a belief which is hedged in such a way as to incorporate any possible disconfirming evidence). In the absence of further convincing examples (but see Anderson 1974, chapter 6, for an attempt to construct another), the appeal of feature counting went away and, with it, much of the apparatus that was intended to support it—not with a bang, but a whimper.

The theoretical problems of the 'classical' period of generative phonology (up to the early 1970s), then, were fundamentally problems of the nature of rules: the design of an appropriate notation for expressing rules, the choice of an adequate set of abbreviatory conventions for sets of rules, the formulation of principles governing the ordering and other interactions of rules within a grammar. Even the central representational issue of the period, the elimination of redundancy from underlying forms, was typically posed as a matter of the status and formulation of morpheme structure rules or some replacement for these. In this context, phonological (and even phonetic) representations were simply assumed to have the properties necessary to enable the rules to function in a maximally general way.

Not long after the appearance of *The Sound Pattern of English* in 1968, however, a number of phonologists began to raise objections from several sides to then-current practice. Most of these objections had their origins in a renewed inquiry into the properties of representations per se, and it is to these developments that we turn in the final chapter.

13

Generative Phonology after
The Sound Pattern of English

There are surely few years that are so clearly marked as watersheds in the history of phonology as 1968. In that year, Chomsky and Halle published their long-awaited work *The Sound Pattern of English*, by far the most comprehensive presentation and exemplification of the theory of generative phonology to appear up to that point (or since, for that matter). The manuscript had circulated in various versions for several years before, but its final appearance made the theory available for much more general analysis and criticism than had hitherto been possible. Although earlier publications had described the theory, as discussed in the previous chapter, 1968 was the year in which generative phonology was finally in complete enough form for substantive scrutiny.

The publication of *SPE* also had another, symbolic importance. It marked the end of an era in which the major works of generative linguistics (in syntax as well as in phonology) were circulated primarily in *samizdat'* form among a small circle of insiders, with those not on the necessary mailing lists confined to secondhand reports and rumors for their information on the shape of theoretical developments. Overt, formal publication of a reasonably definitive description of the principles of the theory made it much more a matter of public property, and enfranchised a much broader audience of potential contributors and critics. And, as this wider accessibility was broadening their audience, generative linguists were increasingly turning to the regular avenues of formal book and journal publication (in some instances, creating their own, such as *Linguistic Inquiry*) rather than to their duplicating machines. The number of significant papers whose reference sections were essentially confined to unpublished work plummeted.

If 1968 was the year in which generative phonology was substantiated and legitimized, it was also the year from which the reaction against the theory must be dated. Before, objection had come largely from those wishing to maintain some form of American (or European) structuralist view; but by the time of the appearance of *SPE*, this had ceased to be an issue for all but a few. From then on, the objections that were raised came from within the general perspective on language that Chomsky and Halle had established, and sought to question generative theory on its own terms. Since much of this discussion continues today, it would be ridiculous to attempt a definitive summary of it and its results; the present chapter aims simply to characterize the most important attempts to revise or replace the theory of *SPE*.

The nature of the *SPE* program

A useful perspective on the issues involved in generative phonology can be gained from a consideration of parallels between the evolution of phonological theory and that of the foundations of mathematics. Let us recall that the nature of a phonological theory as expressed in *SPE* centers on an explicit formal notation for phonological description. In combination with an evaluation function for grammars defined over this notation, this would constitute a comprehensive axiomatization of the subject matter of phonology, in the sense that all problems connected with the discovery of correct (or 'descriptively adequate') accounts of sound structure would thereby be reduced to the mechanical manipulation of expressions in a fully explicit notational system. Of course, Chomsky and Halle (1968) do not claim to have accomplished this goal, but it is nonetheless the program of the theory. The successes achieved within the framework of 'classical' generative phonology were seen as confirmation of the plausibility of such an axiomatization.

In this respect, the program of *SPE* is strikingly similar to that of another fundamental work of twentieth-century thought, Whitehead and Russell's (1910) *Principia Mathematica* (cited as *PM* below). That work enunciated and developed a goal of reducing all of the intellectual content of mathematics to the formal manipulation of expressions in a logistic system by means of fully explicit rules. While the calculus of formal logic in which *PM* proposed to express mathematical propositions is of course quite unlike the descriptive apparatus envisaged by *SPE* for phonological expressions, and Chomsky and Halle never refer to Whitehead and Russell, the intent of expressing all of the content of their respective fields in terms subject to formal manipulation by means of well-established rules is common to the two works.

PM's account of the foundations of mathematics was initially greeted with enthusiasm, since it promised to give a full reconstruction of the traditional notion that the truth of mathematical propositions derives from logic alone, and not from contingent facts about the world. This enthusiasm soon gave way to dissatisfaction, however, as it became apparent that there were fundamental obstacles to the logicist program. In particular, the theory in its basic form was seen to give rise to a number of the paradoxes which had long been troublesomely familiar to mathematicians, such as various forms of the problem of the barber who shaves everyone who does not shave himself, and other apparent self-contradictions. In order to remedy this difficulty, Russell had proposed what is known as the theory of 'types': roughly speaking, a restriction on the kinds of classes that can be referred to in any given expression. Unfortunately, the theory of types itself had undesirable consequences: it rendered many of the basic propositions of number theory unstatable or meaningless. It was thus necessary, in the full system of the *PM*, to appeal to an 'axiom of infinity' and an 'axiom of reducibility', whose plausibility and intuitive appeal are vastly less than that of the rest of the logical system. Since the theory of types seemed unavoidable in the context of the logic of the *PM*, and since it seemed to lead to such counterintuitive emendations of the system, the logicist program for the foundations of mathematics was gradually abandoned.

Partially in response to the perceived failure of this approach, other views of the foundations of mathematics were developed on other assumptions. Among the most important of these alternatives was that presented by Brouwer and others under the title of 'intuitionism'. A primary tenet of this school is the rejection of all expressions purporting to refer to objects that cannot in fact be fully constructed. In particular, expressions that refer to explicitly infinite sets are disallowed, since while one can give directions for enlarging the extension of a set without limit, it is obviously not possible to complete the enumeration of such an object. This move has the immediate consequence that the paradoxes which arise within Russell's system are avoided, since the problematic classes turn out to be impossible to construct within the limits of an intuitionist logic.

Intuitionists have attempted to reconstruct as much as possible of the subject matter of mathematics, while adhering to these strict limitations on the invocation of explicitly infinite classes. In many cases it has proved possible to reformulate classical results in such a way that their essential content can still be derived in these terms. In other areas, however, this cannot be done, and the intuitionists are then led to conclude that these parts of mathematics (including much of traditional analysis) are in fact meaningless: a somewhat controversial result.

In the course of developing the intuitionist program, its practitioners have clearly revealed much about the conceptual basis of mathematical propositions. This program does not really lead to independent advances, however, since its goals are in fact much more conservative ones, and it provides the basis for the development of only a limited portion of mathematical work. Relatively few working mathematicians seem willing to accept the limitations on their subject matter imposed by the premises of intuitionist logic. Although it can be said to have shed light on a (proper) subset of the field, intuitionism cannot be said to have provided a satisfactory replacement for the traditional objects of study and modes of inference in mathematics as a whole.

This history, though tangential to the history of phonology, is rehearsed here because it provides an instructive parallel with the development of phonological discussion in the years immediately after the publication of *SPE*. The substantive similarities between the programs of *SPE* and *PM* have already been pointed out. We will suggest below that the phonetic arbitrariness which was immediately pointed out as a problem with the *SPE* system constituted an Achilles' heel similar to that of the classical antinomies within the framework of *PM*; and that the theory of 'markedness', which was proposed to remedy this defect, was as inadequate a band-aid for phonology as the theory of types was for the mathematical logic of *PM*. Further, in attempting to deal with these problems in more radical ways, some linguists have taken a line quite comparable to that of the intuitionists in mathematics—with comparably limited success.

The problem of phonetic content within the *SPE* theory

The first line of attack on the *SPE* program from within the assumptions of generative grammar is found in the final chapter of the book itself. There it is observed that the purely formal calculus to which phonological expressions are supposed to be reduced is absolutely neutral as to the substantive content of the representations and rules appearing in particular descriptions. The notation, that is, provides a vocabulary in the form of a set of features and a formalism for rules; but within this vocabulary all expressions are essentially homogeneous with respect to the formal measure of evaluation which is intended to reconstruct the linguistic significance of generalizations embodied in particular descriptions.

Central to the formal calculation of this measure is the set of notational conventions: these are intended to capture the extent to which certain sets of rules in fact embody a unitary generalization, and they do so on the basis of a purely formal manipulation of the expressions representing the component rules. Thus, two rules are collapsible by the parentheses notation exactly in the case where the second can be obtained from the first by the omission of a single contiguous substring. Schematically, the rules 'A → B / C D ——' and 'A → B / C ——' can be collapsed as 'A → B / C (D) ——'. This operation (and those implicit in other notational conventions that form part of the evaluation measure) is carried out absolutely without regard for what the rules in question do: it is essential to the 'logicist' goals of the *SPE* program that only purely formal manipulations of well-formed expressions within the system play a role in evaluation, if the claim is to be made that the theory gives a complete reconstruction of the nature of phonological systems.

A fundamental problem with this exclusively formal approach quickly becomes apparent, however. In particular, it leads to the following substantive claim. Suppose we are given a description of some phonological state of affairs (an inventory of segments, a lexicon, a system of phonological rules, etc.). We might then obtain another description from this by consistently substituting, say, the feature [+Round] for the feature [+Consonantal] and vice versa; or consistently interchanging the values '+' and '−' in all cases; or any other such alteration which leaves the lengths of the resulting expressions unchanged and does not alter their susceptibility to abbreviation by the notational conventions of the theory. The two descriptions would then have exactly the same status with respect to their evaluation, and thus they ought to enjoy the same respectability within phonological theory. It is intuitively clear, however, that such formal manipulations can easily relate common and obviously natural states of affairs to ridiculous and impossible ones which could never arise within any natural language. If the theory is so deficient in reconstructing the notion of 'possible phonological system', the argument runs, it is obviously in need of revision.

In the domain of phonological inventories, essentially the same argument can be applied to the question of what is a possible sound system for a natural language. Obviously, a vowel system consisting of the elements /i, e, a, o, u/, which is encountered in a large number of languages is a possible one. If we simply replace the feature [+back] with the feature [−back] (and vice versa) in every vowel, however, we obtain a system consisting exactly of /ɨ, ʌ, æ, ö, ü/—a set of vowels which does not constitute the system of any known language, and which ought perhaps to be excluded in principle.

Similarly, in the domain of phonological rules, we can see that many languages have a rule of voicing assimilation in obstruent clusters, which we might formulate as

$$[+\text{obst}] \rightarrow [\alpha\text{voice}] / \underline{\quad\quad} \begin{bmatrix} +\text{obst} \\ \alpha\text{voice} \end{bmatrix}.$$

If we replace the first occurrence of [+obst] in this rule by [+syllabic], however, and the first occurrence of [αvoice] by [αhigh], we obtain a rule in which the height of vowels 'assimilates' to the value of voicing in a following consonant—again, probably an implausible enough candidate for inclusion in a natural language for us to consider excluding it in principle from our range of descriptive possibilities, but nonetheless a rule with exactly the same formal complexity in the *SPE* system as a banal voicing assimilation process.

It is evident, then, that a formal system of expression for phonological representations and rules (or at least one along the lines of *SPE*) goes badly astray if it is interpreted as constituting an exhaustive definition of what sorts of systems are possible in natural languages. The basis of this deficiency, according to Chomsky and Halle (and all subsequent writers), is the system's principled disregard of the substantive phonetic content of phonological expressions. Only by paying attention to the phonetic interpretation of the features and relations in a phonology, they suggest, is it possible to come to terms with the evident fact that some systems are possible and natural, while others that are formally equivalent are less natural or, indeed, impossible. The formal expression of a voicing assimilation rule may appear in a grammar because voicing assimilation (substantively construed) is something that happens in grammars—while the expression of a formally similar rule such as that concocted above is excluded not because it is formally ill formed but because vowels simply do not take on a value of highness in agreement with the voicing of a following obstruent.

This is obviously a crucial problem for the entire enterprise of *SPE* phonology, as Chomsky and Halle realize. Their solution to it is presented in the form of a theory of 'markedness'. We cannot present the substance of this theory in the present context, but we can note its general form. In essence, the theory consists of a set of 'marking conventions', or definitions of the values 'm(arked)' and 'u(nmarked)' for phonological features in particular contexts. Thus, the unmarked value for the feature [Round] in vowels is whichever value agrees with the value of the feature [Back] for the same segment; the unmarked value of the feature [Voice] in an obstruent followed by another obstruent is whatever value agrees with the voicing of the following one, etc.

These (stipulative) definitions are presented as universally valid, and thus a part of phonological theory rather than language-particular, and they function in two ways. First of all, underlying representations are to be regarded by the evaluation measure as composed of 'm' and 'u' values for features, rather than '+' and '−' values, where 'm' but not 'u' counts as contributing to the complexity of a linguistic element. On this basis, a language with the vowels /i, e, a, o, u/ will have very few marked values for features, while a language with the unlikely vowel system proposed above will have many more. The greater naturalness of the language with the /i, e, a, o, u/ system will thus be reflected directly in the greater simplicity of its representations.

Second, the marking conventions function as 'linking rules', effectively enforcing their unmarked values unless explicitly prohibited from doing so by some statement in the grammar. Chomsky and Halle actually allow only context-free marking conventions (such as the statement that nonlow vowels should agree in backness and rounding) to link, but the extension to context-sensitive phenomena is straightforward. A language with the common sort of voicing assimilation rule, for example, would then typically need no statement of such a rule in its grammar at all: any process that could lead to a cluster of obstruents would have voicing assimilation imposed on this cluster by the marking convention unless the process expressly stipulated that heterogeneous voicing values should be maintained. Such a language would as a result be formally simpler than a language *without* voicing assimilation—and also simpler than a language with the hypothetical pseudo-assimilation formulated above, which would be forced to count every aspect of that rule as contributing to its complexity.

Such a theory is in fact an attempt at exhaustively reducing the considerations of phonetic content that might be relevant to phonology to purely formal expression in the notation (now enhanced by its interpretation through the marking conventions). It is thus entirely consistent with the original *SPE* program of reducing all of the theory of phonological structure to a single explicit formal system including a notation and a calculus for manipulating and interpreting expressions within that notation. This is not to deny that the theory of markedness is an important revision of the proposals made in the rest of *SPE*.

The revision involved, however, was in a more complete working out of the goal of reducing phonology to a formal system rather than a replacement of that goal with some other.

While the theory of markedness was greeted with much initial enthusiasm, it is noteworthy that essentially no substantial analyses of phonological phenomena have appeared subsequently in which this aspect of the theory plays a significant role. One MIT dissertation (Kean 1975) was devoted to further elaboration of the theory, but this remained (like chapter 9 of *SPE*) at the level of a programmatic statement rather than constituting an extended analysis of the phonology of some language(s) in the terms prescribed by the theory.

This general lack of practical repercussions of markedness theory seems to be due at least in part to the fact that the set of marking conventions required to account for the facts of one language (or group of languages) simply do not extend to comparable utility in others. Lass (1972) makes the point that while front rounded vowels may be unnatural in many or even most of the world's languages, there is no reason to believe they are not perfectly well integrated into the phonologies of many Germanic languages. The same can be said of retroflex consonants in the languages of India, clicks in the Khoisan (and Southern Bantu) languages, glottalized stops in the languages of the Caucasus, etc.

The important observation Lass makes is that these problems do not arise simply because an adequate set of marking conventions has not yet been formulated, but because the role of phonetic content in a phonological system can only be analyzed relative to the other properties of the system. If this is true, it is simply not possible to embody this role in a comprehensive and universal way in the definition of the notation in the way foreseen by markedness theory. The purely mechanical problems encountered here are immediately apparent to anyone attempting to formulate a description in markedness terms. It is of course not logically excluded that a system could be constructed that incorporated enough aspects of an entire phonology into the formulation of individual conventions to approach empirical adequacy; but few such global notions of markedness have been proposed, and serious efforts to take account of phonetic content have generally been pursued along quite different lines.

These observations lead us to the conclusion that the phonological importance of phonetic content reveals a fundamental inadequacy of the 'logicist' program for phonology as sketched in *SPE*. Extending the parallel of the previous section, the theory of markedness seems to be an emendation with the same character as Russell's theory of types within the *PM*. In each case, the problem is that available ways of constructing a consistent formal system with the required character lead inevitably to conflicts with the subject matter for which the theories in question are intended to provide an account. Neither a logical basis for mathematics nor a comprehensive notation for the expression and comparison of phonological descriptions is thereby proved to be *wrong*:

they are simply shown to be essentially incomplete as full reconstructions of the domains of thought with which they are concerned.

Now in mathematics the disillusionment with the full logicist program which followed from certain aspects of the *PM* system certainly did not have the effect that serious work on the logical underpinnings of mathematics ground to a halt. On the contrary, the sort of investigation carried out in these terms turned out to constitute an interesting and coherent field of study in its own right. 'Formalist' mathematicians such as Hilbert, von Neumann, Kleene, and others were able to define significant problems to which substantive solutions could be sought, resulting in essential contributions to our understanding of the structure of mathematical ideas. If it is not possible to reduce *all* mathematical questions to a form in which they can be studied within this field, it is still an area of basic importance, and one concerned with very real problems.

There is no reason not to see the situation in phonology as entirely analogous. The formalist program of *SPE* is undoubtedly incomplete as the basis of a comprehensive account of all problems in the sound patterns of natural language; but it still appears to constitute a well-formed and important subpart of that study. There are real problems which can be formulated, addressed, and decided in terms of a system for the formal expression of phonological processes, leading to basic improvements in our understanding of the nature of sound structure in language. Indeed, most of the productive results in phonology in the years since *SPE* have followed directly from attempts to work out exactly the problems posed by that work.

The study of disjunctive ordering among phonological rules presenting particular formal resemblances, for example, has led to the (re)discovery of an important principle of complementarity between relatively specific and relatively general rules which was probably first discussed by Pānini, and which has consequences in a variety of areas of linguistic structure (see Anderson 1974; Kiparsky 1973c; and much of the recent literature on morphological rules for illustrations). The study of the formal properties of so-called 'exchange rules' has led to the observation that these are apparently always conditioned by morphological rather than phonological factors (see Anderson & Browne 1973; McCawley 1974). Examples could easily be multiplied: it is in this area, arguably, that present-day phonologists (owing largely to the neglect of such issues by previous generations, coupled with the fundamental contributions of *SPE*) are best equipped to make substantial progress.

In fact, our growing awareness of the range of problems that cannot be reduced to notational decisions has only been achieved by attempting to carry out the logicist program comprehensively. This has had the effect of refining our understanding of the significance of the results that can be obtained by a study of phonological formalisms, just as the latter contribute to a proper appreciation of the phonological role of phonetic content. Pursuing the mathematical analogy, we can note that Kurt Gödel's classic proof of the essential incompleteness of any axiomatization of arithmetic is a result which can only be stated in the context of a study of the formal properties of mathematical expressions.

In the recent literature (especially during the late 1970s), many phonologists have approached the field as presenting a dichotomous choice between 'substance-based' and 'formal' approaches (see Basbøll 1980 for this distinction); but surely both have their place in an adequate synthesis of our understanding of the nature of language. As it becomes more and more evident that language is a 'modular' system, representing the essential interaction of a number of domains (see Newmeyer 1983 and references there), there is no reason to doubt that sound structure, too, must be approached from several independent perspectives simultaneously.

How abstract are phonological representations?

The objections posed by *SPE* to its own program in the form of the theory of markedness were not the only ones raised in 1968. In the same year, an important paper by Paul Kiparsky asked the question 'How Abstract is Phonology?' in response precisely to the body of analyses represented by *SPE* and other generative work of the 1960s. The paper was initially circulated only in dittoed form; subsequently it was made available through the semiformal channel of the Indiana University Linguistics Club, and it was eventually published formally as Kiparsky (1973a). In a short time, the issues raised by Kiparsky took on central significance in theoretical discussion of the bases of phonology.

We argued in the previous chapter that the abstractness of the relation between underlying and surface forms was not in fact the primary difference between generative phonology and its predecessors; but that does not mean that this abstractness was not an issue. From within the framework of generative assumptions, Kiparsky identified two major areas in which the analytic practices of the 1960s led to counterintuitive (indeed, demonstrably incorrect) results by paths that were not excluded by the theory. In both classes of examples, the cause was identified by Kiparsky as excessive abstractness: the problematic cases involved phonological representations that were insufficiently constrained by the nature of the surface forms to which they correspond.

The first set of apparently too-abstract analyses involved "the diacritic use of phonological features": the positing of an underlying phonological distinction which is never realized as such, but rather serves to differentiate two classes of forms with respect to their behavior under some other rule. If we were to represent the final [f] of *leaf*, which alternates with [v] in *leaves*, as a bilabial fricative [φ] opposed to the (nonalternating) labiodental [f] of e.g. *laugh*, we could then posit a phonological rule converting [φ] to [v], and another rule to merge [φ] and [f]. We would thus avoid any reference to the particular morphemes that undergo voicing of f before the plural ending. The distinction between [φ] and [f], however, would be purely diacritic on this analysis: no instance of [φ] would ever actually surface as such, and the difference between this segment and [f] would serve simply to identify the class of formatives that undergo voicing as opposed to those that do not.

The classic uses of such analyses are probably in descriptions of vowel harmony systems such as that of Hungarian. In this language, certain vowels (e.g., é [e:]) are neutral, in that they can occur either in back-vowel words or in front-vowel words. Stems that contain only neutral vowels usually take front-vowel variants of suffixes that are added to them, but there is a small (closed) class of neutral-vowel words that take back vowel suffixes: e.g., héj 'rind, peel', but héj-am 'my rind', contrasting with kés 'knife', kés-em 'my knife'. One possible description of this state of affairs would be to represent words like héj not with underlying /é/, but rather with an otherwise nonoccurring back counterpart of this vowel: [ə:]. The vowel harmony rule and a (subsequent) rule converting [ə:] into [e:] could then be stated in purely phonological terms—but the putative vowel [ə:] would therefore never appear as such in any surface form, and the difference between it and [e:] would serve simply to distinguish two sorts of behavior words might show with respect to vowel harmony.

Of course, phonological rules must be sensitive to the phonological composition of forms, and it may well be the case that a distinction which conditions the differential behavior of some pair of forms with respect to a given rule is later neutralized. For example, in English, vowel lengthening takes place before voiced obstruents but not before voiceless ones. In the pair *rider* versus *writer*, however, this distinction is later neutralized (in American English, at least) when both /t/ and /d/ in certain environments are replaced by flapped [D]. The difference between this analysis (which we presumably wish to allow) and that in Kiparsky's examples is that the latter but not the former involve *absolute* neutralization. The difference between English /t/ and /d/ appears in many environments, even though it is neutralized in others, but that between e.g. Hungarian /e:/ and /ə:/ would never be manifested except by its effects on other rules.

The second class of cases Kiparsky suggested should be prohibited involve "the phonological use of diacritic features." By this, he refers to analyses in which some nonphonological feature with essentially arbitrary content is assigned to certain forms, and then used to trigger phonological rules which have the effect of differentiating forms with this feature from forms without it in surface structures. Again, vowel harmony provides an example: some analyses had proposed that the phonological composition of words belonging to distinct harmony classes might be identical except for a morpheme-sized harmony feature such as '[±B]' or the like. Thus, Finnish *pouta* and *pöytä* might both be represented as /pOUtA/, with the former marked [+B] and the latter [−B]. The use of such arbitrary features, which have no intrinsic phonetic interpretation but serve only to trigger the operation of rules in the grammar, would defeat the general claim that phonological representations should be nonarbitrary in content.

As a way of prohibiting analyses involving both of these sorts of abstractness, Kiparsky proposed that grammars should be subject to an *alternation condition*. It is not immediately obvious how to formulate such a condition, but among its effects we would like to ensure that morphemes which are always the same have the same phonological representation; and that morphemes which always differ have distinct phonological representations. The first branch of the condition prevents us from encoding a consistent difference of phonological effect as a difference in phonological constituency (as in the Hungarian example), while the second branch prevents analyses in which a consistent difference in phonological composition (such as the difference between front and back vowel words in Finnish) is replaced systematically by some nonphonological diacritic.

Kiparsky argued in favor of the correctness of some form of such a condition on the basis of the fact that a substantial class of the analyses which it excludes can be shown to be incorrect on independent grounds (principally, through the use of evidence from historical change). His points are clearly serious and cogent, and his proposed limitation on the power of analyses was widely (though not universally) accepted. The issue of just how strong such a condition should be, and how it should be formulated, became a prominent topic of discussion for the next several years. One school of thought attempted to defend abstract analyses that constituted at least prima facie counterexamples to the alternation condition (including Hyman 1970 for Nupe; Brame 1972 for Maltese; and Vago 1973 for Hungarian and other vowel harmony systems). Another group of linguists, however, took the opposite tack, maintaining that the excesses of abstractness of *SPE* were much more pervasive than could be dealt with by a limited prohibition such as the alternation condition. We deal briefly with one set of these proposals in the next section.

Kiparsky's own attention centered on the correct delimitation of the original set of problems, and the formulation of a condition that would correctly exclude just these analyses. His subsequent treatment of the problem (Kiparsky 1973b) is interesting in the present context because it is directed toward some sort of balance between formulations involving rules and those involving representations. He notes that his original discussion was couched in terms of preventing certain sorts of representations: thóse in which an underlying distinction is always neutralized, or those in which some consistent phonological distinction is not represented phonologically. This might be stated as a constraint on the operation of rules: 'Neutralization rules cannot apply to all occurrences of a morpheme.'

This condition by itself would not exclude all of the illicit instances of absolute neutralization, however. In the example of English alternating and nonalternating /f/, for instance, the rule neutralizing /ɸ/ and /f/ would not apply to all instances of the morpheme *leaf*, since in some cases /ɸ/ would be replaced by /v/ and thus escape conversion to /f/. The analysis would thus (incorrectly) be allowed. An alternative proposed formulation would require that 'neutralization processes only apply to derived forms,' where 'derived' means that some aspect of the environment which permits the application of a rule must come from a context external to any one single morpheme, or else from the prior operation of some other rule. Such a condition would exclude the analysis of *leaf* as /lijɸ/.

Our interest here is not in the precise formulation of the alternation condition. What is most important historically is simply that phonology came quickly to realize that a purely formal theory such as that of *SPE* was incapable of excluding in principle a large class of apparently incorrect analyses; and to this extent, such a theory was intrinsically deficient as a complete representation of the nature of sound structure in natural language. Some additional conditions, at a minimum, had to be imposed on the theory in order to achieve adequacy in this domain. As a reflection of the fact that generative phonology at this time was based on a conception of sound structure as involving both representations and rules, the correct formulation of such a condition might well involve either aspect of the grammar, or some complex interplay between them.

Constraining representations: 'Natural generative phonology'

For some, the recognition that *SPE* analyses could involve unrealistically abstract relations between underlying and surface forms was not carried nearly far enough by Kiparsky and others in the discussion of possible alternation conditions. One line of argument held that phonological representations ought to keep much closer to surface forms than did *SPE* and other analyses coming from generative linguists at about the same time, such as Lightner's (1965) analysis of Russian, Schane's (1968) description of French, Foley's (1965a) or Harris's (1969) treatment of Spanish, and many others. While the specific conditions of structuralist phonemics (such as the requirement of bi-uniqueness) were by and large discredited, the spirit of a phonological representation which could be directly and unambiguously recovered from surface forms was far from dead.

The most completely articulated version of this program is undoubtedly that originally associated with Theo Vennemann and his students at UCLA in the early 1970s. Interestingly enough, Vennemann's own dissertation consisted of a rather abstract analysis of the phonology of German; but he soon decided that such descriptions were more a matter of the ingenuity of linguists than of the reality of natural language. In a paper presented in 1971, he initiated a program based on the principle that phonological statements should be confined to ones that are literally true of surface forms; and phonological representations should be regarded as largely identical with phonetic forms.

Vennemann's student Joan [Bybee] Hooper was largely responsible for the subsequent elaboration and presentation of this theoretical position to a wider audience; Hooper (1976) remains the most extensive statement of the theory of 'natural generative phonology'. Its central notion is a proposed *True Generalization condition*, which requires that "speakers construct only generalizations that are surface-true and transparent." Such a condition may sound conservative enough, but it has profound consequences for the class of analyses allowed. In particular, it denies the reality of phonological rules that have even a single exception; rules which necessarily apply prior to the operation of some other rule which alters their environment; etc. For instance, the rule of vowel lengthening in English cannot be stated as a phonological rule (or 'P-Rule') in this theory, since a rule of flapping may neutralize the difference between underlying /t/ and /d/. Forms like [ra:jDɚ] (*rider*) versus [rajDɚ] (*writer*) show that vowel lengthening is not surface-true and transparent, and so it cannot be a phonological rule of the language.

In this and many other examples, the result is that phonological relations must be encoded simply as more or less systematic connections between fully-specified lexical entries. Both [rajt] (*write*) and [ra:jd] (*ride*) are entered in the lexicon as such; and the 'rule' of vowel lengthening is reduced to the status of a lexical redundancy rule. Indeed, while details of the nature of lexical relations within the theory vary from one presentation to another, natural generative phonology quite typically maintained that lexical entries are always essentially identical with some occurring surface form. This position, then, is an instance of the 'fully specified surface variant' theory of phonological representations discussed in chapter 2 above, with the exception that in some presentations (e.g., Hooper 1975) a certain amount of completely predictable detail is absent from underlying representations.

The great bulk of the descriptive burden on this view is borne by conditions of well-formedness imposed on lexical representations; but even these can only be stated insofar as they are completely exceptionless and 'surface-true'. Certain systematic relations between forms may be stated in the form of P-Rules, insofar as they are phonologically exceptionless. Other relations between forms may be stated as 'MP' (morphophonemic) rules insofar as they have an exceptionless (and surface-true) character in terms of morphological categories. Regularities that are not exceptionless in either phonological or morphological terms (such as the English vowel shift or velar softening rules) are to be considered unproductive, somewhat anecdotal relations between individual autonomous lexical items (on a par with Baudouin's class of traditional, paleophonetic alternations; see chapter 3 above). These are described (if at all) by means of 'via-rules'.

The program of natural generative phonology is one sort of reaction to the perceived inadequacies of the account of phonetic substance offered by *SPE*. It attempts to remedy the presumed paradoxes resulting from *SPE*'s disregard of these issues by radically restricting the conceptual richness of the theory. As such, it represents a reaction quite analogous in character to that of intuitionist mathematicians to the program of *PM*. Notably, the approach of natural generative phonology has been to require the reconstruction of phonological accounts without appeal to abstract entities or to (putatively) counterintuitive logistic principles such as that of relevant explicit ordering of rules. This constitutes a major retreat from the idealism of *SPE*, to a theory founded insofar as possible on what are (from the point of view of a linguist, if not that of an experimental psychologist) the observable and immediately verifiable aspects of linguistic structure. As such, it is immediately reminiscent of the constructivist basis of intuitionist mathematics.

In fact, the parallel is quite close. Natural generative phonology succeeds in reconstructing a large part of the traditional domain of phonological description, though sometimes in rather unfamiliar terms. In doing so, it has shown much about the conceptual basis of more familiar accounts. On the other hand, there are also many aspects of what has usually been taken to be phonology which are inaccessible on its premises. These areas of phonology are either written off altogether (that is, declared to be linguistically meaningless) or ascribed to the operation of essentially nonlinguistic or unsystematic principles (such as the 'via-rules', essentially a name for the description of those aspects of phonology that cannot be accounted for without recourse to abstract entities).

A program of this sort is effectively impossible to falsify, since it consists not in a potentially verifiable claim about the object of linguistic study but in an externally imposed limitation on the object of such study. It is always possible, of course, to confine one's attention to certain types of fact to the exclusion of others; and to accord the name 'linguistics' only to what can be studied in this way. This procedure, however, should not be confused with a genuinely empirical result about the nature of language, which can only come from the effort to construct substantive explanatory theories for domains whose exact delimitation follows from the scope of the principles that they reveal, rather than being given completely in advance.

Now a consistent advocate of the 'natural generative' theory may well be happy with the result that certain domains are legislated out of consideration, just as a confirmed intuitionist may be convinced of the result that much of classical and modern mathematics is literally meaningless. In both areas, though, the majority of traditional, presystematic practitioners have felt discontent with the limited portions of their field that can be treated within such radically constructivist accounts. A number of detailed examinations of natural generative phonological analyses (such as those of Harris 1978 and Gussmann 1978) have concluded that the theory has the result of throwing out the baby with the bath water. By the mid-1980s, the great majority of phonologists have apparently concluded that whatever *a priori* considerations of 'psychological reality' may motivate it, this way of avoiding the disregard of phonetic substance characteristic of *SPE* is unsatisfactory as a basis for understanding the sound structures of natural languages.

It should be noted that, although advocates of natural generative phonology have consistently portrayed their position as a theory quite distinct from that of generative phonology, a single overall set of underlying assumptions about what sorts of thing constitute evidence and valid modes of inference about theoretical issues is largely common to 'natural' and 'orthodox' (or 'standard theory') generative phonologists. From this, we can conclude that natural generative phonology constitutes an attempt to reform the theory from within, rather than a fundamentally different theory (in the way generative phonology surely constituted a different theory from that of American structuralist theory in the late 1950s and early 1960s). This does not of course trivialize the enterprise; but it does mean that 'natural' and 'orthodox' generative analyses are not as incommensurate with each other as both sides sometimes assert.

This fact is essential to an understanding of the ultimate impact of natural generative phonology. The radical restrictions on phonological analyses proposed in this theory found few advocates, though it is hard to deny that a gradual trend toward more concrete accounts of phonological systems and a reduced reliance on highly abstract mechanisms among generative phonologists in the late 1970s and early 1980s resulted in part from the challenges natural generative phonology mounted to the unrestrained use of the descriptive power of the *SPE* theory. The principal effect has been on the prevailing conception of phonological representations, as is only natural given the rather impoverished notion of phonological rules that natural generative phonologists maintained.

Although there has not yet been any overt agreement on this point in the literature, the descriptive practice of the field has been considerably altered in a more conservative direction as a direct consequence of the arguments of natural generative phonology. An example is the effect on current analyses of French of the work of Tranel (1981). This effect results quite directly from the fact that, at bottom, the positions involved share the majority of fundamental assumptions about how linguistic inquiry is conducted, what constitutes evidence, etc. The specific *a priori* limitations on the field proposed by natural generative phonologists are widely (though not universally) judged to have been misguided, but insofar as specific analyses constructed along these lines can be supported by concrete evidence, they can be directly incorporated into other sets of views.

Constraining rules: Natural phonology

The major thrust of the reaction against the *SPE* theory in the 1970s was that although such a theory might (if appropriately modified, along lines such as those suggested by Kiparsky) capture what is *possible* in the sound systems of natural languages, it is intrinsically incapable of representing what is *natural* about such systems. The very name 'natural generative phonology' was of course intended to imply that any other sort of generative phonology was *not* natural. Other theoretical positions which developed during this period (e.g., the present author's theory of 'natural ordering' in Anderson 1974) similarly attempted to trade on the favorable connotations of the word 'natural'. Among these works purporting to refound phonological thought on bases closer to those of the organic sources of language, surely the most interesting (and most explicit in this regard) is the theory of 'natural phonology' developed by David Stampe.

Stampe starts from a consideration of the same puzzles for a purely formal theory that motivated the theory of markedness in *SPE*: some phonological systems and rules are much more likely to occur in languages than others, and this must somehow be part of the essence of language which it is the business of the theory to capture. Unlike the markedness theory of *SPE*, however, he rejects the attempt to encode these facts about what is and is not natural in the notation (Stampe 1973). Rather, he recognizes that natural rules, as well as effects of the constraints imposed on phonological systems by the nature of language, are nonetheless aspects of the grammars of particular languages. The insight underlying his view is that there are some rules and constraints which are more expensive for a language *not* to have; that is, languages which are not subject to them are in some sense more complex than languages that are. Much of the theory of natural phonology is devoted to an attempt to articulate the sense in which this is true.

The basis of the theory is the claim that our innate phonetic capacity can be represented in the form of a set of very general *natural processes*. These can be classified into two groups: *syntagmatic* processes, which reduce the complexity of articulating particular sequences of segments (as with rules assimilating nasals to following obstruents, or nasalizing vowels before nasal consonants); and *paradigmatic* processes, which highlight or maximize the articulatory or acoustic properties of a single segment (such as a rule specifying that vowels are generally [−nasal], given that nasal vowels are less distinct from one another than are non-nasal vowels). As is evident, these two classes may make contradictory demands on a given segment: a vowel preceding a nasal consonant should be [−nasal] by virtue of the paradigmatic process of denasalization, but [+nasal] by virtue of the syntagmatic process assimilating nasality. Such conflicts are resolved either by general principle ("syntagmatic processes do not apply before contradictory paradigmatic processes") or as a matter of language-particular limitation of one or the other process.

The inventory of natural processes is assumed to constitute part of the genetically determined endowment which the language learner brings to the task of acquisition. In fact, on this view, the essential nature of that task is precisely that of learning to suppress and limit those natural processes which are not fully general in the language to be learned. Thus, a French (but not an

English) child must learn to limit severely the domain of application of vowel denasalization, since nasal vowels appear in that language. The kinds of limitation involved may involve not only complete suppression of a process, or restriction of the range of cases to which it applies, but also the imposition of an ordering relation on it, such that its applicability is limited to forms to which some other process has not yet applied.

In addition to natural processes, languages are also assumed to contain learned *Rules*—but these are taken to be rather limited, ad hoc, and unsystematic constraints that are consequences of the accidental history of the language (comparable to the arbitrariness of the fact that, in English, the word *dog* designates dogs). As such, they are said to fall outside of the explanatory domain of phonology proper, and into the realm of the purely conventional. Natural phonology thus attempts to provide an account of "everything that language owes to the fact that it is *spoken*" (Donegan & Stampe 1979:128), and to "exclude the topic of unmotivated and morphologically motivated alternations" (ibid., p. 127) such as German Umlaut or English velar softening.

In the data of natural languages, alternations naturally do not wear on their sleeves an indicator of the group (natural processes or learned rules) to which they belong. It is thus necessary to establish from the outset what qualifies a given alternation for the status of a natural process, since it is only these that the theory has anything to say about. In this regard, the central point is that natural processes appear "unbidden and unlearned": i.e., positive evidence is not necessary for them to arise, but only the lack of negative evidence. They thus show up in the substitutions children make in the forms of adult language, in rules of casual or fast speech, in historical change—as well, of course, as in rules of adult grammars (where, however, they coexist with learned rules).

The great attractiveness of this theory is quite similar to that of Jakobson's *Kindersprache* (see chapter 5 above): both promise to unify large domains of phenomena that fall outside the strict notion of the 'grammar' of a language but are nonetheless clearly related to the nature of language. This similarity is of course not accidental, since Stampe explicitly models his program on Jakobson's. Such a theory makes very strong claims about the nature of language, and these claims are immediately open to a wide range of potential confirming or disconfirming evidence (assuming they are not simply metaphorical).

Dressler (1974) has examined some of the claims of natural phonology in the domain of historical change, and pointed out a number of difficulties. He cites, for instance, a number of (context-free, or paradigmatic) historical changes of the form [u] > [ü], in which no intermediate stages can be motivated. Such changes have taken place in the history of French, Icelandic, and other languages. The importance of this fact (and a number of comparable ones cited by Dressler) is that it is directly contrary to a presumed hierarchy of naturalness governing vowel systems, according to which front rounded vowels should be replaced either by back rounded or by front unrounded vowels, but not vice versa. In order to incorporate such examples, it is necessary to assume that 'natural processes' are in some sense two-way streets along which substitutions can occur. If true, this would greatly weaken the empirical content of the theory.

One of the most extended analyses of the claims made by the theory of natural phonology is provided by Drachmann (1976) in the context of an examination of putative similarities between child and adult language substitutions. Among Drachmann's points are the following: (1) children tend to substitute stops for fricatives, through the replacement of a gesture of continuous control by a ballistic one—but in adult language such changes are much less common than the reverse process of spirantization of stops. (2) Children typically shorten words by removing their initial syllable(s). The fact that it is final syllables that are retained can be seen as due to a 'recency' effect; but in adult language, phonological rules and historical change operate almost exclusively to reduce or eliminate *final* syllables. (3) In child language acquisition, the very general processes of 'vowel harmony' seem to be suppressed early, while comparable consonantal assimilations across a word persist much longer. In adult language, however, vowel harmony is comparatively common, while consonant harmony (especially on the scale observable in child language) is rare or nonexistent.

All of these points seriously compromise the underlying assumptions of natural phonology, for they suggest that the coherence of the theory is not matched by the facts. The claim that what is natural in the systems of adult languages has its basis in whatever more general aspects of our phonetic capacities operate in other domains (such as child language, casual speech simplifications, historical change, etc.) can only be substantiated by a demonstration that these domains are in fact homologous—and a detailed examination of the evidence suggests that the similarities that do exist are too limited to sustain the weight of a comprehensive theory of phonological naturalness.

If we attempt to limit the explanatory domain of phonology to the set of natural processes in Stampe's sense, the result is that any alternation which is not phonetically motivated, or shows phonetically arbitrary properties, immediately falls into the category of learned rules and thus outside of the theory. In that case, however, a great deal of the descriptive content of the sound systems of natural languages—perhaps, indeed, nearly all of it—is not describable as 'phonology' in this sense at all.

As observed already by Baudouin (see chapter 3 above), even those processes with the most evident phonetic motivation tend to acquire arbitrary aspects once they become part of the grammar of a particular language ('phonologized'). A number of examples of this sort are examined in "Why Phonology isn't 'Natural'" (Anderson 1981); these will not be repeated in detail here, but we can note that the appearance of arbitrary, 'learned' aspects in rules affects even apparently low-level phonetic processes such as vowel lengthening before voiced obstruents in English (whose degree is not phonetically explicable, but must be regarded as an arbitrary fact about English) or velar fronting before front vowels in Icelandic (which applies before some vowels that are no longer phonetically front, though they used to be, and not before others that are front but that come historically from back vowels).

Apparently, then, if we exclude all facts from phonological consideration that show a component of purely language-particular arbitrariness, little will remain. If we furthermore require that the natural processes which constitute the empirical content of the theory operate in a more or less uniform fashion across several domains (child language, etc., as well as the rules of adult language), even less will be left to us. For this reason, the theory of natural phonology has remained at the level of a suggestive hypothesis, though it is one which continues at this writing to be applied to a wide range of empirical phenomena (especially in the ongoing work of Stampe and his colleague Patricia Donegan; see for example Donegan 1978).

There is clearly something general and natural about phonological systems which is not represented in a system of the *SPE* type; and it is plausible to seek explanations of that fact in the organic basis of human phonetic capacities. Where natural phonology and the theory of markedness in *SPE* go astray, we argue, is in trying to incorporate this explanation directly into the descriptive framework for phonology. We should instead recognize the modularity of language: the fact that it represents the intersection of a number of distinguishable domains, each subject to its own principles.

In these terms, it can be suggested, a fundamentally modular theory with a serious claim to genuine explanatory capacity already exists *in posse* in the views of Baudouin and Kruszewski sketched in chapter 3. On that picture, the phonetic capacities of speakers function to determine the 'raw material' for sound change and other substitutions, which serve as the source of synchronic regularities in natural language systems. The impact of such 'natural processes' on phonological systems, however, is a result both of their substantive content and of the interaction of this with the processes of phonologization and historical change—for they are no longer phonetically determined in their essence, once incorporated into the grammar of a language. Many (if not most) of the details of such a theory remain to be developed, but at least in outline it appears to present the possibility of achieving an understanding of the scope of 'phonetic explanation' in phonology, without abandoning the requirements of comprehensive and accurate description.

Though we have suggested above that the theory of natural phonology (as presented in works such as Stampe 1968 and 1969, and most comprehensively in Stampe 1972 and Donegan & Stampe 1979) errs in confusing the projects of description and explanation in phonology, its impact on the field has not been at all negligible. If phonologists in the 1970s became increasingly aware of the need to supplement purely formal theories with an account of substantive considerations, this was not at all exclusively as a result of the theory of

AUTOSEGMENTAL AND METRICAL FORMALISMS / 347

markedness in *SPE*. A suggestive case was made there, but the mechanism proposed seems to have been a dead end. The rather different proposals of natural phonology have tended to remain somewhat programmatic (indeed, some would say, oracular) and have not really been translated into comprehensive descriptions of actual languages; but their much greater empirical scope (in comparison to *SPE*) has tended to keep the problems they address within the attention of the field at large.

Autosegmental and metrical formalisms

The developments we have followed thus far in this chapter constitute attempts to improve the 'naturalness' of generative phonological descriptions, by imposing additional constraints on either the representations or the rules in analyses, or else by relating the primitives of the theory more directly to external phonetically based reality. During the same period, however, a rather different line of thought was being pursued internal to the mainstream of generative phonology, and it too has had important consequences for the way sound systems are thought of. This was the elaboration of richer notions of phonological representation, going beyond the traditional picture of forms as composed at all levels of sequences of segment-sized units. The resulting changes have radically altered the concerns and priorities of phonologists.

Phonological and phonetic representations in *SPE* are quite uniform in their internal formal structure. Each such representation is a sequence of segments which are in principle independent of one another and uniform in size. Units larger than the segment were recognized, but the only elements of this sort were morphological in character (morphemes, words, etc.); and they were represented not directly as structural units but, rather, by the intercalation of segmentoid boundaries in the segmental string so as to delimit one such unit from its neighbors. No structure internal to the segment was recognized (aside from the fact that segments themselves were regarded as internally unordered collections of features), and no structural units larger than segments (such as syllables) had any systematic representational status.

The absence of syllables, etc., from phonological representations was not, as some have suggested, a matter of oversight or ignorance on Chomsky and Halle's part. Rather, it constituted a principled decision: insofar as all generalizations apparently requiring reference to units other than segments could be encoded in terms of segments alone without significant loss of generality, the more limited theory constituted a stronger empirical claim about the nature of language. It seemed to Chomsky and Halle that this was correct; and at minimum it represents a coherent position.

By the early 1970s, however, the study of tonal systems had begun to undermine the monolithic nature of uniformly segment-based theories. Early attempts to incorporate tonal phenomena in generative descriptions, such as the proposals of Wang 1967, described tones as unitary features. In fact, Wang proposed that these features should be attached to syllables rather than to segments, but this aspect of his theory went essentially unnoticed in the literature. There were no such things as syllables in representations; besides, the same results could usually be obtained by associating the tone features with the segment(s) that constituted the nucleus of the syllable.

Wang's claim that tones—especially contour tones, such as the rising, falling, and falling-rising tones of Mandarin Chinese—could be represented as units in a feature system was first seriously challenged in a dissertation by Woo (1969). She demonstrated that such contours should not be regarded as single units but as sequences of (level tone) units. A falling tone is seen not as a single element characterized by some feature such as [+fall] but as a sequence of a high tone followed by a low. On this basis, Woo argued that syllables bearing complex tonal contours always contain at least enough vowel segments (or moras) to support the tones in a one-to-one fashion.

Shortly thereafter, work on the tonal systems of African languages by Leben (1971) and others demonstrated that such contour tones need to be recognized as also occurring on syllables containing only a single, indivisible, short-vowel segment. In consequence, it is necessary to admit the possibility that some phonological features (such as the individual subparts of a contour tone) take as their domain of specification a scope less than a single segment. Segments, in other words, have to be recognized as having significant internal temporal structure. On the other hand, Leben also showed that it is sometimes necessary to recognize a single tonal specification which takes more than a single segment as its domain, possibly spreading over several syllables of a form.

These points were developed at length by John Goldsmith, as a theory of 'autosegmental phonology'. We cannot even summarize the principles of this theory here (cf. Goldsmith 1976, 1979, as well as van der Hulst & Smith 1982c, for survey articles); but it is clear that once we accept the claim that the number of tonal specifications on a given form is not necessarily equal to the number of vowels, the possibility arises of extending the same descriptive formalism to other areas of structure. Nasality, for example, provides a ready analog to the behavior of tones (see Anderson 1976, as well as Goldsmith's work). Others (particularly Clements 1976 and elsewhere) have argued that vowel harmony provides another example of a single phonological feature specification whose scope is not just a single segment, but as much as an entire word.

As a result of these developments, phonologists had come by the late 1970s to regard representations less as a sequence of segmental 'beads on a string' than as analogous to an orchestral score in which the synchronization of each instrument with the other instruments is as much a part of the score as the actual notes each is to play. In phonological terms, the 'instruments' are the various separable components of the speech apparatus: the laryngeal control of pitch, the velum, the tongue body, the lips, etc. A wide variety of phenomena take on a rather different appearance when seen in this way. For instance, rules of assimilation can often be regarded as involving not a change in the features of some individual segment but a reassociation of the features of one segment (the one assimilated to) so that they come to include the other (assimilating) segment in their scope. In fact, there are few rules in the phonologies of the moderately well studied languages whose form remains unaffected when considered in terms of the manipulation of autosegmental structure and associations rather than as changes in the values of features.

At the same time that tonal phenomena were provoking a reconsideration of the status of segments in phonology, other developments were challenging the notion that no significant structure existed above this level. A seminal paper by Liberman and Prince (1977), based largely on Liberman's earlier (1975) MIT dissertation, presented the thesis that instead of being encoded by a feature assigned to segments, stress should be seen as a relation between units (syllables, in particular) organized into a hierarchical structure. Again, the nature of this theory cannot be adequately surveyed in the space available here (see van der Hulst & Smith 1982c, as well as Liberman & Prince 1977); but the consequence of this revision in the conception of stress was to accord important status to such hierarchically organized units as syllables, feet, and prosodic words.

Liberman and Prince's *metrical* theory of stress was soon extended into other domains as well. There had long been a feeling that syllable structure ought to be recognized explicitly in phonological representations; yet the only apparent way of doing that (by the use of intercalated syllable boundaries in the segmental string) seemed cumbersome and unenlightening. The recognition of hierarchical (or metrical) structure in the domain of stress, however, suggested that syllables could be regarded analogously, as units defining a hierarchical organization of segments into a larger structure. The first major step in this direction was taken by Kahn (1976), and was actually formulated in terms of an autosegmental theory, but subsequent development has been more in line with Liberman and Prince's metrical theory.

Here too, there has been a flurry of effort to apply the new formalism to a range of familiar problems. Vowel harmony, for instance, has been described (by Halle & Vergnaud 1981) as involving in some languages the assignment of a harmonic feature to the head of a metrical tree, and its subsequent propagation through the structure by convention. We cannot trace these developments here, but the two-volume collection of papers by van der Hulst & Smith (1982a, 1982b) contains a number of instructive examples. The wisdom of extending metrical formalisms into all of the traditional segmental domains where such formulations have recently been proposed is questioned by Anderson (1982b) and Poser (1982), but it is obvious that these formalisms do have considerable relevance beyond the facts of stress.

In the 1980s, the trend in phonological discussion has been away from the issues of the immediately post-*SPE* period. The problem of how to represent the naturalness of rules and segment inventories, for example, has largely disappeared from the recent literature, as have the notational issues that seemed so prominent in the late 1960s and early 1970s. Even the problem of abstractness is little discussed. None of these areas, it should be stressed, have lost the attention of phonologists because of a feeling that they have been essentially solved: on the contrary, after a little reflection, most linguists would agree that all of these topics still present major unresolved problems. Rather, what has happened seems to be that attention has simply been diverted by the exciting possibilities inherent in the major innovation of recent years: the enrichment of our notion of representation to include autosegmental and metrical structure.

Accompanying this development has come an almost unperceived shift away from the formal rigor of statement that characterized the *SPE* theory. While much of the recent literature is quite explicit and rigorous about its proposals for phonological representations, much less attention has been lavished on achieving comparable explicitness in the description of manipulations of this structure. Rules are often formulated simply in ordinary English, with minimal concern for the maintenance of a conceptually limited vocabulary and formalism for processes comparable to the proposals of *SPE* for segmental rules.

One might perhaps attribute this growing looseness of statement to a general disillusionment with the formalist project of *SPE*: after all, the various other developments we have surveyed in this chapter have all tended to undermine such a formal theory as a comprehensive reconstruction of our understanding of phonological structure. If this is indeed the case, though, it is perhaps time for a reminder of the relative success achieved by the *SPE* program in constructing an explicit and narrowly constrained formalism for rules stated over its comparatively restricted class of possible representations. In fact, the conceptual richness of 'classical' generative phonology should probably be attributed to its more or less balanced picture of sound structure, in which both representations and rules have important roles to play. If current attention to the possibilities of novel sorts of representations leads to a climate in which the importance of explicit formulation of rule-governed regularities disappears from view, the depth of our knowledge of phonology will in all likelihood be the poorer for it. We hope that this book has demonstrated that neither a theory of rules nor a theory of representations constitutes a theory of phonology by itself.

REFERENCES

Abercrombie, David. 1948. Forgotten Phoneticians. *Transactions of the Philological Society* (1948), 1–34.

Allen, W. Sidney. 1951. Some Prosodic Aspects of Retroflexion and Aspiration in Sanskrit. *Bulletin of the School of Oriental and African Studies* 13:939–46.

Anderson, Stephen R. 1973. Remarks on the Phonology of English Inflection. *Language & Literature* (Copenhagen) 1(4):33–52.

———. 1974. *The Organization of Phonology*. New York: Academic Press.

———. 1976. Nasal Consonants and the Internal Structure of Segments. *Language* 52:326–44.

———. 1978. Tone Features. In V. Fromkin (ed.), *Tone: A Linguistic Anthology*, 133–75. New York: Academic Press.

———. 1980. Remarks on the Development of Phonological Theory. *Language and Speech* 23:115–23.

———. 1981. Why Phonology isn't 'Natural'. *Linguistic Inquiry* 12:493–539.

———. 1982a. Where's Morphology? *Linguistic Inquiry* 13:571–612.

———. 1982b. Differences in Rule Type and Their Structural Basis. In van der Hulst and Smith 1982b, 1–25.

———. 1984. A Metrical Interpretation of Some Traditional Claims about Quantity and Stress. In M. Aronoff and R. Oehrle (eds.), *Language Sound Structure*, 83–106. Cambridge: MIT Press.

Anderson, Stephen R., and Wayles Browne. 1973. On Keeping Exchange Rules in Czech. *Papers in Linguistics* 6 (4): 445–82.

Bach, Emmon, and Robert Harms. 1972. How Do Languages Get Crazy Rules? In R. Stockwell and R. Macaulay (eds.), *Linguistic Change and Generative Theory*, 1–21. Bloomington: Indiana University Press.

Basbøll, Hans. 1971, 1972. A Commentary on Hjelmslev's Outline of the Danish Expression System. *Acta Linguistica Hafniensa* 13:173–211, 14:1–24.

———. 1980. Phonology. *Language & Speech* 23:91–113.

Baudouin de Courtenay, Jan. 1871 (1972). Some General Remarks on Linguistics and Language. In Baudouin de Courtenay 1972:49–80.

———. 1888–89. Mikołaj Kruszewski, jego życie i prace naukowe. *Prace Filologiczne* 2 (3): 837–49; 3(1):116–75.

———. 1895 (1972). An Attempt at a Theory of Phonetic Alternations. In Baudouin de Courtenay 1972:144–212.

———. 1963. In V. P. Grigor'ev & A. A. Leont'ev, (eds), *Izbrannye trudy po obščemu jazykoznaniju*, vols. 1–2. Moscow: Akademija Nauk SSSR.

———. 1972. *Selected Writings of Baudouin de Courtenay*, ed. E. Stankiewicz. Bloomington: Indiana University Press.

Bell, Alexander Melville. 1867. *Visible Speech: The Science of Universal Alphabetics*. London: Simplin, Marshall & Co.

Bellugi, Ursula, and Edward Klima. 1979. *The Signs of Language*. Cambridge: Harvard University Press.

Bever, Thomas G. 1963. Leonard Bloomfield and the Phonology of the Menomini Language. Doctoral diss., Massachusetts Institute of Technology.

Bloch, Bernard. 1941. Phonemic Overlapping. *American Speech* 16:278–84 (reprinted in Joos 1957:93–96).

———. 1946. Studies in Colloquial Japanese II: Syntax. *Language* 22:200–248 (reprinted in Joos 1957:154–85).

———. 1950. Studies in Colloquial Japanese IV: Phonemics. *Language* 26:86–125 (reprinted in Joos 1957:329–48).

Bloomfield, Leonard. 1909–10. A Semasiological Difference in Germanic Secondary Ablaut. *Modern Philology* 7:245–88; 7:345–82.

———. 1914. *An Introduction to the Study of Language*. New York: Holt.

———. 1923. *First German Book*. Columbus, Ohio: R. G. Adams.

———. 1925. Why a Linguistics Society? *Language* 1:1–5.

———. 1926. A Set of Postulates for the Study of Language. *Language* 2:153–64 (reprinted in Joos 1957:329–48).

———. 1930. German ç and x. *Le maître phonétique* III 20:27–28.

———. 1933. *Language*. New York: Holt.

———. 1939. Menomini Morphophonemics. *Travaux du cercle linguistique de Prague* 8:105–15.

———. 1944. Secondary and Tertiary Responses to Language. *Language* 20:45–55.

———. 1962. *The Menomini Language*. New Haven: Yale University Press.

Bloomfield, Leonard, and George M. Bolling. 1927. What Symbols Shall We Use? *Language* 3:123–29.

Boas, Franz. 1889. On Alternating Sounds. *American Anthropologist* 2:47–53.

———. 1894. Classification of the Languages of the North Pacific Coast. *Memoirs of the International Congress of Anthropologists*, 339–46.

———, ed.. 1911. *Handbook of American Indian Languages*, vol. 1. Bureau of American Ethnology, Bulletin 40, part 1.

———, ed.. 1922. *Handbook of American Indian Languages*, vol. 2. Bureau of American Ethnology, Bulletin 40, part 2.

———. 1930. *The Religion of the Kwakiutl Indians*. Columbia University Contributions to Anthropology, vol. 10. New York: Columbia University Press.

———. 1947. Kwakiutl Grammar, with a Glossary of the Suffixes. *Transactions of the American Philosophical Society*, 37 (part 3): 201–377.

Boas, Franz, and Ella Deloria. 1939. *Dakota Grammar*. Washington, D.C.: National Academy of Sciences.

Brame, Michael. 1972. On the Abstractness of Phonology: Maltese ʕ. In M.

Brame (ed.), *Contributions to Generative Phonology*, 22–61. Austin: University of Texas Press.

Chao, Yuen-ren. 1934. The Non-Uniqueness of Phonemic Solutions of Phonetic Systems. *Academica Sinica* (Bulletin of the Institute of History and Philology) 4(4):363–97 (reprinted in Joos 1957:38–54).

Cherry, E. Colin, Roman Jakobson and Morris Halle. 1952. Toward the Logical Description of Languages in their Phonemic Aspect. *Language* 29:34–46.

Chomsky, Noam. 1951. The Morphophonemics of Modern Hebrew. Master's thesis, University of Pennsylvania. Published in 1979 by Garland Publishers, ed. Jorge Hankamer.

———. 1955. *The Logical Structure of Linguistic Theory*. Published in 1975 by Plenum Press, New York.

———. 1957. *Syntactic Structures*. The Hague: Mouton & Co.

———. 1959. Review Of B. F. Skinner's *Verbal Behavior*. *Language* 35: 26–57.

———. 1962. A Transformational Approach to Syntax. In Hill 1962: 124–58.

———. 1964. *Current Issues in Linguistic Theory*. The Hague: Mouton & Co.

———. 1966a. *Topics in the Theory of Generative Grammar*. The Hague: Mouton & Co.

———. 1966b. *Cartesian Linguistics*. New York: Harper & Row.

———. 1979. *Language and Responsibility*. New York: Pantheon.

———. 1981. *Rules and Representations*. New York: Columbia University Press.

Chomsky, Noam, and Morris Halle. 1965. Some Controversial Questions in Phonological Theory. *Journal of Linguistics* 1:97–138.

———. 1968. *The Sound Pattern of English*. New York: Harper & Row.

Chomsky, Noam, Morris Halle, and Fred Lukoff. 1956. On Accent and Juncture in English. In *For Roman Jakobson: Essays on the Occasion of His Sixtieth Birthday*, 65–80. The Hague: Mouton & Co.

Christy, Craig. 1983. *Uniformitarianism in Linguistics*. Amsterdam and Philadelphia: Benjamins.

Clements, G. N. 1976. The Autosegmental Treatment of Vowel Harmony. In W. Dressler and O. E. Pfeiffer (eds.), *Phonologica, 1976*, 111–19. Innsbruck: Institut für Sprachwissenschaft.

Culler, Jonathan. 1976. *Ferdinand deSaussure*. New York: Penguin Books.

Darden, Bill J. 1984. Reduplication and the Underlying Consonant System of Southern Paiute. *1983 Mid-America Linguistics Conference Papers*, 120–29. Boulder: University of Colorado.

Diderichsen, Paul. 1960. *Rasmusk Rask og den grammatiske tradition*. Hist.-fil. meddelelser udg. af det Kongelige Videnskabernes Selskab, bind 38(2) København.

Donegan, Patricia. 1978. *On the Natural Phonology of Vowels*. Ohio State University Working Papers in Linguistics, vol. 23.

Donegan, Patricia, and David Stampe. 1979. The Study of Natural Phonology. In D. Dinnsen (ed.), *Current Approaches to Phonological Theory*, 126–73. Bloomington: Indiana University Press.

354 / REFERENCES

Drachmann, Gaberell. 1976. Child Language and Language Change: A Conjecture and Some Refutations. In J. Fisiak (ed.), *Recent Developments in Historical Phonology*, 123–44. The Hague: Mouton & Co.

Dressler, Wolfgang. 1974. Some Diachronic Puzzles for Natural Phonology. In *Natural Phonology* (parasession volume of the Chicago Linguistic Society), 95–102. Chicago: University of Chicago Department of Linguistics.

Dufriche-Desgenettes, A. 1875. Sur la lettre R et ses diverses modifications. *Bulletin de la société linguistique de Paris* 14:71–74.

Engler, Robert. 1968–74. *Édition critique du cours linguistique de Ferdinand de Saussure*. Wiesbaden: Otto Harrassowitz.

Esper, E. A. 1968. *Mentalism and Objectivism in Linguistics: The Sources of Leonard Bloomfield's Psychology of Language*. New York: American Elsevier.

Firth, J. R. 1934a. The Principles of Phonetic Notation in Descriptive Grammar. *Congrès international des sciences anthropologiques et ethnographiques: compte rendu de la première session à Londres*, 325–28.

———. 1934b. The Word "Phoneme." *Le maître phonétique* 46:44–46.

———. 1935a. The Use and Distribution of Certain English Sounds: Phonetics from a Functional Point of View. *English Studies* 17:2–12.

———. 1935b. The Technique of Semantics. *Transactions of the Philological Society*, 36–72.

———. 1936. Phonological Features of Some Indian Languages. *Proceedings of the Second International Congress of Phonetic Sciences held at London in 1935*, 176–82.

———. 1937. The Structure of the Chinese Monosyllable in a Hunanese Dialect. *Bulletin of the School of Oriental Studies* 8:1055–74.

———. 1946. The English School of Phonetics. *Transactions of the Philological Society*, 92–132.

———. 1948a. Sounds and Prosodies. *Transactions of the Philological Society*, 127–52.

———. 1948b. Word-Palatograms and Articulation. *Bulletin of the School of Oriental and African Studies* 12:857–64.

———. 1949. Atlantic Linguistics. *Archivum Linguisticum* 1(2):95–116.

———. 1950. Improved Techniques in Palatography and Kymography. *Bulletin of the School of Oriental and African Studies* 13:771–74.

———. 1956. Linguistic Analysis and Translation. In *For Roman Jakobson: Essays on the Occasion of His Sixtieth Birthday*, 133–39. The Hague: Mouton & Co.

———. 1957a. *Papers in Linguistics 1934–1951*. London.

———. 1957b. A Synopsis of Linguistic Theory: 1930–1955. In J. R. Firth (ed.), *Studies in Linguistic Analysis*, 1–32. Oxford: Blackwell.

Fischer-Jørgensen, Eli. 1965. Louis Hjelmslev, October 3, 1899–May 30, 1965. *Acta Linguistica Hafniensia* 9:iii–xxii.

———. 1966. Form and Substance in Glossematics. *Acta Linguistica Hafniensia* 10:1–33.

———. 1972. Supplementary Note to Hans Basbøll's commentary on Hjelmslev's Analysis of the Danish Expression System. *Acta Linguistica Hafniensia* 14:143–52.

————. 1975. *Trends in Phonological Theory*. Copenhagen: Academisk Forlag.

Foley, James. 1965a. Spanish Morphology. Doctoral diss. Massachusetts Institute of Technology.

————. 1965b. Prothesis in the Latin Verb *sum*. *Language* 41:59–64.

Frachtenberg, Leo J. 1922. Siuslawan (Lower Umpqua). In Boas 1922, 297–429.

Godel, Robert. 1954. Notes inédites de Ferdinand deSaussure. *Cahiers Ferdinand de Saussure* 12:49–71.

————. 1957. *Les sources manuscrits du cours de linguistique générale de F. deSaussure*. Geneva: Librairie Droz.

Goldsmith, John. 1976. An Overview of Autosegmental Phonology. *Linguistic Analysis* 2:23–68.

————. 1979. The Aims of Autosegmental Phonology. In D. Dinnsen (ed.), *Current Approaches to Phonological Theory*, 202–22. Bloomington: Indiana University Press.

Grammont, Maurice. 1933. *Traité de phonétique*. Paris: Delagrave.

Greenberg, Joseph, ed. 1963a. *Universals of Language*. Cambridge: MIT Press.

Greenberg, Joseph. 1963b. Some Universals of Grammar with Particular Reference to the Order of Meaningful Elements. In Greenberg 1963a.

Gussmann, Edmund. 1978. *Explorations in Abstract Phonology*. Lublin: Marie Curie-Sklodowska University Press.

Hale, Kenneth. 1973. Deep-Surface Canonical Disparities in Relation to Analysis and Change: An Australian Example. In T. A. Sebeok et al. (eds.), *Current Trends in Linguistics* 11:401–58.

Halle, Morris. 1957. On the Phonetic Rules of Russian. Unpublished paper read to the Annual Meeting of the Linguistic Society of America, Chicago.

————. 1959. *The Sound Pattern of Russian*. The Hague: Mouton & Co.

————. 1962. Phonology in Generative Grammar. *Word* 18:54–72.

————. 1964. On the Bases of Phonology. In J. A. Fodor and J. Katz (eds.), *The Structure of Language*, 324–33. New York: Prentice-Hall. (Revised version of "Questions of Linguistics," supplement to *Il Nuovo Cimento* 13, Series 10, 1958, 494–517).

————. 1979. Roman Jakobson. In *International Encyclopedia of the Social Sciences*, Biographical Supplement, 335–41. New York: Free Press.

Halle, Morris, and Kenneth Stevens. 1962. Speech Recognition: A Model and a Program for Research. *IRE Transactions on Information Theory*, IT 8: 155–59.

Halle, Morris, and Jean-Roger Vergnaud, 1981. Harmony Processes. In W. Klein and W. Levelt (eds.), *Crossing the Boundaries in Linguistics*, 1–23. Dordrecht: Reidel.

Hamp, Eric. 1953. The Morphophonemes of the Keltic Mutations. *Language* 27:230–47.

Harms, Robert. 1966. Stress, Voice, and Length in Southern Paiute. *International Journal of American Linguistics* 32:228–35.

Harris, James. 1969. *Spanish Phonology*. Cambridge: MIT Press.

————. 1978. Two Theories of Nonautomatic Morphophonological Alternations. *Language* 54:41–60.

Harris, Zellig. 1942. Morpheme Alternants in Linguistic Analysis. *Language* 18:169–80 (reprinted in Joos 1957:109–15).

————. 1944a. Yokuts Structure and Newman's Grammar. *International Journal of American Linguistics* 10:196–211.

————. 1944b. Simultaneous Components in Phonology. *Language* 20:181–205 (reprinted in Joos 1957:124–38).

————. 1945. Navajo Phonology and Hoijer's Analysis. *International Journal of American Linguistics* 11:239–46.

————. 1951a. *Methods in Structural Linguistics*. Chicago: University of Chicago Press.

————. 1951b. Review of Sapir 1949. *Language* 27:288–333.

Haugen, Einar. 1958. Review of Firth 1957a. *Language* 34:498–502.

Henderson, Eugenie. 1948. Notes on the Syllable Structure of Lushai. *Bulletin of the School of Oriental and African Studies* 12:713–25.

————. 1949. Prosodies in Siamese. *Asia Minor* 1:189–215.

Hill, Archibald A. 1962. *Proceedings of the Third Texas Conference on Problems of Linguistic Analysis in English*. Austin: University of Texas Press.

Hjelmslev, Louis. 1928. *Principes de grammaire générale*. Det Kongelige Danske Videnskabernes Selskab, Hist.-filol Medd. XVI. Copenhagen.

————. 1932, 1933, 1935. *Rasmusk Rask, Udvalgte Afhandlinger* I, II, III. Copenhagen: Ejnar Munksgaard.

————. 1935, 1937. *La catégorie des cas*. Acta Jutlandica, vol. VII.1 (vol. 1), IX.2 (vol. 2). Aarhus: Universitetsforlaget.

————. 1943. *Omkring Sprogteoriens Grundlæggelse*. Copenhagen: Ejnar Munksgaard.

————. 1950–51. Commentaires sur la vie et l'œuvre de Rasmus Rask. *Conférences de l'Institut de linguistique de l'Université de Paris* 10:143–57.

————. 1951. Grundtræk af det danske udtrykkssystem med særligt henblik paå stødet. *Selskab for nordisk filologis aårsberetning for 1948 (1951)*, 12–24.

————. 1953. *Prolegomena to a Theory of Language*, trans. Francis Whitfield. Madison: University of Wisconsin Press.

————. 1954. La stratification du langage. *Word* 10:163–88.

————. 1970. Le système d'expression du français moderne. (Summary by E. Fischer-Jørgensen of two lectures to the Linguistic Circle of Copenhagen, 1948–49). *Bulletin du cercle linguistique de Copenhague 1941–1966*:217–24.

————. 1973. *Essais linguistiques*, vol. 2. *Travaux du cercle linguistique de Copenhague*, vol. 14.

————'. 1975. *Résumé of a Theory of Language*. Copenhagen: Munksgaard.

Hjelmslev, Louis, and Hans-Jorgen Uldall. 1935. On the Principles of Phonematics. *Proceedings of the 2nd International Congress of Phonetic Sciences*, 49–54. Cambridge: Cambridge University Press.

————. 1936. *Outline of Glossematics*. (Privately printed and circulated pamphlet, Copenhagen).

Hockett, Charles. 1942. A System of Descriptive Phonology. *Language* 18: 3–21 (reprinted in Joos 1957:97–108).

———. 1947. Problems of Morphemic Analysis. *Language* 23:321–43 (reprinted in Joos 1957:229–42).

———. 1948. A note on structure. *International Journal of American Linguistics* 14:269–71 (reprinted in Joos 1957:279–80).

———. 1951. Review of A. Martinet, *Phonology as Functional Phonetics*. *Language* 27:333–41.

———. 1954. Two Models of Grammatical Description. *Word* 10:210–31 (reprinted in Joos 1957:386–99).

———. 1955. *A Manual of Phonology*. Baltimore: Waverly Press.

———. 1968. *The State of the Art*. The Hague: Mouton & Co.

———. 1970. *A Leonard Bloomfield Anthology*. Bloomington: Indiana University Press.

Hoenigswald, Henry. 1978. The *Annus Mirabilis* 1876 and Posterity. In *The Neogrammarians* (special commemorative volume of *Transactions of the Philological Society*), 17–35.

Hooper, Joan B. 1972. The Syllable in Phonological Theory. *Language* 48: 525–40.

———. 1975. The Archisegment in Natural Generative Phonology. *Language* 51:536–60.

———. 1976. *An Introduction to Natural Generative Phonology*. New York: Academic Press, Inc.

Householder, Fred. 1952a. Review of Jones 1949. *International Journal of American Linguistics* 18:99–105.

———. 1952b. Review of Harris 1951a. *International Journal of American Linguistics* 18:260–68.

———. 1965. On Some Recent Claims in Phonological Theory. *Journal of Linguistics* 1:13–34.

Huddleston, Rodney. 1972. The Development of a Non-Process Model in American Structural Linguistics. *Lingua* 30:333–84.

Hyman, Larry. 1970. How Concrete is Phonology? *Language* 46:58–76.

———. 1975. *Phonology: Theory and Analysis*. New York: Holt, Rinehart & Winston.

———. 1976. Phonologization. In A. Juilland (ed.), *Linguistic Studies Offered to Joseph Greenberg*, 407–18. Saratoga, CA: Alma Libri.

Hymes, Dell. 1961. Review of W. Goldschmidt (ed.), *The Anthropology of Franz Boas*. *Journal of American Folklore* 74:87–90.

———. 1974. *Studies in the History of Linguistics: Traditions and Paradigms*. Bloomington: Indiana University Press.

Hymes, Dell, and John Fought. 1981. *American Structuralism*. The Hague: Mouton & Co. (First published 1975.)

Jackendoff, Ray S. 1975. Morphological and Semantic Regularities in the Lexicon. *Language* 51:639–71.

Jakobson, Roman. 1923. *O češskom stixe, preimuščestvenno v sopostavlennii russkim*. *Sbornik po teorii poetičeskogo jazyka* V. Berlin, Moscow.

———. 1928. Quelles sont les méthodes les mieux appropriées à un éxposé complet et pratique d'une langue quelconque? *Actes du Ier Congrès International de Linguistes du 10–15 avril, 1928.* (reprinted in Jakobson 1962a: 3–6).

———. 1929. *Remarques sur l'évolution phonologique du russe comparée à celle des autres langues slaves.* Travaux du cercle linguistique de Prague 2.

———. 1939. Observations sur le classment phonologique des consonnes. *Proceedings of the 3rd International Congress of Phonetic Sciences,* 34–41.

———. 1941. *Kindersprache, Aphasie, und allgemeine Lautgesetze.* Uppsala Universitets Aarskrift.

———. 1948. Russian Conjugation. *Word* 4:155–67.

———. 1960. The Kazan' School of Polish Linguistics and Its Place in the International Development of Phonology (translation of Polish Original). In Jakobson 1971a:394–428.

———. 1961. Efforts towards a Means-Ends Model in European Linguistics in the Interwar Period. In C. Mohrmann, A. Sommerfelt and J. Whatmough (eds.), *Trends in European and American Linguistics 1930–1960,* 104–8.

———. 1962a. *Selected Writings,* vol. 1. The Hague: Mouton & Co.

———. 1962b. Retrospect. In Jakobson 1962a, 631–58.

———. 1965. An Example of Migratory Terms and Institutional Models. In Jakobson 1971a:527–38.

———. 1970. Saussure's Unpublished Reflections on Phonemes. *Cahiers Ferdinand de Saussure* 26:5–14.

———. 1971a. *Selected Writings,* vol. 2. The Hague: Mouton & Co.

———. 1971b. The World Response to Whitney's Principles of Linguistic Science. In Silverstein (ed.) 1971, xxv–xlv.

Jakobson, Roman, Gunnar Fant, and Morris Halle. 1952. *Preliminaries to Speech Analysis.* Cambridge: MIT Press.

Jakobson, Roman, and Morris Halle. 1956. *Fundamentals of Language.* The Hague: Mouton & Co.

Johns, David. 1969. Phonemics and Generative Phonology. *Papers from the Fifth Regional Meeting, Chicago Linguistic Society,* 374–81. Chicago: University of Chicago.

Jones, Daniel. 1948. The London School of Phonetics. *Zeitschrift für Phonetik* 2:127–35.

———. 1950. *The Phoneme: Its Nature and Use.* Cambridge: Heffer.

———. 1957, 1973. *The History and Meaning of the Term "Phoneme."* Supplement to *Le maître phonétique* (reprinted in W. E. Jones and J. Laver (eds.), *Phonetics in Linguistics: A Book of Readings,* 187–204. London: Longman).

Joos, Martin. 1948. *Acoustic Phonetics. Language* Monograph 23. Baltimore: Waverly Press.

———. 1957. *Readings in Linguistics,* vol. 1. Washington: American Council of Learned Societies.

Kahn, Daniel. 1976. Syllable-Based Generalizations in English Phonology. Doctoral diss., Massachusetts Institute of Technology; circulated by Indiana University Linguistics Club.

Kean, Mary Louise. 1975. The Theory of Markedness in Generative Grammar. Doctoral diss., Massachusetts Institute of Technology.

Kenstowicz, Michael. 1975. Rule Application in Pregenerative American Phonology. In A. Koutsoudas (ed.), *The Application and Ordering of Phonological Rules*, 259–82. The Hague: Mouton & Co.

Kenstowicz, Michael, and Charles Kisserberth. 1975. *Generative Phonology*. New York: Academic Press.

Kent, Roland G. Review of Bloomfield 1933. *Language* 10:40–48.

Kilbury, James. 1976. *The Development of Morphophonemic Theory*. Amsterdam: Benjamins.

Kiparsky, Paul. 1973a. How Abstract is Phonology?, part 1 of Phonological Representations. In O. Fujimura (ed.), *Three Dimensions of Linguistic Theory*, 5–56. Tokyo: The TEC Corporation.

———. 1973b. Abstractness, Opacity, and Global Rules, part 2 of Phonological Representations. In O. Fujimura (ed.), *Three Dimensions of Linguistic Theory*, 57–86. Tokyo: The TEC Corporation.

———. 1973c. "Elsewhere" in Phonology. In S. Anderson and P. Kiparsky (eds.), *A Festschrift for Morris Halle*, 93–106. New York: Holt, Rinehart & Winston.

———. 1979. *Pāṇini as a Variationist*. Cambridge: MIT Press.

Klausenburger, Jurgen. 1978. Mikołaj Kruszewski's Theory of Morphophonology: An Appraisal. *Historiographica Linguistica* 5:109–20.

Koerner, E. F. K. 1973. *Ferdinand de Saussure*. Elmsford, NY: Pergamon Press.

Kruszewski, Mikołai. 1881. *Über die Lautabwechslung*. Kazan'.

———. 1883. *Očerk nauki o jazyke*. Kazan'.

Kuhn, Thomas. 1962. *The Structure of Scientific Revolutions*. Chicago: University of Chicago Press.

Kuryłowicz, Jerzy. 1949. La nature des procès dit 'analogiques'. *Acta Linguistica* 5:121–38.

———. 1964. *The Inflectional Categories of Indo-European*. Heidelberg: Carl Winter.

Ladefoged, Peter. 1980. What are Linguistic Sounds Made of? *Language* 56:485–502.

Lamb, Sidney. 1966. Prolegomena to a Theory of Phonology. *Language* 42:536–73.

Langendoen, D. Terrence. 1968. *The London School of Linguistics*. Cambridge: MIT Press.

Lass, Roger. 1972. How Intrinsic Is Content? Markedness, Sound Change, and "Family Universals." In D. Goyvaerts and G. Pullum (eds.), *Essays on the Sound Pattern of English*, 475–504. Ghent: Story-Scientia.

Leben, William R. 1971. Suprasegmental Phonology. Doctoral diss., Massachusetts Institute of Technology.

Lees, Robert B. 1957. Review of Chomsky 1957. *Language* 33:375–408.

Lehiste, Ilse. 1970. *Suprasegmentals*. Cambridge, Mass.: MIT Press.

Levine, Robert. 1979. Haida and NaDene: A New Look at the Evidence. *International Journal of American Linguistics* 45:157–70.

Liberman, Mark Y. 1975. The Intonational System of English. Doctoral diss., Massachusetts Institute of Technology; circulated by Indiana University Linguistics Club.

Liberman, Mark Y., and Alan Prince. 1977. On Stress and Linguistic Rhythm. *Linguistic Inquiry* 8:249–336.

Lieberman, Philip. 1965. On the Acoustic Basis of the Perception of Intonation by Linguists. *Word* 21:40–54.

Lightner, Theodore. 1965. The Segmental Phonology of Modern Standard Russian. Doctoral diss., Massachusetts Institute of Technology.

———. 1971. On Swadesh and Voegelin's "A Problem in Phonological Alternation." *International Journal of American Linguistics* 37:227–37.

Linnel, Per. 1979. *Psychological Reality in Phonology*. Cambridge: Cambridge University Press.

Lopez, Barbara. 1979. The Sound Pattern of Brazilian Portugese. Doctoral diss., University of California—Los Angeles.

Lounsbury, Floyd. 1953. *Oneida Verb Morphology*. Yale University Publications in Anthropology 48.

Lyons, John. 1962. Phonemic and Non-Phonemic Phonology: Some Typological Reflections. *International Journal of American Linguistics* 28:127–33.

Matthews, Peter. 1972. *Inflectional Morphology*. Cambridge: Cambridge University Press.

McCarthy, John. 1981. A Prosodic Theory of Non-Concatenative Morphology. *Linguistic Inquiry* 12:373–418.

McCawley, James D. 1967a. Le rôle d'un système de traits phonologiques dans une théorie du langage. *Langages* 8:112–23.

———. 1967b. The Phonological Theory behind Whitney's *Sanskrit Grammar*. In *Languages and Areas: Studies Presented to George Bobrinskoy, 1967*, 77–85. The University of Chicago: Division of the Humanities.

———. 1967c. Sapir's Phonologic Representation. *International Journal of American Linguistics* 33:106–11.

———. 1974. Review of Chomsky and Halle 1968. *International Journal of American Linguistics* 40:50–88.

Mead, Margaret. 1928. *Coming of Age in Samoa*. New York: William Morrow.

Miner, Kenneth. 1981. Bloomfield's Process Phonology and Kiparsky's Opacity. *International Journal of American Linguistics* 47:310–22.

Moulton, William. 1947. Juncture in Modern Standard German. *Language* 23:212–26 (reprinted in Joos 1957:208–14).

Murray, S. O. 1981. The Canadian "Winter" of Edward Sapir. *Historiographica Linguistica* 8:63–68.

Newmeyer, Frederick J. 1980. *Linguistic Theory in America*. New York: Academic Press.

———. 1983. *Grammatical Theory: Its Limits and its Possibilities*. Chicago: University of Chicago Press.

Nida, Eugene. 1948. The Identification of Morphemes. *Language* 24:414–41.

Ohala, John. 1979. Universals of Labial Velars and de Saussure's Chess Analogy. *Proceedings of the 9th International Congress of Phonetic Sciences* 2:41–47.

Palmer, Frank R. 1970. *Prosodic Analysis*. London: Oxford University Press.

Percival, Keith. 1977. Review of Koerner 1973, *Language* 53:383–405.

Pike, Kenneth. 1943. *Phonetics*. Ann Arbor: University of Michigan Press.

————. 1947a. *Phonemics: A Technique for Reducing Languages to Writing*. Ann Arbor: University of Michigan Press.

————. 1947b. Grammatical Prerequisites to Phonemic Analysis. *Word* 3:155–72.

————. 1952. More on Grammatical Prerequisites. *Word* 8:106–21.

Poser, William. 1982. Phonological Representations and Action-at-a-Distance. In H. van der Hulst and N. Smith (eds.), 1982b, 121–58.

Postal, Paul. 1964. Boas and the Development of Phonology: Some Comments Based on Iroquoian. *International Journal of American Linguistics* 30:269–80.

————. 1968. *Aspects of Phonological Theory*. New York: Harper & Row.

Powell, J. W. 1891. Indian Linguistic Families of America North of Mexico. *Annual Report* of the United States Bureau of American Ethnography 7:1–142.

Reichler-Béguelin, Marie-José. 1980. Le consonantisme grec et latin selon de Saussure: Le cours de phonétique professé en 1909–1910. *Cahiers Ferdinand de Saussure* 34:17–97.

Robins, R. H. 1957a. Aspects of Prosodic Analysis. *Proceedings of the University of Durham Philosophical Society* Series B. 1:1–12.

————. 1957b. Vowel Nasality in Sundanese: A Phonological and Grammatical Study. *Studies in Linguistic Analysis*, 87–103.

————. 1961. John Rupert Firth. *Language* 37:191–200.

————. 1963. General Linguistics in Great Britain 1930–1960. In C. Mohrmann, F. Norman, and A. Sommerfelt (eds.), *Trends in Modern Linguistics*, 11–37. Utrecht and Antwerp: Spectrum.

————. 1967. *A Short History of Linguistics*. London: Longmans.

————. 1969. Review of Langendoen 1968. *Language* 45:109–16.

Sapir, Edward. 1921. *Language*. New York: Harcourt, Brace & World.

————. 1922. Takelma. In Boas 1922:3–296.

————. 1925. Sound Patterns in Language. *Language* 1:37–51 (reprinted in Joos 1957:19–25).

————. 1930. *Southern Paiute: A Shoshonean Language*. Proceedings of the American Academy of Arts and Sciences, vol. 65, nos. 1–3.

————. 1933. La réalité psychologique du phonème. *Journal de psychologie normale et pathologique* 30:247–65.

————. 1938. Glottalized Continuants in Navajo, Nootka, and Kwakiutl. *Language* 14:248–274.

————. 1949. *Selected Writings of Edward Sapir*, ed. David Mandelbaum. Berkeley and Los Angeles: University of California Press.

Saussure, Ferdinand de. 1879. *Mémoire sur le système primitif des voyelles dans les langues indo-européennes*. Leipzig: Teubner.

————. 1916. *Cours de linguistique générale*. Paris: Payot.

————. 1959. *Course in General Linguistics*, trans. Wade Baskin. New York: The Philosophical Library.

————. 1974. *Cours de linguistique générale*. Édition critique préparée par Tullio deMauro. Paris: Payot.

Schane, Sanford. 1968. *French Phonology and Morphology*. Cambridge: MIT Press.

Schultz, Amelia [Sussmann]. 1977. Boas on Phonemics and Dissertations. *International Journal of American Linguistics* 43:56–57.

Scott, N. C. 1948. The Monosyllable in Szechuanese. *Bulletin of the School of Oriental and African Studies* 12:197–213.

————. 1956. A Phonological Analysis of the Szechuanese Monosyllable. *Bulletin of the School of Oriental and African Studies* 18:556–60.

Silverstein, Michael, ed. 1971. *Whitney on Language*. Cambridge: MIT Press.

Sommerstein, Alan. 1977. *Modern Phonology*. London: Edward Arnold.

Sprigg, R. K. 1955. The Tonal System of Tibetan and the Nominal Phrase. *Bulletin of the School of Oriental and African Studies* 17:134–53.

————. 1961. Vowel Harmony in Lhasa Tibetan: Prosodic Analysis applied to Interrelated Features of Successive Syllables. *Bulletin of the School of Oriental and African Studies* 24:116–38.

Stampe, David. 1968. Yes, Virginia . . . Paper read at the 4th Annual Meeting of the Chicago Linguistics Society.

————. 1969. The Acquisition of Phonetic Representation. In *Papers from the 5th Annual Meeting of the Chicago Linguistics Society*, 443–54.

————. 1972. How I Spent My Summer Vacation. Doctoral diss., University of Chicago.

————. 1973. On Chapter 9. In M. Kenstowicz and C. Kisseberth (eds.), *Issues in Phonological Theory*, 44–52. The Hague: Mouton & Co.

Stankiewicz, Edward. 1972. Baudouin de Courtenay: His Life and Work. Introduction to Baudouin de Courtenay 1972, 3–48. Bloomington: Indiana University Press.

Stanley, Richard. 1967. Redundancy Rules in Phonology. *Language* 43:393–436.

Stark, B. R. 1972. The Bloomfieldian Model, *Lingua* 30:385–421.

Stocking, George. 1974. The Boas Plan for American Indian Languages. In Hymes 1974:454–84.

Studies in Linguistic Analysis (1956). Special Volume of the Philological Society.

Swadesh, Maurice. 1934. The Phonemic Principle. *Language* 10:117–29 (reprinted in Joos 1957:32–37).

————. 1948. Review of Boas 1947. *Word* 4:58–63.

Swadesh, Maurice, and Carl Voegelin. 1939. A Problem in Phonological Alternation. *Language* 15:1–10 (reprinted in Joos 1957:88–92).

Sweet, Henry. 1877. *A Handbook of Phonetics*. Oxford: Henry Frowde.

Teeter, Karl V. 1964. Descriptive Linguistics in America: Triviality vs. Irrelevance. *Word* 20:197–206.

————. 1969. Leonard Bloomfield's Linguistics. *Language Sciences* 7:1–6.

Trager, George L. 1934. The Phonemes of Russian. *Language* 10:334–44.

Trager, George, and Bernard Bloch. 1941. The Syllabic Phonemes of English. *Language* 17:223–46.

Trager, George, and Henry Lee Smith. 1951. *An Outline of English Structure*. Studies in Linguistics, Occasional Papers, no. 3.

Tranel, Bernard. 1981. *Concreteness in Phonology: Evidence from French*. Berkeley and Los Angeles: University of California Press.

Trubetzkoy, N. 1929. Zur allgemeinen Theorie des phonologischen Vokalsystems. *Travaux du cercle linguistique de Prague* 1:39–67.

———. 1931. Gedanken über Morphonologie. *Travaux du cercle linguistique de Prague* 4:160–63.

———. 1933. La phonologie actuelle. *Journal de psychologie* 30:227–46.

———. 1934. *Das morphonologische System der russischen Sprache*. *Travaux du cercle linguistique de Prague*, 5, no. 2.

———. 1939. *Grundzüge der Phonologie*. *Travaux du cercle linguistique de Prague* 7.

———, J. Cantineau, trans. 1939 (1949). *Principes de phonologie*. Paris: Klincksieck.

Twaddell, W. Freeman. 1935. "On Defining the Phoneme." *Language Monograph*, no. 16. Reprinted in Joos 1957:55–80. (All text references are to the Joos reprint).

Uldall, Hans-Jorgen. 1957. An Outline of Glossematics, Part I. *Travaux du cercle linguistique de Copenhague* 10:1–89.

Vago, Robert. 1973. Abstract Vowel Harmony Systems in Uralic and Altaic Languages. *Language* 49:579–605.

van der Hulst, Harry, and Norval Smith, eds. 1982a. *The Structure of Phonological Representations*, vol. 1. Dordrecht: Foris Publications.

———. 1982b. *The Structure of Phonological Representations*, vol. 12. Dordrecht: Foris Publications.

———. 1982c. An Overview of Autosegmental and Metrical Phonology. In van der Hulst and Smith 1982a:1–45.

Vennemann, Theo. 1971. Natural Generative Phonology. Paper read at Annual Meeting of the Linguistic Society of America, St. Louis, MO.

Voegelin, Carl. 1952. The Boas Plan for the Presentation of American Indian Languages. *Proceedings of the American Philosophical Society* 96:439–51.

Voegelin, Carl, and F. M. Voegelin. 1963. On the History of Structuralizing in 20th Century America. *Anthropological Linguistics* 5.1:12–35.

Wang, William S.-Y. 1967. The Phonological Features of Tone. *International Journal of American Linguistics* 33:93–105.

Wells, Rulon. 1949. Automatic Alternation. *Language* 25:99–116.

Whitehead, Albert N., and Bertrand Russell. 1910. *Principia Mathematica*. Cambridge: Cambridge University Press.

Whitney, William Dwight. 1867. *Language and the Study of Language*. New York: C. Scribner & Sons.

———. 1875. *The Life and Growth of Language*. New York: D. Appleton.

———. 1879. *A Sanskrit Grammar*. Leipzig: Breitkopf & Hartel.

Williams, Roger. 1643. *A Key Into the Language of the Americas*. Reprinted 1963. New York: Russell & Russell.

Winteler, J. 1876. *Die Kerenzer Mundart des Kantons Glarus in ihren Grundzügen dargestellt*. Leipzig: C. F. Winter'sche Verlagshandlung.

Woo, Nancy. 1969. Prosody and Phonology. Doctoral diss., Massachusetts Institute of Technology.

Wrenn, C. L. 1946. Henry Sweet. *Transactions of the Philological Society*, 177–201.

INDEX OF NAMES

INDEX OF SUBJECTS

372 / INDEX OF SUBJECTS

Paleophonetic. *See* Alternation, paleophonetic
Paradigmatic processes. *See* Natural Phonology
Paradigmatic relations, 72, 186–88. *See also* Associative relation
Parole, 23–26, 28–31, 35–37, 40, 45, 48, 51, 55, 91
Pattern congruity, 289, 300
Pawnee, 208, 214
Perception, speech. *See* Speech perception
Performance, 24
Phonematemes, 155–56, 159
Phonematic units, 189–92
Phoneme, 45–46, 66–67, 80–82, 93–96, 113, 117–18, 163, 175–76, 183–84, 215, 222, 228–31, 234, 242, 259–62, 266–67, 271–74, 286–96, 299–300
Phonème, 37–40, 48–49, 66, 156–57
Phonemic principle, 57, 65, 172, 265. *See also* Representations, phonemic
Phonemic analysis, 297–99; vs. prosodic analysis, 189–92
Phonemic theory: fully specified basic variant, 38, 45–46, 48, 81, 95, 175, 231, 260, 288; fully specified surface variant, 38, 47–49, 95, 206, 216, 293, 340; incompletely specified, 44–46, 48, 95,117–18, 260; set of variants, 175–76, 292–93, 295, 303
Phonetic(s): change (*see* Change); combinatorial, 39–40, 52 (*see also* Phonologie); modification, 271; and morphology, 66–67; parameters, 265–66; processes, 237; species, 21, 39, 44. *See also* Anthropophonetics; Phonology vs. phonetics; Representations, phonetic
Phonétique, 36–47
Phonological identity, 108–9. *See also* Polysystemic analysis
Phonological representation. *See* Representations, phonological
Phonological system, 96–100
Phonologie, 35–37
Phonologization, 76–77
Phonology: autosegmental. *See* Autosegmental theory; vs. phonetics, 9, 44, 91–93; task of, 89. *See also* Metrical phonology
Phonotactics, 210
Pitch. *See* Suprasegmentals
Plane: of expression, 146–47, 150–53 (*see also* Signifié); of content, 146–47 (*see also* Signifiant)
Pleremes, 155–56

Polysystemic approach, 112–13, 170–71, 180–83
Prague: school, 15, 62, 88–91, 95, 96, 100, 101, 106, 108, 110, 117, 144, 155, 157, 173, 178, 220, 281, 302, 323, 324
Predictability, 10–14, 126–27, 135–39, 182, 206, 216
Principia Mathematica. See Mathematics
Prosodeme, 165–66
Prosodic analysis, 186–93
Prosodic features. *See* Suprasegmentals
Psychological basis of language, 222, 227–28, 254–55, 257–59
Psychological interpretation of langue, 25–26
Psychological nature of phoneme, 80–82, 94, 95, 175, 290–91
Psychophonetic alternation, 65–68, 72–73, 75
Purport, 150–51

Redundancy, 10–14, 35, 47, 125–27, 135–39, 326–27
Reduplication, 248–49
Regularities, 9, 34–35, 41, 48, 55, 87, 214–15, 237–38, 242, 289–90, 300, 301, 308–9, 340
Representations, 80, 94, 104, 122–23, 126–27, 160, 188–89, 209, 233, 262–66, 274, 300, 304, 323, 339–42, 348; lexical, 235–36, 326–27; metrical, 192, 193; morphophonemic, 114–15, 214–15; phonemic, 42, 44–46, 48, 126, 135, 138, 230–33, 236, 266–70, 275–76, 300–301; phonetic, 43–44, 47, 213, 230, 263, 264, 266; phonological, 12, 43–44, 46–47, 111, 114, 138, 288, 319–20, 325, 337–39, 349; vs. rules (*see* Rules, vs. representations); underlying, 242–43, 324–26, 333
Retroflexion, 191–92
Rhotacism, 54
Rules, 44, 46, 47, 52–54, 67–68, 74, 78–79, 127, 156–57, 162–64, 188, 209, 212–14, 231–32, 236–39, 272–75, 300, 323, 325, 331, 342–47, 349; lexical redundancy, 53, 340; morpheme structure, 326–27; morphophonemic, 79–80, 340; phonological, 77, 227, 337–38; order, 188–89, 212, 238–39, 275, 306–8, 335; redundancy, 35, 47; vs. representations, 7–10, 43, 55, 92, 95, 112, 114, 206, 216, 239–43, 303, 321–22, 327, 331–32, 338–39, 347–50. *See also* Laws, euphonic